COPYRIGHT LAW AND THE PUBLIC INTEREST IN THE NINETEENTH CENTURY

Copyright law is commonly described as carrying out a balancing act between the interests of authors or owners and those of the public. While much academic work, both historical and contemporary, has been done on the authorship side of the equation, this book examines the notion of public interest, and the way that concepts of public interest and the rhetoric surrounding it have been involved in shaping the law of copyright. While many histories of copyright focus on the eighteenth century, this book's main concern is with the period after 1774. The nineteenth century was the period during which the boundaries of copyright, as we know it today, were drawn and ideas of 'public interest' were integral to this process, but in different, and complex, ways. The book engages with this complexity by moving beyond debates about the appropriate duration of copyright, and considers the development of other important features of copyright law, such as the requirement of legal deposit, the principle that some works will not be subject to copyright protection on the grounds of public interest, and the law of infringement. While the focus of the book is on literary copyright, it also traces the expansion of copyright to cover new subject matters, such as music, dramatic works and lectures. The book concludes by examining the making of the 1911 Imperial Copyright Act—the statute upon which the law of copyright in Britain, and in all former British colonies, is based. The history traced in this book has considerable relevance to debates over the scope of copyright law in the present day; it emphasises the contingency and complexity of copyright law's development and current shape, as well as encouraging a critical approach to the justifications for copyright law.

Copyright Law and the Public Interest in the Nineteenth Century

Isabella Alexander

•HART•
PUBLISHING

OXFORD AND PORTLAND, OREGON
2010

Published in the United Kingdom by Hart Publishing Ltd
16C Worcester Place, Oxford, OX1 2JW
Telephone: +44 (0)1865 517530
Fax: +44 (0)1865 510710
E-mail: mail@hartpub.co.uk
Website: http://www.hartpub.co.uk

Published in North America (US and Canada) by
Hart Publishing
c/o International Specialized Book Services
920 NE 58th Avenue, Suite 300
Portland, OR 97213-3786
USA
Tel: +1 503 287 3093 or toll-free: (1) 800 944 6190
Fax: +1 503 280 8832
E-mail: orders@isbs.com
Website: http://www.isbs.com

British Library Cataloguing in Publication Data
Data Available

ISBN: 978-1-84113-786-5

Typeset by Hope Services Ltd, Abingdon
Printed and bound in Great Britain by
Lightning Source UK Ltd

Acknowledgements

While accepting full responsibility for all errors in the following pages, there are numerous people whose contributions must be recognised. The book began life as a doctoral dissertation at the University of Cambridge, and the first person to thank is Bill Cornish for supervising with such good humour and generosity. I owe an enormous debt of gratitude to Lionel Bently, who not only examined the PhD, but also read and advised on subsequent drafts, and was a constant source of encouragement and support. In addition, I am grateful to Hector MacQueen, the other PhD examiner; Kathy Bowrey, who first suggested the public interest as a posssible research topic; and Catherine Seville and Jane Ginsburg for helpful conversations along the way. Other people who were kind enough to read various drafts of various parts are Elena Cooper, Jennifer Davis, Jan-Melissa Schramm, and Ellie Turnbull. The project from PhD to book, was made possible by funding from the Association of Commonwealth Universities, the Cambridge Commonwealth Australia Trust, Lucy Cavendish College and the Centre for Intellectual Property and Information Law at the University of Cambridge.

I also thank my parents and sisters for their unwavering generosity and support. I am especially grateful to my husband Matthew for reading numerous drafts, participating in countless discussions, providing technological assistance and exercising endless patience.

Abbreviations

BT	Records of the Board of Trade (held in the National Archives)
HO	Records of the Home Office (held in the National Archives)
JC	*Journal of the House of Commons*
JL	*Journal of the House of Lords*
Parl Deb	Parliamentary Debates

Contents

Table of Cases

Table of Legislation

National

France

United Kingdom

Bilateral Agreements

European Union

International

1

Introduction: Copyright, History, the Public

I. THE PUBLIC INTEREST: BALANCES AND INCENTIVES

THE NOTION OF a balance, or bargain, has become something of a mantra for judges, legislators, policy makers and academic commentators in the modern field of copyright law. Gerald Dworkin expresses the commonly held view succinctly: 'Copyright and the public interest are inextricably linked. All copyright systems seek to strike a balance between the rights of the owner and the public interest'.[1] The preamble to the WIPO Copyright Treaty also emphasises 'the need to maintain a balance between the rights of authors and the large public interest, particularly education, research and access to information'.[2] In the recent decision of the High Court of Australia, the judgment of French CJ, Crennan and Kiefel JJ states, 'Copyright strikes a balance of competing interests and competing policy considerations. Relevantly, it is concerned with rewarding authors of original literary works with commercial benefits having regard to the fact that literary works in turn benefit the reading public'.[3] In the same case, Gummow, Hayne and Heydon JJ likewise assert that

> the purpose of copyright law respecting original works is to balance the public interest in promoting the encouragement of 'literary', 'dramatic', 'musical' and 'artistic works', as defined, by providing a just reward for the creator, with the public interest in maintaining a robust public domain in which further works are produced.[4]

There have been many attempts to try to quantify or locate the proper balance of copyright law. One important tool employed has been the discipline of economics, which was first applied to copyright in 1934 when Arnold Plant published his article, 'The Economic Aspects of Copyright in Books'.[5] Seminal articles have also been written by Stephen Breyer in 1970[6] and by William M Landes and

[1] G Dworkin, 'Copyright, The Public Interest and Freedom of Speech: A UK Copyright Lawyer's Perspective' in J Griffiths and U Suthersanen (eds), *Copyright and Free Speech: Comparative and International Analysis* (Oxford, Oxford University Press, 2005) 154.

[2] World Intellectual Property Organisation Copyright Treaty, adopted by the Diplomatic Conference on 20 December 1996 (SI 2005/3431).

[3] *IceTV Pty Limited v Nine Network Pty Limited* [2009] HCA 14 (High Court of Australia) [24].

[4] ibid [71].

[5] A Plant, 'The Economic Aspects of Copyright in Books' (1934) 2 *Economica* 167.

[6] S Breyer, 'The Uneasy Case for Copyright: A Study of Copyright in Books, Photocopies and Computer Programs' (1970) 84 *Harvard Law Review* 281.

Richard A Posner in 1989.[7] Landes and Posner see the balance of copyright law as poised between the costs of limiting access to a work and the benefits of providing incentives to create in the first place. The overall aim is to 'maximize benefits from creating additional works minus both the losses from limiting access and the costs of administering copyright protection'.[8]

However, other writers on copyright law have been less concerned with 'balance', looking instead for an overarching objective to be fulfilled by copyright law. Jane Ginsburg argues that the opposition of authors and the public is specious in the way it allows the public interest to be redefined as user's interests, because the public interest 'comprises the goals and aspirations of authors *and* users, or public *and* educators, and so forth'.[9] In the European Council's Directive on copyright term, recital 11 claims that protection of copyright 'ensures the maintenance and development of creativity in the interest of authors, cultural industries, consumers and society as a whole'.[10] William Patry asserts definitively that copyright 'is a system created for a very specific social goal, to encourage learning'.[11] Neil Netanel explains that

> the public interest—as reflected in some 300 years of copyright precedent—is for a narrowly tailored incentive for authors to contribute to the store of knowledge and enrich the public domain. Copyright is meant to spur creativity and expressive diversity.[12]

These formulations all appear to prioritise the public interest, or common good, aspects of copyright law. Their views of how this should be achieved, however, are in some cases starkly different. While Netanel argues for a 'narrowly tailored incentive', the European Council, by contrast, asserts that 'the level of protection of copyright and related rights should be high'.[13] This indicates that views of the public interest itself may differ. It is noteworthy that in its Directive on the Information Society, which was in large part concerned with harmonising the exceptions to copyright protection, the European Council referred to the need for balance in copyright law.[14] Thus, the Council implicitly drew attention to tensions

[7] WM Landes and RA Posner, 'An Economic Analysis of Copyright Law' (1989) 18 *Journal of Legal Studies* 325. (Landes and Posner have recently updated their economic analysis of copyright duration in WM Landes and RA Posner, 'Indefinitely Renewable Copyright' (2003) 70 *University of Chicago Law Review* 471.)

[8] Landes and Posner, 'An Economic Analysis' 326.

[9] J Ginsburg, 'Authors and Users in Copyright' (1997) 45 *Journal of the Copyright Society of the USA* 1, 4.

[10] Directive 2006/116/EC of the European Parliament and of the Council of 12 December 2006 on the term of protection of copyright and certain related rights, recital 11.

[11] WF Patry, 'Metaphors and Moral Panics in Copyright: The Stephen Stewart Memorial Lecture, November 13, 2007' [2008] *Intellectual Property Quarterly* 1, 12.

[12] NW Netanel, 'Why Has Copyright Expanded? Analysis and Critique' in F Macmillan (ed), *New Directions in Copyright Law*, vol 6 (Cheltenham, UK, Edward Elgar, 2008) 4.

[13] Directive 2006/116/EC of the European Parliament and of the Council of 12 December 2006 on the term of protection of copyright and certain related rights, recital 11.

[14] 'A fair balance of rights and interests between the different categories of right-holders, as well as between the different categories of right-holders and users of protected subject-matter must be safeguarded' (Directive 2001/29/EC of 22 May 2001 on the harmonisation of certain aspects of copyright and related rights in the information society, recital 31).

in copyright law but sought to smooth them over in its later directive aimed at expanding the rights of owners.[15]

The formulation of copyright's aims and agendas is therefore not without political and commercial significance. Emphasis on balance and goals signals the existence of a contest between competing objectives and in turn leads us into copyright law's heart of darkness: the justification for its existence. The justifications most commonly proposed for having a copyright law are threefold: recognising the natural right of an author to claim ownership of his work; rewarding authors for creating a work; and providing incentives for authors to create and disseminate works. The first justification is often founded upon John Locke's theory that property rights are created when goods previously held in common are mixed with labour.[16] The second is also based upon the notion of labour, because it is through labour that the author comes to deserve the property right.[17] The third is based on utilitarian reasoning. Whereas the first two justifications prioritise the role of the authors or creators of copyright works, the third prioritises the community in general. It is frequently discussed in terms of balance because it establishes a property right that operates in favour of creators and owners in exchange for long-term public benefits. However, except in their most extreme forms, the first two justifications do not deny that the public also has a role in copyright law, as the ultimate beneficiary. It is just that this role is secondary to copyright's main aim.[18]

None of these justifications is immune from attack. However, the object of this book is not to establish which is best or most accurate. Rather, it focuses on the third type of justification and seeks to uncover the historical pedigree of claims that copyright operates in the public interest, whether as an overarching goal, or through the balancing of competing claims. The book concentrates on copyright law in the nineteenth century. This is the period during which copyright law came to take on many of the features that characterise 'modern' copyright law.[19] The nineteenth century has attracted less attention in current historical accounts, with most commentators appearing to prefer the high drama and rhetoric of the previous century's 'Battle of the Booksellers'.[20] The book is, therefore, less concerned with the origins of copyright, and more with the form it came to take in the second, and in modern terms vitally constitutive, century of its existence.

[15] Above, n 13.

[16] J Locke, *The Second Treatise of Civil Government*, ed JW Gough (Oxford, P Blackwell, 1948; reprint of the 1690 edition) Bk 2, ch 5. For contemporary criticism of this theory see P Drahos, *A Philosophy of Intellectual Property* (Aldershot, Dartmouth, 1996) ch 3.

[17] C Hettinger, 'Justifying Intellectual Property' (1989) 18 *Philosophy and Public Affairs* 31, 40–43.

[18] See, eg, the third 'key point' of MacQueen, Waelde and Laurie's introduction to their textbook *Contemporary Intellectual Property*: 'Copyright rewards individuals for their contributions; but this is offset by recognition of the interests—if not the rights—of the wider public in the free dissemination of material in certain circumstances.' H MacQueen, C Waelde and GT Laurie, *Contemporary Intellectual Property: Law and Policy* (Oxford, Oxford University Press, 2008) 43.

[19] B Sherman and L Bently, *The Making of Modern Intellectual Property Law: The British Experience, 1760–1911* (Cambridge, Cambridge University Press, 1999) 3.

[20] See below: ch 2.

Unlike the accounts of the law and economics scholars, or the balancing act theorists, this book does not treat the public interest as a fixed, or somehow ascertainable concept. Instead, it examines the way that lawyers, courts, legislators and interested parties viewed and formulated ideas of the public interest, and the extent to which such ideas did, in fact, influence the development of the law. To borrow the phrase of Mark Rose, the book distinguishes between the *fact* of public interest and what may be called the *discourse* of public interest.[21] Notwithstanding Ginsburg's assertion of its speciousness, it is the contention of this book that the notion of a 'public interest' which diverges from the interests of authors, even if not always opposed to them, has had a significant rhetorical and discursive impact in shaping the law of copyright. However, it will also argue that, contrary to Netanel's suggestion, it is not the case that the law has always developed consistently in this manner.

II. THE STORIES SO FAR . . .

Histories of copyright law to date have tended to focus on either authors or publishers. The first histories of copyright emerged in the nineteenth century, usually as introductory chapters to legal treatises and frequently with some underlying aim in view. Thus, Maugham wrote his treatise on copyright in 1828 with the object of supporting the campaign for reform of the library deposit provisions in the Copyright Acts.[22] His history described the law of copyright as founded upon a perpetual common law right which was no longer recognised, to the detriment of learning in general and the interests of authors and publishers in particular. John Lowndes wrote his treatise with the specific object of endorsing Serjeant Talfourd's attempts to reform the law in favour of authors in the 1830s and unsurprisingly cast his history as one of continuous recognition by the Crown and Parliament of authors' property rights until the House of Lords voted against the existence of a common law right in *Donaldson v Becket.*[23]

In 1867, George Ticknor Curtis, an American lawyer, published a treatise in both the United States and England.[24] Curtis commenced his book with a discussion of the theory of authors' rights, concluding that the author's right of property in the exclusive multiplication of copies of his work was a right founded in natural law.[25] His history followed this formula, identifying a common law right of authors that he assumed to exist up until the case of *Donaldson v Becket* when, in Curtis's view, it was 'lost forever'.[26] Curtis's history culminated in 1842, when Serjeant

[21] M Rose, 'Nine-Tenths of the Law: The English Copyright Debates and the Rhetoric of the Public Domain' (2003) 66 *Law and Contemporary Problems* 75, 77.

[22] R Maugham, *A Treatise on the Laws of Literary Property* (London, Longman et al, 1828).

[23] *Donaldson v Becket* (1774) 2 Bro PC 129. JJ Lowndes, *An Historical Sketch of the Law of Copyright; with remarks on Sergeant Talfourd's Bill* (London, Saunders & Benning, 1840).

[24] GT Curtis, *A Treatise on the Law of Copyright* (London, Maxwell & Son, 1847).

[25] ibid 13–14

[26] ibid 63.

Talfourd's Act restored to authors a small part of their rightful inheritance.[27] Three years later Walter Copinger published the first edition of what was to become copyright's most long-lived textbook, with new editions published at frequent intervals to the present day.[28] His book was heavily reliant on Curtis's work, and adopted many of his views verbatim. Thus, like Curtis, his section on history was heavily focused on the rights of authors.

In 1883, the first edition of another significant treatise appeared when Thomas Edward Scrutton published his Yorke Prize-winning essay on 'The law of property in literary compositions, published and unpublished; the principles that ought to regulate it, and how far such principles have been acted upon in different countries'.[29] Scrutton's original essay had reform and codification of copyright law as its central practical and political objective.[30] Its philosophical objective was an assertion of the private property rights of authors and unease regarding the principles being applied to the law of copyright, which Scrutton characterised as the same as Socialism or Communism in relation to real property.[31] Scrutton based his case on utilitarian theory, claiming that the fundamental question for copyright law was: 'Is it desirable in the interests of the community that the State should create and protect property in literary productions or the results of literary labour?'[32] His affirmative response advocated a broad and enveloping scope of protection that would cover '[t]he results of a man's intellectual labour as put into form by him, whether communicated to the public either by way of writing or orally, or not, unless either expressly or impliedly he waives protection'.[33] For Scrutton, high levels of protection would assist both authors and the community, because they would encourage better books to be produced.[34]

His history reflected his concerns, and was aimed at demonstrating the existence of a common law property right belonging to authors prior to the Statute of Anne, although he did concede that the benefit of the right was more usually vested in the author's assigns, whether printer or bookseller.[35] When the issue was squarely faced by the courts in the middle of the eighteenth century, it was

[27] ibid 69. Curtis noted that authors 'have long had to struggle against a great weight of prejudice and illiberality in the legislature. Every important concession that has been gained from them has been won as a trophy from a well fought field.'

[28] Copinger was a lawyer with a keen interest in bibliography, founding the Bibliographical Society in 1892.

[29] TE Scrutton, *The Laws of Copyright*, 1st edn (London, J Murray, 1883). The prize was awarded in 1882. Scrutton won three other Yorke prizes from Cambridge and went on to become a distinguished commercial lawyer, with a strong copyright practice. He held the Chair of Constitutional Law and Legal History at University College, London, and later became a judge, first of the King's Bench and then the Court of Appeal; WR Cornish, 'The Copyright History of What Must-have-been' in G Roussel et al (eds), *Mélanges Victor Nabhan* (Montreal, Editions Yvon Blais, 2004) 66–67.

[30] In the later editions, which followed in 1890, 1896 and 1903, Scrutton removed the earlier, theoretical chapters.

[31] Scrutton, *The Laws of Copyright*, 1st edn, 291.

[32] ibid 5.

[33] ibid 19.

[34] ibid 8–15.

[35] ibid 91–92, 104.

therefore open and reasonable to find a perpetual right existed. To Scrutton's disappointment, then, the peers in *Donaldson v Becket* were swayed by the eloquence of Lord Camden and, like Curtis and Copinger, Scrutton claimed that the first legislative attempt to advance the interests purely of authors was Talfourd's Bill of 1837.[36]

Scrutton's philosophical dual agenda of linking copyright more closely to authorship and the common law right whilst also developing a theory which elided the interest of authors and the public was given practical application in his legal practice, where he employed such arguments to found claims to new rights in works,[37] as well as claims to rights over new kinds of work.[38] However, he also used them to argue for the limitation of copyright protection to works of some literary originality, as in the case of reports of speeches.[39]

In 1899, Scrutton's contemporary and colleague, Augustine Birrell, published his entertaining and erudite series of lectures on the history of copyright.[40] Birrell had less time for the causes of perpetual property and authors. He referred to the former as 'a cock-and-bull story'[41] and was alert to the tendency of the booksellers to advocate the interests of authors in place of their own. Like Scrutton, Birrell advocated reform of the law, and noted with approval the Bill then before Parliament. Despite his scepticism of the existence of perpetual copyright as an author's right, he recognised that although authors 'did not exactly write for money, [they] took as much money as they thought they could get for what they had written'.[42] Thus, he advocated a limited term of protection, preferably relating to the life of the author.[43]

After Birrell, the study of copyright law's history ceased largely to be a preoccupation of lawyers until the 1960s, when two works told stories of copyright that emphasised the role of the book trade. Benjamin Kaplan's engaging and learned history, originally given as lectures and published in 1967, gave primacy to the interests of the Stationers in the period before and immediately after the Statute of Anne. He suggested that the pre-1710 practices of the Stationers bore a 'merely familial' relationship to copyright.[44] By the nineteenth century, however, the arrival of Romantic literary ideas in England influenced the increasingly strong protection given to literary works.[45]

[36] ibid 107.

[37] Such as the right to prevent infringement by copying in a different medium: *Hanfstaengl v Newnes* [1984] 3 Ch 108, *Hanfstaengl v Empire Palace* [1894] 2 Ch 1, *Hanfstaengl v HR Baines & Co Limited and EJ Mansfield* [1895] AC 20, *Boosey v Whight* [1900] 1 Ch 122, *Boosey v Whight* [1899] 1 Ch 836, *Newmark v National Phonograph Co* (1907) 23 TLR 439, *Moffat and Paige Limited v George Gill and Sons Limited* (1901) 84 LT 452, *Moffat and Paige Limited v George Gill and Sons Limited and Francis Marshall* (1902) 86 LT 465. See ch 6, section II C.

[38] *Exchange Telegraph Company Limited v Gregory & Co* [1895] 1 QB 147. See below: ch 6, section II C.

[39] *Walter v Lane* [1899] 2 Ch 749, *Walter v Lane* [1900] AC 539. See below: ch 6, section II C.

[40] A Birrell, *Seven Lectures on the Law and History of Copyright in Books* (London, Cassell & Co Ltd, 1899).

[41] ibid 112.

[42] ibid 198.

[43] ibid 149.

[44] B Kaplan, *An Unhurried View of Copyright* (New York, Columbia University Press, 1967) 4.

[45] ibid 24.

Lyman Ray Patterson, whose history was published the year after Kaplan's, gave a more institutional view of copyright than Kaplan.[46] Patterson's history commenced with the grant of the Stationers' Company charter in 1557, and followed the legislative history through to the Statute of Anne. He believed a common law right did emerge during this period, but that it was lost upon the enactment of the Statute of Anne which created a publisher's printing right. His history was essentially the story of how copyright came to be considered a merely economic right and he advocated that a true law of authors' rights would involve the recognition of moral rights.

Another history that also focused on the printers and publishers emerged from a different quarter. In 1957, Harry Ransom, professor of English at the University of Texas, published *The First Copyright Statute.*[47] Ransom painted the period between the arrival of the printing press in England and the Statute of Anne as a time of progression, where the ultimate goal of copyright legislation was shaped by a series of statutes aimed at regulating the press. This was a story of trade rivalry and State regulation, in which changes to the law were brought about as a result of challenges to the status quo by those printers, publishers and booksellers who were excluded from power. Ransom provides a useful and detailed history of book trade regulation in the period between 1476 and 1710. However, his analysis is flawed in its assumption of a constant, shared and accepted idea of 'copyright' during those two hundred odd years. This obscures any notion that concepts of literary property and ownership may have been understood in different ways from how they are understood in the twenty-first century. Moreover, it also assumed that the end point reached when the Statute of Anne was passed was not only inevitable, but the outcome towards which previous societies, possibly unbeknownst to themselves, had been striving.

Bibliographers, armed with evidence from the Stationers' Register, also began to look at copyright as it manifested itself in the relations between publishers, printers, authors and actors.[48] In the 1980s, John Feather continued this project, publishing numerous works that placed the history of copyright law firmly in the context of the book trade. Feather focused on the booksellers' political manoeuvres and, in some cases, the role of professional authors, as well as the relationship between the two.[49]

In recent years, attention has turned to the nature of the relationship between copyright law and authors. The impetus for this approach can be found in Foucault's influential essay, 'What is an Author?'[50] Three of those who took up Foucault's gauntlet were Martha Woodmansee, Peter Jaszi and Mark Rose.

[46] LR Patterson, *Copyright in Historical Perspective* (Nashville, Vanderbilt University Press, 1968).

[47] H Ransom, *The First Copyright Statute* (Austin, University of Texas Press, 1956).

[48] See J Loewenstein, *The Author's Due: Printing and the Pre-history of Copyright* (Chicago, University of Chicago Press, 2002) 6–7.

[49] See bibliography for examples.

[50] M Foucault, 'What is an Author?' in JV Harari (ed), *Textual Strategies: Perspectives in Post-Structuralist Criticism* (Ithaca, NY, Cornell University Press, 1979) 141.

Woodmansee places the birth of the author in the eighteenth century.[51] She argues that new ideas of the writer as unique creator of a unique work, which found expression in the work of Edward Young and, later, in the writings of Wordsworth, redefined the nature of writing and provided the foundations for the modern form of authorship. In another essay, 'The Author Effect', Woodmansee argues that copyright law is 'rooted' in the Romantic view of writing as a solitary and individual pursuit.[52] Peter Jaszi takes a similar view, arguing that authorship is 'the most central, and certainly the most resonant, of the foundational concepts associated with Anglo-American copyright doctrine'.[53]

Mark Rose also locates the emergence of modern authorship in the eighteenth century, seeing this as a period of 'major aesthetic realignment in which terms such as "art", "genius" and "originality" were transvalued'.[54] This realignment resulted in the conception of author as originator of a literary text. During the legal battles that culminated in *Donaldson v Becket*, the view of the author as owner and the work as the proper object of property became established and institutionalised in legal discourse. Rose claims that these debates over literary property prepared the ground for the reception in England of German Romantic theory, which characterised the author in terms of originality and uniqueness.

Like these three, David Saunders is concerned with the history of authorship and how it relates to copyright law. However, he is critical of copyright historians such as Woodmansee, Jaszi and Rose, whom he characterises as writing 'Romantic historicist accounts' which seek to portray the history of copyright law as a progression towards realising the legal personality and subjectivity of the author.[55] He notes that even Patterson fell into this trap because, despite emphasising that copyright was nothing more than a trade regulation device, Patterson simultaneously insisted that it should have been an authorial right.[56]

Saunders considers that focusing on the aesthetic personality of authorship neglects the variability and contingency of legal cultural arrangements.[57] He seeks to avoid portraying copyright in terms of progress to a higher ideal or historical mission towards the recognition of authorial rights or personality. His concern is

[51] M Woodmansee, 'The Genius and the Copyright: Economic and Legal Conditions of the Emergence of the Author' (1984) 17 *Eighteenth Century Studies* 425, 426.

[52] M Woodmansee, 'On the Author Effect: Recovering Collectivity' in M Woodmansee and P Jaszi (eds), *The Construction of Authorship: Textual Appropriation in Law and Literature* (Durham, NC; London, Duke University Press, 1994) 27.

[53] P Jaszi, 'Toward a Theory of Copyright: The Metamorphoses of "Authorship"' (1991) *Duke Law Journal* 455, 455. See also P Jaszi and M Woodmansee, 'Introduction' in M Woodmansee and P Jaszi (eds), *The Construction of Authorship* (Durham, NC; London, Duke University Press, 1994) 1.

[54] M Rose, 'The Author as Proprietor: *Donaldson v Becket* and the Genealogy of Modern Authorship' in B Sherman and A Strowel (eds), *Of Authors and Origins: Essays on Copyright Law* (Oxford, Oxford University Press, 1994) 29.

[55] D Saunders, *Authorship and Copyright* (London, Routledge, 1992) 216–23.

[56] ibid 220–21.

[57] D Saunders, 'Dropping the Subject: An Argument for a Positive History of Authorship and the Law of Copyright' in B Sherman and A Strowel (eds), *Of Authors and Origins: Essays on Copyright Law* (Oxford, Oxford University Press, 1994) 108.

with the interaction between notions of copyright and notions of authorship, and to emphasise the complexity, variability and fluidity of the history of authorship.

Ronan Deazley's book, *On the Origin of the Right to Copy*, is a direct response to Saunders' criticism,[58] and provides an empirical and extremely detailed account of the period between 1695 and 1775. He looks at developments in the legislature, including the passing of the Statute of Anne and the legislative attempts which followed. He then examines the litigation of the eighteenth century, culminating in the decisions of *Millar v Taylor* and *Donaldson v Becket*, which he considers in detail. In so doing, he seeks to displace the author from the centre of the story, and to replace him with a concern for the public in general, concluding his work with the following statement:

> What emerges from a close study of the movement of the law during this period is that copyright, with both the passing of the *Statute of Anne* and the factual decision of *Donaldson*, was primarily defined and justified in the interests of society and not the individual. A statutory phenomenon, copyright was fundamentally concerned with the reading public, with the encouragement and spread of education, and with the continued production of useful books. In allocating the right to exclusively publish a given literary work, the eighteenth century parliamentarians were not concerned primarily with the rights of the individual, but acted in the furtherance of these much broader social goals. The pre-eminence of the common good as the organising principle upon which to found a system of copyright regulation is revealed. This element of the public interest, overlooked or perhaps ignored in other historical tales of the origin of copyright, once lay at its very core.[59]

Although *On the Origin* does not overtly engage with contemporary debates on copyright policy, Simon Stokes points out in his review that 'Deazley's book is welcome ammunition to those who would try to reassert the public domain'.[60] Indeed, Deazley's second book, *Rethinking Copyright*, picks up where his earlier book left off and follows some of the policy and theoretical implications of his thesis through the nineteenth century to the present. He brings to the fore his claim that successive misreadings and misinterpretations of *Donaldson v Becket* have created an 'orthodox history'[61] that obscures the central role of the public interest in copyright law.

The present book is, then, a response not only to those for whom the importance of copyright's history lies mainly in its complex relations with authorship, but also to Deazley's view of the 'public interest'. While Deazley is right to highlight the important role played by the public interest in the formation of copyright law, he does not subject it to close examination or question its content. While rejecting the notion that copyright can be traced 'along any single, unfolding axis'[62] when

[58] R Deazley, *On the Origin of the Right to Copy: Charting the Movement of Copyright Law in the Eighteenth Century (1695–1775)* (Oxford, Hart Publishing, 2004) xxiv.

[59] ibid 226.

[60] S Stokes, Book Review [2005] *Entertainment Law Review* 41, excerpted in R Deazley, *Rethinking Copyright: History, Theory, Language* (Cheltenham, UK, Edward Elgar, 2006) 1.

[61] R Deazley, *Rethinking Copyright: History, Theory, Language* (Cheltenham, UK, Edward Elgar, 2006) 6.

[62] Deazley, *On the Origin* 222.

it comes to author's rights, he appears content to substitute a second axis, or 'true movement of the law',[63] in the direction of the public interest.

Another book which places the public interest at the centre of its examination is Gillian Davies' *Copyright and the Public Interest.* Davies' book commences with the sentence:

> The purpose of this study is to discuss the proposition that copyright is a just and proper concept, established in the public interest and to explore the extent to which the notion of the 'public interest' has influenced the copyright laws of a few major jurisdictions from their origins in the eighteenth century to date.[64]

The present book likewise aims to explore the extent to which the notion of public interest has influenced the development of copyright law[65] but it does so in considerably more detail and with greater attention the different shapes that the concept of public interest took in having such influence.

Davies starts from the premise that:

> National laws are only enacted if they are in the public interest, or at least it must be assumed that the enacting body so regards them, since it is the task of the legislator to make laws for society as a whole.[66]

In that vein, Davies unquestioningly jumps on James Madison's oft-quoted statement that 'Copyright is an instance in which the public good fully coincides with the claims of individuals'.[67] There is a sound basis for the general proposition that the law *claims* to be in the public interest,[68] but that neither establishes that the law's claim is correct[69] nor what the public interest is in any given situation. Davies fails to engage with these limitations, constructing a narrative of copyright's history that develops consistently by balancing the public interest against the interests of creators and owners without ever really considering or analysing what that public interest might be, beyond the claim that copyright stimulates creativity. This approach reveals her to be firmly on the side of copyright owners, as it allows her to advocate that copyright laws should be regularly altered to encompass new kinds of works and to respond to new forms of copying. Thus, she argues in favour of strengthening the protection given to copyright owners while all the time asserting that increased protection is in the public interest.

At the end of his essay on copyright, Scrutton admonishes his readers thus:

> And above all, a caution which is most necessary in dealing with questions of so-called 'justice', 'right,' and 'utility,' let us be careful that we understand what we mean by these terms, for though such an investigation may be tedious to our lofty intellects, perhaps

[63] ibid.
[64] G Davies, *Copyright and the Public Interest,* 2nd edn (London, Sweet & Maxwell, 2002) 3.
[65] Although it is concerned only with Great Britain.
[66] Deazley, *On the Origin* 5.
[67] ibid.
[68] See P Soper, 'Law's Normative Claims' in RP George (ed), *The Autonomy of Law: Essays on Legal Positivism* (Oxford, Clarendon Press, 1996) 220.
[69] ibid.

> even fatal to our pet arguments, it will certainly result in greater clearness and brevity, and less idle declamation.[70]

This book is interested in finding out what has been meant by claims regarding the public interest in the past, and how they have been used to further 'pet arguments' and make 'idle' (or perhaps not so idle) 'declamation'. It subjects the notion of 'public interest' to a closer examination than provided by previous commentators, who merely assert its existence or position it as a counterweight to the interests of authors in copyright's famous balancing act. Where much recent historical work has concentrated on the nature and role of authorship in copyright law, this book seeks to focus attention on the concept of public interest, demonstrating that it is as contingent and shifting as the notion of authorship.

III. SCOPE AND STRUCTURE

The focus of the book is on copyright in the nineteenth century. However, it is a 'long nineteenth century',[71] beginning around the turn of the century and ending not with the usual watershed of 1914 but three years earlier in 1911. This is a significant date in the development of copyright, as it is the year in which the Imperial Copyright Act was enacted. This Act brought most of the disparate statutes which regulated the law in relation to creative, aesthetic and informational works under one legislative instrument. It extended to Britain's colonies as well, and the self-governing Dominions either enacted it directly or enacted their own similar but independent Acts.[72] Thus, with the significant exception of the United States of America, the 1911 Copyright Act set the stage for copyright in the common law world.

Nor is the beginning date of this book strictly 1800. Many of the developments charted in these pages have roots stretching back to the eighteenth century, and these are exposed where relevant. Chapter two involves a brief excursion back into the eighteenth century and earlier to consider the origins of the Statute of Anne and the debate over common law copyright that culminated in the landmark decision of *Donaldson v Becket*. As previously noted, this is a period that has been examined by numerous historians of copyright. The aim here is to draw out and highlight some of the themes that emerged in this period and which would continue to influence the development of copyright law. The two most important themes for the purpose of this book are the role and demands of the book trade, the market in which it operated, and the deployment of public interest rhetoric both to conceal this role, and to strengthen those demands.

It is trite to note that the nineteenth century was a period of transformation of British society. Various sub-periods within the century have been identified by

[70] Scrutton, *The Laws of Copyright*, 1st edn, 292.

[71] To borrow the phrase of Eric Hobsbawm.

[72] Although note that Canada did not do so until 1921, see C Seville, *The Internationalisation of Copyright Law* (Cambridge, Cambridge University Press, 2006) 145.

historians, and named as an age of reform,[73] improvement,[74] revolution,[75] capital[76] and empire,[77] to note but a few. While the reigning monarch remained constant for much of the period, little else stood still. The century saw the development of the first industrial nation and the world's most expansive empire, as well as the emergence of a growing official administration, reaching into ever more spheres of society and culture. The population of Britain in 1801 was a little over 10 million; in 1911 it was almost four times that size.[78] From 1832 onwards, the franchise began to be extended and other reforms were made to improve the lives of children, workers, labourers and others. In short, the economic, political, intellectual and cultural scenes of the early twentieth century were dramatically different to those of one hundred years earlier.

The production, trade and consumption of books also experienced great change in this period. In 1800, around 40 per cent of males and 60 per cent of females were illiterate; by 1900 rates of illiteracy were around 4 per cent.[79] This meant a gradually growing market for book publishers and others involved in the book trade, with a concomitant growth in competition. Other major factors were technological advances and increasing mechanisation in the related trades of printing, typesetting and paper making. Many of these developments, such as the steam-driven press, began in the newspaper print rooms, and only slowly moved over to book production.[80] Methods of distribution were also becoming more efficient and cost-effective, with the spread of the railways and alterations to the Post Office system. Dropping costs of transportation assisted in reducing the price of books and, together with improvements in speed and greater geographical reach, new markets opened up and existing ones expanded.[81] Between 1846 and 1916, book production increased fourfold and book prices reduced by half.[82] During the nineteenth century a mass market for reading was born.[83]

A further transformation took place in relation to the kinds of books that were being written, published and sold. The nineteenth century is known as the golden age of the novel, but it also saw the development of children's books as an import-

[73] L Woodward, *The Age of Reform 1815–1870* (Oxford: Clarendon Press, 1962).

[74] A Briggs, *The Age of Improvement 1737–1867*, 2nd edn (Harlow, UK, Longman, 2000).

[75] E Hobsbawm, *The Age of Revolution 1789–1848* (London, Weidenfeld and Nicholson, 1962).

[76] E Hobsbawm, *The Age of Capital 1848–1875* (London, Weidenfeld and Nicholson, 1975).

[77] E Hobsbawm, *The Age of Empire 1875–1914* (London, Weidenfeld and Nicholson, 1987).

[78] BR Mitchell, *British Historical Statistics* (Cambridge, Cambridge University Press, 1988) 11.

[79] D Vincent, *The Rise of Mass Literacy: Reading and Writing in Modern Europe* (Cambridge, Polity Press, 2000) 9–10.

[80] For more detail on these changes, see D McKitterick, 'Changes in the Look of the Book' in D McKitterick (ed), *The Cambridge History of the Book in Britain*, vol 6: *1830–1914* (Cambridge, Cambridge University Press, 2009) 75–116 and A Weedon, *Victorian Publishing: The Economics of Book Publishing for a Mass Market, 1836–1914* (Aldershot, UK, Ashgate, 2003).

[81] For more detail on changes in distribution, see W Colclough, 'Distribution' in D McKitterick (ed), *The Cambridge History of the Book in Britain*, vol 6: *1830–1914* (Cambridge, Cambridge University Press, 2009) 238–80.

[82] Weedon, *Victorian Publishing* 57.

[83] The classic text on the birth of this development is RD Altick, *The English Common Reader: A Social History of the Mass Reading Public 1800–1900* (Chicago, University of Chicago Press, 1957).

ant category of literature.[84] It was also the time in which the newspaper came of age, and saw an infrequently recognised boom in the publishing of factual information.[85] Another new and increasingly important market that emerged was for educational works and textbooks.[86] Changes in the status of authors and the way that they were remunerated, however, came slowly. Outright sale of copyrights continued to be the dominant business model for most of the century, although half-profits agreements and commission publishing were also common. By the 1880s, royalty agreements had gradually taken over as the standard method of payment[87] and by the same period authorship had come to be considered as a professional activity, helped by the 'super-star' status of a few prominent figures like Charles Dickens and the efforts of the Society of Authors.[88]

Changes in the book trade, and their relationship to copyright law, are considered in greater detail throughout this book. Each of chapters three to six considers a different aspect of copyright law's development in the nineteenth century, in a broadly chronological manner. Chapter three looks at two aspects of copyright that are not commonly considered to be 'core' elements of the law: the legislative provisions for depositing copies of published books in certain designated libraries; and the legal principle that emerged in the early decades of the century which denied copyright protection to works that were immoral, seditious or libellous. Both are set against the background of developments in the book trade around the turn of the nineteenth century.

The debates over the legal deposit provisions are not often thought of as an aspect of the history of copyright law, with the notable exception of John Feather's work. However, the theme of tension between private property rights and the public interest that so often emerges in copyright debates was also a central feature of the legal deposit discussions. The principle that immoral works would not be protected by copyright raises the same tension, but in a different context and an examination of the social and legal context in which this principle developed is fascinating for the light that it sheds on notions of public interest and its relationship to education, books and social order in Regency England. The two issues of library deposit and the principle of non-protection of immoral, seditious or libellous books may seem to have little in common beyond their relationship to copyright law- a relationship that in the case of legal deposit is sometimes said to be an 'accident'.[89] However, both issues raised the question, of considerable importance to Regency society, of how best to encourage learning, or whether it

[84] B Alderson and A Immel, 'Mass Markets: Children's Books' in D McKitterick (ed), *The Cambridge History of the Book in Britain, vol* 6: *1830–1914* (Cambridge, Cambridge University Press, 2009) 382–415.

[85] A Fyfe, 'The Information Revolution' in D McKitterick (ed), *The Cambridge History of the Book in Britain,* vol 6: *1830–1914* (Cambridge, Cambridge University Press, 2009) 567–94.

[86] See Weedon, *Victorian Publishing,* ch 5.

[87] P Leary and A Nash 'Authorship' in D McKitterick (ed), *The Cambridge History of the Book in Britain,* vol 6: *1830–1914* (Cambridge, Cambridge University Press, 2009) 206.

[88] For more on the Society of Authors, see below: ch 5.

[89] J Feather, *Publishing, Piracy and Politics: An Historical Study of Copyright in Britain* (London, Mansell, 1994) 97.

was even desirable. This chapter thereby demonstrates that the concept of 'public interest' has played a role in many aspects of copyright law, and that while it has long been central to copyright law, its formulation is not only different in different eras, but also varies between social groups and depends heavily upon the context in which it is employed.

Chapters four and five trace the growth of copyright law over the course of the century. The expansion of copyright law's reach has been denounced in recent decades by many commentators[90] and has inspired such significance-laden metaphors as 'the second enclosure movement'.[91] Neil Netanel notes that '[c]opyright legislation has long been notorious for its embodiment of successful industry rent-seeking'.[92] These two chapters illustrate that industry rent-seeking was a feature of development of copyright law and policy in the nineteenth century. However, they question the extent to which this could always be said to have been 'successful', highlighting the competing discourses and inevitable compromises.

One obviously important aspect of copyright's expansion is the question of its duration. Clearly, the term for which copyright protection lasts is central to the tension between the rights of owners and the interests of the public. Considerable historical work has already been done on this aspect of copyright law, with particular attention being lavished on the common law copyright cases of the mid-eighteenth century. However, this is not the sole context in which the claims of copyright owners and the alleged public interest came into conflict. Chapter four also examines the extension of copyright to cover the spoken word, in the form of plays and lectures, its reach over the Channel, to cover the works of foreign authors, and the belated formation of professional groups to advance their own agendas. It also considers the process of reform that led to the 1842 Copyright Act. The history of this Act has been thoroughly examined by Catherine Seville[93] and so this chapter does not address the Act's background in great detail. Instead, it focuses on the arguments employed in the debates surrounding the Act, particularly the rhetoric of public interest and its constructed opposition to the natural rights of authors. The chapter goes on to discuss another arena in which the philosophical justifications for copyright were discussed in the years following 1842—the law courts, where the issue arose in relation to cases brought by foreign authors, or rather their publishers, claiming copyright protection in Britain.

Chapter five looks at a second forum in which copyright law was discussed at length in the second half of the century. This was the Royal Copyright Commission, appointed in 1875 to investigate the law of copyright. Several of the witnesses

[90] eg, P Drahos with J Braithwaite, *Information Feudalism* (New York, New Press, 2003), J Litman, *Digital Copyright* (New York, Prometheus Books, 2001) and NW Netanel, 'Why Has Copyright Expanded? Analysis and Critique' in F Macmillan (ed), *New Directions in Copyright Law*, vol 6 (Cheltenham, UK, Edward Elgar, 2008) 3–34.

[91] J Boyle, 'The Second Enclosure Movement and the Construction of the Public Domain' (2003) 66 *Law and Contemporary Problems* 33.

[92] Netanel, 'Why Has Copyright Expanded?' 4.

[93] C Seville, *Literary Copyright Reform in Early Victorian England* (Cambridge, Cambridge University Press, 1999).

appearing before the Commission raised the question whether copyright law should be abolished entirely, thereby giving rise to considerable discussion as to the law's objects and the best way to achieve them. In all of these areas of expansion, the concept of public interest as well as the ideology of romantic authorship played important roles. However, this chapter demonstrates that although both forms of rhetoric were employed extensively by various actors in the legislative process, neither could be said to have driven, nor to have held back, copyright's expansion in this period.

Chapter six examines the development of the law of infringement, particularly the exceptions to infringement. Infringement sets the borders of the scope of the rights conferred by copyright. The exceptions are frequently said to represent the 'public interest', by curtailing the copyright owner's exclusive rights in favour of certain specified uses. Laddie et al characterise the permitted acts as 'the rights of the public',[94] while Paul Torremans states that 'These defences exist in order to restore the balance between the rights of the owner of copyright and the rights of society at large'.[95]

Numerous other scholars, as well as judges, have situated the fair-dealing exceptions at the heart of copyright's balancing act.[96] One of the objects of this book is to contribute to contemporary debate over the role of fair dealing by excavating its historical foundations. A related debate with which this chapter engages is whether the fair-dealing principle evolved as a judicial limitation on the expansive rights of copyright owners[97] or as a judicial expansion of the limited rights granted to copyright owners.[98] An important first step in engaging with these issues is to recognise that the principle that a fair dealing with a work would be allowed for certain specified uses did not emerge as a separate principle prior to the 1911 Copyright Act. Decisions as to the kinds of uses that were to be permitted were bound up with other issues, such as the amount taken and whether protection would be conferred at all. Consequently, this chapter considers the development of the law of infringement more broadly, in terms of the general issue of determining which parts of a work should be protected and which should not.

An examination of the law of infringement over two hundred years reveals a slow process of expansion in favour of copyright owners who were increasingly able to trace their investment into different markets for different formats. By the

[94] H Laddie et al, *The Modern Law of Copyright and Designs* (London, Butterworths, 2000) 737.

[95] P Torremans, *Holyoak and Torremans Intellectual Property Law*, 4th edn (Oxford, Oxford University Press, 2005) 248.

[96] See eg: Gibson LJ described s 30(2) in the Copyright, Designs and Patents Act 1988 as aiming to strike 'a proper balance between protection of the rights of a creative author [and] the wider public interest, of which free speech is a very important ingredient' in *Newspaper Licensing Agency v Marks & Spencer* [2001] Ch 257, 271. See also J Griffiths, 'Copyright Law After Ashdown: Time to Deal Fairly with the Public' (2002) *Intellectual Property Quarterly* 240; K Garnett, G Davies, G Harbottle, *Copinger and Skone James On Copyright*, 15th edn (London, Sweet & Maxwell, 2005) [9-01]; K Puri, 'Fair Dealing with Copyright Material in Australia and New Zealand' (1983) *Victoria University of Wellington Law Review* 277, 290.

[97] M de Zwart, 'Seriously Entertaining: *The Panel Media* and the Future of Fair Dealing' (2003) 8 *Media and Arts Law Review* 1, 3.

[98] R Burrell and A Coleman, *Copyright Exceptions: The Digital Impact* (Cambridge, Cambridge University Press, 2005) 253–56.

end of the nineteenth century, the physical artefact of the 'book' as locus of protection had begun to be replaced by the more abstract, and economically constructed, 'work'. However, it is not possible to discern any simple patterns in achieving this expansion, such as effective deployment of the ideology of romantic authorship, nor of resistance in the form of public interest rhetoric. While some cases do display evidence that the claims of either, or both, authors and the public influenced the judges' reasoning, this is by no means consistently the case. Instead, these claims were frequently subsumed into an assessment based on competition in the marketplace.

Chapter seven looks at the final stages leading up to the enactment of the 1911 Copyright Act, starting with the efforts of the music publishers to increase their protection against piratical sheet music sellers. It then moves on to consider the international developments that made reform necessary, and the domestic negotiations that led to the passing of the Imperial Copyright Act in 1911. The 1911 Act marks the end of this book, but the Act was far from the culmination of a long process of reform. It resolved the most pressing issue of international compatibility, but left unresolved many other issues to plague copyright lawyers and litigants of the future. Investigating the discussions and developments leading up to the Act, this chapter reveals that once again the rhetoric of public interest was employed to mask a variety of private interests. However, even where the claims of the public were genuinely and disinterestedly advanced, they proved to have only limited effect in holding back the expansion of copyright law that was achieved by its codification in 1911.

The central object of this book is to examine in detail the role that the concept of the public interest has had in shaping copyright law. Its central argument is that the role played by the public interest has often been important, but in ways that are far from straightforward. The notion of 'public interest' is not a single or unified concept—its content will vary depending upon who is considered to make up 'the public' and who is articulating its interests. At times different interests may come into conflict, and at other times they may be complementary. The very opacity of the concept is both strength and weakness: strength because the simpler a rhetorical appeal can be made, the more likely it will resonate with its audience; weakness because it can be used as a cloak for private interests and thereby discredited. By exposing the contingency and variability of the concept of public interest in its historical context, this book seeks to construct a more nuanced and multi-dimensional history of copyright's development than is encapsulated in simple assertions that copyright has always been about the public interest or about balancing the public interest against the claims of authorship.

2

Copyright before the Nineteenth Century

I. PRE-HISTORY OF THE STATUTE OF ANNE

THE 1710 STATUTE of Anne[1] is the obvious starting point for a modern history of copyright law, particularly one that seeks to expose the role of the public interest. The Statute is frequently invoked by modern judges and academics as embodying the utilitarian underpinnings of copyright law. In the recent decision of *IceTV v Nine Network*, the High Court of Australia noted that the title and recitals of the Statute of Anne 'echoed explicitly the emphasis on the practical or utilitarian importance that certain seventeenth century philosophers attached to knowledge and its encouragement in the scheme of human progress'.[2] However, the Statute was itself spun from even older thread and has long been the subject of criticism and competing claims over its true objectives. Augustine Birrell believed it was set in motion 'not by an irate populace clamouring for cheap books (as a generation later they were to clamour for cheap gin), but by the authors and their proprietors, the booksellers'.[3] However, he attacked it as a 'perfidious measure "rigged with curses dark" ',[4] that 'gave away the whole case of the author'[5] and thus forestalled further development of common law copyright.[6] Victor Bonham-Carter, on the other hand, believes that the Statute was 'the foundation of copyright as we know it. It established the author's right to his own property, and thereby gave him the power to bargain for better terms'.[7]

Other scholars have emphasised the role of the book trade in influencing the timing and content of the Statute. John Feather considers that the Act was a booksellers' Act, and was seen by them as continuing their existing rights.[8] LR Patterson interprets the Act as 'a trade-regulation statute enacted in order to bring order to the

[1] An Act for the Encouragement of Learning by Vesting the Copies of Printed Books in the Authors or Purchasers of such Copies 1710 (8 Anne c 19).

[2] *IceTV Pty Limited v Nine Network Pty Limited* [2009] HCA 14 (High Court of Australia), [25] (per French CJ, Crennan, Kiefel JJ).

[3] A Birrell, *Seven Lectures on the Law and History of Copyright in Books* (London, Cassell & Co Ltd, 1899) 22.

[4] ibid 19.

[5] ibid 21.

[6] ibid 22.

[7] V Bonham-Carter, *Authors by Profession* (London, Spottiswoode Ballantyne Press, 1978) 6.

[8] J Feather, *A History of British Publishing* (London, Routledge, 1988) 55.

chaos created by the final lapse in 1694 of its predecessor, the Printing Act of 1662, and to prevent a continuation of the booksellers' monopoly'.[9] David Saunders concurs with Patterson that the purpose of the legislation was 'to break the Company's 150-year-old monopoly on the publishing of books in England'.[10] Ronan Deazley, on the other hand, sees the Act as having a broader purpose, stating:

> The legislators were not concerned with the recognition of any pre-existing right, nor were they primarily interested in the regulation of the bookseller's market, but rather secured the continued production of useful books through the striking of a culturally significant social bargain, a trade-off involving the author, the bookseller and the reading public.[11]

For Deazley, the central plank of the Statute of Anne was the 'cultural *quid pro quo*'.[12]

So, was the Statute an Act for authors, for booksellers, or for the public? The short answer is: all three. Its ancestry lay in the dual concerns of trade regulation and censorship that had become increasingly intertwined over the previous 150 years.[13] Since the reign of Henry VII, the Crown had engaged in granting patents or privileges to individuals to print certain documents and books. Under Elizabeth I book patents were complemented by a licensing system revolving around the Stationers' Company, a London guild granted its Charter by Mary I in 1557. The Charter provided that nobody had the right to engage in the trade of printing in the realm unless he was first a member of the Company. Books were inspected by Company officers and entered in a register. The objective of the Crown was to control print media, and thereby to stamp out political and religious dissent. The objective of the Stationers' Company was to regulate the trade, so as to prevent multiple reprints of the same work and concentrate power among its members. The two objectives worked in tandem for many years and were enforced by several Star Chamber decrees.

When the Star Chamber was abolished in 1641, the Company's power began to decline, but censorship did not end. The Long Parliament passed several ordinances and Acts to control the Press, and Cromwell also exercised the Protectorial prerogative for book trade and censorship regulation. In 1662, two years after Charles II came to the throne, an Act for Preventing the Frequent Abuses in Printing Seditious, Treasonable, and Unlicensed Books and Pamphlets; and for the Regulating of Printing and Printing Presses was passed.[14] This Act was the first

[9] LR Patterson, *Copyright in Historical Perspective* (Nashville, Vanderbilt University Press, 1968) 25.

[10] D Saunders, *Authorship and Copyright* (London, Routledge, 1992) 26. The reference is to the Stationer's Company, for detail on which see the following paragraph.

[11] R Deazley, 'The Myth of Copyright at Common Law' (2003) 62 *Cambridge Law Journal* 106, 108.

[12] ibid.

[13] For a detailed and fascinating study of this story, see C Blagden, *The Stationers' Company: A History 1403–1959* (London, George Allen & Unwin Ltd, 1960) chs 1–9.

[14] An Act for Preventing the Frequent Abuses in Printing Seditious, Treasonable and Unlicensed Books and Pamphlets, and for Regulating of Printing and Printing-Presses 1662 (13 & 14 Car II c 33) (Licensing Act 1662).

not to rely on the authority of the prerogative, but sought to give press regulation the greater authority conferred by being an Act of the King in Parliament.[15]

The Licensing Act of 1662, as it is often called, was expressed to last for only two years. However, it was renewed several times before finally lapsing in 1695.[16] Thereafter, numerous attempts were made to re-introduce press regulation. The Stationers lobbied for regulation to protect their interests, but made little progress. One significant stand of opposition flowed from a general and widespread distrust of monopolies. By the time of James I, the royal use of monopolies had become one of Parliament's main grievances. This was intensified in the first two decades of the seventeenth century when the English economy sank into a deep recession that many blamed on patents and monopolies.[17] In 1624, Parliament enacted the Statute of Monopolies, declaring monopolies to be void, but making certain exemptions which included patents for invention and patents for printing.[18]

Despite the printing exemption, however, the distrust of patents extended to the book trade. A temporary financial downturn in the 1690s intensified concerns that the Stationers' Company was abusing its power through the use of State-granted patents.[19] John Locke was among those concerned by the monopolising practices of the Stationers' Company and he campaigned strongly against renewal of the Licensing Act in the 1690s. Locke considered it ridiculous that the writings of long-dead authors should be treated as the property of particular booksellers. For living authors, he considered that the property should be limited to a term of 50 or 70 years.[20] A number of members of the book trade were also opposed to renewal of the Licensing Act. In a petition of February 1693, a group of independent booksellers, printers and bookbinders complained that the Act prevented them from exercising their trades.[21] Moreover, the Bills that were unsuccessfully introduced in the period after 1695 also sought to break the London-based hold of the Stationers' Company on the trade by providing that presses could be set up in other cities if they registered with specified authorities.[22]

Some historians of copyright have portrayed the lapse of the Licensing Act in 1695 as giving birth to the 'public domain'—a halcyon period of six years when

[15] M Treadwell, 'The Stationers and the Printing Acts at the End of the Seventeenth Century' in J Barnard and DF Mackenzie (eds), *The Cambridge History of the Book in Britain*, vol 4: *1557–1695* (Cambridge, Cambridge University Press, 2002) 755.

[16] (1664) 16 Car II c 8; (1685) I Jac II c 17; (1692) 4 & 5 Wm & M c 24.

[17] M Kishlansky, *A Monarchy Transformed: Britain 1603–1714* (London, Penguin Books Ltd, 1996) 99.

[18] An Act concerning Monopolies and Dispensations with Penal Laws and the Forfeitures thereof 1624 (21 Jac I c 3). For more on the role of monopolies, see O Bracha, 'Owning Ideas: A History of Anglo-American Intellectual Property' (unpublished SJD Dissertation, Harvard Law School, 2005) at www.obracha.net/oi/oi.htm.

[19] J Raven, *The Business of Books: Booksellers and the English Book Trade 1450–1850* (New Haven, Yale University Press, 2007) 86.

[20] R Astbury, 'The Renewal of the Licensing Act in 1693 and its Lapse in 1695' (1978) 33 *The Library* 286, 309. See also R Deazley, *On the Origin of the Right to Copy: Charting the Movement of Copyright Law in the Eighteenth Century (1695–1775)* (Oxford, Hart Publishing, 2004) 1–5.

[21] Astbury, 'Renewal of the Licensing Act'.

[22] ibid 310–13

all were 'free to do with the work as they wished'.[23] What this assessment overlooks is the practical operation of the book trade at the time, and the strength of the non-statutory mechanism that shored up the booksellers' monopolies. For, while the lapse of the Licensing Act may have further eroded the Stationers' Company, there was no sudden throwing open of the gates of culture and learning. Instead, a new structure emerged, replacing the established authority of the Stationers' Company. This system was based on a form of trade organisation, known as congers,[24] which drew on the experience of co-operative publishing employed by the English Stock,[25] but relied on economic power rather than royal authority. The first named conger, known as the Wholesaling Conger, dated from the 1690s. However, Blagden places the birth of the idea as early as 1683, around the time that the Licensing Act lapsed for the first time.[26]

The congers were a response to changes in the book trade, particularly the uncertainty over its future regulation during the reign of Charles II and thereafter.[27] The congers shared ownership of the most valuable copyrights, and the conger members were the most prominent members of the London book trade. Their membership overlapped significantly with the senior ranks of the Stationers' Company, demonstrating that although the organisational power base had changed those holding the power had not. If a conger work was pirated, there would be 15 or 16 victims. The conger could then retaliate by refusing to supply the pirate with books, or to purchase from him, which could cause considerable damage to an individual business, and possibly even close it down.[28] Congers also provided other benefits to their members. Given the high-risk levels associated with printing ventures, due to factors such as the costliness of paper and lack of market awareness, the sharebook systems embodied in the congers were effective in spreading and minimising the risk to participants. They also helped to create stability in the book trade by controlling prices.

[23] R Deazley, *Rethinking Copyright: History, Theory, Language* (Cheltenham, UK, Edward Elgar, 2006) 160–61.

[24] The word 'conger' is sometimes claimed to derive from the conger eel, which swallowed up all the smaller fish: AS Collins, *Authorship in the Days of Johnson: Being a Study of the Relationship between Author, Patron, Publisher and Public, 1726–1780* (London, Robert Holden & Co Ltd, 1927) 19, quoting the late 17th- early 18th-century bookseller John Nichols. See also quote from Dunton in N Hodgson and C Blagden, *The Notebook of Thomas Benet and Henry Clements* (Oxford, University Press, 1956) 76. More recent commentators suggest it derived from the word 'conjure', or sworn agreement, of the kind which guilds had used to preserve their 'mysteries' or trade secrets: W St Clair, *The Reading Nation in the Romantic Period* (Cambridge, Cambridge University Press, 2004) 95.

[25] In 1603, the Stationers' Company had raised a fund allowing it to purchase the royal patents for psalters, almanacs, law books and school books. The Committee of the Stock spread the printing among the printers of London and distributed profit among the whole trade by means of dividends on the Stock. Its success led the Company to establish a Latin Stock, an Irish Stock and a Scottish Stock. See G Pollard, 'The English Market for Printed Books: The Sandars Lectures 1959' (1978) 4 *Publishing History* 8, 23.

[26] Blagden, *The Stationers' Company* 78–81.

[27] Hodgson and Blagden, *The Notebook* 76. Booksellers were not alone in seeking to manage trade instability in this period. Other industries were also developing risk sharing schemes, such as simple insurance against fire and marine disasters, and joint stock companies were also appearing on the scene, see M Treadwell, 'The Stationers and the Printing Acts' 773–74.

[28] Hodgson and Blagden, *The Notebook* 77.

II. THE STATUTE TAKES SHAPE

Recognition of the important role played by the congers in stabilising the book trade following the decline of the Stationers' Company undermines the view of copyright historians, like Patterson, that the decline led to trade chaos requiring urgent legislative intervention.[29] However, while the booksellers might have had the London trade sewn-up, matters were different outside the capital. Provincial piracy had long been a target of the Stationers' Company,[30] and one of the major effects of the lapse of licensing was the establishment of printing houses in the provincial centres.[31] Foreign markets also represented a threat, as the lower price of paper on the Continent meant that books could be more cheaply produced there and imported to England where they undercut domestic products.[32] Such external issues could only be dealt with by legislation.

In the first decade of the eighteenth century, the London booksellers abandoned their attempts to re-establish legislative control over the trade through the traditional link with censorship, and began to focus simply on trade regulation.[33] Consequently, their arguments began to centre on their business interests. This had already begun in 1694 when the Stationers' Company petitioned Parliament for a new licensing ordinance, complaining that 'if their Property should not be provided for by the said Bill, not only the Petitioners, but many Widows, and others, whose whole Livelihood depends upon the Petitioners' Property, will be utterly ruined'.[34] In 1707, some of the most prominent members of the trade petitioned the House of Commons, referring to books as their 'property' by which they had made provision 'for their Widows and Children' and complaining that piracy was causing 'great Damage'.[35] A number of the same booksellers petitioned again in 1709, asserting their property rights, by claiming that

> it has been the constant Usage, for the Writers of Books, to sell their Copies to Booksellers, or Printers, to the end they might hold those Copies as their Property, and enjoy the Profit of making, and vending, Impressions of them, [but that lately several persons had taken to reprinting such books] to the great Injury, of the Proprietors, even to their utter Ruin.[36]

At the same time, the booksellers supplemented such arguments with an appeal to the interests of the public in the spread of learning. This rhetorical approach

[29] Patterson, *Copyright in Historical Perspective* 143.

[30] J Barnard and M Bell, 'The English Provinces' in J Barnard and DF Mackenzie (eds), *The Cambridge History of the Book in Britain*, vol 4: *1557–1695* (Cambridge, Cambridge University Press, 2002) 665.

[31] Treadwell, 'The Stationers and the Printing Acts'.

[32] PG Hoftijzer, 'British Books Abroad: The Continent' in J Barnard and DM Mackenzie (eds), *The Cambridge History of the Book in Britain*, vol 4: *1557–1695* (Cambridge, Cambridge University Press, 2002) 736.

[33] Patterson, *Copyright in Historical Perspective* 141.

[34] ibid 139.

[35] *JC* vol 15, 313 (26 February 1707).

[36] *JC* vol 16, 240 (12 December 1709).

resonated with Enlightenment ideals regarding the importance of scientific inquiry and the dissemination of knowledge. This tactic had also been used earlier in relation to petitions concerned with censorship. In a petition of 1641, the Stationers claimed that their objective was 'the advancement of wholesome knowledge'.[37] Similarly, in a petition of 1707, the booksellers asserted that the pirates' actions were 'to the great Discouragement of persons from writing Matters that might be of great Use to the Publick, and to the great Damage of Proprietors'.[38] In 1709, the booksellers began with their claim to property rights as stated above, but quickly followed by noting that as well as causing ruin to the booksellers, piracy was resulting in 'the Discouragement of all Writers in any useful Part of learning'.[39]

These appeals to the public interest in learning and the production of useful books were linked to a third strand of persuasion: the claims of authorship. Mark Rose has noted that this strategy was probably suggested to the booksellers by Defoe's references to the relationship between authors and property rights in the debate over censorship and the renewal of the Licensing Act.[40] Both the 1707 and the 1709 petitions referred to the useful knowledge produced by books, but they also explicitly included the writers of such books as having a claim upon the legislature's attention alongside that of the books' printers and vendors.

Once it became apparent that the end of the licensing regime had not opened the book trade up to small-scale enterprises, smaller traders also began to support the introduction of legislation. A pamphlet published in 1709 by the bookseller turned publisher John How[41] demonstrates the way that the rhetoric of learning and social benefit could be employed in ways diametrically opposed to the interests of the conger member booksellers.[42] How railed against the practice of piracy in the trade, placing it firmly at the door of the wealthiest traders. He noted that:

> First, Because the great Traders can make what Impressions of Books as they please, and can vend them with as much Ease and Privacy as they printed them.
>
> Secondly, They can justify their Oppressions in the Face of the World, because they are rich.
>
> Thirdly, The small Traders cannot prosecute them for usurping their just, equitable, and undoubted Right, because they are poor: Upon which Account, the great Dealers have ingros'd the most profitable and best part of the Trade, and made a Monopoly of those Priviledges and Immunities, which were granted by Royal Favour to the Company of Stationers, and for the common Good of the Whole, and for the particular Advantage and Interest of every individual Member of the Community.[43]

[37] Patterson, *Copyright in Historical Perspective* 128.
[38] *JC* vol 15, 313 (26 February 1707).
[39] *JC* vol 15, 240 (12 December 1709).
[40] M Rose, *Authors and Owners: The Invention of Copyright* (Cambridge, Mass, Harvard University Press 1993) 34–35.
[41] For background on How, see D-J Dugas, 'The London Book Trade in 1709 (Part Two)' (2001) 95 *Papers of the Bibliographical Society of America* 157.
[42] J How, *Some Thoughts on the Present State of Printing and Bookselling* (London, 1709).
[43] ibid 4.

How linked unfair competition practices in the trade with fears of monopoly and rhetoric based on the public good. He advocated a return to trade regulation through the Stationers' Company, which he considered the best way of protecting the interests of all members of the trade, and particularly small-scale enterprises. He also argued:

> It is, besides, a great Discouragement to Learning, that when a Gentleman has had a thousand Pounds or more laid out on his Education, and has no Dependence in the World left but his Learning, which has cost him so much Time and Money, that he cannot have a Reward for his Labours, because he is unable to make the Buyer any secure Title to his Copy.[44]

How's pamphlet, therefore, wove together several different appeals. An encouragement to authors to write and sell learned books was linked to financial considerations, while education was expressed to be an investment in both the author himself and his society.

Thus, by 1709, support for some form of legislation regulating the printing industry was widespread throughout the book trade. The rhetoric of the wealthy London booksellers and that of the small traders coincided in the public advantages to be gained by legislation, but their proposals as to how this was to be achieved were quite different. Eventually, a Statute was enacted and, inevitably, the result was a compromise.

Some provisions of the Statute of Anne clearly responded to the booksellers' concerns. The title was 'An Act for the Encouragement of Learning, by Vesting the Copies of Printed Books in the Authors or Purchasers of such Copies, during the Times therein mentioned'. The preamble, however, commenced with the problems suffered by 'Printers, Booksellers and other Persons' due to the lack of regulation, leading 'to their very great Detriment, and too often to the Ruin of them and their Families'.[45] The next part of the preamble moved on to the reason for the legislation: 'For Preventing therefore such Practices for the future, and for the Encouragement of Learned Men to Compose and Write useful Books'.[46] The booksellers' tactic of linking their trade interests to more general social interests in encouraging learning was thus enshrined in legislation, with consequences that would emerge again and again over the next two centuries.

Other parts of the Act likewise favoured the booksellers, as well as incorporating elements of the previous licensing regimes. The prohibition on printing and reprinting extended to importation, thereby addressing the booksellers' fears that English books would be brought in from the Continent, where they could be printed much more cheaply, to undercut the domestic market.[47] A similar prohibition had featured in the 1662 Licensing Act.[48] The operation of the Act was also extended to Scotland, which addressed concerns about the burgeoning Scottish

[44] ibid 12.
[45] Statute of Anne 1710, Preamble.
[46] ibid.
[47] This concern was expressed by How, *Some Thoughts* 15.
[48] Licensing Act 1662 s 9.

printing industry.[49] The Register of the Stationers' Company was retained, and entry of the title of books therein was to be the indicia of ownership and a prerequisite for the recovery of the Act's penalties.[50] However, the rationale for retaining this feature of the licensing system was re-characterised as performing the public service of informing people which books were claimed as property.[51]

At the same time as recognising the interests of the booksellers, the legislature also responded to concerns regarding monopolistic practices by placing certain limits on the rights granted to them. One of the most dramatic changes from the previous regime was to limit the right to print books to a period of 21 years, in the case of books already in existence, and to a period of 14 years, in the case of books not yet printed.[52] Disputes over the rights were no longer to be handled within the Stationers' Company, but were to give rise to an action at law.[53] Still more significantly, ownership of rights in copies was no longer limited to booksellers and other members of the Company, but was to be vested first of all in the authors of such books and, as a secondary matter, in booksellers as their assignees. Moreover, the final section of the Act provided that if the author were living at the end of 14 years, the sole right of printing or disposing of copies would return to him for another 14 years.[54]

Three other elements of the Act sought to place limitations on the booksellers' monopoly. First, there was a section which made provision for complaint to be made to certain persons, including the Archbishop of Canterbury and the Lord Chancellor, in the event that any book were sold at an unreasonably high price.[55] Second, the number of copies of every published book to be given free to libraries in England and Scotland was increased from three to nine.[56] Third, the operation of the Act was not to extend to prohibit the importation and sale of books in Greek, Latin and foreign languages.[57] Importation of foreign-language books had long been allowed, on the basis that this market could not be satisfactorily supplied by the English booksellers.[58] As well as limiting the booksellers' monopoly, these three provisions could be interpreted as serving a second purpose of ensuring that books were accessible and affordable, and thereby encouraging learning. However, there was no explicit link between that encouragement and these provisions in the Act,

[49] Statute of Anne 1710 s 6.
[50] ibid s 2.
[51] ibid.
[52] ibid s 1.
[53] The Stationers' Company had made efforts to keep disputes in-house, although from time to time disputes had gone before the courts. A 1678 ordinance of the Company provided that members who commenced suits at law, rather than bringing an application to the Court of Assistants of the Company, would be fined £10. See H Ransom, *The First Copyright Statute* (Austin, University of Texas Press, 1956) 80–81.
[54] Statute of Anne 1710 s 11.
[55] ibid s 4.
[56] ibid s 5. The Licensing Act 1662 provided that three copies of every printed book had to be delivered to the Royal Library and the libraries of the two universities: Licensing Act 1662 s 17.
[57] Statute of Anne 1710 s 7.
[58] J Barnard, 'Introduction' in J Barnard and DM Mackenzie (eds), *The Cambridge History of the Book in Britain*, vol 4: *1557–1695* (Cambridge, Cambridge University Press, 2002) 6. Licensing Act (1662) s 9.

and the connection is made to seem even more tenuous when it is remembered that both the library deposit and foreign-language book provisions had appeared in the 1662 Licensing Act.[59] In addition, the price control provisions were repealed after only a few years.[60]

The attitude of the legislature towards authors themselves was far from clear. Despite Feather's claim that authors are not mentioned at all in the Act,[61] the author in fact made several appearances. In the scheme of the Act, the author was someone to be encouraged to write books (as a 'learned man'), someone who had initial rights in a copy which could either be transferred to a bookseller or exercised by himself, and someone with a reversionary interest at the expiry of 14 years in any book he had written.

Patterson claims that the introduction of the author was a weapon against the booksellers' monopoly, and that the draftsmen were effectively turning the booksellers' promotion of the author in their own interest against them.[62] Certainly he is correct in identifying that the most radical change of the Statute was not that it gave *authors* rights in their own works. Authors had always had at least the right to consent to publication by virtue of their physical ownership of the manuscript. What was new in the Act was that these rights could be assigned by authors to *anyone*, not just members of the Stationers' Company.[63] This was further emphasised by section 3 of the Act, which was intended to provide for penalties against the Clerk of the Company if he refused to enter the title of a book into the Register.[64]

Practically speaking, the right to print was of little use to authors, unless they happened to own a printing press of their own and have access to a distribution network. The main objective of an author in 1710, and for almost 200 years afterwards, was to obtain a sum of money from a bookseller in exchange for his work, and there was little thought of retaining any rights in respect of it. It seems likely that the rationale behind section 11 of the Act, which gave living authors a reversionary interest in their books after the expiry of 14 years, was to protect authors who may have parted with their rights for too little consideration in the light of later popularity. Alternatively, it may have been to prevent a single publisher from benefiting from one book for an extended term of 28 years. Whatever the reason, the section was of little use in protecting authors, as in practice it was interpreted restrictively by the courts.[65]

59 Licensing Act 1662 ss 9, 17.

60 An Act for Prohibiting the Importation of Books reprinted Abroad and first composed or written and printed in Great Britain, and for repealing so much of an Act made in the 8th year of the reign of Her Late Majesty Queen Anne as Impowers the Limiting the Prices of Books 1739 (12 Geo II c 36) s 3.

61 J Feather, *A History of British Publishing* 74–75.

62 Patterson, *Copyright in Historical Perspective* 147.

63 ibid 145.

64 Statute of Anne 1710 s 3. See Deazley, *On the Origin* 47–49 for a discussion of the poor drafting of this section.

65 In 1786, Lord Thurlow LC found that the wording 'he conveys all his interest in the copyright' included conveyance of the second term: *Carnan v Bowles* (1786) 2 Bro CC 80, 83–84. In *Rundell v Murray* (1821) Jac 311, the Court assumed that general wording would not suffice to pass the second term, but that specific words, like those used in *Carnan v Bowles*, would do so.

The lack of any real coherent rationale underlying the Statute of Anne can be seen in the conflicting objectives of its various provisions. The Statute appears to represent an attempt by Parliament to recognise the conflicting interests of different booksellers, as well as the claims of authors and more general social concerns. The result was, in the words of Scrutton, 'an unfortunately worded compromise'.[66] But presenting the Statute as a societal 'quid pro quo' or bargain aimed at ensuring the continued production of books, as Deazley does,[67] is overstating the matter.[68] Although many of the elements that would later come to be key features of copyright contests were present, they were insufficiently developed in the legislation to be clearly recognisable as trade-offs between competing interests.

The notion of public interest was particularly vague. The Statute may have referred to the 'encouragement of learning', but this was the age before mass literacy and only a small fraction of the population had any learning at all. The link between granting property rights and the encouragement offered to authors was effected only by their juxtaposition in the Act's preamble and the pre-Statute rhetoric of the booksellers, and was not developed with any greater sophistication. Moreover, David Lieberman has noted that, in the eighteenth century, statements as to the legislature's intention in preambles were not considered to add anything to the meaning of an Act. Quoting from Daines Barrington's authoritative *Observations on the More Ancient Statutes*, that most preambles 'dwelt upon a pretence, which was not the real occasion of the law', Lieberman notes that 'any attempt to interpret the law by this means was likely to mistake the legislature's intention, as well as the state of the law when the Act was passed'.[69] The overlap between trade interests, public interests and authors' interests that occurred in the Statute of Anne was therefore contingent and unformed. However, it was far from being without real effect. The three had been loosely woven together into a trade regulation Act and as time passed the bonds between them would draw ever tighter.

The Statute of Anne has been retrospectively christened the world's first copyright Act. However, it seems that in the years following its enactment, it had little effect on the book trade. After an initial period of compliance with the registration and library deposit provisions, both activities declined,[70] and, while some authorial contracts recognised the new limited period of 14 years,[71] many did not.[72] The

[66] TE Scrutton, *The Laws of Copyright,* 1st edn (London, J Murray, 1883) 114.

[67] Deazley, *On the Origin* 46.

[68] As Kathy Bowrey and Natalie Fowell have noted, Deazley gives 'an enormous foundational significance on what [he] describes as a "poorly drafted piece of legislation" . . . It also suggests cohesion or accord amongst those supporting limits to literary property.' K Bowrey and N Fowell, 'Digging Up Fragments and Building IP Franchises' (2009) 31 *Sydney Law Review* 185, 201.

[69] D Lieberman, *The Province of Legislation Determined* (Cambridge, Cambridge University Press, 1989) 19. Lieberman also notes that Blackstone did not include use of the preamble in his ten rules for the construction of statutes, in W Blackstone, *Commentaries on the Laws of England,* 4 vols, 1st edn (Oxford, Clarendon, 1765) Book 1, pp 87–92.

[70] D McKitterick, *Cambridge University Library. A History. Eighteenth and Nineteenth Centuries* (Cambridge, Cambridge University Press, 1986) 29.

[71] eg, Pope's contract for the sale of *The Iliad,* entered into in 1713 or 1714 was expressly limited to 'such time and terme of years as he or his heirs enjoyed such rights'. See St Clair, *The Reading Nation* 92.

[72] See, eg, St Clair, *The Reading Nation* 94.

booksellers could afford to ignore the Statute of Anne due to the stability of the book trade at that time. A shift in the organisation of the book trade meant that it relied less on traditional forms of authority and more on economic power. The congers which had formed prior to the Statute continued in operation until the second decade of the eighteenth century and other new congers were formed, some of which were concerned with specialist works such as law books.[73] By the second half of the century, the term 'conger' had come to be used loosely as a synonym for publishing in partnership.[74]

The cohesion of the congers was maintained through trade sales, at which shares in copies were exchanged. Although the earliest sales took place shortly after the passing of the Statute of Anne,[75] and lasted until several years before *Donaldson v Becket*,[76] the prices paid for shares at the sales give no indication that the booksellers believed they were not buying a perpetual right.[77] Even the failure of the booksellers' attempts to secure legislation increasing the term of copyright protection in 1735 and 1737 did not seem to affect prices or sales adversely.[78]

In the first half of the century, then, the book trade was dominated by a small number of wealthy and powerful booksellers, almost all of whom were wholesalers who did not necessarily run retail operations.[79] The conger system has been criticised for its monopolistic tendencies.[80] However, despite the strong hold it exercised over the trade, the conger system can be seen as a realistic response to prevailing market conditions. The advantages of the system in sharing and spreading risk as well as discouraging piracy have been noted above. Printing and bookselling served a luxury market, which was particularly vulnerable to vicissitudes of fortune among its customers, and therefore to unstable social conditions. The eighteenth-century economy revolved around delicate webs of credit between producers, distributors, consumers, masters and apprentices.[81] In good times this was unproblematic, but when the bubble burst, as in the South Sea case, major liquidity crises would ensue.[82] In such cases the hardest hit would be tradesmen, shopkeepers and retailers because they found it hardest to realise their assets.[83]

73 Hodgson and Blagden, *The Notebook* 94–96.

74 ibid 96.

75 Pollard believes that the first trade sale occurred in 1689, but both Blagden and Belanger place the earliest sale in 1718: G Pollard, 'The English Market for Printed Books' 32; C Blagden, 'Booksellers' Trade Sales 1718–1768' (1951) 5 *The Library*, 5th series, 243; T Belanger, 'Booksellers' Trade Sales, 1718–1768' (1975) 30 *The Library* 281.

76 *Donaldson v Becket* (1774) 2 Bro PC 129.

77 Blagden, 'Booksellers' Trade Sales' 255.

78 ibid.

79 T Belanger, 'Booksellers' Sales of Copyright: Aspects of the London Book Trade 1718–1768' (PhD Dissertation, Columbia University, 1970) 1–3.

80 St Clair, *The Reading Nation* 106.

81 J Brewer, 'Commercialisation and Politics' in N McKendrick, J Brewer and JH Plumb (eds), *The Birth of a Consumer Society: The Commercialisation of Eighteenth-Century England* (London, Hutchinson, 1983) 205.

82 ibid 209.

83 ibid 211.

This was also a society in which credit depended on individual relationships of trust.[84] Those who could demonstrate such relationships, such as the Rivingtons, Robinson, Strahan and Cadell, were best served in such a financial atmosphere, and it was beneficial for others to be associated with them.[85] Conger groupings also aided distribution of books, as each share-owner received a certain number of copies, which he or she could then sell himself, pass on to retailers or exchange for the books of other retailers and other conger groups.

Yet, inevitably, the conger system caused dissatisfaction among other traders as well as authors and members of the public. In 1735, a group of eminent and educated gentlemen, including George Sale, the orientalist, Roger Gale, the antiquary, George Lewis Scott, the mathematician, and several distinguished doctors, formed the Society for the Encouragement of Learning, under the presidency of the Duke of Richmond.[86] The aim of the society was

> to supply the want of a regular and publick encouragement of learning; to assist authors in the Publication, and to Secure to them the entire Profits of their own works; to institute a republick of letters, for the promoting of arts and sciences, by the necessary means of profit, as well as by the nobler motives of praise and emulation.[87]

The Society published several scholarly books but, despite its noble motives, it did not prosper and was dissolved in 1749.[88] Its failure can largely be attributed to the hostility of the booksellers, who refused to promote books in which they had no interest or to work together with the Society which did not follow the usual custom of exchanging books and giving trade discounts. The Society, for its part, failed to appreciate the booksellers' extensive knowledge of the book market.[89] This short-lived but worthy attempt to alter the prevailing conditions of bookselling in Britain illustrates the stranglehold of the London booksellers over the trade at the time.

III. CHARTING THE BOUNDARIES OF THE STATUTE OF ANNE

One thing that does seem to emerge clearly from the text of the Act is that the minds of the legislature and parliamentary draftsmen were fixed firmly upon the particular problem of multiple people wishing to print and publish the same book. As part of the objective of shifting the power base away from the Stationers' Company, redress for breaches of the Act was made the subject of an action at common law. However, this limited approach to the subject of literary property did not address many of the questions that were to arise in the following years. As

[84] J Raven, 'The Book Trades' in I Rivers (ed), *Books and their Readers in Eighteenth Century England: New Essays* (London, Leicester University Press, 2001) 10.

[85] ibid.

[86] C Atto, 'The Society for the Encouragement of Learning' (1938) 19 *The Library* 261, 265.

[87] ibid 264.

[88] ibid.

[89] ibid 272–82.

Jane Ginsburg has written, in terms of delineating what would be treated as property from what was in the public domain, 'the realm of copyright was a shoreline of uncertain contours. The Statute of Anne may have separated the waters from the lands, but it did not clearly tell us which was which'.[90]

Many questions regarding the scope of the Act were to come before the courts of common law and equity in the following years. Did the Act extend beyond 'books'? In particular, did it apply to unpublished works? Did the Act affect grants of patent rights? Were the remedies available for breaches limited to the penalties set out in the Act? Did the Act apply if the work had not been registered at Stationers' Hall? Did the Act apply only where an *identical* copy of the book was published? And finally, and most controversially, did the Act entirely cover the field of rights to print and publish books or did common law rights exist alongside the Act's sphere of operation?

From the 1720s, the booksellers began testing the limits of the Act before the courts. The question of whether the printing patents fell within the Statute was the earliest to be addressed. As Deazley shows, the courts appeared to consider that the Statute had no effect on these royal grants.[91] Indeed, in 1734 Parliament filled the gap left in the Statute of Anne regarding domestically printed books in Greek or Latin by granting Samuel Buckley the right to print a work in Latin for a period of 14 years.[92]

The question of remedies beyond the statutory penalty[93] was the next to be considered. Appeals to the Court of Chancery for interim injunctions were successful in a number of cases,[94] even after the statutory periods of protection had expired.[95] An account of profits and perpetual injunction were also awarded in one case.[96] Claims for damages proved more problematic, and became bound up with the question of common law copyright.

The willingness of the Court of Chancery to look expansively upon the wording of the Statute and to grant interim injunctions and even an account of profits demonstrates that the legal world was not approaching the Statute in an overly positivistic, or formalistic, manner in the first half of the eighteenth century. Nonetheless, as the statutory periods of protection began to run out, the booksellers began to seek extensions of their valuable monopolies. They began by approaching the Legislature, and brought several Bills into Parliament between 1735 and 1738. None of these, however, was successful in extending the term of protection. After 1739, the booksellers turned their attention to the courts. The

[90] J Ginsburg, '"Une Chose Publique"? The Author's Domain and the Public Domain in early British, French and US Copyright Law' [2006] *Cambridge Law Journal* 636, 642.

[91] Deazley, *On the Origin* 52–57.

[92] ibid 87–88.

[93] Statute of Anne (1710) s 1.

[94] eg, *Burnett v Chetwood* (1721) 2 Mer 441; *Knaplock v Curl* (1722) 2 Eq Ca Abr 523. See also Deazley, *On the Origin* 59–65.

[95] *Eyre v Walker* (1735); *Motte v Falkner* (1735); *Walthoe v Walker* (1736), and *Tonson v Walker* (1739)—all referred to in *Millar v Taylor* (1769) 4 Burr 2303, 2325.

[96] *Baller v Watson* (1737), referred to in *Tonson v Collins* (1761) 1 Black W 301, 305–06. See Deazley, *On the Origin* 62–69.

booksellers' legal campaign for perpetual copyright, and common law damages for incursions of their rights, has been covered by numerous commentators, from a variety of perspectives.[97] Birrell's name for the period, 'The Battle of the Booksellers', encapsulates the highly aggressive tactics employed by the London booksellers in their attempts to drive the Scottish booksellers out of the domestic and foreign book trade.[98]

Asserting the existence of common law copyright provided not only the basis of a claim for damages, but also the foundation for an argument that the property rights in printing and selling books were perpetual. The argument was raised but not resolved in *Millar v Kincaid*,[99] which began in Scotland in 1743 and ended in the House of Lords in 1751. Common law copyright was also discussed at length in the King's Bench in 1761 in *Tonson v Collins*,[100] again without resolution. In 1769, the King's Bench, with Lord Mansfield as its Chief Justice, accepted the existence of common law copyright in the case of *Millar v Taylor*.[101] Lord Mansfield found in favour of the common law right and granted the damages sought by the plaintiff. Two of the other judges, Willes and Ashton JJ, followed him but, to Lord Mansfield's chagrin, Yates J, who had acted for the defendants opposing such a right in the earlier case of *Tonson v Collins*, dissented.[102] At last it appeared that the booksellers had their perpetual common law copyright and their common law damages.

This happy state was not, however, to last. In 1773, the Scottish Court of Session ruled that no such common law right existed in Scotland in *Hinton v Donaldson*.[103] Even more significantly, two years earlier another action had been commenced in England against Alexander Donaldson, an enterprising Scottish bookseller who had recently set up shop in London. Thomas Becket, now claiming ownership of the right to print Thomson's *The Seasons* (the same book which had been at issue in *Millar v Taylor*), sought an injunction against Donaldson for printing the book without permission. Donaldson appealed the injunction to the

97 Birrell, *Seven Lectures*; Patterson, *Copyright in Historical Perspective*; HB Abrams, 'The Historical Foundation of American Copyright Law: Exploding the Myth of Common Law Copyright' (1983) 29 *Wayne Law Review* 119; Rose, *Authors and Owners*; RS Tompson, 'Scottish Judges and the Birth of British Copyright' (1992) *Juridical Review* 18; D Saunders, *Authorship and Copyright* (London, Routledge, 1992); T Ross, 'Copyright and the Invention of Tradition' (1992) 26 *Eighteenth Century Studies* 1; Deazley, 'The Myth of Copyright'; R Deazley, 'Re-reading Donaldson (1774) in the Twenty-First Century and Why it Matters' [2003] *European Intellectual Property Review* 270; Deazley, *On the Origin*.

98 One such tactic was the establishment of a fighting fund to meet the costs of any bookseller bringing an action against a printer or seller of piratical editions: Saunders, *Authorship and Copyright* 62.

99 *Millar v Kincaid* (1743–51) Also known as *Midwinter v Hamilton*. See Deazley, *On the Origin*, 115–32.

100 *Tonson v Collins* (1761) 1 Black W 321.

101 *Millar v Taylor* (1769) 4 Burr 2303.

102 Yates was soon moved to the Common Pleas, from which he shortly retired, due to ill health; WR Cornish, 'The Author's Surrogate: the Genesis of British Copyright' in K O'Donovan and GR Rubin (eds), *Human Rights and Legal History* (New York, Oxford University Press, 2000) 254, 261 fn.

103 *Hinton v Donaldson* (1774) recorded in 'The Decision of the Court of Session Upon the Question of Literary Property in the case Hinton against Donaldson, &c, Published by James Boswell' in S Parks (ed), *The Literary Property Debate: Six Tracts 1764–1774* (New York, Garland Publishing Inc, 1975). Voting 11 to 1 (Lord Monboddo dissenting), the Court of Session found in favour of Donaldson and held that there was no common law copyright in Scotland.

House of Lords, which summoned the twelve common law judges to attend the House, hear the argument and deliver advisory opinions.[104] All 12 of the judges delivered a separate opinion, responding to three questions set by the Lord Chancellor, Lord Apsley, and two questions added by Lord Camden. Having heard the opinions, several of the Lords also addressed the House, and the House then voted to overturn the injunction granted against Donaldson. The revisionist work of Abrams, Rose and Deazley has established, with some differences between their interpretations, that the opinions of the judges were misreported, leading to the incorrect view that the majority had voted against the common law right. In fact, the majority of the judges were of the opinion that the common law right existed, and was not abridged by the Statute of Anne.[105] This meant that the vote of the Lords was contrary to the judges' advisory opinions—a very rare occurrence.[106]

Several days after the decision was handed down, the London booksellers petitioned the House of Commons for legislation which would extend the term of the printing right. A Bill was introduced and passed by the House of Commons, but it was blocked in the House of Lords, with both the Lord Chancellor and Lord Camden speaking strongly in opposition to it.[107]

The issues raised in these cases were discussed and debated extensively outside the courts, as well as within them. Numerous pamphlets and essays were published in the 1740s and 1750s exploring the philosophical and legal foundations and implications of conferring property upon something in a way that was disconnected to its physical and tangible existence.[108] The argument in favour of common law copyright based on authors' rights relied on the interweaving of two strands of discourse. The first revolved around ideas of Romantic authorship. Both Martha Woodmansee and Mark Rose have identified the emergence around this time of ideas that an original author has a special relationship to his work that could be called proprietorial.[109] The second strand was based upon natural law and, in particular, Locke's theory of property rights. The natural jurisprudence of the Dutch philosopher Grotius, and those, such as Locke, who were influenced by him, had a great impact on social and legal thought in seventeenth- and eighteenth-century Britain. In the absence of clear-cut case law regarding literary

[104] For the appellate jurisdiction of the House of Lords, see R Stevens, *Law and Politics: The House of Lords as a Judicial Body, 1800–1976* (London, Weidenfeld and Nicolson, 1979); T Beven, 'The Appellate Jurisdiction of the House of Lords' (1901) 17 *Law Quarterly Review* 155; W Holdsworth, *A History of English Law*, 3rd edn (London, Methuen & Co, 1922) vol 1, pp 370–77.

[105] Rose, *Authors and Owners* 98–192, App B; Abrams, 'The Historical Foundation' 1166; Deazley *On the Origin* 196–205. Deazley disagrees with Rose and Abrams as to the voting on the first question; see Deazley, 'Re-reading Donaldson' 272–73.

[106] See Deazley, *On the Origin* 194.

[107] Patterson, *Copyright in Historical Perspective* 178–79.

[108] See M Rose, 'The Author as Proprietor: *Donaldson v Becket* and the Genealogy of Modern Authorship' in B Sherman and A Strowel (eds), *Of Authors and Origins: Essays in Copyright Law* (Oxford, Clarendon Press, 1994) 47–51; Deazley, *On the Origin*, ch 6.

[109] See Rose, 'The Author as Proprietor' and M Woodmansee, 'The Genius and the Copyright: Economic and Legal Conditions of the Emergence of the Author' (1984) *Eighteenth Century Studies* 425.

property, natural law was the obvious place to turn in order to locate common law principles. Consequently, it is not surprising to find extensive use being made of such jurisprudence by the supporters of perpetual common law copyright.

Although, as noted above, Locke himself had not advocated a perpetual copyright, Blackstone adapted his theory of property rights in order to formulate such an argument in his *Commentaries on the Laws of England*:

> There is still another species of property, which, being grounded on labor and invention, is more properly reducible to the head of occupancy than any other; since the right of occupancy itself, (a) is supposed by Mr Locke, and many others, (b) to be founded on the personal labor of the occupant.[110]

He traced this right back to Locke's property theory, Roman law, legislative recognition of copyright, Chancery injunctions and the patent cases.[111]

The natural law argument was also influentially expressed by Lord Mansfield in *Millar v Taylor*. Rejecting the argument that the common law of literary property could be found in custom, Mansfield proceeded to locate it in relation to unpublished works as follows:

> . . . because it is just, that an author should reap the pecuniary profits of his own ingenuity and labour. It is just, that another should not use his name, without his consent. It is fit that he should judge when to publish, or whether he will ever publish. It is fit he should not only chose the time, but the manner of publication; how many; what volume; what print. It is fit, he should choose to whose acre he will trust the accuracy and correctness of the impression; in whose honesty he will confide, not to foist in additions: with other reasonings of the same effect.[112]

Lord Mansfield held that these same reasons continued after publication for, if they did not, then the work could be pirated and the author could reap no pecuniary profit.[113]

Despite the coincidence of the growing influence of ideals of Romantic authorship and the rhetorical appeal of natural law arguments, the House of Lords voted against the perpetual common law copyright. Deazley claims that this was because the 'House of Lords understood the copyright regime, first and foremost, as addressing the broader interests of society'.[114] However, what precisely those interests might be was not a matter of simple consensus, nor was the way in which they were best served. Both those who favoured the perpetual right and those who opposed it asserted that they had the best interests of the public at heart.

On the part of those who supported the perpetual right, natural rights-based arguments were closely aligned to appeals to the public interest. In *Donaldson v*

[110] W Blackstone, *Commentaries on the Laws of England*, 4 vols, 1st edn (Oxford, Clarendon Press, 1765–69) Book 2, p 405 (c 26 s 8).

[111] ibid 407. Note that the 'Gentleman of the Inner Temple' (see below: n 115) reporting *Donaldson v Becket* substituted this statement from the *Commentaries* when reporting Blackstone's judgment, on the grounds that his original judgment was repetitive of Nares and Ashurst JJ.

[112] (1769) 4 Burr 2303, 2398.

[113] ibid.

[114] Deazley, 'The Myth of Copyright' 132 and Deazley, 'Re-reading Donaldson' 278.

Becket, Aston J noted: 'our Common Law hath its Foundation in private Justice, moral Fitness, and public Convenience; the natural rights of every subject are protected by it'.[115] The public convenience Aston J had in mind is found in his earlier decision in *Millar v Taylor*, where he noted the intersection of the property right and the public interest:

> Publication therefore is the necessary act, and only means, to render this conferred property useful to mankind, and profitable to the owner: in this, they are jointly concerned.
>
> Now, to construe this only and necessary act to make the work useful and profitable, to be 'destructive, at once, of the author's confessed original property, against his express will,' seems to be quite harsh and unreasonable.[116]

Similarly, in *Millar v Taylor*, Willes J stated:

> It is certainly not agreeable to natural justice, that a stranger should reap the beneficial pecuniary produce of another man's work . . . It is wise in any state to encourage letters, and the painful researches of learned men. The easiest and most equal way of doing it, is, by securing to them the property of their own works.[117]

Lord Lyttelton, addressing the House of Lords in *Donaldson v Becket*, also made use of the language of public benefit. He is quoted as stating:

> It is of infinite Importance to every Country, that Arts and Sciences should be cultivated and encouraged; where Men of Letters are best protected, the People in general will be more enlightened, and where the Minds of Men are enlarged, where their Understandings are equally matured in Perception and Judgment, there the Arts and Sciences will take their residence.[118]

Those lawyers and judges who were opposed to the common law property right formulated two rationales: first, that there was no property right capable of inhering in literary works; and second, that such a property would be against the interests of the community and learning in general. The first argument focused on the differences between literary property, which consisted of ideas, and the way that property was traditionally understood and characterised by natural lawyers, generally by reference to the archetypal form of property—land. Literary property could not be analogised to land, argued the opponents of the common law right. Therefore, the only way that literary works could be protected was through the Statute of Anne. This view was endorsed by Yates J who stated that property was founded on occupancy, and that no such occupancy could be asserted in respect of intellectual ideas.[119] He held that 'To extend this argument, beyond the

[115] 'The Cases of the Appellants and Respondents in the Cause of Literary Property wherein the Decree of Lord Chancellor Apsley was Reversed, &c, by a Gentleman of the Inner Temple' in S Parks (ed), *The Literary Property Debate: Six Tracts 1764–1774* (New York, Garland Publishing Inc, 1975) 39

[116] (1769) 4 Burr 2303, 2341.

[117] ibid 2334–35.

[118] 'The Cases of the Appellants and Respondents by a Gentleman of the Inner Temple' 55–56.

[119] See *Tonson v Collins* (1761) 1 Black W 321, 333. Yates J points to statements of Bynkershock and Pufendorf that property must be capable of physical possession.

manuscript, to the very ideas themselves, seems to me very difficult, or rather quite wild'.[120]

The second head of argument bolstered the first: there could not be a common law property right, as such a property right was not in the interests of the public. Yates J also employed this reasoning, stating:

> 'That every man is intitled to the fruits of his own labour,' I readily admit. But he can only be intitled to this, according to the fixed constitution of things; and subject to the general rights of mankind, and the general rules of property. He must not expect that these fruits shall be eternal; that he is to monopolize them to infinity; that every vegetation and increase shall be confined to himself alone, and never revert to the common mass. In that case, the injustice would lie on the side of the monopolist, who would thus exclude all the rest of mankind from enjoying their natural and social rights.[121]

Edward Thurlow, arguing for the defendant in *Tonson v Collins*, pointed out that 'public utility, &c points one way as well as the other. It is useful to the public, that a monopoly should be abolished'.[122] Lord Kames spoke even more strongly against the common law right in the Scottish Court of Session in *Hinton v Donaldson*, stating:

> Such a monopoly, so far from being founded on common law, is contradictory to the first principles of society. Why was man made a social being, but to benefit by society, and to partake of all improvements of society in its progress toward perfection?[123]

Lord Kames was one of the few jurists who looked specifically to the commercial consequences of a perpetual right, claiming that books would become cheaper at the end of the monopoly, which was also beneficial to the public.[124] He also focused on the role of copyright as providing economic incentives, thereby fleshing out the Statute of Anne's simplistic claim to encourage learning. He noted:

> The Statute of Anne is contrived with great judgment, not only for the benefit of authors, but for the benefit of learning in general. It excites men of genius to exert their talents for composition and it multiplies books both of instruction and amusement. And when, upon expiration of the monopoly, the commerce of all those books is laid open to all, their cheapness, from a concurrence of many editors, is singularly beneficial to the public.[125]

Concern with a broadly expressed public interest in learning is also evident in the Lords' speeches in *Donaldson v Becket*. Lord Camden stated: 'If there be any thing in the World, my Lords, common to all Mankind, Science and Learning are in their nature *publici juris*, and they ought to be as free and general as Air and Water'.[126] However, as Trevor Ross has pointed out, the views of Camden and

[120] (1769) 4 Burr 2303, 2357.
[121] ibid 2359–60.
[122] (1761) 1 Black W 301, 306.
[123] 'The Decision of the Court of Session Upon the Question of Literary Property published by Boswell' 18–19.
[124] ibid 19–20.
[125] ibid.
[126] 'The Cases of the Appellants and Respondents by a Gentleman of the Inner Temple' 53.

Kames are based on different views of society. Camden valued literature in a 'patrician and gentlemanly'[127] way, and 'resisted the commodification of writing that is explicit in the term "intellectual property"'.[128] Kames, on the other hand, realised that 'the value of literature is determined within a dynamic scheme of production relations'.[129] Both prioritised the interests of the public but while Camden took a more traditional, didactic approach towards society, Kames conceived of it as a forum for the exchange of commodities.

The Bishop of Carlisle took a similar approach to that of Lord Camden, noting that the intention of the Statute of Anne was to encourage learning and opposing the perpetual right on the grounds that it was 'too feeble to be safely relied on for promoting the general service of the public, or for supporting any true, valuable interests of literature in particular'.[130] Lord Howard, however, took a different point of view again, claiming that perpetual copyright posed a danger to constitutional rights, and linking it to liberty of the press.[131] Employing an argument which harked back to copyright's early ties to censorship, but which also has considerable modern resonance, he described the situation of a pamphlet describing 'some despotic matter'[132] involving a Member of Parliament, all the copies of which were bought up by the Minister concerned, 'thereby choking the Channel of public information'.[133]

The development of opposing discourses of the nature of the property right and its relation to society in general had an important effect that went beyond the mere question of how the property should be described. For the first time, the interests of authors and owners were pitted against those of the public in general. Although the parties in each case were rival booksellers, one of the most notable aspects of the series of cases which culminated in *Donaldson v Becket* was to achieve the identification of the interests of authors with those of the booksellers. Alexander Wedderburn, as counsel for Tonson in *Tonson v Collins*, explicitly adopted this tactic, stating: 'The right of authors in general is now to be determined; not of any particular bookseller'.[134]

As a result, those who opposed the common law right contrasted the interests of authors to those of the public. Both Thurlow and Joseph Yates took this approach in *Tonson v Collins*. Thurlow argued that, 'The establishment of copyright may tend to the advantage of authors; not of the public'.[135] Yates, also appearing for the defendant in that case, continued the theme, stating:

127 T Ross, 'Copyright and the Invention of Tradition' (1992) 26 *Eighteenth Century Studies* 1, 11.

128 ibid 11.

129 ibid.

130 'The Cases of the Appellants and Respondents by a Gentleman of the Inner Temple' 59.

131 Thurlow had raised this in argument before the judges. Given that the Licensing Acts of the previous centuries had been aimed at suppression of the press, this was a powerful argument, although little seems to have been made of it.

132 'The Cases of the Appellants and Respondents by a Gentleman of the Inner Temple' 59.

133 ibid 59.

134 (1761) 1 Black W 301, 301.

135 ibid 306.

> I wish all due encouragement to ingenious authors, consistent with the principles of law, and the rights of the subject. But if their claim tends to a monopoly, is contrary to the provisions of the Legislature, or the good of the community; if it introduces any change or novelty into the common law, they must excuse me.[136]

Moreover, some lawyer and judges pointed out that there was a difference between authors and booksellers. In *Hinton v Donaldson*, Lord Coalston pointed out that:

> This is not a question in which authors are much concerned; for whether their exclusive right of publication is supposed to be perpetual, or temporary to subsist for the space of twenty-eight years, will make no great difference as to the extent of the price which will be paid to the author.[137]

Lord Coalston correctly realised that the vast majority of authors in the eighteenth century parted with all their rights in a manuscript to booksellers for a fixed lump sum. Thurlow, in his argument on behalf of Donaldson, claimed that the only reason that the booksellers introduced the author into their claims was because they found it necessary 'to give a colorable Face to their Monopoly'.[138] Lord Kames also emphasised that the relationship in issue was between booksellers and the public, and suggested that the perpetual right might actually harm authors. He stated:

> Our booksellers, it is true, aiming at present profit, may not think themselves much concerned about futurity. But it belongs to judges to look forward; and it deserves to be duly pondered whether the interest of literature in general ought to be sacrificed to the pecuniary interest of a few individuals.[139]

On this basis, he said: 'I am for dismissing this process as contrary to law, as ruinous to the public interest, and as prohibited by the statute'.[140]

It is thus overly simplistic to claim, as Deazley does, that in *Donaldson v Becket* the peers voted against the majority of the judges because they conceived copyright as operating in the interests of the public.[141] There was no single view of what the 'interests of the public' might comprise, nor whether society was best served by a limited or a perpetual copyright. If the vote of the House of Lords appears to have prioritised the interests of society in general over those of authors and/or booksellers, then that is because that is how the issues came to be framed during the course of legal argument.

This complexity is emphasised by the fact that it was not only the booksellers who petitioned Parliament in the wake of *Donaldson*. The universities were also

[136] ibid 340.

[137] 'The Decision of the Court of Session Upon the Question of Literary Property, . . . published by Boswell' 27.

[138] 'The Case of the Appellants and Respondents by a Gentleman of the Inner Temple' 20.

[139] 'The Decision of the Court of Session Upon the Question of Literary Property, . . . published by Boswell' 20.

[140] ibid 21.

[141] See above: n 114.

fearful of the effect that the decision might have on their printing prerogatives and lobbied for a Bill which would recognise their right to print books bequeathed to them in perpetuity.[142] An Act was accordingly passed, granting perpetual printing rights in the limited circumstances of books bequeathed to the universities under trusts directing that any profits arising from the sale of such books should be appropriated as a 'Fund for the Advancement of Learning, and other beneficial Purposes of Education within the said Universities and Colleges'.[143] The right only applied to books that had been bequeathed in perpetuity, and not those bequeathed for a limited term.

Thus, it seems that the House of Lords was not opposed to printing monopolies per se, merely to those which were in the hands of the wealthy London booksellers. This suggests that it was not against the public interest to recognise perpetual copyright itself, rather it was against the public interest that such a perpetual right should be held by private traders. Monopolies in the hands of educational bodies that were to be exercised for charitable educational purposes rather than for private profit were acceptable. However, even the universities were not to be granted complete *carte blanche* in the field of printing. In the year following the decision in *Donaldson*, Thomas Carnan's challenge to the Stationers' monopoly on almanacks was successful.[144] By way of response, the Stationers convinced the universities, who also suffered from the breaking of the monopoly, to support a Bill vesting the sole right to print almanacks in the Universities of Oxford and Cambridge and the Company of Stationers.[145] Carnan petitioned against the Bill[146] and it was defeated in the Commons by 45 votes.[147] Therefore, it is reasonable to suppose that the vote of the peers in *Donaldson* was both a reaction against the London booksellers' monopoly and based on the belief that limited duration would serve a public purpose. The notion that the laws regulating literary property should serve a public interest was affirmed, but its precise nature remained unclear.

Unfortunately, we can never know from a mere vote precisely what motivated the Lords to decide *Donaldson v Becket* as they did—whether they considered that there was no common law copyright, that there was a common law copyright but that it was lost upon publication, or that upon publication it was limited by the Statute of Anne. The most we can say from the decision to continue the injunction is that the Lords did not consider that there was a perpetual common law copyright that survived the passing of the Statute of Anne. The result of this uncertainty and the subsequent misinterpretations of the decision, from the point of view of

142 Deazley, *On the Origin* 215.

143 An Act for enabling the Two Universities in England, the Four Universities in Scotland, and the several Colleges of Eton, Westminster and Winchester to hold in perpetuity their Copy Right in Books given to or bequeathed to the said Universities and Colleges, for the Advancement of useful Learning, and other Purposes of Education (1775) 15 Geo III (c 53, Preamble).

144 *Stationers' Company v Carnan* (1775) 2 Black W 1004.

145 *JC* vol 37, 338 (10 May 1779).

146 *JC* vol 37, 355 (29 April 1779).

147 For the full story, see C Blagden, 'Thomas Carnan and the Almanack Monopoly' (1961) 14 *Studies in Bibliography* 23, 24–45, 35.

precedent and posterity, is that what was *not* decided in *Donaldson v Becket*, became as important as what *was* decided. The question of literary property may have been determined as a limited right, but the legal and philosophical basis of the finding was unstable. A majority of the common law judges believed that a common law right existed, and the House of Lords' reason for rejecting that finding was not apparent. An attractive and persuasive theory for the basis of copyright according to natural law principles as well as ideals of authorship had been constructed and, although it had been rejected by the House of Lords, no satisfactory foundation was asserted in its place. Consequently, the spectre of common law copyright would continue to appear, in various guises, throughout the next 150 years.

IV. UNFINISHED EDGES

The House of Lords in *Donaldson* resolved the comparatively narrow question of whether copyright lasted beyond the statutory period. However, it left two important questions that demanded immediate answers. The first was the issue of common law damages, which had been awarded in *Millar v Taylor.* The peers did not address this question and their vote to overturn the injunction rendered it irrelevant. The question was soon resolved, but with none of the fanfare that attended the common law copyright decisions. In the 1798 case of *Beckford v Hood*[148] Lord Kenyon CJ, Ashurst and Grose JJ all found that damages were available under the Statute of Anne. Furthermore, they held that this remedy would be available even if the formality of registering the work at Stationers' Hall had not been complied with.

The second unresolved question was the status of unpublished works. This question had first come before the courts in 1741, when Alexander Pope brought an action against Edmund Curl for the unauthorised publication of Pope's letters.[149] According to the printed report, Lord Hardwicke LC held that unpublished letters did come within the 'grounds and intention' of the Statute of Anne, despite the fact that he believed that Pope had not intended to publish the letters.[150] In the following years, injunctions were also granted to prevent publication of a manuscript[151] and an unpublished play.[152] A month after the decision in *Donaldson*, Lord Chancellor Apsley granted an interim injunction in *Thompson v Stanhope*[153] and in 1818, in *Gee v Pritchard*, Lord Eldon held that he was bound to

[148] *Beckford v Hood* (1798) 7 TR 621.

[149] For the full story, see M Rose, 'The Author in Court: *Pope v Curl* (1741)' in M Woodmansee and P Jaszi (eds), *The Construction of Authorship: Textual Appropriation in Law and Literature* (Durham, NC, Duke University Press, 1994) 211–30.

[150] *Pope v Curl* (1741) 2 Atk 342.

[151] *Duke of Queensbury v Shebbeare* (1758) 2 Eden 329.

[152] *Macklin v Richardson* (1770) Amb 694.

[153] *Thompson v Stanhope* (1774) Amb 737.

grant an injunction following Lord Hardwicke in *Pope v Curl*[154] and Lord Apsley in *Thompson v Stanhope*, despite having some personal doubts as to the jurisdiction of the Court with respect to unpublished works.[155] Lord Eldon appears to have endorsed the view of Lord Hardwicke that unpublished letters come within the Statute, although he merely referred to the letters being the subject of property.

What can be seen here is the common law seeping in to fill gaps left by the legislation. It is the language of property that allowed this to happen, and this language can be traced back to the Statute of Anne itself (as well as the petitions that preceded it). Although the booksellers had failed to convince the House of Lords of a proprietary right existing outside the Statute, the extended debates over the precise nature of the right were not without effect. As Sherman and Bently have argued, 'the mere fact that literary property was discussed so widely and in so much detail had the effect that its normative status was effectively rendered incontestable'.[156] The courts of law and equity were able to build upon this property right to decide cases that did not fall squarely within the confines of the Act. In *Beckford v Hood*, for example, Lord Kenyon noted:

> On the fair construction of this Act, therefore I think it vests the right of property in the authors of literary works, for the times therein limited, and that consequently the common law remedy attaches, if no other be specifically given by the Act.[157]

Lord Ashurst likewise stated in the same case:

> I can only consider the action for the penalties given to a common informer as an additional protection, but not intended by the Legislature to oust the common law right to prosecute by action any person who infringes this species of property, which would otherwise necessarily attack upon the right of property so conferred.[158]

However, the status of unpublished works would continue to be contentious, and would lead the common law copyright debates to be re-opened repeatedly in the nineteenth century. Consequently, despite Deazley's observation that the decision in *Donaldson v Becket* ought to have closed the book forever on claims of common law rights,[159] the courts both before and after that decision continued to draw on the common law to supplement the wording of the Statute. Interpretation of the Statute of Anne was never confined to literalism.

This necessarily brief survey of copyright in the eighteenth century demonstrates that the notion of public interest being mobilised by booksellers, lawyers and others in this period should be understood as a more complex construction

[154] *Pope v Curl* (1741) 2 Atk 342.

[155] *Gee v Pritchard* (1818) 2 Swans 408. In 1813, the Vice-Chancellor had refused to continue an injunction in *Perceval v Phipps* 2 V & B 19 in respect of unpublished lectures, although the basis of the decision is unclear. However, he appeared to suggest that not all letters would attract protection, as some letters could not be described as a 'literary work' (at 28).

[156] B Sherman and L Bently, *The Making of Modern Intellectual Property Law: The British Experience, 1760–1911* (Cambridge, Cambridge University Press, 1999) 40.

[157] (1798) 7 TR 621, 628.

[158] ibid 628.

[159] Deazley, 'Re-thinking Copyright' 64.

than Deazley suggests when he writes that the Statute of Anne and *Donaldson* were 'primarily defined and justified in the interests of society'.[160] Although the Statute of Anne was overtly expressed in utilitarian terms as aiming to 'encourage learning', it was never solely about the public interest in the spread of knowledge. Other broader public interest concerns, such as dislike of monopolies, can also be discerned in its text, but so can concerns regarding the protection of private property and regulation of the book market. Nor can *Donaldson v Becket* be interpreted simply as the triumph of public interest over natural rights. Arguments based on the public interest had been advanced on both sides of the debate and the advancement of learning was argued to flow both from a perpetual right and a limited right. Indeed, the blank nature of the Lords' votes means that we can never know if they were motivated by the public interest in the spread of learning or that in free communication. Alternatively, some or all of them could have found against the common law right on purely legal grounds or been reluctant to give too much credence to property claims of such uncertain scope. Finally, they may have been motivated by antipathy to the booksellers' trade practices and market dominance. This latter also reflects a public interest but is conceived much more broadly in terms of free competition.

By the end of the eighteenth century many of the recurrent themes and tensions in copyright law had been in circulation for some time in the various law-making fora. The real flashpoint was the duration of the right to print and publish, and this would re-emerge as copyright's most explosive issue in the middle of the next century. However, this was not the only context in which the claims of copyright owners came into conflict with the alleged interests of the public and the arguments and rhetoric developed in the course of the debates over duration and common law copyright impacted in significant ways on other aspects of the law's development. It is these aspects to which the book now turns.

[160] Deazley, *On the Origin* 226.

3

Copyright, the Book Trade and the Reading Public

I. CO-OPERATION AND CORPORATISM IN THE BOOK TRADE

THE LONDON BOOKSELLERS may have been defeated in *Donaldson v Becket*[1] in their desire for a perpetual common law copyright, but this by no means marked the end of their attempts to re-negotiate the hand that they had been dealt in the Statute of Anne. They continued to look for ways to circumvent the three elements of the Act which were most displeasing to them: the inadequate penalties, the limited term and the library deposit provisions.

The first of these was the most easily dealt with, although it did not occur for some decades after the decision in *Donaldson v Becket* was handed down. As was noted in the previous chapter, the Court of the King's Bench held in *Beckford v Hood*[2] that damages could be recovered at common law, even in respect of a book which had not been registered at Stationers' Hall.[3] Kenyon CJ considered that the legislature could not have intended the only remedy to be the penalties provided for in the Statute of Anne, not only because of the inadequacy of the sum involved, but because they were recoverable by any common informer, which might leave the aggrieved party without any remedy.[4]

The second problem facing the booksellers was the loss of the perpetual right. As noted in chapter two, their first reaction was to petition Parliament, unsuccessfully, for a new statute. The booksellers claimed in their petitions that the decision would ruin them. However, their adeptness in structuring their affairs in ways that would mitigate, if not exclude, the effects of legislation, once again came to the fore. Many of their contemporaries were under no illusions as to the effect of *Donaldson v Becket*. Oliver Goldsmith noted that 'The London booksellers talk of

[1] *Donaldson v Becket* (1774) 2 Bro PC 129.

[2] *Beckford v Hood* (1798) 7 TR 620.

[3] Previously there had been some confusion about this—see Mansfield J's reference to *Tonson v Clifton* (1722) in *Tonson v Collins* (1761) 1 Black W 321, 330, in which an injunction was granted in respect of 'The Conscious Lovers', although it had never been registered at Stationers' Hall. Mansfield J interjected that entry was only necessary in order to claim the penalties. Likewise in *Blackwell v Harper* (1740) 2 Atk 93; Barn C 210 Lord Hardwicke stated that it was necessary to register a book in order to receive the penalties. However, in Atkyn's report he is also reported to have stated that 'property cannot vest without entry': 2 Atk 93, 95.

[4] ibid 627.

ruin but they know better. In fact, that species of trade which they possess by occupancy will still continue to be theirs in a great measure'.[5] James Boswell observed in 1791 that 'honorary copyright' was still preserved among the London booksellers 'by mutual compact, notwithstanding the decision of the House of Lords against the perpetuity of Literary Property'.[6]

The 'honorary copyright' to which Boswell referred, was maintained by the sharebook system, which had taken over from the conger system after the 1730s. The sharebook system was based upon the congers, as it effectively created a separate conger for each publication. Graham Pollard, called this 'copyright *de facto*',[7] and describes it as

> just as real and profitable a form of occupancy of literary property as legal copyright; but it depended not on the normal sanctions of the law, but on those which the book trade was itself to apply. These depended on the cohesion of the London book trade; as long as all the principal publishers and wholesalers in London would refuse to sell any books to retailers who dealt in any editions that were not copyright editions (as defined by the London trade), then the retailer whether in town or country was practically helpless. If he printed an edition of Shakespeare, or of any other book not copyright in the legal sense, he would be cut off from his supply of all other books at trade rates. As no single bookseller could reprint all the books he might want to sell, the combined London trade had a stranglehold on all retail booksellers.[8]

The *de facto* copyright system was probably not as entirely effective as Pollard suggests.[9] Although some publishers, such as Andrew Strahan, went on trading shares in copyright-expired books as though nothing had changed,[10] others began to concentrate on the top end of the market, producing high quality products and making up in profit margins what they lost in volume.[11] The booksellers also briefly experimented with forming an 'Association of the Booksellers for the Preservation of their Trade', which appears to have been a more official plan to deal with pirates and undersellers collectively.[12] However, it is likely that the strength of the sharebook system made more official organisations unnecessary.[13] Moreover, suggestions that the publishers were operating a '*de facto*' copyright system were still being made as late as the 1830s.[14]

[5] Quoted in G Walters, 'The Booksellers in 1759 and 1774: The Battle for Literary Property' (1974) 29 *The Library* 287, 309.

[6] Quoted in RB Sher, 'Corporatism and Consensus in the Late Eighteenth-Century Book Trade: The Edinburgh Booksellers' Society in Comparative Perspective' (1998) 1 *Book History* 32.

[7] G Pollard, 'The English Market for Printed Books: The Sandars Lectures, 1959' (1978) 4 *Publishing History* 8, 28.

[8] ibid 28–29.

[9] See H Amory, '"*De facto* Copyright?" Fielding's *Works* in Partnership, 1769–1821' (1984) 17 *Eighteenth Century Studies* 449.

[10] Sher, 'Corporatism and Consensus'; see also Pollard, 'The English Market for Printed Books' 34.

[11] Amory, '"*De facto* Copyright?"' 468.

[12] N Hodgson and C Blagden, *The Notebook of Thomas Benet and Henry Clements* (Oxford, University Press, 1956) app 15; Amory, '"*De facto* Copyright"' 462.

[13] Sher, 'Corporatism and Consensus' 37.

[14] Parl Deb HC vol 42 cols 563–64 (25 April 1838); vol 45 cols 941–42 (27 February 1839).

The London booksellers' tendencies towards co-operation and corporatism continued in the practice of private sales and auctions, as well as regular meetings at the Chapter Coffee House. A register separate to that of the Stationers' Company, which was now regulated by the Statute of Anne, was also held at the Chapter Coffee House, where booksellers were encouraged to enter titles.[15] As will be discussed below, the Stationers' Register was out of favour due to its link with library deposit but the existence of an alternative register demonstrates that registration was still seen as an important aspect of trade regulation. These co-operative tendencies were soon echoed by the booksellers of Dublin and Edinburgh, who also began to form organisations to combat reprinting and under-selling.[16]

The decision in *Donaldson*, however, did lead to new opportunities at the lower end of the book market. The publisher John Bell had considerable success with the publication of small, cheap volumes of Shakespeare and other plays, as well as *The Lives of the Poets*, which so angered the London booksellers.[17] A new breed of bookseller arrived on the scene, epitomised by the careers of James Lackington and Thomas Tegg, both of whom started with nothing but built hugely successful businesses, based on the purchasing and re-selling of remaindered stock and the publication of reprints.[18] Tariq Baloch has also argued that the law book trade saw an 'explosion in publication' from the final decade of the eighteenth century.[19]

Other changes were also occurring in the trade. Most important was the shift from small, independent but co-operative booksellers to large corporate enterprises, comprising a number of partners and employees.[20] Alongside this change in business structure came the rise of the publisher. The bookseller of the eighteenth century was both wholesaler and retailer, as well as frequently the commissioner of books and the purchaser of copyrights. But from the beginning of the nineteenth century some booksellers began to sell only their own publications.[21] This development can be traced to the increased need for capital, as prices at every level of book production increased. Booksellers simply did not have the resources

[15] Sher, 'Corporatism and Consensus' 43–44.

[16] ibid 45–73. Ironically, the members of the Edinburgh Booksellers' Society included James Donaldson, son of Alexander, and John Bell, who had so angered the London booksellers by proposing to publish cheap volumes of *The Poets of Great Britain* that they retaliated by publishing the book known today as Johnson's *Lives of the Poets*.

[17] R McKeen Wiles, 'The Relish for Reading in Provincial England Two Centuries Ago' in PJ Korshin (ed), *The Widening Circle: Essays on the Circulation of Literature in Eighteenth-Century Europe* (Philadelphia, University of Pennsylvania Press, 1976) 95. See also TF Bonnell, 'John Bell's *Poets of Great Britain*: The "Little Trifling Edition" Revisited' (1887) 85 *Modern Philology* 128.

[18] J Raven, 'Selling One's Life: James Lackington, Eighteenth-Century Booksellers and the Design of Autobiography' in OM Brack (ed), *Writers, Books and Trade* (New York, AMS Press, 1994); JJ Barnes and PP Barnes, 'Reassessing the Reputation of Thomas Tegg, London Publisher, 1776–1846' (2000) 3 *Book History* 45.

[19] T Baloch, 'Law Booksellers and Printers as Agents of Unchange' [2007] *Cambridge Law Journal* 389.

[20] LF Chard, 'Bookseller to Publisher: Joseph Johnson and the English Book Trade, 1760–1810' (1977) 32 *The Library* 138, 138.

[21] Pollard, 'The English Market for Printed Books' 35.

required for such broad operations, particularly as competition increased and the reading public grew. Specialisation was required, and publication of one's own books became increasingly common.[22]

The shift can also be seen in the use of better methods for advertising and supply. The improvement in the quality of reviews in the magazines, such as the *Quarterly* and the *Edinburgh Review*, increased their sale and popularity and assisted in creating both knowledge of, and appetite for, new books. The London publishers began communicating with the provinces by sending out commercial travellers, and also by issuing catalogues and prospectuses (although the latter practice only came after the introduction of the penny post in 1840). These developments meant that wholesalers became less essential to the London trade, and gradually began to die out, leaving the two categories of retail booksellers and publishers that still exist today.[23]

Technological changes were also arriving on the scene. By the late eighteenth century little had changed in printing methods since the days of Caxton. Type was set by hand, and printing presses operated by unskilled labour. In 1798, Charles Mahon, third Earl Stanhope, patented a new version of the printing press, made by a Mr Walter.[24] The real improvement, however, came with the application of steam, and from the 1810s stereotype plates and steam presses began to be put into use.[25] Stereotype plates lasted indefinitely so it was now possible for a printer or publisher to produce reprints as soon as a book went out of print, should there be further demand for it.[26] This lessened the publisher's risk and cut production costs dramatically. Paper-making machines first came into use in 1803. However, it must be noted that adoption of the new technology was far from immediate. Most printers did not employ the new machines in the early decades of the century, as print runs were not so large as to justify the expense. As a result, the earliest adopters tended to be the newspapers, and only slowly did the rest of the trade move from hand to machine production.[27]

Thus, notwithstanding these advances and the growing market for cheap books, books were becoming increasingly expensive at the turn of the century. During the Napoleonic Wars prices rose sharply and a new novel, which had cost 3s or 3s 6d in 1780 cost 10s 6d in 1815.[28] By the 1820s novels sold in the standard 3 volumes cost 31s 6d.[29] These prices put the purchase of books well out of reach of the working and lower-middle classes.

[22] Chard, 'Bookseller to Publisher' 150–51.

[23] Pollard, 'The English Market for Printed Books' 36–42.

[24] M Plant, *The English Book Trade: An Economic History of the Making and Sale of Books*, 2nd edn (London, Unwin & Allen Ltd, 1965) 272–73.

[25] ibid 273.

[26] ibid 184.

[27] See D McKitterick, 'Changes in the Look of the Book' in D McKitterick (ed), *The Cambridge History of the Book in Britain*, vol 6: *1830–1914* (Cambridge, Cambridge University Press, 2009) 75–86.

[28] Pollard, 'The English Market for Printed Books' 42.

[29] ibid; W St Clair, *The Reading Nation in the Romantic Period* (Cambridge, Cambridge University Press, 2004) 203.

The dissemination of books to those who could not afford them was taken up as an issue by various social reformers. The Evangelist Hannah More began writing and distributing her Cheap Repository Tracts and, in 1826, Henry Brougham formed the Society for the Diffusion of Useful Knowledge. This Society issued fortnightly volumes of the *Library of Useful Knowledge*, published by Charles Knight who also had a strong commitment to cheap publications for the masses. In 1829, the Society launched the Library of Entertaining Knowledge, and in 1832–33 Knight launched the *Penny Magazine* and the *Penny Cyclopaedia.*[30] The social aims of these efforts are discussed further below. Here, their significance lies in the fact that the success of these ventures alerted less socially minded publishers to the existence of a new market. Archibald Constable, the publisher of Scott, commenced his *Miscellany*, which consisted of a cheap volume every month, in 1826.[31] In 1829, John Murray imitated him with his *Family Library*, but in 1834 he was compelled to sell it to Tegg who turned it into a commercial success.[32]

The bank crisis of late 1825 affected the book trade in ways that had a lasting effect on popular memory. Constable was made bankrupt, and even John Murray suffered some reversals of fortune.[33] While Charles Knight alleged that the crash led to trade paralysis, and other commentators asserted that a considerable proportion of booksellers were driven out of business, it seems that times were not as tough as many, at the time and subsequently, made them out to be.[34] Nonetheless, it was a bad year for business and the unsettled economic atmosphere may have contributed to the major London booksellers' next move.

Despite a growing awareness of differentiated price markets for books, the London booksellers were still keen to maintain price stability for new books. In 1828, a new organisation was formed to bring about the control of retail prices. Known as the Booksellers' Committee, this organisation included Longman and his partners, John Murray, the Rivingtons and Simpkin, Marshall & Co, the largest firm of wholesalers.[35] Regulations were drawn up by which members had to abide, forbidding the sale of new books or reprints below their published prices. The punishment for doing so was that the other members would refuse supply of their books. Exceptions were made for cash customers, who could receive a discount of 10 per cent, and for book clubs and reading societies, which could be given a discount of 15 per cent on the retail price.[36] Within a year, 650 members of the trade had agreed to abide by the Regulations.[37]

[30] St Clair, *The Reading Nation* 269–70.

[31] AS Collins, *The Profession of Letters: A Study of the Relation of Author to Patron, Publisher, and Public, 1780–1832* (London, George Routledge & Sons Ltd, 1928) 199.

[32] ibid 188, 200.

[33] His principal author, Byron, had also died in 1824.

[34] See J Sutherland, 'The British Book Trade and the Crash of 1826' (1987) 9 *The Library* 148.

[35] W Pickering, *Booksellers' Monopoly, Address to the Trade and the Public* (London, Whittingham, 1832) 2.

[36] ibid 1.

[37] ibid.

The Committee only recognised those who had a formal retail shop as being entitled to trade privileges.[38] It also sought to limit entry to the trade by compelling new entrants to buy licences and carrying out inspections of premises to see if the applicant qualified as a retail shop.[39] The tactics employed by the Committee against those who did not fall in line included refusal to supply them with books, printing the share works in which they had shares without consulting them or giving a share of the profit, and circulating placards casting aspersions on their credit and reputation as a trader.[40] Other tactics included refusing admission to trade sales and demanding cash for all transactions.[41]

For a couple of years, the existence of this agreement was known only to the trade. However, in 1832 William Pickering, as revenge for being blacklisted by the Committee, exposed it to the public by publishing a pamphlet setting out the situation in some detail and providing the names of the Committee members. Pickering stated that he had no objection to the Committee opposing his editions by printing rival ones 'equally good and cheap' on the grounds that it was fair competition.[42] What he objected to were the more underhand and secretive tactics they employed, arguing that it was 'for the Public to consider whether open trade or a monopoly is deserving of its support'.[43]

Although Pickering and others accused the booksellers of attempting to uphold their monopoly of the trade during this period out of self-interest and greed, this was not the whole truth. Many of those involved with the book trade expressed fear of the danger of unrestrained competition flooding the market and causing widespread damage. For some this represented merely self-interest. Others, such as Strahan, envisaged corporate order in the book trade as a social goal that required individuals to curb their drives towards material acquisition for the common good. In a letter written to a fellow publisher Strahan claimed that his interest in the perpetual property cases had not stemmed from a desire for personal profits, as most of his books were still within copyright, but 'from a Desire of saving the Trade in general from universal Destruction, as we cannot conceive how it can honestly or beneficially be carried on, on the Plan of old [literary] Property being laid open'.[44]

According to this theory maintaining order in the book trade would allow the continued production and distribution of books, leading in turn to social benefits. This demonstrates, once again, that the booksellers' monopolistic practices should not only be seen in terms of the stark contrast between public and private interests. Nor were their opponents as disinterested as they liked to portray themselves. The booksellers' practices to some extent neutralised the limited duration

[38] JJ Barnes, *Free Trade in Books: A Study of the London Book Trade since 1800* (Oxford, Clarendon Press, 1964) 8.

[39] ibid 10–11.

[40] Pickering, *Booksellers' Monopoly* 2.

[41] Barnes, *Free Trade in Books* 15.

[42] Pickering, *Booksellers' Monopoly* 3.

[43] ibid.

[44] Sher, 'Corporatism and Consensus' 54.

provided for in the Statute of Anne and set them at odds with those who wished more and cheaper books to be made available to more people. While some of the advocates of cheap books, such as Brougham and Knight were motivated by the ideology of reform, others, such as Tegg, were motivated as much by self-interest as the most monopolistic of the established booksellers. Thus, the picture of self-interested monopolists versus publicly minded cheap book producers is not as black and white as it may at first appear.

II. THE BATTLE OVER LEGAL DEPOSIT

A. The Origins of Legal Deposit

The third element of the Statute of Anne that was most displeasing to the booksellers was the provision which required them to deliver nine copies of each published book to the Warehouse Keeper of the Stationers' Company for the use of the Royal Library (being the British Museum), the libraries of the Universities of Oxford and Cambridge, the four universities in Scotland, the library of Sion College and the library of the Faculty of Advocates in Edinburgh.[45] If these books were not delivered within 10 days after being demanded by the libraries, the statute provided that the person defaulting (be it the proprietor, publisher or Warehouse Keeper) would forfeit the value of the copies and the sum of £5 for every undelivered copy.[46]

That copyright and legal deposit were linked at all was not quite an historical 'accident',[47] but it was an anachronism. The Licensing Act of 1662 required every printer to deliver three copies of every book to Stationers' Hall, for subsequent delivery to the Royal Library and the libraries of the Universities of Oxford and Cambridge.[48] The object of that statute was literary censorship and the deposit provision seems more likely to have been intended to assist with enforcement than to express goodwill towards the universities.[49] The deposit provisions were continued in subsequent Licensing Acts, until the lapse of the last of them in 1695.[50]

Reluctance on the part of the printers to provide the copies required was a constant complaint of the libraries.[51] But a right which was frequently breached was better than no right at all and, following the lapse of the final Licensing Act, the

[45] Statute of Anne 1710 s 5.

[46] ibid.

[47] cp J Feather, *Publishing, Piracy and Politics: An Historical Study of Copyright in Britain* (London, Mansell, 1994) 97.

[48] Prior to this, in 1610, Sir Thomas Bodley had entered into an agreement with the Stationers' Company according to which it would deliver books printed by its members to the library at Oxford.

[49] The libraries of Oxford and Cambridge were under the control of the Church, while the Royal Library was under the inspection of Court officials. Sedition, blasphemy and libel could therefore be quickly detected by the authorities most concerned by them. See RCB Partridge, *The History of the Legal Deposit of Books* (London, The Library Association, 1938) 24.

[50] ibid 25–31.

[51] ibid.

librarian of Oxford and the Royal Librarian made some efforts to renew the provisions relating to deposit.[52] When the prospect of a literary property statute arose again as a real possibility in 1707, the library of Oxford and other libraries around the country began lobbying for inclusion of a library deposit clause. Nine of these libraries achieved their object and were granted the right to receive a copy of every book printed in England.[53]

After an initial period of compliance with the registration provisions on the part of booksellers, and insistence on their rights on the part of the libraries, activity in both areas fell off drastically.[54] Factors contributing to this decline included the administrative unwieldiness of the provisions, lack of co-operation on the part of the booksellers and lack of industry on the part of university staff.[55] The libraries were clearly involved in the drafting of the Bills of 1735 and 1737, which sought to add a further five libraries to the list of deposit libraries, being the law libraries of the Inner and Middle Temples, Lincoln's Inn, Gray's Inn and the Advocates at Doctor's Commons.[56] These Bills also provided that the legislature's protection would be dependent on depositing these copies.[57]

These Bills were not enacted, but the libraries had more luck in 1774. While the booksellers were unsuccessful in their efforts to convince Parliament to pass legislation overturning the result in *Donaldson v Becket*, Lord North, the Chancellor of the University of Oxford introduced a Bill which both conferred perpetual protection on copyrights owned by the universities and reinforced the duty of delivery to the nine libraries.[58] The clause spelt out the nature of the libraries' complaint, stating that the provision in the Statute of Anne 'has not proved effectual, but the same hath been eluded by the Entry only of the Title to a single Volume, or of some Part of such Book or Books so printed and published, or reprinted and republished, as aforesaid'.[59] The Bill found another supporter in the

[52] D McKitterick, *Cambridge University Library. A History. The Eighteenth and Nineteenth Centuries* (Cambridge, Cambridge University Press, 1986) 27 fn.

[53] The Cottonian Library and St Paul's Cathedral also lobbied for inclusion but were unsuccessful. See ibid 28.

[54] ibid 29 ff.

[55] The staff of the University Library at Cambridge, for example, devoted most of its energy towards housing and setting in order the massive library of John Moore, which had been donated to the library. See McKitterick, *Cambridge University Library* 42; JCT Oates, 'Cambridge University and the Reform of the Copyright Act, 1805–1813' (1972) 27 *The Library* 275, 276.

[56] Partridge, *The History of the Legal Deposit of Books* 39.

[57] Deazley, *On the Origin of the Right to Copy: Charting the Movement of Copyright Law in the Eighteenth Century (1695–1775)* (Oxford, Hart Publishing, 2004) 98, 105.

[58] An Act for enabling the Two Universities in England, the Four Universities in Scotland, and the several Colleges of Eton, Westminster and Winchester, to hold, in perpetuity, their Copy Right in Books given or bequeathed to the said Universities and Colleges for the Advancement of Useful Learning and other Purposes of Education; and for amending so much an Act of the Eighth Year of the Reign of Queen Anne, as relates to the Delivery of Books to the Warehouse Keeper of the Stationers Company for the Use of the several Libraries therein mentioned 1775 (15 Geo III c 53) (Universities Copyright Act 1775) s 6. See *JC* (1775) vol 35, 299, 325, 351, 370, 381; *JL* (1775) vol 34, 451, 454, 458, 462, 463, 470. See also H Carter, *A History of the Oxford University Press*, vol 1 (Oxford, Clarendon Press, 1975) 367.

[59] Universities Copyright Act 1775 s 6.

Lords in Edmund Law, Bishop of Carlisle and former librarian of the University of Cambridge. Prior to his speech in *Donaldson v Becket*, Law had published a pamphlet of observations on the question of literary property in which he had noted that very few books of value had been obtained by the libraries under the Statute of Anne. The reason for this was that the booksellers interpreted the Statute as requiring only the deposit of books that were registered, and many preferred to forego all benefit of the Act by not registering their works, than to register and deposit the nine copies. As a result, Law claimed, the libraries had been deprived of the benefits they should have received under the Act.[60] The 1775 Act provided that nobody should be subject to the penalties in the Statute of Anne unless the book in question was registered and all nine copies deposited with the relevant libraries.[61]

Despite this legislative reinforcement, by the end of the century the deposit clauses had ceased to function at all. An aggravating factor came in the case of *Beckford v Hood*[62] which, by establishing that damages could be obtained by a party who had not registered at Stationer's Hall, cemented the practices of those booksellers who sought to avoid deposit by failing to register. In 1801, when an Act to extend the operation of the Statute of Anne to Ireland following the Act of Union was passed, two more libraries were added to the list of deposit libraries.[63] In passing this Act, the legislature reflected the decision in *Beckford* by providing damages could be awarded at the suit of the proprietor of a book.[64] However, the Act also appeared to be attempting some kind of compromise by further providing that the penalty of three pence a sheet (raised from a penny a sheet in the Statute of Anne) would only be available if registration had occurred.[65] Since the penalties were rarely claimed or awarded, this provision had little effect.

B. Villiers' Bill

Things really began to go wrong for the booksellers in 1805 when Basil Montagu, a barrister and well-known radical campaigner for law reform, was irritated to find that the Cambridge University Library did not have a law report he wished to consult.[66] He published a pamphlet calling for better enforcement of the deposit laws.[67]

[60] E Law, *Observations Occasioned by the Contest about Literary Property by Dr Law, Bishop of Carlisle* (Cambridge, J Archdeacon, 1770) 3, 5.

[61] Universities Copyright Act 1775 s 6.

[62] (1798) 7 TR 621.

[63] An Act for the further Encouragement of Learning, in the United Kingdom of Great Britainand Ireland, by securing the Copies and Copyright of printed Books, to the Authors of such Books and their Assigns for the Time herein mentioned 1801 (41 Geo III c 107) s 6. The libraries were Library of the College of the Holy Trinity, Dublin, and the Society of King's Inn, Dublin.

[64] ibid s 1.

[65] ibid s 4.

[66] Ironically, Montagu recalled, the volume of law reports that he had wished to consult had contained the case of *Beckford v Hood.*

[67] B Montagu, *Enquiries and Observations Regarding the University Library* (Cambridge, 1805).

Two years later, Edward Christian,[68] Downing Professor of Law at Cambridge, was similarly annoyed to discover that the University Library did not contain the law books he wanted. Christian also went into print on the subject, publishing his *Vindication of the Right of the Universities of Great Britain to a Copy of Every New Publication* in 1807.[69] Key to Christian's argument was the claim that prior to the case of *Beckford v Hood*[70] authors and booksellers had obeyed the deposit provisions in the Statute of Anne but, following that decision, they had realised they could avoid the deposit requirements merely by neglecting to register their books at Stationers' Hall.

As described above, it was not correct that the registration and deposit provisions had been complied with prior to this decision. Moreover, Christian's assumption that authors would be happy to pay this 'equitable tax upon the republic of learning . . . as a debt of justice and gratitude, for the benefit which he must or might have derived from these common fountains of science',[71] as well as his insistence that the matter had nothing whatsoever to do with booksellers or publishers, demonstrated how naïve and unrealistic his expectations were. Nonetheless, Christian's pamphlet was to spark off a national examination of the deposit question. He achieved this by passing it along to John Charles Villiers, a Member of Parliament and former Cambridge student.

Villiers met with the most prominent booksellers and publishers to discuss the issue with them, and then introduced a Bill into Parliament. The Bill provided for the delivery of deposit copies to 11 libraries but it also increased the duration of copyright protection to a single term of 28 years, replacing the previous split term, in which the second 14 years depended on the life of the author. Both Christian and Villiers were under the impression that the trade had agreed at the meeting not to contest the Bill in return for the certainty of a single 28-year term.[72] However, the booksellers were under no such apprehension and resolved to press for the Bill's adjournment on 24 June 1808.[73] Signatories of the resolution included Joseph Butterworth, whom Villiers had claimed was his principal negotiator, and other leading publishers such as John Murray, Lackington, Allen & Co, Thomas Tegg, Cadell & Davies, Longman, Hurst, Rees & Brown and others.[74]

The Bill met with little support in the House of Commons. It was opposed by Charles Watkin Williams Wynn, a Tory and friend of Robert Southey, and Samuel Romilly, a Whig with a strong interest in law reform, particularly of the criminal law.[75] Romilly supported the increase in duration, but called the deposit

[68] Christian was the elder brother of Fletcher Christian, the *Bounty* mutineer, and related by marriage to Edmund Law. See above n 60.

[69] E Christian, *A Vindication of the Right of the Universities of Great Britain to a Copy of Every New Publication* (Cambridge, University Press, 1807).

[70] (1798) 7 TR 620.

[71] Christian, *Vindication* (1807) 8.

[72] Minutes of Evidence taken before the Select Committee on the Copyright Acts of 8 Anne c 19; 15 Geo III c 53; 41 Geo III c 107; 54 Geo III c 116 (1818) 280, 84, 93.

[73] ibid 349–50.

[74] ibid.

[75] Parl Deb HC vol 11 cols 988–90 (22 June 1808).

provisions a tax upon authors.[76] The Bill's progress stalled when Parliament was prorogued, and Villiers was then sent to Portugal on an official mission, where he remained until 1810, returning to England only to retire from Parliament two years later due to ill health.[77]

Meanwhile, the University of Cambridge followed Christian's original suggestion that it should bring legal proceedings against the defaulting booksellers.[78] A defendant, Henry Bryer, was selected around whom the prominent booksellers rallied, engaging Henry Brougham as counsel on his behalf.[79] Brougham claimed that if a book had not been registered at Stationers' Hall then there was no requirement of deposit.[80] The Court of the King's Bench did not accept this argument, finding that the two requirements were separate. Lord Ellenborough CJ (the son of Edmund Law) based his decision on an interpretation of the Statute of Anne as having two aims: the protection of copyright and the encouragement of learning. The first sections of the Act, which gave the right to authors and their assigns, served the first objective; while the provisions on prices (since repealed) and library deposit served the second.[81] Deposit encouraged learning by making books more readily available: 'for the books might have been of such considerable price, as not to be easily attainable by scholars of ordinary means'.[82] The University had its victory, but at a considerable cost. It had outlaid £250, and gained £6 16s.[83]

C. The Act of 1814: Deposit and Duration

The book trade could have adopted an approach of attrition at this point, on the basis that the costs of suing individual offenders would soon become prohibitive, but they took this opportunity to launch a counter-attack. At the end of 1812, the booksellers began petitioning Parliament once again,[84] complaining of the burden placed on them by delivery of 11 copies, especially in the case of small print runs of expensive books. They argued that deposit represented a serious diminution of the reward that authors and booksellers hoped to receive for their labour and risk.[85] In addition, they requested a single 28-year term, not reliant on the author remaining alive, noting the hardship caused to the families of authors by the loss of the second term of 14 years in the case of the author's death.[86] The booksellers found a valuable sponsor in Davies Giddy, an active supporter of the Liverpool

[76] ibid col 990.
[77] Oates, 'Cambridge University' 281.
[78] *The University of Cambridge v Bryer* (1812) 16 East 317.
[79] Oates, 'Cambridge University' 281–82.
[80] *The University of Cambridge v Bryer* (1812) 16 East 317, 318.
[81] ibid 321.
[82] ibid.
[83] Oates, 'Cambridge University' 284.
[84] Parl Deb HC vol 24 col 308 (16 December 1812); vol 25 col 12 (11 March 1813).
[85] Parl Deb HC vol 25 col 762 (9 April 1813).
[86] Parl Deb HC vol 24 col 310 (16 December 1812).

Government, whose political influence was instrumental in persuading Parliament to establish a committee to deal with the matter.[87]

The Committee, with Giddy in the Chair, began taking evidence from witnesses on 23 March 1813 and continued until 16 June 1813.[88] Almost all of the witnesses were booksellers or printers, and the Committee was presented with considerable detail about the inner workings of the book trade. In particular, the booksellers and printers were anxious to establish that the loss suffered by delivery was greater than the cost of the paper printed upon, as had been assumed by Christian and other supporters of the libraries. In fact, they claimed, the loss was the retail price of the book delivered, because undelivered books would be sold.[89]

The booksellers were also concerned to emphasise that the effect was felt most greatly in respect of books with small print runs. As these were usually the most expensive to print, the burden was doubly heavy.[90] They claimed that the need to deposit 11 copies would so eat into their profits that they would hesitate to publish such works at all.[91] As one witness, the printer Richard Taylor, argued, enforcing the provisions would prevent the publication of 'those works which are most calculated to advance knowledge'.[92] This turned the reasoning of Lord Ellenborough on its head, by suggesting that library deposit actually *discouraged* learning.

The evidence of the witnesses was sometimes exposed as flawed. When asked by the Committee whether the cost of the deposit copies could be recouped through increasing retail prices, all of the publishers were opposed to such an action. Longman noted that, with prices of books so much complained of in recent years, he always expected an increase of price to diminish sales.[93] However, under further questioning he was forced to concede it was not easy to prove that the increase in price directly caused such diminution.[94] Longman was also the only witness to be questioned on the proposed extension of term to 28 years in Villiers' Bill. Longman claimed that he had been present at the meeting to discuss the Bill, but that he had not considered the extension would compensate for the loss of the 11 copies by delivery.[95]

Given the homogeneity of the witnesses and their evidence, which was consistently opposed to depositing 11 copies, the Report of the Committee must have been a surprise and a disappointment to the booksellers and printers. Although it recommended that the term of copyright be increased to a fixed term of 28 years,

[87] J Feather, 'Publishers and Politicians: The Remaking of the Law of Copyright in Britain 1775–1842 Part I: Legal Deposit and the Battle of the Library Tax' (1988) 24 *Publishing History* 49, 55.

[88] Minutes of Evidence taken before the Committee on Acts respecting Copy Right of Printed Books (1812–13) 341, 1003.

[89] Davies Giddy, Report from Committee on Acts of 8 Anne and 15 & 41 Geo III for the Encouragement of Learning by Vesting the Copies of Printed books in the Authors or Purchasers of such Copies (1812–13) 292, 3, 16.

[90] ibid 1, 16, 19.

[91] ibid 28.

[92] ibid 32.

[93] ibid 6.

[94] ibid 7.

[95] ibid 12.

it also followed the reasoning of Lord Ellenborough and recommended that the substance of the deposit laws should be retained, on the grounds that it 'will tend to the advancement of learning, and to the diffusion of knowledge, without imposing any considerable burden on the Authors, Printers, or Publishers of such works'.[96] Some small changes to ease the burden on booksellers were proposed, such as ceasing to require that the books delivered must be on the best quality paper, but were counteracted by recommendations to increase the penalties for non-compliance.[97]

Agitation for change continued outside the parliamentary process, as the opponents of legal deposit began printing pamphlets putting forward their views. Sharon Turner, legal advisor to John Murray, and witness before the Committee, Richard Duppa, an artist and writer, JG Cochrane, a bookseller, and John Britton, antiquary and topographer, all published pamphlets focusing on the claims of authors. Each characterised deposit as a tax and an unfair invasion of property interests, basing this on the existence of a perpetual common law copyright which had been taken away by the Statute of Anne.[98] Duppa wrote, 'the author's copyright ought to be considered as an inviolable right'.[99] Britton, likewise, quoted Dr Johnson's complaint that

> the poorest manual operations should be more valued than the noblest products of the brain! That it should be felony to rob a cobbler of a pair of shoes, and no crime to deprive the best author of his whole subsistence.[100]

They also argued, as witnesses had before the Committee, that the deposit provisions were inimical to learning. Cochrane characterised the libraries as the 'discouragers, the task-masters and the oppressors of literature'.[101] Turner turned the arguments of the universities as the encouragers of knowledge against them, asserting that the real encouragers were authors themselves. He finished his piece with the rhetorical flourish:

> Few will dispute that literature is the dearest treasure which any nation can possess: it is the source and preserver of eloquence, knowledge and wisdom. The interests of its authors ought therefore to be dear to everyone; and every mind, that has been improved by them, should be proud to stand forward as their advocate and protector.[102]

[96] ibid 999, 1000.

[97] ibid 999.

[98] S Turner, *Reasons for a Modification of the Act of Anne respecting the Delivery of Books and Copyright* (London, Nichols, Son and Bently, 1813); R Duppa, 'An Address to the Parliament of Great Britain on the Claims of Authors to their own Copyright' (1813) 2 *The Pamphleteer* (published anonymously); JG Cochrane, *The Case Stated Between the Public Libraries and the Booksellers* (London, J Moyes, 1813); J Britton, *The Rights of Literature; or an Inquiry into the Policy and Justice of the Claims of Certain Public Libraries on all the Publishers and Authors of the United Kingdom for Eleven Copies on the Best Paper of Every New Publication* (London, AJ Valpy, 1814).

[99] Duppa, 'An Address to the Parliament' 179.

[100] Britton, *The Rights of Literature* 67.

[101] Cochrane, *The Case Stated* 20.

[102] Turner, *Reasons for a Modification* 60.

The supporters of the libraries were not as energetic, but they made some contribution to the pamphlet war. In 1813 Montagu re-issued his pamphlet of 1805, and the following year Christian published a new and updated edition of his *Vindication*. The University of St Andrews also responded by publishing a *Memorial against the Protest of the London Booksellers* refuting allegations that the library abused the privilege by selling deposited books, pleading inadequate resources and pointing out that the only other public library was forty miles away in Edinburgh.[103]

On 10 May 1814, Davies Giddy sought leave to bring in a Bill.[104] The Bill commenced by appealing to the general public interest in learning, with the preamble stating that delivery was 'a very heavy expense to the Authors or Proprietors of such Books and a discouragement to Literature'.[105] It repealed the parts of the Statute of Anne and the 1801 Act that related to deposit, instead requiring printers to send 11 copies to libraries upon demand being made for them. Second editions could not be demanded unless they contained 'material additions'. In committee, several further clauses were added, providing that the libraries had to pay a third of the retail price for any books they wanted delivered.[106] Another addition provided that any publisher who wished to waive copyright protection did not need to deliver copies of the book to any library except the British Museum.[107] Giddy also included the consolidation of the two 14 year terms into a single term of 28 years.

The Bill had a tortuous passage through the House of Commons, being recommitted and altered several times. Numerous petitions were introduced: the universities were largely opposed to the Bill;[108] the booksellers in favour.[109] However, the retention of delivery, even if offset by payment, meant that some members of the book trade were opposed to it.[110] Of interest is the fact that two petitions in favour of the Bill were made by 'authors and composers of books'.[111] Deazley has plausibly suggested that these petitions were in fact drafted by Sharon Turner, solicitor to John Murray and also to Henry Bryer, in his case against the universities.[112]

In the Commons, some Members also remained opposed to the Bill, including Wynn and Sir Samuel Egerton Brydges, a writer and publisher.[113] Others, how-

[103] P Ardagh, 'St Andrews University Library and the Copyright Acts' (1948–55) 3 *Edinburgh Bibliographical Society Transactions* 183, 191.

[104] Parl Deb HC vol 27 cols 810–11 (10 May 1814).

[105] A Bill to Amend the Several Acts for the Encouragement of Learning, by Securing the Copies and Copyright of Printed Books to the Authors of such Books or their Assigns HC (1813–14) [184].

[106] ibid.

[107] ibid.

[108] *JC* vol 69, 329 (6 June 1814), 344 (13 June 1814), 355 (15 June 1814), 365 (20 June 1814), 396 (28 June 1814), 419 (4 July 1814), 435 (6 July 1814).

[109] *JC* vol 69, 363 (17 June 1814), 381 (24 June 1814), 476 (18 July 1814).

[110] *JC* vol 69, 470 (15 July 1814).

[111] *JC* vol 69, 396 (28 June 1814).

[112] R Deazley, 'Commentary on *Copyright Act* 1814' in L Bently and M Kretschmer (eds), *Primary Sources on Copyright (1450–1900)* www.copyrighthistory.org.

[113] Brydges was a genealogist, who became interested in the area following his own unsuccessful claim to the title of Baron Chandos. He also had a keen interest in literature and bibliography, and in 1810 he bought the Lee Priory Press which specialised in republishing rare and forgotten works of

ever, supported it. Croker, a Tory politician and essayist, informed the House 'that all authors must be proud of contributing to the supply of those great reservoirs of literature, which enabled so many of them to write for the public advantage, and their own credit'.[114] Horner, a Whig member and economist who had been involved with Brougham in establishing the *Edinburgh Review*, likewise thought the opponents underestimated the advantage gained by supplying public libraries with books, which enabled all authors to find 'all the materials of knowledge'.[115] Over the course of its progress through the Commons and various committees, changes were made so that what had begun as a Bill aiming to improve the position of the booksellers soon began to look like a Bill shoring up the position of the libraries.[116] Supporters of the booksellers were unhappy with the final version. Before the Bill left the Commons, Wynn spoke strongly against the entire concept of free delivery and Giddy expressed his complete agreement with such sentiments.[117]

Despite continued resistance, the Bill was finally passed and carried to the House of Lords. Just before it left the Commons, however, a significant and easily overlooked amendment was made. On the 18 July, Brydges gave notice that he would bring a motion the next day for an extension of copyright.[118] No discussions surrounding such an amendment are noted in the record of parliamentary debates, but by the time the Bill arrived in the Lords it had a new clause in it, which provided that if the author of a book were still living at the end of 28 years, he would retain the right to print and publish his book until the end of his life.[119] The Lords made further amendments extending the benefit of the increased term to authors of books that had already been published at the time of the passing of the Act. For authors living at the time of the Act, but who died during the first 14 years of protection, the right to print and publish the book for another 14 years would pass to their assigns, while authors who survived the full 28 years would

literature; KA Manley, 'Brydges, Sir (Samuel) Egerton, First Baronet, styled Thirteenth Baron Chandos (1762–1837)' in *Oxford Dictionary of National Biography* (Oxford, Oxford University Press, 2004) www.oxforddnb.com/view/article/3809.

114 Parl Deb HC vol 28 col 754 (18 July 1814).

115 ibid col 753.

116 A number of changes were made in committee. The second draft altered the Preamble to state that deposit was 'a very great expense and inconvenience to the Authors or Proprietors of Books, without producing any adequate encouragement to Learning' (A Bill to Amend the several Acts for the Encouragement of Learning, by Securing the Copies and Copyright of Printed Books to the Authors of such Books or their Assigns HC (1813–14) [214]). This part of the Preamble was dropped in the third draft (A Bill to amend the several Acts for the Encouragement of Learning, by Securing the Copies and Copyright of Printed Books to the Authors of such Books or their Assigns HC (1813–14) [321]). The second draft also changed the amount that the libraries had to pay to a fifth of the retail price, but this requirement was also dropped in the third draft. The third draft also removed the provision for publishers who wished to waive copyright protection.

117 Parl Deb HC vol 28 cols 751–52 (18 July 1814).

118 ibid col 751.

119 Brydges' hitherto overlooked role in inserting the residuary life term is uncovered by Ronan Deazley in Deazley, 'Commentary on *Copyright Act* 1814'.

retain the rights to print and publish for the rest of their lives.[120] This latter clause also provided that the new rights should not affect any contracts which had already been concluded.[121] The House of Lords passed the Bill in the space of three days, the House of Commons approved the amendments and the Bill became law on 29 July 1814.[122]

This new Act reinforced the interests of the libraries in receiving deposit copies, and made only small attempts to recognise the interests of booksellers. One concession was that the 11 libraries would receive only the books they requested;[123] another was that they would not receive subsequent editions of books unless they contained alterations and additions, and such additions could be printed in a separate book and delivered in that form.[124] The clause proposed by Giddy, on behalf of the booksellers, that the libraries be prevented from selling or otherwise disposing of their deposit copies did not appear in the final version, nor did the requirement of part payment.[125]

However, the booksellers had not lost everything. The term of copyright was increased to 28 years, and thereafter to the remainder of the author's life, if still living.[126] Indeed, with hindsight and the knowledge of the furious debates that the issue of increasing the term of copyright would ignite 25 years later, the lack of discussion in either House of Parliament over the introduction of a term which for the first time made copyright dependent on the life of the author is quite astonishing. What prompted Brydges to insert it is something of a mystery, but Lionel Bently plausibly contends that the clause reflected his commitment to an ideology of romantic authorship. Brydges was himself a poet, as well as a publisher, and corresponded with writers such as William Haley, Robert Southey and Sir Walter Scott. He also corresponded with Wynn, who in turn had been the recipient of Southey's views that copyright should be perpetual.[127] Bently further surmises that the lack of resistance offered to Brydges' amendment suggests that the Members and Lords considered it to be fair and unobjectionable.[128]

[120] An Act to Amend the several Acts for the Encouragement of Learning by securing the Copies and Copyright of Printed Books to the Authors of such Books or their Assigns 1814 (54 Geo III c 156) (Copyright Act 1814) ss 8, 9.

[121] ibid s 9. Responsibility for the insertion of these clauses was claimed by Edward Christian, who asserted in the 1818 edition of his *Vindication* pamphlet that he had suggested their insertion to Lord Redesdale at the last minute, and the Speaker had agreed they could be inserted. See E Christian, *A Vindication of the Right of the Universities of Great Britain to a Copy of Every New Publication,* 3rd edn (Cambridge, University Press, 1818) 161.

[122] *JL* vol 49, 1129–30 (26 July 1814); *JC* vol 49, 517 (29 July 1814).

[123] Copyright Act 1814 s 2.

[124] ibid s 3.

[125] See Parl Deb HC vol 27 col 810 (10 May 1814).

[126] Copyright Act 1814 s 4.

[127] L Bently, '*R. v The Author*: From Death Penalty to Community Service' (2008) 32 *Columbia Journal of Law & the Arts* 1, 68–71.

[128] ibid 70.

D. Continuing Discontent and the 1818 Committee

The effect of the 1814 Copyright Act on delivery of copies was immediate. In 1813, 350 entries were made at Stationers' Hall, in 1814 this had increased to 541 and, by 1815, the number was 1,244.[129] The libraries made arrangements with George Greenhill, Warehouse Keeper at Stationers' Hall for order and delivery, and deposits were made with increasing frequency.[130] However, it was not long before the publishers were again attempting to evade the statute by failing to register, and in 1816 representatives from all the libraries met at Sion College to discuss enforcement.[131] An original plan to bring legal proceedings was abandoned in favour of applying pressure to defaulting individuals through the threat of legal action.[132]

Prior to the passing of the legislation the publishers had been assured that the libraries would not claim every new book.[133] They were, therefore, angry when the libraries began to demand reprints of several large and expensive subscription publications.[134] In March 1817, the publishing firm of Lackington sent a letter to Brydges complaining of the injury to them in providing these costly works;[135] the following June Brydges published a pamphlet complaining of the Act.[136] His next tactic was to move in Parliament that a Bill be brought in to amend the Copyright Act.[137] Brydges reiterated the complaints that the publishers had placed before the Select Committee of 1813 and contended that authors and publishers had a property right in books which the state was bound to protect. He was supported by Romilly, as well as Sir Francis Burdett and Henry Brougham. Brydges' motion was lost narrowly by a single vote,[138] but he continued his campaign and the following March he moved again in Parliament for an amending Bill.[139]

Some Members expressed opposition but, in the first few weeks of April, Parliament was presented with numerous petitions from various publishers, engravers, authors and printers.[140] Most of the petitions made arguments that were by now familiar. However, one new objection emerged in the petition of certain authors and composers of books on 8 April 1818.[141] This objection drew on general contemporary concerns regarding the nature of reading matter, and fears

[129] McKitterick, *Cambridge University Library* 414.
[130] ibid 414–15; Feather, *Publishing, Piracy and Politics* 112–13.
[131] McKitterick, *Cambridge University Library* 417.
[132] ibid 420.
[133] ibid 63.
[134] Partridge, *The History of the Legal Deposit of Books* 63.
[135] ibid.
[136] E Brydges, *Reasons for a further Amendment of the Act Geo III c 156 being an Act to amend the Copyright Act of Queen Anne* (London, Nichols, Son and Bently, 1817).
[137] Parl Deb HC vol 36 col 1063 (19 June 1817).
[138] *JC* vol 72, 372 (19 June 1817).
[139] Parl Deb HC vol 37 col 756 (3 March 1818).
[140] Parl Deb HC vol 37 cols 1190–93 (6 April 1818), cols 1212–18 (8 April 1818), cols 1225–28 (9 April 1818); *JC* vol 73, 217 (6 April 1818), 219 (8 April 1818), 226 (9 April 1818), 229 (10 April 1818).
[141] Parl Deb HC vol 37 col 1214 (8 April 1818).

that immoral and irreligious works could harm the moral fabric of society.[142] The author petitioners claimed they had been surprised to note that all but two of the libraries collected books indiscriminately, so that a 'promiscuous medly of modern publications should be incorporated with the important works that were formerly deposited in libraries'.[143] They further added that many such books were unfitted to 'the impressible minds of the educating youth'.[144] Sir Egerton Brydges echoed these complaints in another pamphlet publication, claiming that the Copyright Act brought together in 11 libraries:

> all that is seditious, all that is lascivious and obscene, all that is irreligious and atheistical, to attract the curiosity and mislead the judgment and passions of those, for whose cultivation of solid learning and useful knowledge these gratuitous supplies are intended to be enforced. Nothing short of such a law could have brought many of these contemptible, disgusting and contagious publications out of obscurity, in which they would otherwise have perished.[145]

Petitions opposing the amending Bill were presented by several of the university libraries.[146] The strength of feeling on the matter was such that, on 17 April, the proposed Bill was referred to a Select Committee.[147] While the matter was before the Committee, petitioning continued both for and against an amending Bill on similar lines as before.[148] Outside Parliament, pamphlet publication recommenced. Christian published a third edition of his *Vindication*, adding the history of the last four years on the matter of legal deposit, including the enacting of the 1814 Act.[149] The Syndics of the University of Cambridge published a pamphlet which consisted mainly of reproductions of Christian's *Vindication*,[150] and Sir Egerton Brydges published three more pamphlets in response.[151] Sion College also circulated a letter to each fellow and incumbent of the College, asking that every effort be made to halt Brydges' Bill.[152]

[142] This theme is discussed further in section III below.

[143] Parl Deb HC vol 37 col 1217 (8 April 1818).

[144] ibid. Deazley's research has uncovered evidence that this petition was also composed by the indefatigable Sharon Turner, see Deazley, 'Commentary on *Copyright Act* 1814'.

[145] E Brydges, *A Summary Statement of the Great Grievance imposed on Authors and Publishers and the Injury Done to Literature by the Late Copyright Act* (London, Longman, et al, 1818) 16. Interestingly, Christian had pre-empted such arguments in 1807, claiming that libraries would exercise judgement as to which books they took: Christian, *Vindication* (1807) 13–14.

[146] *JC* vol 73, 129 (4 March 1818), 141 (6 March 1818), 186 (16 March 1818), 218 (6 April 1818), 247 (15 April 1818).

[147] Parl Deb HC vol 38 cols 154–62 (17 April 1818).

[148] *JC* vol 73, 260 (20 April 1818), 263 (20 April 1818), 293 (28 April 1818), 296 (29 April 1818), 305 (30 April 1818), 309 (4 May 1818), 317 (5 May 1818), 334 (13 May 1818), 338 (14 May 1818), 350 (18 May 1818), 352 (18 May 1818).

[149] Christian, *Vindication* (1818).

[150] W Webb, *Observations on the Copyright Bill, printed by order of the Vice-Chancellor, Heads of College &c of the University of Cambridge* (1818).

[151] E Brydges, *A Summary Statement*; E Brydges, *A Vindication of the Pending Bill for the Amendment of the Copyright Act, from the Misrepresentations and Unjust Comments of the Syndics of the University Library at Cambridge* (London, Longman, Hurst, Rees, Orme and Brown, 1818); E Brydges, *Answer to the Further Statement ordered by the Syndics of the University of Cambridge* (London, Barnard and Farley, 1818).

[152] Partridge, *History of the Legal Deposit of Books* 67.

All this activity outside Parliament was mirrored by the investigations of the Select Committee, which began work on 27 April 1818. It was chaired by Charles Williams Wynn, long-time advocate of book trade interests, who was joined by Davies Giddy (who had now taken the name of Gilbert) and Sir Egerton Brydges. Joseph Butterworth, head of the publishing house of that name, was also a member. Other members, however, were closely allied with the universities, including Henry Bankes, who was a Trustee of the British Museum, and William Scott, Robert Peel, Lord Palmerston, JH Smyth and William Plunkett were all university members.[153] The witnesses appearing before the Committee were drawn from all sides of the debate, and included a large number of booksellers, such as Owen Rees and John Murray, as well as an engraver and some printers. Representatives from the libraries appeared, as did John Villiers, the Vice-Chancellor of Cambridge University and Edward Christian.

Almost all of the booksellers and printers complained of the great burden placed upon them by the delivery of 11 copies. Much of the evidence was contradictory and disingenuous. Owen Rees gave evidence that the 1814 Act had cost him £3,000 in delivery copies, and further claimed that he had been unable to publish other books due to the loss of the libraries as assured customers.[154] He also argued that the presence of books in public libraries discouraged members of the public from buying them.[155] Under further questioning from the Committee, however, he admitted that the presence of books in libraries acted to increase sales, because it diffused a taste for reading.[156] It became clear that Rees's real objection was the loss of the profit he could have made on the books he delivered to the library.

The booksellers also wanted to have it both ways on other arguments. One of their claims related to the practice of printing books in multiples of 250. This had been identified as problematic in 1814, with some booksellers arguing that the extra 11 copies would be charged to them by the printer as an extra 250 copies. However, John Matthews, the foreman of the University of Cambridge printing house, gave evidence that he had consulted the printers themselves and they had conceded that they would be prepared to charge only for the extra 11 copies, upon reasonable remuneration, but only because the copies were required by law.[157]

Another interesting aspect of the evidence of the booksellers was their insistent, and possibly disingenuous, denial that they had received any advantage at all from the extension of copyright term. Owen Rees claimed that not one book in fifty retained any value after 27 years, and not more than a quarter had any value after a few years.[158] Robert Baldwin claimed he would give a higher price to the author of a book for its copyright for the extra 14 years in about one-third of cases,[159] but

[153] J Feather, *Publishing, Piracy and Politics* 115–16.

[154] Minutes of Evidence taken before the Select Committee on the Copyright Acts of 8 Anne c 19; 15 Geo III c 53; 41 Geo III c 107; 54 Geo III c 116 (1818) 280, 3–6.

[155] ibid 3–6.

[156] ibid 14.

[157] ibid 67.

[158] ibid 9.

[159] ibid 45.

John Murray suggested such occasions for him would be extremely rare, stating not five out of a hundred works had any value after the first 14 years.[160]

The witnesses appearing for the universities were equally adamant that their interests were best served by continuing the delivery provisions. The Reverend William Webb, Vice-Chancellor of Cambridge, rejected any suggestion of monetary compensation, stating: 'We want books, we do not want money; we want books for the benefit of the University and literature in general; we want a regular supply'.[161]

The Select Committee's Report was delivered on 5 June 1818 and was highly favourable to the book trade. It recommended that the British Museum be retained as the only deposit library and that a fixed allowance be granted to the other institutions; or, in the alternative, that only the British Museum and the libraries of Oxford, Cambridge, Edinburgh and Dublin, be retained; that all books of prints be exempted; that all books in respect of which the claim to copyright is abandoned be exempted; and that the obligation imposed on printers to retain a copy of each work printed by them cease, and be replaced by the copy delivered to the British Museum.[162]

These proposals recognised the major complaints of the booksellers and followed their suggestions for improvement. The recommendation regarding the waiver of copyright had been raised by witnesses before both Select Committees, as well as featuring in early versions of the 1814 Act, and related to the practice of not registering large and expensive books, on the grounds that it would be too expensive to reproduce them illegally anyway.[163] The booksellers could afford to look generous in such cases, due to the practical barriers to piracy in the form of expense.

The Committee's Report had been carried by a small majority[164] and no legislation was introduced in that session. The University of St Andrews instructed its solicitor to draw up a statement on behalf of the universities of Scotland, which was circulated amongst Members of Parliament. The Librarian of St Andrews also sent a letter to its Chancellor, Viscount Melville, asking him to bear their interests in mind if amendments were proposed in the House of Lords.[165] The following March saw the London booksellers petitioning Parliament again for repeal of the 1814 Act, but Brydges was no longer in the House, and the Commons showed little interest in pursuing the matter.

160 ibid 61.

161 ibid 89. See also 118, 123.

162 Report from the Select Committee on the Copyright Acts of 8 Anne c 19; 15 Geo III c 53; 41 Geo III c 107; 54 Geo III c 116 (1818) 402, 5.

163 Minutes of Evidence (1818) 129.

164 Parl Deb HC vol 38 col 1262 (5 June 1818).

165 Ardagh, 'St Andrews University Library' 197.

E. The 1836 Act: Final Resolution?

Over the next 17 years the booksellers continued to find ways to evade deposit, and the libraries experimented with different ways of enforcing it.[166] An important development came during the course of the Royal Commission of Inquiry into the Universities of Scotland in 1831. The Commission's Chair was Lord Rosebery, and the Commissioners concluded in their report that, although the deposit privilege was of great value, the libraries would derive greater benefit from an arrangement which paid a proportional compensation to the Universities for each book. Moreover, under such an arrangement 'the operation of the privilege would be less felt by the authors and publishers of the works to which it applies'.[167] In March 1832 Lord Rosebery asked the University of St Andrews in confidence whether it would consider giving up its deposit rights in return for compensation. The University said it would consider the offer if it applied to all universities, but was informed that only St Andrews was to be asked to surrender its privilege. The University refused and in July a similar proposal was made in respect of Marischall College of the University of Aberdeen, as part of a scheme of exchange of books between France and Britain. Marischall College agreed to surrender its privilege in return for £460 a year, but in the end the proposals came to nothing.[168]

The apparent willingness of some libraries to commute their privilege for money, however, signalled that change was in the air and, in 1836, the issue was addressed again by Parliament. This time, the initiative was taken by James Silk Buckingham, a prolific writer, traveller, enthusiastic social reformer and temperance advocate, who had been involved in the debate to abolish stamp duty on newspapers, and strongly supported freedom of the press.[169] Buckingham drew a parallel between the taxes on knowledge that had been the subject of previous debates before the House, and the deposit provisions.[170] Identifying the problem of deposit with the current issues of the day allowed him to feed into existing frameworks of support for reform in Parliament.

Buckingham's Bill, as it was first drafted, gave the right to copies only to the British Museum, but provided that these would be paid for at the wholesale price by the Museum, using money given to it by Parliament, in accordance with a yearly estimate.[171] The 10 other libraries were to receive 'grants for the encouragement of learning' of between £200 and £500 each[172]. The Trustees of the

[166] McKitterick, *Cambridge University Library* 433–40. See also Ardagh, 'St Andrews University Library' 194–203.

[167] Report made to His Majesty by a Royal Commission of Inquiry into the State of the Universities of Scotland, Report (1831) 310, 84.

[168] Parl Deb HC vol 14 cols 896–98 (28 July 1832). See also Partridge, *The History of the Legal Deposit of Books* 74.

[169] Feather, *Publishing, Piracy and Politics* 118.

[170] Parl Deb HC vol 33 col 440 (28 April 1836).

[171] *JC* vol 91, 339 (10 May 1836).

[172] A Bill to Repeal so much of an Act of the fifty-fourth year of King George the Third, commonly called 'the Copyright Act,' as Requires the Gratuitous Delivery of Eleven copies of every Published

British Museum argued that they had a duty to preserve all books for posterity, even those new editions with only slight alterations.[173] This would have required Parliament to provide such a huge sum that an amended version removed the provision as to payment by the British Museum and altered the compensation arrangements for the other libraries.[174] Finally, after much lobbying and many revisions, delays, deferrals and discussions,[175] the libraries of Oxford and Cambridge, the Faculty of Advocates in Edinburgh and Trinity College, Dublin, were restored to the Bill as deposit libraries, and the Bill was passed in the House of Commons on 16 August.[176] Three days later it was passed without amendment by the Lords, and received Royal Assent on 20 August 1836.[177] The booksellers and publishers had been partially successful in their struggle to get rid of legal deposit as in the end the number of deposit libraries was reduced from 11 to 5. The new arrangement in fact suited some libraries better than the old. Sion College, for example, focused mainly on theological works and a sum of money was therefore preferable to receiving all books indiscriminately.[178]

The history of legal deposit, although infrequently told, is significant in the history of copyright law. Today, legal deposit is considered a separate issue from the rights encompassed by copyright law, and the inclusion of deposit in the copyright legislation is characterised as an historical accident. However, an examination of its history reveals that the link between copyright and deposit was no accident, and that its relationship to the bundle of rights encompassed by copyright law had an important historical function. The decisions of *Beckford v Hood*, and *University of Cambridge v Bryer* were instrumental in separating the functions of registration, deposit and property rights. However, old habits died hard, and the use of copyright term as a bargaining chip meant that they remained linked in the debates until after 1818. It is also noteworthy that, unlike in the common law copyright cases of the previous century, it seems that increasing the term of protection was of more interest to authors themselves than it was to publishers.

The interlinking of the three issues was also achieved by the choice of rhetoric of the debate's participants. Those who opposed the claims of the libraries employed the language of private property rights, as well as the existence of

book to Eleven of the Public Libraries of the Kingdom, in the said Act named, and to Provide other means for the Encouragement of Learning (1836) [252] s 5.

[173] Partridge, *The History of the Legal Deposit of Books* 756.

[174] A Bill to repeal so much of an act of the fifty-fourth year of King George the Third, commonly called 'the Copyright Act,' as requires the gratuitous delivery of eleven copies of book to eleven of the public libraries of the kingdom, in the said act named, and to provide other means for the encouragement of learning (1836) [441] s 2.

[175] *JC* vol 91, 432 (6 June 1836), 441 (8 June 1836), 795 (11 August 1836), 798 (12 August 1836), 801 (13 August 1836).

[176] ibid 819.

[177] An Act to Repeal so much of an Act of the fifty-fourth year of King George the Third, respecting Copyright, as requires the Delivery of a Copy of Every Published Book to the Libraries of Sion College, the Four Universities of Scotland, and of the King's Inns in Dublin 1836 (6 & 7 Will IV c 110).

[178] EH Pearce, *Sion College and Library* (Cambridge, Cambridge University Press, 1913) 314. Philip Ardagh also suggests that a lump sum must have had its attractions for St Andrews, as it would have allowed greater purchasing of foreign works. P Ardagh, 'St Andrews University Library' 204.

common law copyright based on natural law and Lockean labour theory that had been so prevalent in the eighteenth-century 'Battle of the Booksellers'. Once again, authors were cast as the victims of the piece, despite the fact that the main protagonists were booksellers and publishers. This language was therefore close to hand and rhetorically powerful. In addition, authors were characterised as disseminators of learning and it was argued that, if publishers and booksellers were unable to afford the cost of deposit, fewer books would be printed and society as a whole would suffer. Although it is necessary to exercise caution in assigning statutory intention using the Preamble of an Act,[179] that of the 1836 Act does suggest that these appeals did resonate with the legislature. It stated that the provisions of the 1814 Act 'have in certain respects operated to the Injury of Authors and Publishers, and have in some Cases checked or prevented the Publication of Works of great Utility and Importance'.[180]

However, the rhetoric was not powerful enough to convince Parliament that deposit should be abandoned altogether, as five libraries continued to receive copies. Supporters of the libraries had appealed to the public interest in encouraging learning. They argued that libraries were places where literature and knowledge were nurtured and that compulsory delivery of books would further these aims. In the end, it seems that the vision of the public libraries as nurturers of both literature and authors was enough to persuade Parliament that the deposit should continue. Perhaps also there remained some suspicion among the Members of Parliament as to the motives of the booksellers and their never-ending search to maximise financial returns. It became clear during the evidence before both Committees that for all the booksellers' protestations at the chilling effect of deposit on the publication of advantageous and publicly desirable works, their real fear was of the chilling effect on their calculations of profit.

III. BOOKS CONTRARY TO THE PUBLIC INTEREST

A. The Reading Public in the Regency Period

The role of the Stationers' Company in suppressing potentially dangerous, subversive or immoral works ended with the final lapse of the Licensing Act in 1695. Despite various attempts to re-introduce licensing at the turn of the century, none succeeded,[181] and in 1710 the Statute of Anne was passed to regulate the printing trade, but without re-enacting pre-publication licensing. The influence of the Stationers' Company had waned after 1695, and although warrants were sometimes issued to them for the arrest of libellers, this was infrequent and it was soon decided to employ individuals specifically tasked with discovering the authors and

[179] See above: ch 2, n 69.

[180] Copyright Act 1836, Preamble.

[181] See R Astbury, 'The Renewal of the Licensing Act in 1693 and its Lapse in 1695' (1978) 33 *The Library* 296.

publishers of libel.[182] Indeed, one interpretation of the provision in the Statute of Anne preventing the Clerk of the Stationers' Company from refusing registration to any author or proprietor is that it aimed at emphasising that the Stationers no longer had any role in pre-publication licensing of books.[183] The history of prosecutions for libellous and other 'dangerous' books in the following years is not a concern of this book, which picks up the story at the end of the eighteenth century, when censorship again began to intersect with copyright law.

The final years of the eighteenth century saw a growing concern among the middle and upper classes for the education of the poor.[184] Until this period, learning had largely been the province of the higher echelons of society. However, after 1780, the Sunday School movement began to provide religious-based education for the children of the poor, and was soon joined by the schools of Lancaster and Bell. Moves towards adult education were also made, first by the Society for the Promotion of Christian Knowledge, then through the Sunday Schools, and finally by the Mechanics' Institutes. The latter originated in Glasgow, when George Birkbeck, professor of natural philosophy and chemistry, began holding lectures for working men. Birkbeck left Glasgow for London where he founded the London Mechanics' Institute, and other Mechanics' Institutes were soon set up in other towns.[185]

Another leading supporter of the Mechanics' Institutes was Henry, later Lord, Brougham. Brougham believed that it was:

> highly useful to the community that the true principles of the constitution, ecclesiastical and civil, should be well understood by every man who lives under it. The peace of the country, and the stability of the government could not be more effectually secured than by the universal diffusion of this kind of knowledge.[186]

Brougham also sought to encourage education for the masses by means of cheap publications. In 1826, he established the Society for the Diffusion of Useful Knowledge, and began to issue monthly publications with the publisher Charles Knight. The first volume of the *Penny Magazine*, as it was called, included short articles on Van Dieman's Land, the Zoological Gardens and the history of beer, as well as an extract of the poetry of the recently deceased Rev. George Crabbe. It also contained several homilies, of varying length, no doubt intended to edify, improve and instruct in the value of scientific knowledge.[187] Brougham and Knight then started the Society for the Diffusion of Useful Political Knowledge.

[182] L Hanson, *Government and the Press 1695–1763* (Oxford, Oxford University Press, 1936) 39.

[183] Statute of Anne 1710 s 3. See above: ch 2, n 64.

[184] For the history of education of the lower classes see M Sturt, *The Education of the People: A History of Primary Education in England and Wales in the Nineteenth Century* (London, Routledge & Kegan Paul, 1967); SJ Curtis, *History of Education in Great Britain*, 7th edn (London, Maxwell & Son, 1967).

[185] EL Woodward, *The Age of Reform* (Oxford, Clarendon Press, 1962) 494–95.

[186] H Brougham, *Practical Observations on the Education of the People, Addressed to the Working Classes and their Employers* (London, Richard Taylor, 1825) 5.

[187] An example of such a homily is as follows: 'When the air-balloon was first discovered, someone flippantly asked Dr Franklin what was the use of it? The doctor answered this question with another: "What is the use of the new-born infant? It may become a man"' (*Penny Magazine* 1:1 (1823) 8).

Around the same time, the radicals Hume, Grote, Warburton, Place and Roebuck founded the Society for the Diffusion of Political and Moral Knowledge. Although these two latter bodies had short life-spans, their establishment demonstrates that working class education had moved firmly onto the radical agenda.

The objectives of most schools aimed at working-class children were limited. As the evangelist Hannah More noted, 'My object has not been to teach dogmas and opinions, but to form the lower classes in habits of industry and virtue'.[188] However, even with such limited aims, education remained an object of concern and fearfulness to more conservative members of society. When the French Revolution broke out, fear of the power of the masses reached new heights. In 1792, a Royal Proclamation against seditious writings was passed, and led to a number of state trials. Blame for the unsettled state of society was laid on the Sunday Schools, which had been the most prominent advocates of working-class education.[189]

In 1797, the *Gentleman's Magazine* worried that

> [a] little learning makes a man ambitious to rise, if he can't by fair means then he uses foul . . . A man of no literature will seldom attempt to form insurrections, or form idle schemes for the reformation of the state.[190]

The destabilising potential of print appeared, to the upper classes, to be realised in the unprecedented sales and dissemination of Tom Paine's response to Edmund Burke, *The Rights of Man*. Although first published at 3s, a price that the Tories considered high enough to keep the book out of the reach of the lower classes, copies spread like wildfire.[191] When Paine dropped the price to 6d, and arranged for the distribution of copies among workers in manufacturing cities, the Government panicked. Having refused 1,000 guineas for the purchase of the copyright, Paine was convicted *in absentia* of seditious libel, and several booksellers who had been selling the pamphlet were prosecuted.[192]

Reading matter was subject to the same duality of attitudes as education and most attacks focused on the novel. This was not entirely a nineteenth-century development. In 1750, Samuel Johnson wrote of novels,

> These books are written chiefly to the young, the ignorant, and the idle, to whom they serve as lectures of conduct, and introductions into life. They are the entertainment of minds unfurnished with ideas, and therefore easily susceptible of impressions . . . not informed by experience, and consequently open to every false suggestion.[193]

188 Sturt, *The Education of the People* 13.

189 RD Altick, *The English Common Reader: A Social History of the Mass Reading Public 1800–1900* (Chicago, Chicago University Press, 1957) 72, 73.

190 Sturt, *The Education of the People* 4.

191 Altick, *The English Common Reader* 69. Altick states that within weeks the first volume had sold 50,000 copies and by 1793 an estimated 200,000 copies were in circulation. By 1802, Paine estimated that 400,000 to 500,000 copies were being circulated, and seven years later there were thought to be 1,500,000 copies of Part 2 alone (pp 69–72). St Clair considers that such claims were greatly exaggerated: St Clair, *The Reading Nation* 256. However, even allowing for hyperbole, the circulation of the pamphlet was unprecedented, especially judging by the Government's reaction.

192 St Clair, *The Reading Nation* 256.

193 *The Rambler* (31 March 1750) quoted in P Brantlinger, *The Reading Lesson: The Threat of Mass Literacy in Nineteenth-Century British Fiction* (Bloomington, Indiana University Press, 1998) 27.

Women were seen as particularly vulnerable to corruption by novels. Hannah More believed that, for women, novel reading 'prepares for the surrender of virtue'.[194] She attempted to counteract the effects of novel reading, as well as the bawdy chapbooks carried around by hawkers, by producing the Cheap Repository Tracts series. These little books were priced at the same low prices as chapbooks and were peddled by the same hawkers, but their content combined Bible teaching and moral lessons.[195] This view of books as both poison and antidote encapsulates the ambiguity of the attitudes of the middle and upper classes towards the education of the lower classes.[196]

Similar contradictions are apparent in relation to the circulating libraries. The libraries serviced and supported the rapidly expanding novel-reading market, particularly for those who could not afford to purchase new books, and were in consequence considered by many as the wellspring of decadence. However, Mudie, the proprietor of the largest and most powerful of these libraries, exercised a firm hand of censorship over the novels he stocked. His influence and market power were such that if he refused to stock a book, it would remain unsold and unknown.[197]

In 1816, Samuel Coleridge characterised the reading public as 'the misgrowth of our luxuriant activity'.[198] Learning and reading, he implied, should be limited to the upper classes, and the creation of a mass reading public merely debased them. However, the relationship between class and morality was more nuanced than the simple dichotomy between a virtuous middle and upper class and the depraved masses which was so often asserted. This was demonstrated by the moral crusading movement that emerged at the end of the eighteenth century. Associations such as Wilberforce's Proclamation Society, the Society for the Suppression of Vice, and Wellington's Constitutional Association, sought to improve public morals generally by focusing on the middle and upper classes as an example. The most influential of these was the Society for the Suppression of Vice, or Vice Society as it was called, which passed information to magistrates and brought actions itself against works of pornography (obscene libel), as well as blasphemous libel, such as Paine's *Age of Reason*.[199] Fear of immoral books reached such heights that even Shakespeare was not immune. Thomas Bowdler bequeathed his surname to the English language when he produced his 'Family Shakespeare' in 1818 with the aim of producing an

[194] St Clair, *The Reading Nation* 283.

[195] J Feather, *A History of British Publishing* (London, Routledge, 1988) 162; Altick, *The English Common Reader* 73–75.

[196] Brantlinger notes that the contradiction inherent in trying to address the poisonous effects of reading with books of curative power is reminiscent of Derrida's analysis of the *pharmakon* in Plato's *Phaedrus*; Brantlinger, *The Reading Lesson* 7.

[197] On Mudie, see GL Griest, *Mudie's Circulating Library and the Victorian Novel* (Newton Abbot, Devon, David & Charles (Publishers) Ltd, 1970) and JA Sutherland, *Victorian Novelists and Publishers* (London, Athlone Press, 1976).

[198] *Lay Sermons*, 36, quoted in Brantlinger, *The Reading Lesson* 3.

[199] D Thomas, *A Long Time Burning: The History of Literary Censorship in England* (New York, Frederick A Praegar, 1969) 200–01.

edition of Shakespeare that a father could read to his daughters 'without incurring the danger of falling unawares among words and expressions which are of such a nature as to raise a blush on the cheek of modesty'.[200]

These were also years of considerable political unrest among the working classes, characterised by renewed interest in Major Cartwright's Hampden Club and outbreaks of machine breaking and rioting. In the wake of the French Revolution the State sought to bring reading matter under control by increasing the amount of the newspaper stamp. The first Stamp Act to apply to newspapers had been introduced in 1712,[201] although stamp duty had applied to paper and other documents for over a decade prior to that.[202] The Stamp Act of 1712 raised tax on newspapers, pamphlets and advertisements as well as paper and was calculated according to size.[203] Its main aim was to raise money to pay for Marlborough's foreign wars.[204] Contemporary writers, such as Swift, identified a secondary objective of discouraging the periodical press and the opposing political views it expressed.[205] Certainly, numerous publications were forced to shut down by the Act, but many survived and found ways to circumvent its operation. Following the French Revolution, numerous radical publications were surreptitiously printed and circulated among the working class, leading to what became known as the war of the unstamped press.

In 1819, the 'massacre of Peterloo' and the subsequent political unrest led the Government to pass the Six Acts. Two of these were directly aimed at press control by further increasing the price of the newspaper stamp, as well as the publications to which it applied, and by giving magistrates greater search and seizure powers in relation to blasphemous and seditious literature. In the same year, the Attorney-General brought 33 prosecutions against radical publishers, and local magistrates continued to apprehend and punish hawkers of radical pamphlets.[206] In 1820, the Prince Regent succeeded his father as George IV, and soon had his wife tried for adultery before the House of Lords. The radical press rallied to the Queen's support, and further prosecutions for seditious libel ensued.[207] In the minds of the ruling classes during this period immorality, profanity and civil disorder were all intrinsically linked, not only with each other, but also with books as the conduit by which they were spread.

[200] ibid 186.

[201] An Act for Laying Severall Duties upon all Sope and Paper &c, 1712(10 Anne c.18).

[202] D Foxon, *The Stamp Act of 1712: Sandars Lectures 1978* (unpublished, copy in Cambridge University Library) 3.

[203] Over the course of the eighteenth century further stamp acts were introduced to close loopholes, assist with enforcement and increase the level of the tax, before finally being repealed in the middle of the nineteenth century: FS Siebert, *Freedom of the Press in England* (Urbana, University of Illinois Press, 1952) 318–22.

[204] Foxon, *The Stamp Act of 1712* 2.

[205] ibid; Siebert, *Freedom of the Press* 304.

[206] D Thomas, *A Long Time Burning* 163.

[207] ibid 164–65.

B. Litigating 'Dubious' Books

It was against this background of political unrest and contradictory attitudes towards education, reading matter and public order that Lord Eldon formulated the principle that no copyright would subsist in immoral, libellous or blasphemous books. Lord Eldon's key role came about partly as a result of the central function of the Court of Chancery in eighteenth- and nineteenth-century copyright litigation. The Statute of Anne[208] had provided for penalties recoverable at common law,[209] but what copyright owners really wanted was to prevent their books being copied, multiplied and distributed. The best remedy was, therefore, an injunction from the Court of Chancery.[210]

The procedure followed in the Court of Chancery required the plaintiff to commence his suit with a Bill, in the nature of a petition, usually addressed to the Lord Chancellor.[211] The Bill could complain of an injury actually suffered, or of a threatened wrong.[212] The Bill required answer by the defendant, upon oath, which would take the form of a demurrer, a plea or an answer. The plaintiff would respond with a replication, which would usually conclude the pleadings.[213] The remedy sought by most plaintiffs was an injunction, and there were three possible types that the Court could award: first, an injunction designed to last until the defendant could make a 'full and perfect' answer;[214] second, an injunction lasting until a full hearing could be held; and, third, a perpetual injunction, granted following a full hearing.[215] However, as Willes J noted in *Millar v Taylor*, 'Few bills against pirates of books are ever brought to a hearing. If the defendant acquiesces under the injunction, it is seldom worth a plaintiff's while to proceed for an account; the sale of the edition being stopped'.[216] For the same reason, very few

[208] And its successor, An Act for the Further Encouraging of Learning in the United Kingdom of Great Britain and Ireland, by Securing the Copies and Copyright of printed Books to the Authors of such Books or their Assigns for the Time herein mentioned 1801 (41 Geo III c 107) s 1.

[209] Statute of Anne 1710 s 1. These penalties could be sued for by a common informer, who would receive half the amount awarded, with the other half going to the crown.

[210] As Eden wrote in 1821, 'The jurisdiction of the courts of equity in interposing by injunction to restrain the violation of copyright has been assumed merely for the purpose of making effectual the legal right': R Eden, *A Treatise on the Law of Injunctions* (London, Butterworth & Cooke, 1821) 264.

[211] J Mitford, *A Treatise on the Pleadings in Suits in the Court of Chancery by English Bill* (London, Owen, 1780) 1.

[212] ibid 2.

[213] ibid 3.

[214] There is inconsistency in the authorities as to whether the plaintiff needed to show a clear right in order to be granted an injunction. In *Millar v Taylor*, Willes J stated that a clear right was necessary and if the right was doubtful an injunction would be improper: 4 Burr 2303, 2324. However, Lord Eldon cast doubt on this proposition, noting that injunctions were sometimes granted in cases where the right was not clear: *The Universities of Cambridge and Oxford v Richardson* (1802) 6 Ves 689, 707.

[215] T Gomez-Arostegui, 'What History Teaches Us about Copyright Injunctions and the Inadequate-Remedy-at-Law Requirement' (2008) 81 *Southern California Law Review* 1197, 1230–33. In 1737, the Court of Chancery held that a perpetual injunction could be accompanied by an account of profits but this order was not repeated. See Deazley, *On the Origin* 66–69.

[216] *Millar v Taylor* (1769) 4 Burr 2303, 2334.

injunctions were ever made perpetual.[217] In 1817, Sir William Grant MR expressed considerable annoyance towards a plaintiff seeking a perpetual injunction at hearing in a case where the defendants had not challenged the interim injunction. The Master of the Rolls claimed that he could recall no instance where such a request had been granted, and he dismissed the Bill.[218] Over the course of the eighteenth century, it became increasingly common for Lord Chancellors granting injunctions to order also that the plaintiff proceed to establish his legal title at law.[219] Sometimes, an injunction was suspended until after the plaintiff established such title.[220] In practice, however, it was unusual for parties to continue to law and so the Lord Chancellor's decision generally ended the litigation.

The first case involving a work of dubious political tendency to come before Lord Eldon was *Walcot v Walker*.[221] In 1802 John Walcot, a former physician and clergyman, better known by his pseudonym Peter Pindar under which he published satirical works that frequently targeted George III, was granted an interim injunction against two booksellers for publishing two editions of his works without consent. Walcot applied to make the remedy permanent, but Lord Eldon entertained suspicions that the works were libellous. He suggested that if they were libellous then an action would not lie and the court of equity would give no account of profits, stating that 'the Court ought not to give an account of the unhallowed profits of libellous publications'.[222] Nor, it seemed, would it give an injunction, for he dissolved the injunction already awarded unless the books were brought into court so that he could inspect them.[223]

The authority that Lord Eldon relied on for his view that no action would lie in respect of libellous works was a case involving Dr Priestley, the well-known scientist, dissenter and republican sympathiser, who had brought an action against the hundred for damage sustained as the result of the Birmingham riots of 1791.[224] Among the property he had claimed was destroyed were certain unpublished manuscripts, and he offered to lead evidence of what booksellers would have paid

217 The reporter of *Whittingham & Others v Wooler & Anor* (1817) 2 Swans 428 notes only two instances: *Manley v Owen* (1755) and *Gay's Case (Baller v Watson)* (1737) 2 Swans 431. See also Deazley, *On the Origin* 62–65 and Gomez-Arostegui, 'What History Teaches Us about Copyright Injunctions' 1232–37, who locates more examples of perpetual injunctions but confirms their rareness. His research also establishes that interim injunctions were granted in the vast majority of infringement cases.

218 *Whittingham v Wooler* (1817) 2 Swan 428.

219 At common law a claim could be made for the recovery of damages, which was preferable to the penalties provided for by the Statute of Anne which were low and half of which had to go to the crown.

220 For an outline of this practice, in the context of a patent case, see *Bacon v Jones* (1839) 4 My & Cr 433, 436; 41 ER 167, 169, per Lord Cottenham LC.

221 *Walcot v Walker* (1802) 7 Ves 1.

222 ibid 2.

223 ibid.

224 The ability of citizens to bring actions for damages against the hundred dated back to the ancient principle that the individual inhabitants of the hundred were liable for damages to any person who had sustained harm from a robbery or other felony unless they raised the hue and cry and captured the criminal within forty days: W Holdsworth, *A History of English Law*, vol 4, 3rd edn (London, Methuen & Co, 1922) 521. This was extended to cover damages caused by rioting by an Act of George I (1 Geo I c 5). See also 19 Geo I c 22, 41 Geo III c 24, 52 Geo III c 130, 56 Geo III c 125, 57 Geo III c 19 and 3 Geo IV c 33 (consolidation and reform).

for them. Counsel for the hundred alleged that the works were seditious. Lord Eyre CJ held that if counsel for the hundred had produced evidence of the claim, then he would have allowed it to be received 'as against' the plaintiff's claim.[225]

There was, however, an earlier case to which Lord Eldon could have looked for authority for a different approach. In 1720, a work of dubious morality had come before the Court of Chancery:[226] *Archaelogica Philosophica*, by the (then deceased) well-known natural philosopher Dr Thomas Burnett, was written in Latin and claimed that the Bible's stories were allegorical, thereby threatening the divine authority of the scriptures. Dr Burnett had taken steps to suppress the book during his lifetime and, after his death, his son sought an injunction to prevent the book's publication in English. The view taken by Lord Macclesfield LC distinguished between knowledge in the hands of the upper and lower classes. Having read the book, he concluded that it 'contained strange notions, intended by the author to be concealed from the vulgar in the Latin language, in which language it could not do much hurt, the learned being better able to judge of it'.[227] He granted the injunction, on the basis that the Court of Chancery had 'superintendency over all books, and might in a summary way restrain the printing or publishing any that contained reflections on religion or morality'.[228] This case therefore provided authority for the granting of an injunction to prevent publication of immoral works, where such injunction would prevent publication altogether. Such a situation would come before Lord Eldon 15 years later, but in the interim several cases involving immoral works were brought before the common law courts.

In 1803, the case of *Hime v Dale*[229] came before Lord Ellenborough in the King's Bench. The case involved the alleged piracy of the words of a song, and counsel for the defendant argued that the song was libellous against the Government. Lord Ellenborough was clearly influenced by Lord Eldon's decision in *Walcot* because, although he found that the song was not libellous, he stated by way of obiter dictum that if it were a libel 'so gross as to affect public morals' the Court of Chancery would grant no injunction and he would advise a jury to grant no damages.[230]

Several months before Lord Eldon's decision in *Walcot v Walker*, the case of *Fores v Johnes*[231] had been heard by the court of King's Bench. In that case the plaintiff brought an action of assumpsit to recover the value of several caricature prints he had sold to the defendant but which the defendant had refused to receive on the grounds that some of them were libellous and obscene. Lawrence J held that the plaintiff could not recover for those prints which were obscene, libellous or immoral or for which a criminal action could be brought. Lord Ellenborough also

225 Noted by counsel in *Southey v Sherwood* (1817) 2 Mer 435. It is not clear whether 'as against' means as a bar to or as a defence to the plaintiff's claim.
226 *Burnett v Chetwood* (1720) 2 Mer 441.
227 ibid 441.
228 ibid.
229 *Hime v Dale* (1803) 2 Camp 27 fn.
230 ibid.
231 *Fores v Johnes* (1802) 4 Esp 97.

heard two actions involving claims for damages in respect of works of dubious content. In 1810, Du Bost brought an action for damages against Beresford, who had destroyed Du Bost's painting of Beresford's sister and her husband.[232] The defendant claimed that the picture was libellous and Lord Ellenborough accepted that evidence, instructing the jury that damages could be awarded only for the cost of the canvas and paint, and not in respect of any anticipated profits from its exhibition. In the 1817 case of *Gale v Leckie*[233] Lord Ellenborough suggested he would have allowed evidence of the libellous nature of the books to be brought as a defence against an action of assumpsit to recover damages against a printer who had refused to print a book. It is not clear from these three cases whether the principle emerging was that no property could subsist in an immoral or libellous work, or whether works of such a nature could not claim the protection of the law for other, possibly public policy-based, reasons.

Nor was clarity reached in the next case to come before Lord Eldon, *Southey v Sherwood*.[234] Twenty-three years earlier, Southey had left a poem entitled *Wat Tyler*, expressing the radical views of his youth, in the hands of a publisher. In 1817 the publisher Sherwood began to print and sell the poem to embarrass him, as Southey was by now a Tory and Poet Laureate. Southey sought an injunction to restrain publication. Lord Eldon read the poem and refused the injunction until Southey had established his right to the property at law. As Southey wanted to suppress publication entirely, this case could have fallen within Lord Macclesfield's judgment in *Burnett v Chetwood*.[235] However, Lord Eldon made no mention of it. Once again, he referred to Lord Eyre CJ as having 'expressly laid it down that a person cannot recover damages for a work which is, in its nature, calculated to do injury to the public'.[236] At the same time, however, Lord Eldon seems also to have based his decision on the fact that Southey had left his work in the hands of the publisher for so long that he could no longer complain if it were published—presumably, though not explicitly, relying on the notion of acquiescence or waiver of rights, or possibly even abandonment.[237]

The next work to come before Lord Eldon was by a much more controversial poet: Lord Byron. Lord Eldon and Lord Byron represented the two extremes of Regency England. One, cautious, conservative and highly moral, the son of a coal factor who ended up as the highest legal officer in the land; the other, a hereditary peer and flamboyant flouter of almost every moral, and sexual, code. Both Byron and his publisher Murray had been reluctant to seek the protection of Chancery, despite the fact that Byron's poems were extremely popular targets for the pirates. Murray feared prosecution for publishing an immoral work, and went to the lengths of publishing it anonymously. Byron's anxiety stemmed from fear of the

232 *Du Bost v Beresford* (1810) 2 Camp 411.

233 *Gale v Leckie* (1817) 2 Stark 107.

234 *Southey v Sherwood* (1817) 2 Mer 435.

235 (1720) 2 Mer 441. See above: text to n 226. *Burnett v Chetwood* was at that time unreported but was later appended to the report of *Southey v Sherwood* by the reporter Merivale.

236 (1817) 2 Mer 435, 439.

237 ibid 440.

effect that refusal to protect his poem, based on its immorality or blasphemy, might have on his right to custody of his daughter, Ada.[238] This concern was not unreasonable. In 1817, Lord Eldon had refused Byron's friend Shelley custody of his children due to his 'highly immoral conduct', established in part by reference to his poem *Queen Mab*.[239]

Although Murray had considered taking action against the numerous piracies of *Don Juan*, in the end he brought an action in respect of *Cain* against the radical political publisher William Benbow.[240] Advice was sought from Lancelot Shadwell, King's Counsel and later Vice-Chancellor, and Shadwell consented to lead the case, considering the poem no worse than *Paradise Lost*.[241] However, Shadwell's view was not shared by Lord Eldon. The Lord Chancellor considered that Milton's poem promoted Christianity, rather than bringing it into disrepute, and he doubted that Byron's work had the same innocent intent. Implying that no action would lie in respect of a work which undermined Christianity, he refused the injunction.[242]

Lord Eldon expanded upon this view a month later, in respect of Lawrence's *Lectures on Physiology, Zoology and the Natural History of Man*, which contained some metaphysical and theological argument.[243] Lord Eldon held that the law gave no protection to those who contradicted the Scriptures. Since he had a 'rational doubt' as to whether the book violated the law, he was unable to say definitively that the plaintiff had a right of property in the book and, consequently, was unable to continue the injunction. In this case, as in *Murray v Benbow*, he suggested that the plaintiff could seek to establish his right at law, and apply for an injunction again if the action were upheld.[244]

An action to halt the piracy of Byron's *Don Juan* was eventually brought before the Court of Chancery by Wakefield, acting for Lord Byron, in 1823. Sir John Leach, the Vice-Chancellor, granted an injunction against the publisher Hodgson,

[238] See LA Marchand (ed), *Byron's Letters and Journals*, vol 7 (London, John Murrary, 1976) 238.

[239] *Shelley v Westbrooke* (1817) Jac 266 fn.

[240] *Murray v Benbow* (1822) Jac 474 fn and 6 Petersdorff Abr 558 fn. Murray's biographer, Smiles, states that an injunction was sought in respect of *Don Juan* in 1819 and granted, as do Robinson Blann and Hugh J Luke Jnr; however, I have been unable to locate a reported or unreported case concerning *Don Juan* at this time. In 1823, when Byron did bring an action against Hodgson for publishing cantos 6, 7 and 8 of *Don Juan*, his counsel assured the court that no injunction had ever been sought in respect of the whole work. The Vice-Chancellor was particularly insistent upon the point, stating he had been under the impression that an injunction had been sought in the past, but Wakefield firmly denied it. Moreover, the piracy of *Don Juan* continued at the same high levels in the period after 1819, and Byron's concerns about his daughter were not assuaged. See S Smiles, *A Publisher and his Friends: Memoir And correspondence of the Late John Murray*, vol 1 (London, John Murrary 1997) 408; R Blann, *Throwing the Scabbard Away: Byron's Battle Against the Censors of 'Don Juan'* (New York, Peter Lang, 1991) 72; JH Luke Jnr, 'The Publishing of Byron's *Don Juan*' (1965) 80 *Publications of the Modern Language Association of America* 199, 202; Marchand, *Byron's Letters and Journals*, vol 7, p 238. Also *The Times* (19 July 1823, 2 July 1823).

[241] Smiles, *A Publisher and his Friends* vol 1, p 428.

[242] *Murray v Benbow* (1822) 6 Petersdorff Abr 558 n.

[243] *Lawrence v Smith* (1822) Jac 471.

[244] ibid 474.

which Hodgson did not contest.[245] Several days later, Shadwell sought an injunction on behalf of Murray against another publisher, Dugdale, for publishing *Beppo*. This time, Shadwell was able to persuade a rather reluctant Lord Eldon that there was nothing objectionable about the poem and the injunction was granted.[246]

A month later, Wakefield, acting for Byron, sought an injunction against Dugdale for publishing cantos 6, 7 and 8 of *Don Juan*.[247] Sir John Leach V-C granted the application, but Dugdale moved for its dissolution, arguing that the work was 'immoral in the highest sense of the word, most calculated to taint the minds of the public, licentious, in every way dangerous, and most destructive of the morals of the community at large'.[248] Pleading inexperience, Sir John Leach consulted with Lord Eldon before delivering his decision, which was to refuse the requested injunction. Leach stated that the rule was:

> Wherever, therefore, a court of law would grant a reparation by damages for the piracy of a work, there, as a general principle, the court of equity would grant a more perfect remedy to prevent further injury of the property. Where, on the contrary, a court of law would refuse a reparation by damages, it necessarily followed that a court of equity must withhold its injunction.[249]

The rule established in this series of cases was clear: where it was doubtful whether a work was of an 'innocent' character, the Court of Chancery would grant no injunction. The basis for the rule was, however, less clear. Sometimes Lord Eldon had suggested that no action at common law would lie because there could be no property in such a book, while at other times he had suggested that no damages would be granted at common law, which was the aspect emphasised by Leach V-C. If the former were the case, no equitable remedy would be available as they lay only to protect property rights; if the latter view was adopted, then Lord Eldon's refusal to grant an injunction rested either on the principle that no right exists without a remedy, or on the principle that if no damages would be awarded then the injunction would not be protecting against anything, or on a combination of the two. The significance of the distinction was probably lost on the plaintiff who was denied his injunction. However, it was raised when the issue was squarely considered by a common law court for the first time in 1826.

This case involved the memoirs of the well-known Regency courtesan, Harriette Wilson.[250] Harriette is famous today for having been told by the Duke of Wellington to 'publish and be damned' but, in the event, it was her publisher who suffered when the memoirs were pirated.[251] Harriette persuaded Henry,

[245] *The Times* (19 July 1823, 22 July 1823).

[246] *The Times* (23 July 1823).

[247] *Byron v Dugdale* (1823) *The Times* (2 August 1823).

[248] *Byron v Dugdale* (1823) *The Times* (9 August 1823).

[249] *Byron v Dugdale* (1823) *The Times* (11 August 1823).

[250] *Stockdale v Onwhyn* (1826) 5 B & C 173; 2 Car & P 163.

[251] However, it is hard to feel too sorry for Stockdale, who had used the argument that the book was obscene in order to avoid paying the printer, Poplett. When Poplett brought an action in Common Pleas to recover the amount Stockdale owed him, Best CJ refused the assistance of the court to 'the person who lends himself to the violation of the public morals and laws of the country', adding that he

later Lord, Brougham, her friend and former lover, to act for her in exchange for keeping his name out of her book. At the hearing, Lord Abbott CJ held that: 'The law cannot recognize as property the history of the low amours of a notorious courtezan'.[252]

Brougham moved for a new trial, this time founding his argument on the distinction between refusing an injunction on the basis that damages would not be granted, and holding that no action would be maintainable.[253] He claimed that the principle that no property existed in such a work was sustained only by a dictum of Lord Eyre CJ.[254] In addition, Brougham argued that the decisions of the Lord Chancellor were no authority for the court and that the question was still open and worthy of further consideration.[255] The significance of Brougham's argument was that, if the court accepted that the correct principle was that property subsisted prima facie in all publications, then the burden of proof fell upon the person denying or defending the infringement.

The reports of the case differ slightly. However, it is clear in all of them that even in the absence of clear authority, Lord Abbott CJ was in no doubt as to what the law should be. Although he agreed with Brougham that the cases in equity provided no authority for the courts of law, he considered that

> upon the plainest principles of common law, founded as it is, where there are no authorities, upon common sense and justice, this action cannot be maintained. It would be a disgrace to the common law could a doubt be entertained upon the subject; but I think no doubt can be entertained, and I want no authority for pronouncing such a judicial opinion.[256]

The other three judges of the court of King's Bench concurred.

C. A Knot Twisted by a Single Hand?

Unsurprisingly, in light of the strong feeling surrounding the moral content of books and the widespread discontent with Chancery practice and procedure in this period, Lord Eldon's judgments were attacked in the periodical press. These attacks mixed proprietarian concerns that the decisions undermined private property rights, utilitarian fears regarding the practical effects of the decisions, and more general stabs at the Court of Chancery and the role of the Lord Chancellor. The *Quarterly Review*, which was, incidentally, owned by John Murray, claimed that

would not 'take an account between two robbers on Hounslow Heath': *Poplett v Stockdale* (1825) Ry & Mood 337, 338, 339.

252 *The Times* (12 January 1826).
253 *Stockdale v Onwhyn* 2 Car & P 163, 168.
254 ibid 167.
255 *The Times* (28 January 1826).
256 *Stockdale v Onwhyn* 5 B & C 173, 176.

> no sooner was it whispered that there was no property in 'Don Juan' than ten presses were at work, some publishing it with obscene engravings, others in weekly numbers and all in a shape that brought it within the reach of purchasers on whom its poison would operate without mitigation.[257]

Pirated copies of *Don Juan* and *Cain*, it warned, would be exposed to 'thousands totally unfitted by knowledge and habits of thinking to grapple with its difficulties',[258] thereby echoing the judgment of Lord Macclesfield 100 years before.[259] The reviewer also worried that the rule would have a chilling effect on freedom of the press, as learned men such as Malthus and Locke might be discouraged from writing books for fear of suffering the stigma of the disapprobation of Chancery.[260] The *Edinburgh Review*, which numbered Brougham among its founders, argued that the rule would result in the whole property of modern literature turning 'on the pendulous oscillations in the mind of the person who, for the time being, may hold the Great Seal'.[261] The reviewer also considered that 'the single hand that twisted [the knot] is of itself competent to untie it . . . we believe that Lord Eldon, should he have occasion to review his own decisions, will find no authority but that of Lord Eldon which it will be necessary to overrule'.[262] The lawyer Joseph Parkes also condemned Lord Eldon's rule, stating:

> Two extraordinary and recent stretches of the prerogative of a Lord Chancellor cannot pass unnoticed, viz: the assumption of the offices of *Licensor of the Press*; and of *Censor*, an office of the Roman Emperors who in the height of their power styled themselves *morum praefecti*.
>
> In the former jurisdiction nothing can be more anomalous than the effect of Lord Eldon's interference under the powers given him as the arbiter of copyright. His Lordship would not *protect* a bad book, but assisted to bring (what he deemed) licentiousness and irreligion into notice by cheap pirated publications, thus stimulating and disseminating that which otherwise would be smothered in its own obscurity and insignificance. The liability to error in the selection of the judge, and the possibility of error in his judgment, unite to make this a dangerous power in the hands of any individual.[263]

These accusations of judicial overreach and capriciousness would have been particularly galling to Lord Eldon, who had explicitly sought to endow equity with principles as settled as those of the common law. In 1818, in *Gee v Pritchard*, he famously noted:

[257] 'Cases of *Walcot v Walker*, *Southey v Sherwood*, *Murray v Benbow* and *Lawrence v Smith*' (1822) 27 *Quarterly Review* 127, 128 (The authorship of this article has been attributed to either Southey or Nassau Senior).

[258] ibid 128.

[259] In *Burnett v Chetwood* (1720) 2 Mer 441 and see above: text to n 226.

[260] 'Cases of *Walcot v Walker*' 136.

[261] 'Late Judgments of the Lord Chancellor' (1823) 38 *Edinburgh Review* 300.

[262] ibid 314.

[263] J Parkes, *A History of the Court of Chancery* (London, Longman, Rees, Orme Browne and Green, 1828) 438.

> I cannot agree that the doctrines of this court are to be changed by every succeeding judge. Nothing would inflict on me greater pain in quitting this place, than the recollection that I had done anything to justify the reproach that the equity of this court varies like the Chancellor's foot.[264]

Set against the argument that refusal of injunctions would lead to greater and cheaper numbers of such books being printed was the claim that denying publishers the profits from their works would discourage such works from being printed at all. *Blackwood's Magazine* claimed that in this way, Lord Eldon's rule had 'kept a flood of improper books from the market, without recurring to the unpopular method of prosecution, and has neutralized the power of those which have already crept in'.[265]

In fact, it seemed that those who attacked the rule were correct. Lord Eldon's refusal to protect books against piracy had indeed operated to multiply such books and to drive down prices. Southey's *Wat Tyler*, which would normally have sold for 10s 5d, was sold in Sherwood's pirated edition for 2s in 1817, but within the year had dropped to 3d.[266] Southey's son estimated the total sale of the book to be 60,000 copies, making it twice or three times as popular as the rest of Southey's poems put together. *Don Juan* had a similar fate, with copies appearing in the year of its first publication for 4s, an eighth of Murray's original asking price.[267]

Lord Eldon was undoubtedly aware that his decisions would result in increased circulation of these works, as this was argued by plaintiffs in almost every case that came before him. In *Walcot v Walker*, he appeared to endorse the opposing argument (that refusal to protect books would mean that publishers could no longer afford to print them) when he noted that he would not protect 'the unhallowed profits of libellous publications'.[268] However, in later cases Lord Eldon emphasised that instrumentalist questions were not the concern of his court. In *Southey's case*, he noted 'It is very true that, in some cases, it may operate so as to multiply copies of mischievous publications', but held that he had nothing to do with such a question.[269] In *Murray v Benbow*, he pointed out that 'the duty of stopping the work does not belong to the court of equity, which has no criminal jurisdiction, and cannot punish or check the offence'.[270]

For Lord Eldon, the public interest was reflected in the law's obligation to uphold a well-ordered constitutional monarchy and Christian society. It could not, therefore, be used to protect works that undermined it. In *Stockdale v Onwhyn*, Bayley J suggested that a practical solution to the dissemination problem would be for the Court of Chancery to grant an injunction, requiring at the same time an

[264] *Gee v Pritchard* (1818) 2 Swan 402, 414; 37 ER 670.

[265] 'Letters of Timothy Tickler to Eminent Literary Characters' (1823) 9 *Blackwood's Edinburgh Magazine* 214, 217.

[266] St Clair, *The Reading Nation* 318.

[267] ibid 317, 324.

[268] *Walcot v Walker* (1802) 7 Ves 1, 2.

[269] *Southey v Sherwood* (1817) 2 Mer 435, 439–40.

[270] *Murray v Benbow* (1822) Petersdorff Abr 558 fn, 559 fn.

undertaking by the owner not to publish the work himself.[271] Such an approach would not have accorded with Lord Eldon's ideas about the role of the Court of Chancery.

An important corollary of Lord Eldon's position was that criminal prosecutions would be undertaken against publishers, whether piratical or not. This did occur in some cases. William Clark was prosecuted by the Vice Society for piratically publishing Shelley's *Queen Mab*, and John Hunt was prosecuted for legitimately publishing Byron's *Vision of Judgment*. A second supplementary element of Lord Eldon's view was that he was not denying all relief to the plaintiff, who was always free to bring an action at common law to establish his right and then return to Chancery for his injunction. However, the fear of criminal prosecutions, combined with financial considerations, meant that, with the exception of *Stockdale v Onwhyn*, no plaintiffs took their cases to the common law courts, and the Court of Chancery decision *was* the final settlement of the matter.

It was for this reason that the American lawyer George Ticknor Curtis argued in his mid-nineteenth-century treatise on copyright law that it would be a far sounder rule to hold that every work was entitled to protection prima facie, unless malicious or mischievous intention appeared on its face, and if no such intent appeared then it rested on those who relied on the intent to establish it.[272] He particularly objected to Lord Eldon's decision in *Southey v Sherwood*, arguing that the right to publish or withhold from publication a manuscript was a common law right of possession and control, and the question of the work's innocence or otherwise did not arise, because that question related only to the right to publish and make a profit.[273]

Joseph Story, Dane Professor of Law at Harvard University, was also critical of Lord Eldon's decisions. In his *Commentaries on Equity Jurisprudence*, published in the United Kingdom in 1839, Story stated that Lord Eldon's view that equity would not protect immoral, irreligious or blasphemous books was correct, and he agreed that the effect of such a finding on the book's circulation should be no concern of the court of equity.[274] However, Story noted that the rule was difficult to apply in practice and expressed concern that conferring an absolute power on a court of equity over the subject of literary property might 'sap the very foundations' of the law of literary property and 'retard, if not entirely suppress the means of arriving at physical as well as metaphysical truths'.[275]

[271] *The Times* (28 January 1826).

[272] GT Curtis, *A Treatise on the Law of Copyright* (London, Maxwell & Son, 1847) 165–66.

[273] ibid 157–61.

[274] J Story, *Commentaries on Equity Jurisprudence*, 2nd edn, vol 2 (London, Maxwell, 1839) 193.

[275] ibid 194. Between the mid-nineteenth and mid-twentieth centuries, some United States courts took that view that copyright protection would be denied to obscene works: see Z Chafee, 'Coming into Equity with Clean Hands' (1947) *Michigan Law Rreview* 1065, 1065–67 and B Wilkinson, 'Recent Developments' (1978) *Fordham Law Review* 1037. Interestingly, an alternative justification sometimes offered for refusing protection in the USA was that it arose from the limitations in the Constitution, which provided that copyright must 'promote the Progress of Science and the Useful Arts'. See eg *Martinetti v Maguire* (1867) 16 F Cas 920 (CCD Cal 1867) (No 9, 173). However, the principle of non-protection was decisively abandoned in the 1979 case of *Mitchell Brothers Film Group v Cinema Adult Theater*

After the decision in *Stockdale v Onwhyn*, the principle of non-protection of immoral and blasphemous works moved sideways, and was applied to refuse protection to deceptive and fraudulent books.[276] In 1848, an injunction was refused in respect of a libellous book,[277] and Kekewich J dismissed an action without costs relating to two indecent pictures in 1899, with very little discussion of the principle.[278] The last time that the principle was directly considered and applied was in the 1915 case of *Glyn v Western Feature Film Company*.[279] In that case, Younger J noted:

> It may well be that the Court in this matter is now less strict than it was in the days of Lord Eldon, but the present is not a case in which in the public interest it ought, as it seems to me, to be at all anxious to relax its principles.[280]

The hand that tied the knot may have been Lord Eldon's but the rope with which he was supplied was woven from the particular ideals, fears, and political pressures of Regency England. Although books continued to be viewed as morally corrosive and a threat to social order into the Victorian era, the copyright cases challenging the moral and religious content of individual books ceased after 1826. This may be due to a change of political atmosphere. The threat of immoral and irreligious works had been closely linked to the cause of radical reform because it was largely the radical publishers, such as Dugdale and Benbow, who were involved in the piracies. These publishers were not averse to publishing the works of living writers who might forward the radical agenda.[281] Nor were they averse to linking piracy and reform. In 1822, following his success against Murray, Benbow wrote:

> The enormous high price of books has long prevented the humble in place and purse from acquiring information, and we are not sorry to see the 'gates of knowledge' opened, so that all ranks may enter therein for a mere trifle; and, we trust, that cheap editions of dear and valuable works will rapidly proceed from the press, in spite of threats and animadversions.[282]

(1979) 604 F 2d 852. See also MB Nimmer and D Nimmer, *Nimmer on Copyright: A Treatise on The Law of Literary, Musical and Artistic Property, and the Protection of Ideas* (New York, Matthew Bender, 1996) §2.17.

[276] *Wright v Tallis and Anor* (1845) 1 CB 893; 135 ER 794; *Slingsby v Bradford Patent Truck and Trolley Company* [1906] WN 51.

[277] *Clark v Freeman* (1848) Beav 112; 50 ER 759.

[278] *Baschet v London Illustrated Standard Co* [1900] 1 Ch 73.

[279] *Glyn v Western Feature Film Co* [1916] 1 Ch 261.

[280] ibid 269. Although the case has never been explicitly overruled in the United Kingdom since this time, it has long since ceased to be applied in relation to immoral, blasphemous and even pornographic works. The rule of non-protection of immoral works, in fact, might have completely slipped off the judicial radar if it had not been referred to approvingly in 2001 by Aldous LJ in *Hyde Park v Yelland* as belonging to the inherent jurisdiction of the court; [2001] Ch 143, 161. In *Attorney-General v Guardian*, Lords Griffiths and Jauncey also considered that *Glyn v Western Feature Film* was good law: [1990] 1 AC 109, 275–76, 294. Although this was obiter dictum, it was implicitly adopted by Lord Phillips MR in *Ashdown v Telegraph Group* when he concluded that Aldous LJ's approach to the public interest defence was too restrictive; [2002] Ch 149, 171. The principle of non-protection of immoral works was also recently discussed in the Australian case of *Venus Adult Shops Pty Ltd v Fraserside Holdings Ltd* [2006] FCAFC 188, but the Federal Court held that no such principle existed under the Australian Copyright Act.

[281] Luke, 'The Publishing of Byron's *Don Juan*', 199.

[282] ibid 205–06.

After Dugdale's victory over Lord Byron, a pseudonymous writer, probably either Dugdale or Benbow, wrote a letter directed at Byron's publisher John Hunt for publication in Benbow's *Rambler Magazine*:

> I trust that the next excellent thing you bring out will spread in similar manner to Don Juan and disappoint the avarice of such fellows as you, who think, that knowledge should be given only to them who can afford to buy it at high price.[283]

After 1820 prosecutions for seditious libel also began to drop off. One explanation for this could be that following Castlereagh's replacement by Canning as leader of the Commons in 1822, the Tory administration took on a new tone, gradually becoming more open to reform.[284] Perhaps more significantly, Michael Lobban has also demonstrated that the law of seditious libel had become increasingly unworkable from the late eighteenth century and, after the 1820s, the authorities looked increasingly to the law of unlawful assembly to control threats to public order. Physical force, not radical ideas, thus became the main focus of conservative fear.[285]

The relationship between copyright law and immoral or blasphemous works in the early nineteenth century reveals that the public interest in the encouragement of learning proclaimed by those involved in debates over copyright law was a deeply complex and ambivalent issue. In the words of Brantlinger, the threat posed by reading matter in this period was 'of mass literacy producing the opposite of enlightenment'.[286] The principle of non-protection subordinated private property rights to a concept of public interest. However, it was not the public interest championed by the radical publishers of making cheap books available to the masses that triumphed, but rather Lord Eldon's notion that the law should serve the public interest in an altogether stricter and more principled sense by refusing to grant property rights over books that undermined public order, morality and religion.

IV. CONCLUSION

Developments in copyright law in the first four decades of the nineteenth century took place against a background of incipient change in the book trade. New technologies for production were appearing on the scene and new markets were beginning to be identified. Overall, the trade remained conservative and leading members sought to maintain stability through traditional tactics of co-operation and exclusion. In society at large, social reform and the education of the lower

[283] ibid 207–08. The comment was unfair, as Hunt had attempted to avert the threat of piracy by issuing the new cantos in a 1s for an 18mo edition, advertising the cheap edition as 'a substitute for the Lord Chancellor's protection'.

[284] D Thomas, *A Long Time Burning* 173; Woodward, *The Age of Reform* 69.

[285] M Lobban, 'From Seditious Libel to Unlawful Assembly: Peterloo and the Changing Face of Political Crime c1770–1820' (1990) *Oxford Journal of Legal Studies* 10.

[286] Brantlinger, *The Reading Lesson* 3.

classes were moving onto the political agenda. While this remained the concern of a minority, as a movement it was gathering momentum. Other sectors of society strongly resisted such moves, fearing the potential destabilising effects of too much, or the wrong type of, education.

Consideration of this background exposes links between two areas of copyright law that might otherwise seem to have little in common. Library deposit and the principle of non-protection of 'dubious' books both fed in to concerns about encouraging learning, how it was best achieved, or whether it was even desirable. Both areas engaged the economic interests of booksellers and pitted them against the broader claims of society as a whole. When the controversies moved from Parliament (in the case of library deposit) and the courts (in the case of the non-protection principle) into the wider public sphere through the publication of pamphlets and the periodical press, the rhetoric of private rights opposing the public interest became more explicit still. In this way, much of the rhetoric of conflicting interests that had been developed in the previous century was simply transposed into new copyright contexts. However, it is also important to note that while the 'interest' identified in both areas was the interest in education, ideas about the nature of the access to be given to educational materials were far more problematic in the case of immoral books. Moreover, the 'public' envisaged in each case also differed. In relation to legal deposit, the public whose interests were being advocated was generally an educated, or seeking to be educated, and literate public, which frequented public and university libraries and might be expected to engage in acts of authorship itself. In relation to the question of whether immoral or otherwise subversive books should be protected, the public in mind was a less educated, impressionable, and generally belonging to the lower classes.

4

Extension and Expansion

OVER THE COURSE of the nineteenth century copyright law was both extended and expanded. By the end of the century, copyright had increased in length, breadth and strength, becoming more and more recognisable to modern eyes as the copyright law we know today. This enlargement is sometimes Whiggishly presented as inexorable or inevitable. However, the following chapters will demonstrate that this is far from being the case. This chapter traces support for, and resistance to, extension and expansion of literary copyright law as the copyright statutes of the eighteenth century were first supplemented, and then supplanted, by new legislative regimes which covered new types of subject matter and addressed the growing pressures of an increasingly international market for books, plays and music. It focuses on the first three quarters of the nineteenth century, with chapter five picking up the story with the Royal Copyright Commission of 1875–78.

This chapter covers three main developments in the law during this period: first, the application of copyright to the spoken word, in the form of plays and lectures; second, the 1842 Copyright Act; and, third, the court cases and debates that considered the question of whether, or how, copyright should apply to foreign authors. In each of these areas, it will consider the role played by public interest considerations, demonstrating that at times the public was made up of theatregoers, at times of attendees at educational lectures; it might be readers of newspapers, working men anxious to improve themselves, lower class readers unable to afford expensive books, printers, reprinters, importers, Britons or foreigners. Different versions of the 'public' had different interests, which sometimes aligned with, and at other times were opposed to, the interests of authors or publishers.

I. COPYRIGHT IN THE SPOKEN WORD

A. Plays

In chapter two, it was noted that one of the significant matters left unaddressed by *Donaldson v Becket* was the status of manuscripts not published as books. A related issue was whether copyright law could protect the spoken word, as manifested in plays and lectures, whether or not they also took form as manuscripts. Clearly, such matters did not fall within the narrow, literal, confines of the Statute of Anne and yet they too were valuable articles of commerce. Consequently, it is not surprising that towards the end of the eighteenth century dramatists and theatre managers began to look to the Statute of Anne to provide them with protection against their rivals in the marketplace.

The history of dramatic copyright, like that of copyright in books, has its roots in censorship and monopoly. Censorship of the theatres stretches back to the Tudors, but the central instrument for censorship in the eighteenth and nineteenth centuries was Walpole's Stage Licensing Act of 1737.[1] This Act supported the monopolies of the two patent theatres, Drury Lane and Covent Garden, which had been granted exclusive rights to perform 'legitimate' drama by Charles II. The Stage Licensing Act required a copy of every new play to be submitted to the Lord Chamberlain, who could prohibit performance of the play if he saw fit. The powers of the Lord Chamberlain extended to the City of Westminster, which comprised the two patent theatres, as well as the Haymarket, which was granted a royal patent in 1766, and the King's Theatre. Other theatres, which grew steadily in numbers throughout the eighteenth century, were, in theory, restricted to performing plays containing singing, dancing and 'spectacles'. However, they too submitted manuscripts to the Lord Chamberlain regularly. Theatres outside the City of Westminster were subject to supplementary licensing regimes.[2]

The system of censorship and licensing, however, did not inhibit various sharp practices between rival theatres, as managers sought to obtain copies of successful plays, in order to stage them for their own profit. One popular method was to purchase a copy of the prompt book from the prompter,[3] or to send in several agents to join the audience over several nights, each tasked with recording a particular character or characters. By the 1830s, the practice had evolved to sending in shorthand writers to take down the script as it was performed.[4] In 1770, the actor and dramatist Charles Macklin, who had taken the precaution of never printing any copies of his play *Love à la Mode* and always took the copy away from the prompter, sought an injunction from the Court of Chancery against just such practices.[5] The defendants were the proprietors of a magazine called the *Court Miscellany*, rather than a rival theatre, and they published the play's first act in their magazine, promising that the second was to come in a subsequent edition. Macklin brought a Bill seeking an account of profits and injunction against further publication of the first act, and the promised publication of the second. Lord Camden initially stood the case over until after the decision in *Millar v Taylor*[6] should be given.

[1] An Act to explain and amend so much of an Act made in the twelfth year of the Reign of Queen Anne &c as relates to common Players of Interludes, 1737 (10 Geo II c 28).

[2] JR Stevens, *The Censorship of English Drama 1824–1901* (Cambridge, Cambridge University Press, 1980) 5–7.

[3] A prompter is a person who stands next to the theatre stage, but out of sight, so as to prompt the actors, should they forget their lines.

[4] JR Stevens, *The Profession of the Playwright* (Cambridge, Cambridge University Press, 1992) 86.

[5] *Macklin v Richardson* (1770) Amb 694.

[6] *Millar v Taylor* (1760) 4 Burr 2303.

As was discussed in chapter two, the court in *Millar v Taylor* found that there was a common law copyright existing outside the Statute of Anne. Macklin sought to rely on this precedent, arguing that representing a play in a theatre did not amount to making a gift of it to the public, and that the defendants' publication thereof amounted to an invasion of the plaintiff's property right. The defendants, however, asserted that representing a farce on the stage gave a right to the audience to 'carry away what they could and make any use of it'.[7] Moreover, they alleged that the publication occasioned no damage to Macklin as he could still receive profits from the acting of the piece. Lord Commissioners Smythe and Bathurst rejected these arguments, finding that the printing of the play did occasion damage to the plaintiff and granted a perpetual injunction.[8]

However, the Court of the King's Bench took a different approach in the subsequent case of *Coleman v Wathen*.[9] Colman (as it is usually spelt), was the manager of the Haymarket theatre and claimed that he had purchased the copyright (presumably meaning the rights conveyed by the Statute of Anne) of John O'Keeffe's play, *The Agreeable Surprise*. In 1793, he brought an action against Wathen, of the Richmond Theatre, for performing the piece without permission. Although the Statute of Anne used the words 'printing and reprinting', the report of the case suggests that the parties used the word 'publication' to refer to the statutory rights, presumably in the hope that its broader meaning would result in a broader interpretation of the Statute. Thomas Erskine (later Lord Chancellor), acting for the plaintiff, argued that a representation should amount to a 'publication' within the meaning of the Statute, for if it was not 'all dramatic works might be pirated with impunity'.[10] As an alternative, should the court not accept that the Statute covered performances, he argued that it had been held in *Millar v Taylor* that an author had a property in his works independent of the Statute of Anne. Lord Kenyon CJ did not accept this argument. By this stage, *Donaldson v Becket*[11] had been decided by the House of Lords, and Lord Kenyon held that 'the statute for the protection of copyright only extends to prohibit the publication of the book itself by any other than the author or his lawful assignees. It was so held in the great copyright case by the House of Lords'.[12] He further held that there had been no 'publication'.[13]

In his 1828 treatise on literary property, Robert Maugham suggested that the differing results in the two cases could be traced to the fact that the plaintiff in the latter case was seeking statutory penalties, rather than bringing an action for damages, with the result that he was bound by the express provisions of the Statute of Anne, which were, as penal provisions, construed strictly.[14] This seems to be borne

[7] *Macklin v Richardson* (1770) Amb 694, 696.
[8] ibid 696–97.
[9] *Coleman v Wathen* (1793) 5 TR 245.
[10] ibid 245.
[11] *Donaldson v Becket* (1774) 2 Bro PC 129.
[12] *Coleman v Wathen* (1793) 5 TR 245, 245.
[13] ibid.
[14] R Maugham, *A Treatise on the Laws of Literary Property* (London, Longman et al, 1828), 155.

out by the greater success of later plaintiffs in Chancery. In 1820, David Morris, also a manager of the Haymarket, obtained an injunction from Lord Eldon in respect of another of John O'Keeffe's plays, *Young Quaker*. Lord Eldon was satisfied by the production of an affidavit stating that the copyright of the play had been assigned to Morris in writing, and granted the injunction against the actress Maria Kelly and Samuel Arnold, proprietor of the English Opera House.[15] Morris was also successful in obtaining injunctions against the patent theatres for other plays by O'Keeffe.[16]

However, when the Lord Chancellor referred the case of *Murray v Elliston* to the Court of the King's Bench, that Court found against the plaintiff.[17] This case was brought by John Murray, the publisher and assignee of Byron's *Marino Faliero*, against the manager of the Theatre Royal, Drury Lane, who was advertising a performance of the poem. Once again, counsel for the plaintiff argued that the question did not depend on the Statute of Anne, but was an invasion of Murray's property right in the poem. Counsel for the defendant relied on *Donaldson v Becket* as deciding that the author had no remedy except that provided by the Statute, as well as the authority of *Coleman v Wathen*. He argued that 'The safe rule for the Court to lay down is, that an author is only protected from the piracy of the book itself, or some colourable alteration of it'.[18] The judgment of Abbott CJ, Bayley and Holroyd JJ is briefly reported as finding that the action could not be maintained for publicly acting and representing the poem.[19] It is not clear, from the report, whether they came to this conclusion because they accepted Elliston's argument that the performance was an acceptable abridgment, or the argument that there was no reprinting within the meaning of the Statute of Anne.[20]

A number of defensive practices grew up in response to this uncertain situation. The managers of theatres would often buy the 'copyright' in a play from the dramatist but, rather than printing and publishing these plays, they would hoard the manuscripts, both to protect the script and as a long-term investment. Often the manuscript would be later sold to a publisher. An informal system of spying on competitors also grew up.[21] The method of remunerating authors changed at the start of the nineteenth century. The old system which involved authors taking a share of box office takings on the 'benefit' nights (the third, sixth and ninth nights) began to give way to the more certain system of payment by a lump sum, which might include an allowance for the copyright, and might include bonus amounts on certain nights, should the play run that long.[22] However, by the 1820s and 1830s the theatres were in a general decline and this was reflected in decreasing

[15] *Morris v Kelly* (1820) 1 Jac & W 481.

[16] Select Committee to inquire into Laws affecting Dramatic Literature HC (1831–32) 679, 153 (hereinafter 'Dramatic Literature Select Committee').

[17] *Murray v Elliston* (1822) 5 B & Ald 657.

[18] ibid 660.

[19] ibid 661.

[20] For more on abridgments, see ch 6.

[21] JR Stevens, *Profession of the Playwright* 86–87.

[22] ibid 25–26.

amounts paid to authors. Reasons for the decline were variously identified as incompetent management, excessive actors' salaries, the fashion for late dinner hours, the absence of Royal encouragement and the opposition of religious sects.[23]

The fact that the surreptitious copying of plays as they were performed had become a considerable industry is illustrated by the observation of the well-known playwright Douglas Jerrold that 'Mr Kenneth, at the corner of Bow Street, will supply any gentleman with any manuscript on the lowest of terms'.[24] The dramatist JR Planché claimed in his autobiography the honour of being the first to try to address this unsatisfactory situation. He alleged that he was given the impetus to seek reform of the law following an incident involving William Murray, lessee of the Theatre Royal in Edinburgh.[25] According to Planché, Murray had refused to pay the entirely reasonable sum of £10 for the privilege of staging Planché's drama *Charles XIIth* pleading poverty, and then obtained an unauthorised copy and staged that instead.[26] However, the Bill that Planché convinced Lamb to introduce in 1830 was continually deferred and Lamb eventually dropped it.[27]

Interestingly, this was not in fact the first attempt to convince the legislature to take action to protect dramatic authors. In 1814, in the course of debate regarding legal deposit,[28] Davies Giddy, a scientist and MP for Bodmin, suddenly proposed including a clause that would protect the interests of authors in the habit of writing plays 'intended merely for the closet'.[29] Apparently, a gentleman of his acquaintance had described to him the lack of protection for dramatic authors against theatre managers putting on plays without the author's permission. It was objected that the clause was too disconnected to the rest of the Bill and Giddy let the suggestion drop.

In 1832, however, the matter was taken up by Edward Bulwer Lytton.[30] This time, the matter of dramatic copyright was raised alongside reform of theatrical London. Bulwer Lytton, a Whig radical and novelist of growing popularity, had become an MP the year before. He objected to the system of dramatic licensing and considered that the original reason for suppressing the minor theatres, namely their disorderly state during the time of Charles II, no longer existed. In his view, the system was the direct cause of deterioration in national drama.[31] Moreover, he

[23] JR Stevens, *Profession of the Playwright* 31 and Dramatic Literature Select Committee 3.

[24] Dramatic Literature Select Committee, 157.

[25] Apparently no relation to the publisher John Murray.

[26] JR Planché, *The Reflections and Recollections of JR Planché*, 2 vols (London, Tinsley Brothers, 1872) vol 1, pp 148–49. See also Dramatic Literature Select Committee, 214.

[27] Parl Deb HC vol 22, col 918 (24 February 1830); *JC* vol 85, 161 (10 March 1830), 167 (11 March 1830), 174 (13 March 1830), 222 (24 March 1830); Parl Deb HC vol 13, col 252 (31 May 1932).

[28] See above: ch 3, section II C.

[29] Parl Deb HC vol 28, col 685 (13 July 1814).

[30] Edward Lytton Bulwer changed his name to Bulwer Lytton in 1843, according to the terms of his mother's will. In 1866 he became Baron Lytton of Knebworth. For ease and consistency he will be referred to in this book as Bulwer Lytton. For more on Bulwer Lytton's involvement in copyright law, see C Seville, 'Edward Bulwer Lytton Dreams of Copyright: "It might make me a rich man"', in F O'Gorman (ed), *Victorian Literature and Finance* (Oxford, Oxford University Press, 2007) 55–72.

[31] Parl Deb HC vol 13, cols 239–41 (31 May 1832).

considered the censorship powers exercised by the Lord Chamberlain over all dramatic performances to be unconstitutional.[32]

Bulwer Lytton believed that a revival in English drama would result from relieving theatres and dramatic works from the restrictions under which they operated and from conferring on dramatic authors similar rights to those enjoyed by literary authors under copyright law. In calling for the Select Committee, Bulwer Lytton explicitly invoked the ideology of romantic authorship and natural rights claims. He stated:

> The state of the laws regarding dramatic copyright alone, would long be a proof how indifferent that House had been to the general claims of that property, which ought to be the most sacred of all, because it encouraged all—because it ennobled all—because it produced all—the property that derived from intellectual exertion.[33]

His motion to appoint a Select Committee to look into these matters was agreed to by the House of Commons, and the Committee began to take evidence on 13 June 1832. All the dramatic authors who appeared before the Select Committee were of the opinion that granting copyright protection to published plays as well as a right to consent to performances of their plays, whether published or unpublished, would benefit them and lead to an increase in the amount they were paid.[34] Moreover, they considered that granting these rights would encourage people with greater literary talents to write for the stage, instead of working on better paid periodical literature and novels.[35]

As well as being anxious to receive payment for performances of their plays, dramatists were also concerned with the effects of such unauthorised performances upon their reputations. This issue had been raised in *Murray v Elliston* by Murray's counsel James Scarlett, who had argued that Bryon had expressly stated that he did not want his tragedy to be performed, and claimed that the play's failure would hurt Byron's feelings as well as his fame.[36] As Douglas Jerrold put it before the Select Committee, unauthorised performances constituted a

> double injury [to authors]: in the first place, they are not paid for their pieces, and in the next place, they are represented by the skeleton of their dramas; so that, as it was emphatically said by a sufferer, the author was not only robbed but murdered.[37]

The argument was not pressed, but represents an instance of the impetus to lay claim to author's rights going beyond mere pecuniary interest.[38]

Despite the opposition of theatre managers and proprietors to a scheme that would give authors of plays control over their performance, the Committee

[32] ibid col 244.
[33] Parl Deb HC vol 13 col 246 (31 May 1832).
[34] Dramatic Literature Select Committee, 142, 156, 176, 190, 194, 214, 227, 228.
[35] ibid 143, 157, 176.
[36] *The Times* (4 May 1822) 3e.
[37] Dramatic Literature Select Committee, 157.
[38] Bulwer Lytton made a similar point before the House of Commons: Parl Deb HC vol 13 col 246 (31 May 1832).

recommended that the authors of plays should possess the same legal rights as the authors of any other literary production, as well as the right to grant consent to performances.[39] In its report, the Select Committee invoked the claims of the public to support their recommendations on behalf of authors, as well as those recommendations on censorship and licensing. The Committee stated that 'the Public' would be 'equally benefited' because

> it is probable that the ordinary consequences of competition, freed from the possibility of licentiousness by the confirmed control and authority of the Chamberlain, will afford convenience in the numbers and situation of theatres, and cheap and good Entertainment in the Performances usually exhibited.[40]

In March 1833, Bulwer Lytton introduced a Bill[41] into Parliament to this effect, noting that 'dramatic authors possessed no control over their property, such as was very properly given to other labourers in the field of literature by the law of copyright'.[42] Bulwer Lytton initially proposed the penalty for representing a play without permission to be a minimum of £10 and maximum of £50 for each representation, although this was altered in his Bill to the simple figure of £50 per representation. The Select Committee had taken considerable evidence on the amount of money a dramatist could expect to receive in respect of performance of his plays and it seemed that the amount varied greatly, depending on the type of play and the theatre involved. Charles Lamb supported Bulwer Lytton's Bill but objected that £10 would be too great a minimum of damages in cases, such as for the manager of a company of strolling players.[43] The House of Commons reduced the penalty drastically to 40s.[44] With a few other small amendments the Bill was passed in the House of Commons and the House of Lords made no further changes. The Bill received royal assent in June 1833 and passed into law.[45] On the matter of censorship, the Committee's recommendations were modest: rather than abandoning the office of censor, it advocated extending the Lord Chamberlain's jurisdiction to cover the minor theatres, but removing the privileges of the patent theatres.[46] Bulwer Lytton introduced the censorship provisions in a second Bill, but it was far more contentious than the Dramatic Copyright Bill and had to be dropped.

Bulwer Lytton's Act sought to clarify the confusing situation that had resulted from the different approaches taken to unauthorised performances by the courts of Chancery and law. The statute provided that the author or assign of any 'tragedy,

[39] Dramatic Literature Select Committee 150, 209–13, 5. The right was to last for 28 years, and if the author were still alive at the end of the period, it would last for the rest of his life, just as it was for literary works under the 1814 Copyright Act.

[40] ibid 6.

[41] Bill to amend Laws relating Dramatic Literary Property (1833) [73].

[42] Parl Deb HC vol 16 col 560 (12 March 1833).

[43] ibid 561.

[44] *JC* vol 88, 246 (2 April 1833), 310 (26 April 1833), 470 (10 June 1833).

[45] An Act to amend the Laws relating to Dramatic Literary Copyright 1833 (3 Will IV c 15).

[46] Dramatic Literature Select Committee 3–5. The Lord Chamberlain's role as licenser of theatres lasted until 1968.

comedy, play, opera, farce or any other dramatic piece or entertainment' should have the sole liberty of performing or representing the piece at any place of dramatic entertainment. The right applied to books that had been composed but not published or printed and books that would in the future be composed but not printed and published. The right also applied to the authors and assigns of plays printed and published within 10 years before the passing of the Act and any plays printed and published after the passing of the Act. For plays that were not printed, the right granted was perpetual; for printed plays it followed the provisions of the 1814 Copyright Act, lasting for 28 years from the date of first publication and, if the author were still alive at the end of that period, for the rest of his life.[47] The penalty for breaching the Act was to be 40s, or the amount of benefit derived from the representation, or the loss occasioned by the plaintiff.[48]

B. Lectures

The position of lecturers was not dissimilar to that of dramatic authors, as they too relied on oral communication as a source of income, possibly to be followed by publication in print. The first case to arise with respect to lecturers came before the courts in 1825 and involved Thomas Wakley's pioneering medical journal, *The Lancet*. Wakley's central aim in founding the journal was to make medical knowledge available to a wider audience.[49] He chose the name carefully: a lancet was not only a surgical instrument used to open abscesses, but also an arched window for letting in light.[50] The first edition had been largely devoted to publishing a lecture by Sir Astley Cooper, who dropped by his former pupil's house and caught Wakley in the act of correcting proofs.[51] Cooper allowed the publication to go ahead, but several years later another surgeon, John Abernethy, took a stronger line regarding publication of his lectures, and sought an injunction and an account of profits from the publishers of the *Lancet* in the Court of Chancery.[52]

Counsel for Abernethy based his argument on the common law right that existed apart from the Statute of Anne, stating:

> [W]e submit, that although the lectures may exist incorporeally, and merely in language and ideas unembodied and unfit for use, still they have a right to the protection of the Court, independently of any question on the statute of Anne, as the law existed and was administered in this court long before that statute was introduced.[53]

47 Dramatic Copyright Act 1833 s 1.
48 ibid s 2.
49 *The Lancet* (22 February 1896) 504.
50 WF Bynum, 'Wakley, Thomas (1795–1862)', *Oxford Dictionary of National Biography* (Oxford University Press, 2004) www.oxforddnb.com/view/article/28425.
51 ibid.
52 *Abernethy v Hutchinson* (1825) SC 3 LJ Ch (OS) 209; 1 H & Tw 28.
53 *Abernethy v Hutchinson* (1825)SC 3 LJ (OS) 209, 212.

Lord Eldon gave some consideration to this argument, and drew a distinction between a lecture delivered from a written composition and one that was purely oral. He stated that he should have no difficulty in making his decision if Mr Abernethy were to produce in court the notes on which his lectures were based, so that they could be compared with what was published in the journal.[54] However, as Abernethy did not produce his notes, the Lord Chancellor found he was obliged to consider the case on the basis of the second alternative—a lecture delivered orally.

In considering this question, Lord Eldon referred back to *Millar v Taylor*. He did not refer to *Donaldson v Becket*, but appeared to elide the two cases by referring to *Millar v Taylor* as being 'first before the King's Bench, and afterwards before the House of Lords'.[55] He noted that in these cases there was 'a great deal said with respect to a person having a property in sentiments and language'[56] but that the Lords did not make any explicit finding on the point and there had been no decision on the legal question since. Consequently, he found it was not open to a court of equity to grant an injunction on the point. Lord Eldon also noted a point of practical difficulty arising from sustaining actions over publication of orally delivered lectures, which was the question of proving that what was published was the same as what was delivered orally. However, in this case, the matter did not arise because the editor admitted he had published the lectures of Abernethy.[57]

Lord Eldon ultimately granted Abernethy's injunction but not on the basis of the property argument. Instead, he found that there was an implied contract between Abernethy and his students that they could take notes of his lectures and make any use of them, except publishing them for profit. This principle extended to the editors of the *Lancet* for the purposes of granting the injunction.[58] However, the *Lancet* was ultimately successful. When Abernethy resigned his post as surgeon, Wakley capitalised on this change in circumstances to apply for a dissolution of the injunction. He argued that Abernethy's lectures were the property of the public because they were delivered in a public capacity as surgeon to a public charity. Abernethy did not oppose the dissolution and Lord Eldon granted Wakley's application.[59]

This case provided a basis for preventing the unauthorised publication of lectures, but through the common law of implied contract, rather than through any common law copyright. Ten years later, Henry Brougham, who had acted for the *Lancet* in that case, introduced into the House of Lords a Bill for Preventing the Publication of Lectures Without Consent.[60] The Bill provided that the author of

[54] ibid 216–17 It seemed Lord Eldon would have been prepared to protect the notes as a 'literary composition' if they had been reproduced in the journal, presumably, although he did not say so, because he believed that unpublished works could be protected.

[55] ibid 213.

[56] ibid 217.

[57] ibid 215.

[58] ibid 219.

[59] *The Lancet* (7 March 1896) 643–46. The end of the story is told in *The Lancet* but I have not found any legal report of these proceedings.

[60] A Bill intituled An Act for preventing the Publication of Lectures without Consent HL (1835) 456. See also *JL* vol 67, 542 (10 August 1835).

a lecture, and any person to whom he had conveyed a copy of a lecture in order to be delivered in any college, school, seminary or other institution, should have the sole right to print or publish it.[61] Anyone who took down the lecture by shorthand, or in some other manner, and printed it or copied and published it without the consent of the author would forfeit the lecture together with a penny for every printed sheet.[62]

Brougham's motivation in bringing this Bill is unclear.[63] His role in *Abernethy v Hutchinson* would have familiarised him with the issues involved and he may have been unhappy with the strained solution arrived at by Lord Eldon. However, the Bill followed Lord Eldon's approach by providing that a person attending a lecture for a fee should not be deemed to have been licensed to print or make copies of lectures, merely by having leave to be present.[64] In addition, Brougham's involvement with the Mechanics' Institutes and educational lecturing must have made him alert to the existence of publishers who sought to make profits from lectures intended to be cheap or free. In his 1825 pamphlet, *Practical Observations upon the Education of the People*, Brougham was explicit about his views of the importance of lectures, writing:

> The preparation of elementary works is not the only, nor at first, is it the most valuable service that can be rendered towards economising the time of the labouring classes. The institution of lectures is, of all the helps that can be given, the most valuable, where circumstances permit; that is, in towns of a certain size.[65]

During the 1835 session, Brougham was also heavily involved in campaigning against the newspaper stamp, which intensified the hostility between him and Barnes, the editor of *The Times*.[66] Newspapers were one of the main culprits in the unauthorised publication of lectures, and the second clause of the Bill specifically included them in the prohibition.[67]

The Bill was passed in the House of Lords with some amendments and sent to the Commons, where it met with opposition from Thomas Wakley, now a Member of Parliament.[68] Wakley claimed that the Bill was intended not only to prohibit publication of lectures, but also publication of criticism of lectures.[69] In his view, the Bill would be acceptable if it applied only to private lectures, but if it applied to public ones it would act to shield them from public inspection.[70]

[61] A Bill intituled An Act for preventing the Publication of Lectures without Consent HL (1835) s 1.

[62] ibid s 1.

[63] It does not appear that he introduced the bill with a speech and, although the Lords Journal notes that changes were made by the House, there is no record of any discussion accompanying those changes: *JL* vol 67, 574–75 (17 August 1835).

[64] A Bill intituled An Act for preventing the Publication of Lectures without Consent HL (1835) s 2.

[65] H Brougham, *Practical Observations upon the Education of the People, addressed to the Working Classes and their Employers* (London, Richard Taylor, 1825) 11.

[66] C Seville, *Literary Copyright Reform in Victorian England* (Cambridge, Cambridge University Press, 1999) 55–58.

[67] A Bill intituled An Act for preventing the Publication of Lectures without Consent HL (1835) s 2.

[68] *JL* vol 67, 559 (14 August 1835); 574–75 (17 August 1835); 576 (18 August 1835).

[69] Parl Deb HC vol 30 col 953 (24 August 1835).

[70] ibid 953.

Warburton, another radical member, agreed with Wakley that the Bill should be judged in terms of the 'public good' and, on that basis, public lectures should not be shielded from criticism.[71] On this basis, when the Bill went into Committee, Wakley moved to omit the clause which applied to newspapers, but the House did not agree and the clause remained.[72] The Bill also received criticism in an article in the *Legal Observer*, reprinted in *The Times*, which argued that the legislation was unnecessary, as lecturers were already protected by the authority in *Abernethy v Hutchinson*, and that the Bill only added additional conditions which would be burdensome.[73] The burdensome condition was the requirement that the Bill would only apply if two days' notice was given to two Justices, living within five miles from the place where the lecture should be delivered.[74] Moreover, it would not apply to lectures delivered in any university, public school, college or according to a gift, foundation or endowment.[75]

In the House of Commons, the Lord Advocate John Archibald Murray,[76] a friend of Lord Brougham and patron of the arts, spoke in favour of the Bill. Murray argued that 'every man had as much right to claim security for his lectures, as for his books, as any other fruit of his labour or his ingenuity'.[77] He described lectures as 'the lecturer's own property' and noted they might be worth up to £1,000 to the lecturer.[78] Recourse to the rhetoric of romantic authorship by drawing an analogy between lectures and books based on labour giving rise to property rights seems to have persuaded the House of Commons. After some minor amendments,[79] the Bill was passed by both Houses and received royal assent on 9 September 1835.[80]

In the space of three years, two new rights had been created to protect against the publication of the spoken word. For the first time, copyright had been extended to protect something that did not take a physical form.[81] In seeking these extensions, the ideology of romantic authorship and natural rights were invoked and, as both Bills were passed with only minimal debate, it seems likely that at least a majority of members were amenable to such arguments. The public interest was used as a counter argument in relation to the Lectures Act, but without success. Indeed, as Lord Brougham's extra-Parliamentary writings show, it could equally be adduced in favour of protecting lectures. The 'public' appealed to here was a

71 ibid 954.
72 Parl Deb HC vol 30 col 977 (26 August 1835).
73 *The Times* (3 September 1835) 7a.
74 An Act for preventing the Publication of Lectures without Consent 1835 (5 & 6 Will IV c 6) s 5.
75 ibid.
76 No (direct) relation to John Murray, the publisher.
77 Parl Deb HC vol 30 col 954 (24 August 1835).
78 ibid.
79 *JC* vol 90, 604 (28 August 1835); 633 (2 September 1835); 646 (4 September 1835); 657 (9 September 1835).
80 Lectures Publication Act (1835).
81 Note that when Lord Mansfield held that music could be protected against reprinting, it was on the basis that music fell within the Statute of Anne, which covered 'other writings' as well as books: *Bach v Longman* (1777) 2 Cowp 623.

lower-class public, seeking to improve and inform itself by attending educational lectures. In relation to dramatic copyright, the 'public' was more broadly conceived as the people who might attend the theatre, although the effect that what they saw might have on them was also considered in somewhat patrician terms. In these debates, the interests of the public were characterised as coinciding with those of dramatic authors, as it was argued that encouraging authors would lead to the production of better dramatic literature.

II. THE COPYRIGHT ACT OF 1842

A. An Ambitious Scheme

Two years later, Serjeant Talfourd commenced his campaign to bring about a complete overhaul of the law of copyright. This attempt at reform resurrected many of the questions regarding the nature of literary property and the reasons for protecting it which had been raised during the common law copyright debates and left unresolved after *Donaldson v Becket*. The main objective of Talfourd, himself the author of several plays and close friend of many of the foremost literary talents of the day, was to fashion a copyright law that would adequately reward authors and artists for the products of their genius and labours. In his phrase, this would constitute 'justice to learning'.[82] Central to achieving this justice was increasing the term of protection and Talfourd, realising that the time had passed for claiming a perpetual right, proposed, in the spirit of compromise, the term of life plus 60 years.[83]

The question of duration was the most controversial element of Talfourd's proposal and the debates in Parliament over the desired term of protection generated considerable heat. When Talfourd introduced his first Bill into Parliament in 1837 it ran into immediate opposition. Revised versions were introduced every year thereafter, and Talfourd was soon forced to concede many of his main objectives. Duration was the main sticking point for a number of MPs and when Lord Mahon took over responsibility for the Bill he changed the term to life plus 25 years. The compromise eventually reached, after five years of debate, was a term of life plus 7 years, with a minimum of 42 years.[84]

However, Talfourd's aims were more far-reaching than merely extending the copyright term, as he sought to consolidate all the different statutes relating to different types of copyright material into a single Act.[85] In addition, he also wished

[82] Parl Deb HC vol 38 col 872 (18 May 1837).

[83] ibid 873.

[84] An Act to amend the Law of Copyright 1842 (5 & 6 Vict c 45) s 3.

[85] This is demonstrated by the preamble of the 1837 Copyright Bill, dated 6 June 1837, which commenced: 'Whereas it is expedient to consolidate and render uniform the Laws relating to copyright in Printed Books, Musical composition, Acted Dramas and Engravings'. A Bill to consolidate and amend the Laws relating to Copyright in Printed Books, Musical Compositions, Acted Dramas and Engravings, to provide Remedies for the Violation thereof, and to extend the Term of its Duration HC (1837) [380].

to clarify certain other aspects of the common law that had grown up around the Statute of Anne and its successors. The resulting Act was to fall far short of his lofty ambitions. The provisions relating to engravings were dropped after 1837,[86] and the sections seeking to codify the law of infringement were also abandoned in 1842.[87] Dramatic and musical works were brought within the fold of the 1842 Act, but the Acts dealing with the performing rights continued in operation, and the provisions relating to lectures were abandoned by 1840.[88]

One of Talfourd's initiatives which survived related to the formalities associated with copyright registration. Talfourd did not wish to make any great changes to the current system of registration at Stationers' Hall, but he did wish to extend the system that prevailed for books to cover engravings, etchings, maps and charts.[89] He also proposed that, before any action could be brought in respect of copyright, the owner should deposit a copy of the book and register his ownership thereof. Further, he proposed that any transfers of ownership should be registered.[90] As this would be a greater burden on the Stationers' Company, he proposed increasing the fees for registration.[91]

As was noted in chapter three, registration was one of the areas where the common law had seeped into the interstices of the Statute of Anne.[92] Talfourd's Bills replicated the common law position to some extent; the provision that became section 24 of the Act provided that the proprietor of copyright would not be able to maintain any action or suit at law or in equity, or any summary proceedings, unless he had first registered his work, but added that failure to register would not affect the copyright in the book, but merely the right to bring proceedings for infringement.[93] This provision in fact went further than the common law, making the ability to bring any action, whether at law or equity, conditional upon prior registration, in the correct manner.[94] It did not, however, apply to the representation of dramatic works.[95]

Clauses 11 and 13 of the 1842 Act also gave copyright owners the ability to enter assignments and licences of copyright in the Registry Book at Stationers' Hall. The formalities required for such instruments had come before the courts several times. Under the Statute of Anne, the courts had held that an assignment

[86] Parl Deb HC vol 39 col 1092 (14 December 1837).

[87] These are discussed in more detail in ch 6 below.

[88] Seville, *Literary Copyright Reform* 254.

[89] Parl Deb HC vol 38 col 871 (18 May 1837).

[90] ibid 871, 872.

[91] ibid 871.

[92] The case of *Beckford v Hood* (1798) 7 TR 620 had held that failure to register a work affected only the availability of the penalties under the Statute of Anne, but did not prevent the copyright owner from bringing an action at common law for damages. See above: ch 3 n 62.

[93] 1842 Copyright Act s 24.

[94] See,eg, *Wood v Boosey* (1867–68) LR 3 QB 223, *Mathieson v Harrod* (1868) LR 7 Eq 270 and *Page v Wisden* (1869) 17 WR 483. However, it did not matter if the registration occurred on the same day as the writ was issued, as long as it occurred *before* the action was commenced: *Warne v Lawrence* (1886) 54 LT 371.

[95] Copyright Act 1842 s 24. See also *Lacy v Rhys* (1864) 4 B & S 873.

must be in writing and attested by two witnesses.[96] It was then held by the Exchequer Chamber that the 1814 Act had altered this principle to dispense with the need for two witnesses.[97] Clause 15 of the 1842 Act continued the rule that assignments must be in writing, likewise making no mention of the need for two witnesses.[98]

Talfourd, however, was not so fortunate in his ambitions to place authors in a stronger position regarding remedies. Clause 24 of the 1841 Bill sought to give the power to grant injunctions to a judge of any court, including the upper courts of judicature in the British dominions, as well as awarding an account of profits. When the clause was debated in the House of Commons, Godson explained that the aim was to allow a plaintiff to get an injunction and damages in the same court.[99] Thomas Wakley objected strongly, asserting that plaintiffs should be prevented from going to the Court of Chancery at all.[100] The clause proved so divisive, even to the Bill's supporters, that Lord Mahon suggested that it be omitted and it was deleted in the House of Lords.[101]

B. Opposition in the Book Trade

Talfourd's Bills excited considerable opposition, both inside and outside Parliament. He also had many supporters, particularly among authors, but their support tended to be less visible, due in part to reluctance on the part of many of them to be seen as campaigning for their own interests, and also to the lack of any peak professional body to serve as an organising point.[102] The extended debate polarised opinions and rhetoric, and the claims of authors to property rights were frequently contrasted to a general public interest in dissemination of learning.

Much of the opposition to reform came from the book trade. First the printers began to petition and lobby against the Bill of 1837 and, as time passed, they were joined by other elements of the trade: compositors, pressmen, newspapermen, machinemen, bookbinders, papermakers and others.[103] Changes to copyright law attacked the established order of the trade, already under threat from the growing numbers of booksellers involved in the provision of cheap books.[104] There was a fear among printers that increasing the monopoly right for authors would make

[96] Statute of Anne 1710 s 1. See *Power v Walker* (1814) 3 M & S 7; 4 Camp 8 and *Davidson v Bohn* (1848) 6 CB 456.

[97] *Cumberland v Copeland* (1862) 1 H & C 194.

[98] These provisions were interpreted by the courts as alternatives: an assignment or licence would be valid if it was in writing *or* if it were registered, see *Leyland v Stewart* (1876) Ch 419, *Hole v Bradbury* (1879) LR 12 Ch D 866.

[99] Parl Deb HC vol 62 col 894 (20 April 1842).

[100] ibid.

[101] ibid.

[102] Seville, *Literary Copyright Reform* 29–30.

[103] For more detail on this, see ibid 68–99.

[104] See above: ch 3.

books scarce and expensive and that, in consequence, printing presses would fall into disuse.[105]

The booksellers and publishers were also opposed to Talfourd's early Bills. For those like Thomas Tegg, who specialised in cheap editions and remaindered works, the extension of term would have severely restricted his trade, and he remained implacably opposed to copyright reform at all times.[106] The opposition of the established booksellers and publishers to the early Bills is initially more difficult to comprehend. It was still overwhelmingly the case that the copyright of authors was purchased outright for a single lump sum and so they should have welcomed the extension of term. However, as the negotiations over the issue of legal deposit revealed, the booksellers did not value increases in copyright duration as highly as other factors which contributed to the stability of the trade and their direct profit margins. The expansive scope of Talfourd's early Bills would not have appealed to them. Even more importantly, Talfourd sought to prioritise authors and their families over the interests of the book trade through the insertion of a retrospective clause which would have prevented the assignee of a copyright from reaping the benefit of the extension at all. It was this clause to which the booksellers and publishers were particularly opposed.[107]

Talfourd's first version of the retrospective clause in the 1837 Bill gave the extended period of duration to authors who had retained any part of the copyright in existing works. Moreover, in the case of those who had assigned their entire right, copyright would return to them after the expiration of 28 years (the initial period of copyright protection under the 1814 Copyright Act[108]). Changes were made in the Bills of 1838 and 1839 to try to placate the publishers, providing that the extended term would apply in cases where the author had assigned copyright to any person 'in consideration of natural love and affection' but that it would expire after 28 years where the copyright had been assigned for something other than natural love and affection. This removed the reversionary interest but did not satisfy the publishers who would still not receive the benefit of the extension for existing works.[109]

In 1840, a compromise was finally reached which would allow the author, or his personal representative, and the publisher to enter into a written agreement that both parties would 'accept the benefits' of the Act with respect to a particular book.[110] If such an agreement were entered into, copyright would continue for the full term of the Act. This allowed some scope to renegotiate the terms between the author and publisher if, for example, the book had become surprisingly successful and profitable. Once this compromise had been reached, many of the booksellers

105 Seville, *Literary Copyright Reform* 23.

106 T Tegg, *Remarks on the Speech of Sergeant Talfourd on Moving for Leave to Bring in a Bill to Consolidate the Laws relating to Copyright and to Extend the Term of its Duration* (London, Thomas Tegg & Son, 1837) 9.

107 See, eg, the letter to the *The Times* from W and R Chambers (25 April 1838) 3c, and the statement of Messrs Longman & Co, *The Times* (16 May 1838) 7a.

108 See above: ch 3.

109 Seville, *Literary Copyright Reform* 228–29.

110 A Bill to Amend the Law of Copyright (1840) [61] s 4.

and publishers, including the prestigious house of Longman & Co, began to support the legislation.[111] This clause was enacted in the 1842 Copyright Act.[112]

C. The Rhetoric of Opposing Interests

Although their opposition was driven largely by self-interest, the different elements of the book trade were not averse to employing public interest rhetoric. The printers of Carlisle, for example, expressed in a petition of 1838 their anxiety over a Bill which would be 'highly injurious to the interests of the community, the literature of the country, and more particularly to the interests of your Petitioners'.[113] Likewise, the Petition of the Stationers Company of Glasgow noted that the effect of the Bill 'will be to benefit only a very few particular individuals, and deeply to injure all the rest of society'.[114] The reprinter Thomas Tegg, in a letter to Sir Robert Peel, protested against any extension of term that went beyond what would induce an author to write, stating:

> The great advantage of literature is in its effects on the public, by facilitating their instruction, extending their information, enlarging their mental powers, inculcating just, honourable and religious principle, and affording a refined species of entertainment. Its operation in this way is eminently conducive to the public good, and would be best promoted by the unrestricted liberty of publication.[115]

The effect of these attempts to broaden the subject matter of the Bill beyond a mere trade dispute by invoking issues of monopolism and the diffusion of knowledge was to bring copyright within the radical political agenda. The opposition of radical parliamentarians focused on the increased costs that the increased term would impose on the public and on the printing and publishing trades. Some, such as Warburton, Wakefield and Hume, characterised copyright as another 'tax on knowledge' and an extension of an undesirable monopoly.[116] Since 1820 the Newspaper Stamp Duties Act, one of the infamous Six Acts, had required the printer and publisher of a newspaper to enter into recognisances of £300 in the case of London newspapers, and find sureties for the same amount.[117] The

[111] Seville, *Literary Copyright Reform* 122, 229.

[112] Copyright Act 1842 s 4. A small change was made in 1841 to provide that the terms of the agreement should be entered in the book of registry.

[113] Appendix to the Twenty-Fourth Report of Public Petitions, Petition 4629, presented 9 April 1838, App 389 (95 signatures).

[114] ibid, Petition 4631, presented 11 April 1838, App 396 (56 signatures).

[115] Tegg, *Remarks on the Speech of Sergeant Talfourd* 9.

[116] Seville, *Literary Copyright Reform* 22. 'Taxes on knowledge' was the phrase used by radicals to describe the three kinds of duties payable on newspapers between 1815 and 1836: 4d on every sheet printed; 3s 6d on all advertisements (which was reduced in 1833 to 1s 6d); and an excise duty on paper of 3d a pound: W Thomas, *The Philosophic Radicals: Nine Studies in Theory and Practice 1817–1841* (Oxford, Clarendon Press, 1979) 316–17. Charles Dickens considered that the window tax, which reached its highest level between 1808–23 was an even more formidable tax on knowledge than the stamp duties. See RD Altick, *The English Common Reader: A Social History of the Mass Reading Public 1800–1900* (Chicago, University of Chicago Press, 1957) 92.

[117] W Thomas, *Philosophic Radicals* 316–17.

radicals claimed that these taxes kept the prices of newspapers high and out of the hands of the working classes.[118] Thus, when the question of extended copyright protection arose, they characterised it as yet another circumstance which would raise book prices. Another Member of Parliament who opposed the Bill on the grounds that it would impose increased costs, thereby inhibiting the dissemination of knowledge, was Henry Brougham. As noted earlier, Brougham had a long involvement with cheap publications as well as education.[119] Objections were also expressed by free-traders, who advocated the application of free market principles to the book trade, again on grounds of public welfare.[120]

The most effective opposition came from Lord Macaulay who, as a successful author himself, was a shock entry to the ranks of Talfourd's opponents. Macaulay was a skilled orator and the rhetoric he employed in his speeches against the Bill in 1841, which drew heavily on concepts of public interest, was responsible for the Bill's demise that year.[121] He opened by stating that he was convinced that the Bill would 'inflict grievous injury on the public, without conferring any compensating advantage on men of letters'.[122] He also invoked anti-monopoly sentiment by emphasising copyright's monopolistic qualities.[123] Although Macaulay preferred the system of copyright as a means of remunerating literary men over that of patronage, he thought the term proposed was too long, favouring a shorter term of 20 years.[124] According to Macaulay, the evil of a monopoly was proportional to its length.[125] He also drew upon radical sympathies by calling copyright 'a tax on readers for the purpose of giving a bounty to writers'.[126] Finally, he invoked the spectre of censorship, arguing that the increased term would give authors or their assigns, whether descendants or publishers, the power to suppress books.[127]

The rhetoric employed by Talfourd and his supporters centred on arguments of justice and fairness, and drew upon the ideology of romantic authorship. The latter can be seen in Talfourd's first speech in favour of his Bill in 1837, when he referred to 'the property of men of letters in the results of their genius and industry'[128] as well as painting a picture of the author of literature, persevering 'in his high and holy course, gradually impressing thoughtful minds with the sense of truth made visible in the severest forms of beauty'.[129] Talfourd's depiction of such

[118] ibid 323–24. Although some radicals had called for complete abolition of the duties, most were satisfied with the reduction achieved in 1836, which retained the last penny as a postal charge.

[119] Brougham in fact introduced his own version of a Copyright Bill into the House of Lords in 1838, but it did not proceed far: Seville, *Literary Copyright Reform* 58.

[120] ibid 24.

[121] ibid 67.

[122] Parl Deb HL vol 56 col 344 (5 February 1841).

[123] 'Copyright is a monopoly and produces all the effects which the general voice of mankind attributes to monopoly . . . I believe, Sir, that I may safely take it for granted that the effect of monopoly generally is to make articles scarce, to make them dear, and to make them bad' (ibid 347–48).

[124] ibid.

[125] ibid 348.

[126] ibid 350.

[127] ibid 353–55.

[128] Parl Deb HC vol 38, cols 866–67 (18 May 1836).

[129] ibid col 877.

an author as deserving of greater protection also raised once more the notion of authors' natural rights. In the same speech, Talfourd harked back to the common law copyright debates, arguing that:

> By the common law of England, as solemnly expounded by a majority of seven to four of the judges in the case of 'Donaldson v Beckett,' and as sustained by the additional opinion of Lord Mansfield, the author of an original work had for ever the sole right of multiplying copies, and a remedy by action, incident to every right, against any who should infringe it.[130]

Talfourd then took the Members through a potted history of copyright, the starting point being that

> [i]n truth, the claim of the author to perpetual copyright was never disputed, until literature had received a fatal present in the first act of Parliament for its encouragement—the 8th Anne, c19, in which the mischief lurked, unsuspected, for many years before it was called into action to limit the rights it professed, and was probably intended, to secure.[131]

In this way, Talfourd sought to employ the long-standing uncertainty as to the authority of the outcome in *Donaldson v Becket* to his own advantage in arguing for an increased duration for authors, concluding, 'I see no reason why authors should not be restored to that inheritance which, under the name of protection and encouragement has been taken from them'.[132]

For Talfourd, the natural entitlement of authors to the products of their labours fundamentally underpinned his reform. The view he took of the common law copyright debates was that a perpetual right had existed prior to the Statute of Anne, but that this and subsequent statutes had abridged the common law right. Indeed, he argued before Parliament that

> [i]f we should now simply repeal all the statutes which have been passed under the guise of the encouragement of learning, and leave it to be protected by the principles of the common law, and the remedies which the common law could supply, I believe the relief would be welcome.[133]

This might be seen as incongruous when placed alongside his attempts to strengthen the place of formalities in the system.[134] However, it is important to remember that Talfourd's main aim was to bring order and consistency to the law of copyright through clear legislation. Although Talfourd spoke little about his motivation in retaining registration, it is apparent that for him the registration system would sit on top of an underlying common law copyright, albeit one abridged by statute. This explains the provision in the Act that allowed copyright

[130] ibid col 867.
[131] ibid col 868.
[132] ibid cols 872–73.
[133] Parl Deb HC vol 38 col 868 (18 May 1837).
[134] See, eg, Ginsburg's discussion of formalities in J Ginsburg, '"Une chose publique"? The Author's Domain and the Public Domain in Early British, French and US Copyright Law' [2006] *Cambridge Law Journal* 636, 644–46.

to continue to subsist, in the absence of registration, despite the unavailability of statutory remedies.

Even those who were less convinced by the common law right could agree on the benefits of registration. Richard Godson, MP, a supporter of Talfourd's Bills and author of a treatise on copyright and patent law, may have feared that the deadlock over term extension would never be overcome, as he introduced his own Bill dealing solely with issues of registration early in the 1842 session.[135] Godson's treatise of 1823 shows that he was more ambivalent about the common law right than many of his contemporaries, as when writing on the subject he concluded: 'Hence, all literary property or copyright is either founded by constitution on the statute of 8 Anne, or given by positive provisions of other acts of parliament'.[136] Godson's proposal differed somewhat to that of Talfourd, in that he proposed that registration be carried out through the office of the Registrar of the Court of Chancery and went into greater detail on the system. When introducing his Bill, Godson explained that his aim was

> property being thus made more secure, authors having the advantage of their own works, and the public the benefit of knowing in whom the Copyright existed if they wished to make a new edition of it, or to introduce it in a work of greater extent or invention.[137]

Where Talfourd focused heavily on arguments of property, right and justice, others among his supporters emphasised the claim that increasing copyright protection would encourage learning and thereby result in social benefit. In 1842, Lord Mahon commended the measure to the House,

> conscious that we, the promoters of it, have no selfish or sordid objects in view. I commend it, persuaded that if you provide due and adequate rewards for literature, and encouragement to it as a career—if you raise it in the social scale, and adorn it with marks of public gratitude—you will bestow not merely on those who cultivate that literature a personal boon, but on the nation at large a public blessing.[138]

Likewise, the author and MP Richard Monckton Milnes, another staunch supporter of the Act refuted the accusations of Wakley and others that the proposed Bill gave no thought to the public, noting that no evidence had been raised to show that the public would be injured by the extension of copyright. On the contrary, he alleged that the cheapest books were copyright books and that lack of copyright meant that great works became scarce and out of print.[139] John Lowndes, in his

[135] A Bill for the Registering of Copyright and Assignments thereof, and for the better securing the Property therein HC (1842) [9], 8 February 1842. See also Parl Deb HC vol 60 col 191, (8 February 1842), 730 (21 February 1842).

[136] R Godson, *A Practical Treatise on the Law of Patents for Inventions and of Copyright, with an Introduction book on Monopolies*, 1st edn (London, Butterworth & Sons, 1823) 206–07. See also the discussion of treatise writers in R Deazley, *Re-Thinking Copyright: History, Theory, Language* (Cheltenham, Edward Elgar, 2006) 41.

[137] Parl Deb HC vol 60 col 191 (8 February 1842).

[138] Parl Deb HC vol 56 col 1363 (6 April 1842).

[139] ibid col 1387.

treatise devoted to supporting Talfourd's campaign, combined the interests of authors and the public, arguing that the response to the objection that the legislation would injure the public was that 'the public can have no right to demand that anyone should devote his life *gratuitously* to their service'.[140]

The debates surrounding Talfourd's copyright Bills once again pitted the discourse of common law copyright and the natural rights of authors against that of public interest. In this context, common law copyright was resuscitated to provide the justification for legislative reform and, somewhat ironically, thereby became part of the process of codification. However, as Bently has observed, 'even at the height of romanticism, the rhetoric of romantic authorship did not carry sufficient power to win the day'.[141] While the radicals made little headway in relation to the earlier extensions to dramatic works and lecture, when it came to wholesale copyright reform the radicals' views of the public interest were bolstered by the book trade's self-interest, and together they operated as a powerful force of resistance. Once again, the result was compromise. The term of copyright was extended and some consolidation did take place, but the Act fell far short of Talfourd's dream of a uniform, consistent, codified law of copyright. Overall, the law remained fractured and incoherent.

III. FOREIGN AUTHORS AND THE CASE OF *JEFFERYS V BOOSEY*

A. The Problem of Foreign Authors

The next context in which issues regarding the foundations of copyright law arose was the question of whether copyright protection extended to foreign authors. From the earliest days of printing, the place of foreigners had been contentious in the book trade. Many of the first printers in England had brought their craft over from the Continent, and at first they were exempted from the general restrictions to which aliens who sought to practise other trades were subject.[142] However, protectionist concerns for domestic industry forced many of them out of the trade in the sixteenth century, while those who remained were resented.[143] The problems caused by foreign printers located overseas was considered a censorship issue, and at regular intervals governments would become concerned about the importation of books printed on the Continent which might undermine the censorship regime because of their seditious or heretical content.[144] Concerns likewise arose on the part of the British booksellers regarding the threat posed by foreign books

[140] JJ Lowndes, *An Historical Sketch of the Law of Copyright* (London, Saunders & Benning, 1840) 102.

[141] L Bently, '*R. v The Author*: From Death Penalty to Community Service' (2008) 32 *Columbia Journal of Law & the Arts* 2, 78.

[142] See C Blagden, *The Stationers' Company: A History 1403–1959* (London, George Allen & Unwin Ltd, 1960) 24–25.

[143] ibid 25–26.

[144] ibid 29–31.

and foreign printers to local trade and price structures.[145] However, there was always a certain tolerance displayed towards foreign language books due to the recognition that this market could not be filled solely by domestic printers, as the Statute of Anne's provisions allowing their importation demonstrates.[146]

During the nineteenth century the problems posed by cross-border book trade became even more pressing, and raised two interrelated issues. First was the problem of pirate editions of books by British authors printed and sold overseas, and this was particularly acute in the case of the United States, due to the size of its market for English language books. Under American legislation it was not possible for foreign authors, such as the British, to acquire copyright protection unless they were permanently resident in that country.[147] In the early years, and again after the depression of 1837–1843, American publishers adopted a practice known as 'courtesy of the trade', whereby the first publisher to reprint a book in America would receive recognition of priority from other publishers who would not then reprint the same book.[148] Under this system, authors who provided advance sheets would receive payment.[149] Both Sir Walter Scott and Edward Bulwer Lytton availed themselves of this system.[150] However, the system soon collapsed, and most British authors ceased receiving even token amounts of remuneration for American reprints. Several concerted efforts were made by amalgamations of British authors, publishers and politicians to convince Congress to enter into an international copyright agreement, but without success.[151]

The second issue was whether or not the works of foreign authors would receive copyright protection in Britain. While all British publishers agreed on the desirability of securing copyright protection for their authors overseas, not all of them were of the same opinion regarding copyright for foreigners at home. Two strong publishing markets for foreign works emerged in the early nineteenth century. One was for musical pieces by Continental composers, such as Bellini, Mendelssohn and Kalkbrenner; the other was for books by American authors. As always, the existence of popular markets resulted in feverish competition, followed by litigation. Some publishers, such as the book publishers Murray and Bentley and the music publishers Chappell and Boosey, sought to purchase or license the works of foreign authors in much the same manner that they would do for domestic authors. This,

[145] ibid 164, 170. This is reflected in the various statutory prohibitions on importation in the 1662 Licensing Act, the Statute of Anne and the 1739 Printing Act. See above: ch 2.

[146] J Barnard, 'Introduction' in J Barnard and DF McKenzie (eds), *The Cambridge History of the Book in Britain*, vol 4: *1557–1695* (Cambridge, Cambridge University Press, 2002) 6; Statute of Anne s 7.

[147] An Act for the Encouragement of Learning, by Securing Copies of Maps, Charts, and Books, to the Authors and Proprietors of Such Copies, during the times therein mentioned 1790 (1 Stat 124) s 1.

[148] JJ Barnes, *Authors, Publishers and Politicians: The Quest for an Anglo-American Copyright Agreement 1815–1854* (London, Routledge & Kegan Paul, 1974) 84.

[149] ibid 52–53.

[150] For details of Edward Bulwer Lytton's dealings with American publishers, see Seville, 'Edward Bulwer Lytton' 63–64.

[151] For more on such attempts in the 1850s, see Barnes, *Authors, Publishers and Politicians* and for a detailed history of the copyright relations between Britain and the United States, see C Seville, *The Internationalisation of Copyright Law* (Cambridge, Cambridge University Press, 2006) esp ch 5.

however, exposed them to considerable risk at the hands of less fastidious publishers, such as Routledge and Bohn in the book trade, and Purday in the music trade, due to the uncertain legal position of foreign authors.

In the 1830s and 1840s, a considerable number of cases involving foreign authors went before the various courts. The majority of these related to musical works. The different courts did not take the same approach towards the rights of foreigners seeking to publish in Britain. The Courts of Chancery,[152] Common Pleas[153] and the Queen's Bench[154] were generally sympathetic to foreign authors and their assigns, as long as the work was first published in England.[155] The Court of Exchequer, on the other hand, changed its position over time.[156] In the 1835 case of *D'Almaine v Boosey*, the English assignee of Auber, a French composer, was granted an injunction by Abinger CB to prevent publication of the works by Boosey.[157] The Chief Baron held that the question of whether a foreigner could acquire copyright in Britain had been settled as long ago as 1777, in the case of *Bach v Longman*.[158] However, he also noted that the question did not, strictly speaking, arise because D'Almaine was not a foreigner but had merely acquired the copyright from a foreigner, and he was the first to publish it anywhere in the world.

In his 1837 Bill, Serjeant Talfourd had included a provision confirming this decision, but he was persuaded to drop it so that the Government could take up the matter and pass the International Copyright Act in 1838.[159] Under this Act, Her Majesty, by Order in Council, could grant copyright within the Dominions to authors of books first published abroad, on condition that reciprocal protection was granted by the foreign state to British authors. No Order in Council was ever made and in 1844 it was repealed and a second Act was passed.[160] This Act provided that Her Majesty, by Order in Council, could direct that books, prints,

[152] In *Delondre v Shaw* (1828) 2 Sim 237 Shadwell V-C held that the common law did not protect the rights of foreigners. However, in *Bentley v Foster* (1839) 10 Sim 329, he seemed to have changed his mind and asserted that protection was given to any work first published in Britain, whether it was written abroad or not. In *Guichard v Mori* (1831) 2 Coop T Cott 216 Lord Brougham LC suggested a foreigner who published first in England could assert copyright. See also *Ollendorf v Black* (1850) 4 De G & Sm 209 and *Buxton v James* (1851) 5 De G & Sm 80.

[153] In *Cocks v Purday* (1848) 5 CB 860, Wilde CJ held that a foreigner who publishes in Britain before any publication abroad has copyright under the 1842 Copyright Act, which may be assigned.

[154] In 1824, Bayley J held that a foreign composer who had first published his work overseas could not claim copyright in Britain: *Clementi v Walker* (1824) 2 B & C 861. In *Boosey v Davidson* (1849) 13 Q.B. 257, Patteson J followed *Cocks v Purday* (above n 153), finding for the copyright owner, Purday, when the work was first published in Britain.

[155] JC Bach had been granted copyright protection by the King's Bench for a work first published in England in 1777: *Bach v Longman* (1777) 2 Cowp 263.

[156] It is not clear why the publishers continued to bring actions before the Court of the Exchequer when they had obtained favourable results in the other courts. After 1835, the equity side of the Exchequer was declining, and in 1841 it was abolished altogether. See WH Bryson, *The Equity Side of the Exchequer* (Cambridge: Cambridge University Press, 1975) 160–65.

[157] *D'Almaine v Boosey* (1835) 1 Y & C 288.

[158] *Bach v Longman* (1777) 2 Cowp 623.

[159] Seville, *Internationalisation* 46. An Act for Securing to Authors in Certain Cases the Benefit of International Copyright 1838 (1 & 2 Vict c 59).

[160] An Act to amend the Law relating to International Copyright 1844 (7 Vict c 12).

sculptures and works of art first published in a foreign country could be protected for the same term as works first published in the United Kingdom.[161] It also applied to dramatic pieces and musical compositions first performed abroad.[162] Again, the Act would only apply if reciprocal protection was offered by the foreign state.[163]

Meanwhile, cases continued to come before the domestic courts. In the 1841 case of *Chappell v Purday*,[164] Abinger CB again held that the foreign author of a work unpublished in France might assign his right to a British subject who could then acquire copyright. However, he found against Mrs Chappell, the assignee of Auber's work, as he found that the work had been published in France and imported into Britain prior to the plaintiff having acquired the copyright.[165] In 1845, the case was appealed, and Pollock CB, delivering the judgment of the Court, was rather less certain in his conclusions, stating the Court thought it 'doubtful whether a foreigner not resident here can have an English copyright at all'.[166] and that he certainly could not if the work had been already published abroad. In 1846, Prussia became the first country to conclude a treaty with the United Kingdom under the 1844 International Copyright Act, a factor which probably assisted Pollock CB to come to the conclusion, in 1849, that under the common law, on construction of the relevant statutes, any foreigner who sent a work over to be first published in England would receive no copyright protection.[167]

While the music publishers were bringing their cases, Murray was also pursuing Bohn and Routledge, both having published works by Washington Irving in their respective cheap 'Library' series.[168] In August 1850, Knight Bruce V-C refused to grant Murray an injunction, but suggested that Murray bring an action at common law against the two publishers.[169] The Vice-Chancellor commented in the case that 'The point in dispute was a very important one beyond all doubt, and one which, some day, must reach the House of Lords'.[170]

It did reach the House of Lords, but it was not Murray who took it there. The decisive case had begun in 1849 when Boosey once again sought to defend his right to publish Bellini's *La Sonnambula*.[171] Bellini had composed the work in Milan and assigned his copyright in the work to the publisher Ricordi, who was also resident in Milan at the time. Ricordi went to London where he assigned his interest in the composition to Boosey, who entered the work in the Stationers' Register and

[161] International Copyright Act 1844 s 1.
[162] ibid s 5.
[163] ibid s 14.
[164] *Chappell v Purday* (1841) 4 Y & C 485.
[165] ibid 495.
[166] *Chappell v Purday* (1845) 14 M & W 303, 321.
[167] *Boosey v Purday* (1849) 4 Ex 145, 157.
[168] Murray had paid £10,000 for Irving's works in the 1820s. Seville, *Internationalisation* 177.
[169] For Murray's dealings with Bohn and Routledge, see Barnes, *Authors, Publishers and Politicians* 153–65.
[170] *Murray v Bohn; Murray v Routledge* (1850) *The Times* (8 August 1850) 7d.
[171] This piece of music had previously been the subject of litigation in *Boozey v Tolkein* (1848) 5 CB 476, *Boosey v Davidson* (1849) 13 QB 257 and *Boosey v Purday* (1849) 4 Ex 145.

printed it. This was accepted as the first publication of the work.[172] In 1849, Boosey brought an action in the Court of Exchequer against Jefferys for publishing the work and Rolfe B directed the jury to find a verdict for the defendant.[173] Boosey then appealed to the Exchequer Chamber, the forum where appeal cases from each common law court were heard. Lord Campbell CJ delivered the judgment of the Court, holding that a foreigner who published his work first in Great Britain, even if he continued to reside abroad, was entitled to copyright protection.[174]

The unanimous opinion of a number of the highest judges in the land might have been considered to be the end of the matter. However, at this point the two interrelated issues relating to foreign copyright, namely the copyright granted to British authors overseas and the copyright granted to foreign authors in Britain, began to come together. Despite the 1844 International Copyright Act, those countries who presented the most significant threat to the home market, namely France, Belgium and the United States, had yet to conclude treaties with the United Kingdom. Jefferys and Bohn, whose common cause made them natural allies, arranged for a meeting to be called, which was held at the start of July 1851 and chaired by Sir Edward Bulwer Lytton. Also in attendance were the humourist George Cruikshank, authors William Howitt and Richard Hengist Horne and the publisher Henry Colburn.[175] The meeting adopted a resolution stating that the decision in *Boosey v Jefferys* would have a prejudicial effect on British literature and would remove a material inducement to foreign states to grant copyright to British authors.[176]

In addition, the meeting decided that the expense of appealing the decision to the House of Lords should not be borne by one person alone, and Bohn and others present formed a society to finance this undertaking, called 'The Society for Obtaining an Adjustment of the Law of Copyright'.[177] Bolstered by this support, Jefferys appealed the decision to the House of Lords. Faced with such a difficult and, by now, contentious decision, the House of Lords called in the common law judges to advise them, as they had in *Donaldson v Becket*.[178] However, the practice of the House of Lords when hearing appeals had changed since the days of *Donaldson v Becket*. After *O'Connell*'s case in 1844, it was no longer acceptable for lay lords to vote in appeals.[179] The three Law Lords who sat in this case were Lord Cranworth (who, as Baron Rolfe, had found for the defendant in the Court of Exchequer), Lord Brougham and Lord St Leonards.

172 *Jefferys v Boosey* (1854) 4 HLC 815, 816–17.

173 *Boosey v Jefferys* (1851) 6 Ex 580, 581.

174 *Boosey v Jefferys* (1851) 6 Ex 580. The other judges were Patteson, Maule, Wightman, Cresswell and Williams JJ.

175 *The Times* (3 July 1851) 8f.

176 ibid.

177 Barnes, *Authors, Publishers and Politicians* 168.

178 The judges who attended were Jervis CJ, Maule and Williams J from the Court of Common Pleas, Coleridge, Crompton, Erle and Wightman JJ from the Queen's Bench, and Pollock CB, Parke B and Alderson B from the Court of Exchequer. Several of these judges had presided over the earlier cases on foreign authors.

179 See R Stevens, *Law and Politics: The House of Lords as a Judicial Body, 1800–1976* (London: Weidenfeld and Nicolson, 1979) 33.

Jefferys v Boosey inspired a rare example of concurrence of opinion between these three Law Lords.[180] Although six of the common law judges, being a majority, were of the opinion that a valid copyright had been assigned to Boosey and was therefore enforceable, Lord Cranworth, Lord Brougham and Lord St Leonards sided with the minority and voted to reverse the judgment of the Exchequer Chamber.[181] The Lords considered that the Copyright Acts applied only to British authors, and gave no protection to foreigners. Only foreign authors who first published their work in England at the same time as being resident there would receive copyright protection for their works.

B. Rhetoric, Authors and the Public

The issue of whether a foreign author was entitled to copyright protection in Britain led many of the litigants and judges involved in the cases to consider the underlying justifications for copyright law and the phoenix of common law copyright rose once again from the ashes. Common law copyright was an important argument for the supporters of foreign authors because if they could establish a natural right to copyright held by all authors then foreign authors would come within its protection as a matter of course.[182]

Establishing the existence of common law copyright required its proponents to rely heavily on the decision of *Millar v Taylor*, as well as the advisory opinions of the majority of judges in *Donaldson v Becket*. It also required the actual result in the latter case to be side-lined or contradicted. This process has been described by Deazley as 'the cult of *Millar* and the re-branding of *Donaldson*'.[183] An example of this reasoning is found in the argument of Boosey's counsel, Bovill, before the Exchequer Chamber:

> Copyright is a species of property which existed at common law; indeed it is difficult to find anything more in the nature of property than the produce of a person's own intellect. That such a right existed at common law was affirmed in the year 1769 by the judgment of Willes J., and Aston J., in the celebrated case of *Millar v Taylor* . . . If the test of property be control and possession, it can make no difference whether the work be

[180] In the years 1853–54, these three judges had been the most active in the hearing of appeals. However, their inability to agree with one another and perceived lack of professionalism led to a number of criticisms being levelled against the House of Lords appellate jurisdiction. After several inquiries and considerable debate, the system was reformed in 1876, when a separate court was established, still called the House of Lords, but with the sole purpose of hearing appeals. See R Stevens, *Law and Politics* 38–67.

[181] *Jefferys v Boosey* (1854) 4 HLC 815.

[182] France was the first country to give protection to foreigners against unauthorised publication, in the Revolutionary decrees of 1791 and 1793. Protection was extended to non-resident foreigners who had first published outside France in 1852: A Strowel, '*Droit d'auteur* and copyright: Between History and Nature' in B Sherman and A Strowel (eds), *Of Authors and Origins: Essays on Copyright Law* (Oxford: Clarendon Press, 1994) 247. See below ch 5 text to nn 206 ff for more detail.

[183] Deazley, *Re-Thinking Copyright* 53.

> written in Great Britain or abroad, or whether it be brought here by the author or his deputy or transferee.[184]

Recourse was also made to the Blackstonian/Lockean theory of literary property by Erle J in his opinion in *Jefferys v Boosey*. He stated:

> The origin of property is in production. As to works of imagination and reasoning, if not of memory, the author may be said to create, and, in all departments of mind, new books are the product of the labour, skill, and capital of the author. The subject of property is the order of words in the author's composition; not the words themselves, they being analogous to the elements of matter, which are not appropriated unless combined, nor the ideas expressed by those words, they existing in the mind alone, which is not capable of appropriation.[185]

Wightman, Maule and Coleridge JJ also supported the existence of common law copyright, but they limited their remarks to the legal position of unpublished works. They held that if the author had a right in an unpublished manuscript, which had been settled by the Queen's Bench in *Millar v Taylor* and the majority of judges in *Donaldson v Becket*, then the common law would protect it as property.[186] However, as noted in chapter two, the status of unpublished works was one issue that *Donaldson v Becket* had signally failed to resolve.

Those who did not favour the rights of foreign authors dismissed the existence of the common law right. However, they were not content to rely merely upon the vote of the House of Lords in *Donaldson v Becket*. Jefferys' counsel referred back to some of the arguments made by Yates as counsel in *Tonson v Collins* against the right, stating,

> Literary property is, in truth, a property in ideas only; it is not the subject of possession or occupation, and therefore never could have been a subject of a Common Law right; nor could it exist upon general principles of property; it could only be created by the express provisions of the legislative power.[187]

Lord Brougham also believed that it was permissible to revisit the debates due to the differences of opinion in *Donaldson v Becket*, and he expressed the view that if Lord Mansfield had given his opinion, there would have been a majority in favour of the right and the House of Lords would have voted the other way.[188]

Lord Brougham himself was prepared to assume that authors did have a right prior to publication, but the right he envisaged appeared more like a property right in the physical copy. He stated:

> The right of the author before publication we may take to be unquestioned, and we may even assume that it never was, when accurately defined, denied. He has the undisputed

[184] (1851) 6 Ex 580, 583–5; 676–77. For similar reasoning, see *Boozey v Tolkein* (1848) 5 CB 476, 481 and *Boosey v Purday* (1849) 4 Ex 145, 152.

[185] 4 HLC 815, 867.

[186] ibid 883–84, 888 (per Wightman J), 893 (per Maule J) 903 (per Coleridge J).

[187] 4 HLC 815, 821, 824. For Yates' opposition to the common law right, see above: ch 1.

[188] 4 HLC 815, 961. See above: ch 2, for discussion of the incorrect count of the judges' votes and the subsequent misinterpretation of the decisions.

> right to his manuscript; he may withhold, or he may communicate it, and, communicating, he may limit the number of persons to whom it is imparted, and impose such restrictions as he pleases upon their use of it. The fulfilment of the annexed conditions he may proceed to enforce, and for their breach he may claim compensation.[189]

Brougham considered that this initial right was abandoned by publication. The Statute of Anne, however, clothed the published work with the 'qualities of property' and gave it the protection refused by the common law.[190]

Lord St Leonards also distinguished between an author's 'right to his manuscript and to any copy which he may choose to make of it as his property, just like any other personal chattel, and the right to multiply copies to the exclusion of every other person',[191] noting that 'Nothing can be more distinct than these two things'.[192] Lord Cranworth LC was equally definite that there was no common law copyright, although he was slightly more equivocal on the position prior to the Statute of Anne. He stated that copyright 'if not the creature; as I believe it to be, of our statute law, is now entirely regulated by it, and therefore in determining its limits we must look exclusively to the statutes on which it depends'.[193]

In addition to re-igniting the common law copyright debates, the foreign author cases also contributed to the development of the public interest discourse of copyright law. Both supporters and opponents of the rights of foreign authors made reference to public interest concerns. The argument in favour of granting copyright to foreign authors who first published in Britain was linked to the public interest in encouraging learning as well as benefits to British trade. This approach is illustrated in the judgment of Bayley J in the case of *Clementi v Walker*:

> [T]he Legislature must be supposed to have legislated with a view to British interests and the advancement of British learning. By confining the privilege to British printing, British capital, workmen and materials would be employed, and the work would be within reach of the British public. By extending the privilege to foreign printing, the employment of British capital, workmen, and materials might be suspended, and the work might never find its way to the British public. Without very clear words, therefore, to shew an intention to extend the privilege to foreign publications, I should think [the Statute of Anne] must be confined to books printed in this kingdom . . . Whether the act of printing and publishing abroad makes the work at once publici juris is not necessary now to decide; but we have no doubt that it becomes publici juris if the author does not take prompt measures to publish here. To hold to the contrary would discourage British enterprise, and stop avenues of British knowledge.[194]

Maule J expressed a similar opinion in *Jefferys v Boosey*: 'British industry and talent will be encouraged by conferring a copyright on a foreigner first publishing in England; industry, by giving it occupation; and talent, by furnishing it with

189 4 HLC 815, 962.
190 ibid 968.
191 ibid 978–79.
192 ibid 979.
193 ibid 954.
194 2 B & C 861, 867–68, 870.

valuable information and means for cultivation'.[195] Wightman J also appealed to the public interest, but emphasised the social benefits of education, rather than manufacturing and the economy, stating:

> [The Statute of Anne] professes to be an Act for the encouragement of learning generally, and for the encouragement of learned men to compose and write useful books, without reference to any country or persons. Literature and learned men are of no particular age or country, and the benefit to be derived by this country from the encouragement of learned men would be greatly reduced if the operation of the statute was restricted to native authors.[196]

These judges considered that the interests of authors coincided with those of the public. However, Erle J took a different view. He considered that there was an inherent conflict between the two and that, by limiting the duration of the right, the Statute of Anne had sacrificed the interests of authors to those of the public:

> The Legislature under Queen Anne had the double purpose of encouraging both learners and authors; and as the monied interests of the two parties conflict, the learner wishing the book at the lowest, and author at the highest price; therefore, for the benefit of learners, the author's perpetuity in his property is reduced, as to future publications, to 14 years, with a contingent increase, and as to existing publications, to 21 years; the larger term being due for the loss of a vested right, and the price of books is to be lowered, if certain officers judge it to be too high. On the other hand, for the benefit of authors, the power of fining pirates and confiscating their piratical property during the statutable term of copyright, as also the mode of proving proprietorship, and licenses under the proprietor, by means of registration with the Stationers' Company, are restored almost as they had existed from the 13th and 14th of Charles the 2d, till late in the reign of William the 3d.
>
> The Judges, in construing the 8th of Anne, in *Millar v Taylor*, advert to its Parliamentary history, as brought in to secure copyright, and altered in its progress to destroy it. But without going upon such a construction, it is legitimate to observe, from the statute itself, that it appears to have proceeded from the conflicting interests of readers and authors.[197]

He added that, in finding that the very clause which appeared to protect authors actually stripped them of their perpetual right, the decision of *Donaldson v Becket* 'created such a sacrifice of the author's interest as I may assume has been thought inconvenient, seeing that the Legislature made one restoration to authors of their property by 54 Geo 3, and another by 5 and 6 Vict'.[198]

By contrast, Parke B, Jervis CJ and Lord Brougham considered that the Statute of Anne had sacrificed the interests of the public to those of authors.[199] Consequently, they believed, such encouragement did not extend to foreign authors, as this would unduly burden the public. Parke B noted:

[195] 4 HLC 815, 896. See also the argument of Boosey's counsel and the opinion of Williams J: 4 HLC 815, 842, 863.
[196] ibid 886–87.
[197] 4 HLC 815, 874.
[198] ibid 875.
[199] ibid 947, 970.

> It is rather a startling proposition that the Parliament of Queen Anne meant to foster and encourage foreign authors at the expense of the British public. It is said that learning would be encouraged by the introduction of foreign books which might not otherwise be imported, but it is expressly declared in the Act itself, that it is for the encouragement of learned men to *compose and write*, not for the encouragement of the importers of books. It would be of small advantage to the community, and an inadequate reward to the first importer, to allow him to have a monopoly, and thereby increase the value of the book to the public; for if the book was of real value, doubtless it would be imported for the use of British readers. And if the introduction of books had been the object, why not give the exclusive right of printing to the first *importers*? It was indisputably the intention of the framers of the Act to reward *authors* not importers; and what benefit could the British public derive from the encouragement of foreign *authors*?[200]

Lord Brougham constructed a similar narrative of the Statute of Anne's history:

> The encouragement of learning, by encouraging learned men to write useful books, is declared to be the object of the statute, and that object it pursues by giving the author and his assigns a monopoly for a limited period. The Legislature gives this encouragement at the expense of its own subjects, to whom the monopoly raises the price of books.[201]

Based on this theory, foreign authors would not receive protection. Brougham pointed out that:

> It can hardly be contended that, a century and a half ago, the Parliament was minded to encourage learning at home, by encouraging foreigners to write books at the expense of the British purchaser; that a monopoly in our market was to be established for the sake of foreign writers who might thus be induced to write, and thereby benefit our people.[202]

Lord Brougham located the Statute of Anne's concern for the public interest in the price-control provisions contained therein,[203] stating:

> [I]n truth no one can read the provision touching prices without drawing a further inference from it, that very crude and narrow principles then prevailed on these subjects; and we could hardly expect that the same Legislature which appointed an authority with stringent liberal powers to keep down prices would entertain such large and enlightened views as it must have had, if it encouraged foreigners, at the temporary and immediate cost, at all events, of its own subjects, for the sake of multiplying the number of useful works, and so benefiting those subjects on the whole.[204]

Of the three Law Lords, Lord Brougham's speech engages most closely with the public interest elements of copyright law. The two other judges found that the Statute's operation was limited to British subjects on a more literal interpretation of the text, although Lord St Leonards quoted Bayley J's statement in *Clementi v*

200 ibid 927.
201 ibid 970.
202 ibid.
203 Statute of Anne s 4.
204 4 HLC 815, 971–72.

Walker[205] with approval. Thus, Lord Brougham and, to a lesser extent Lord St Leonards, explicitly favoured the interests of the reading public and British manufacturers over the claims of authorship.

By the time that *Jefferys v Boosey* was decided, the question of granting copyright protection to European authors was rapidly becoming less a question for domestic courts, and more a matter of international law. In 1851, Britain concluded a treaty with France in which each country undertook to offer the same protection to the authors of works published in the other country that they offered to works published in their own country.[206] The 1844 International Copyright Act had to be modified in respect of translations and, in 1852, the British enacted legislation to bring the convention into force.[207] Under this Act, similar protection could be offered to other countries by the Queen's Order in Council, and Prussia and the other German states entered into a new treaty with Britain on the basis of this Act, as did Belgium, Spain, Sardinia and Italy.[208]

However, similar progress was not made in relation to the United States and the decision in *Jefferys v Boosey* was a serious blow for British publishers who had paid large amounts of money to publish works by American authors on the basis that first publication in Britain would secure their rights. Their legal advisors carefully analysed the decisions and came to the conclusion that remarks of Lord Cranworth had left open the possibility that first publication in the British dominions might be sufficient to secure copyright for a foreign author.[209] This theory was tested when the American author Maria Cummins sent her manuscript to the publishers Sampson Low and travelled to Montreal for the time of publication. When Routledge reprinted the work, Sampson Low was successful in seeking an injunction from the Court of Chancery. The decision was appealed to the House of Lords, which upheld the decisions of the courts below and found in favour of Sampson Low.[210]

The reasons for this finding, however, differed. Lords Cranworth and Chelmsford (with Lord Colonsay briefly concurring) held that, following the decision in *Jefferys v Boosey*, copyright could be awarded to any foreign author first publishing in Britain, while resident in Britain or in any part of the dominions. However, Lord Cairns LC and Lord Westbury were prepared to go further and, in so doing, they relied on arguments based on the public interest. Lord Cairns took as his starting point that 'The great object of the law of copyright is to stimulate by means of the protection secured to literary labour, the composition and publication to the world of works of learning

[205] *Clementi v Walker* 2 B & C 861, 867–68, 870 (noted above).

[206] Convention between Her Majesty and the French Republic for the establishment of international copyright (signed 3 November 1851, Paris).

[207] An Act to enable Her Majesty to carry into effect a Convention with France on the Subject of Copyright; to extend and explain the International Copyright Acts; and to explain the Acts relating to Copyright in Engravings 1852 (15 Vict c 12). See below ch 5, text to n 207.

[208] JHG Bergne, 'The International Copyright Union' (1887) 3 *Law Quarterly Review* 14, 23.

[209] See Seville, *Internationalisation* 197–98.

[210] *Routledge v Low* (1869) LR 3 HL 100.

and utility'.[211] Noting that *Jefferys v Boosey* had been decided upon the basis of the Statute of Anne, he held that it did not apply to the 1842 Copyright Act, which could be interpreted more broadly so as to grant copyright protection to any author who publishes in the United Kingdom, wherever he may reside. This was because the 1842 Act 'professes to aim at affording greater encouragement to the production of lasting benefit to the world' than did the Statute of Anne. He linked this back to notions of public interest:

> The intention of the Act is to obtain a benefit for the people of this country by the publication to them of works of learning, of utility, of amusement. This benefit is obtained, in the opinion of the Legislature, by offering a certain amount of protection to the author, thereby inducing him to publish his work here. This is, or may be, a benefit to the author, but it is a benefit given, not for the sake of the author of the work, but for the sake of those to whom it is communicated. The aim of the Legislature is to increase the common stock of the literature of the country; and if that stock can be increased by the publication for the first time here of a new and valuable work composed by an alien, who has never been in the country, I see nothing in the wording of the Act which prevents, nothing in the policy of the Act which should prevent, and everything in the professed object of the Act, and in its wide and general provisions, which should entitle, such a person to the protection of the Act, in return and compensation for the addition he has made to the literature of the country.[212]

Lord Westbury similarly held that *Jefferys v Boosey* was not binding, because it was based on the Statute of Anne, and similarly considered that the 1842 Act should be more broadly construed. He found that it contained

> an invitation to men of learning in every country to make the United Kingdom the place of first publication of their works; and an extended term of copyright throughout the whole of the British dominions is the reward of their so doing. So interpreted and applied the Act is auxiliary to the advancement of learning in this country.[213]

Routledge v Low was followed several months later in *Low v Ward*,[214] in which case Giffard V-C seemed to follow the narrower approach of Lords Cranworth, Colonsay and Chelmsford. In a brief judgment, he held that the case was authority for the proposition that a foreigner who published a work in the United Kingdom while temporarily resident in Canada should be in the same position as a British subject.

The various arguments and judicial decisions made in the foreign author cases of the mid-nineteenth century reinforced the notion that copyright law gave rise to a tension between the claims of authors and those of the public. The point of contention was which side should take supremacy. On the side of foreign authors, common law copyright was employed and the public interest claim of encouraging learning was cast as the encouragement of authors and making greater numbers

211 ibid 108.
212 ibid 110–11.
213 ibid 118.
214 *Low v Ward* (1868) LR 6 Eq 415.

of works available to readers. Another public interest consideration was also raised, namely, the support of British manufacturing and trade. Arguing against the protection of foreign authors, copyright was characterised as a monopoly, which raised prices, and should be as limited as possible in the interests of the reading public. Once again, the rhetoric of romantic authorship was far from providing a knock-out blow for those arguing in favour of the protection of foreign authors. However, these cases demonstrate that the issue was not *whether* copyright should serve the public interest, but *which version* of the public interest should take priority, and how it should interact with property rights. Drawing a line between domestic and foreign authors represented a temporary solution, but it was far from providing closure of the issues.

5

Examination and Internationalisation

I. THE ROYAL COPYRIGHT COMMISSION OF 1878

THE SHIFTING SAND upon which copyright law had been built became apparent once again in the late 1870s, when copyright was subjected to the most searching analysis in the United Kingdom to date or since. There had, however, been two earlier attempts to achieve the consolidation of copyright law that Talfourd had sought in the 1830s and early 1840s. In 1857, Felix Johns Hamel, solicitor for Her Majesty's Customs, tired of being approached by customs officers bewildered by the variety of contradictory and conflicting separate Acts, drafted a consolidating statute.[1] This was taken up by the Government but both its sponsors died before anything was done in the matter.[2] In 1864, the matter was taken up by the publisher Adam Black.[3] Black's Bill was based on Hamel's consolidating measure, but it included two significant new sections. The first provided for a right of dramatisation of works of fiction,[4] while the second encapsulated a version of what today would be referred to as the 'idea/expression dichotomy'. This latter section provided that

> [n]othing herein contained shall prejudice the Right of any Person to copy or use any Work in which there shall be no Copyright, or to represent any Scene or Object, notwithstanding that there may be Copyright in some other Representation of such Scene or Object.[5]

Black was a prominent and enterprising Edinburgh publisher, who had purchased the *Encyclopaedia Britannica* from Archibald Constable when the firm went bust in 1827 and the remaining years of Sir Walter Scott's copyrights in 1851. It seems likely that his experiences with these two major works inspired these statutory innovations. Compiling the *Encyclopaedia* relied on giving new expression to existing information, while Sir Walter Scott's works were frequently dramatised.[6] Black's Bill was sent to a Select Committee but made no further progress. Eleven

[1] Copyright Acts Consolidation Bill HC (1857) [142].

[2] Report of the Select Committee on the Copyright (No 2) Bill; together with the Proceedings of the Committee, and Minutes of Evidence (1864) 441, 7, 8.

[3] Parl Deb HC vol 173 col 563 (15 February 1864), vol 174 col 503 (6 April 1864).

[4] Copyright (No 2) Bill HC [59] s 6.

[5] ibid s 9.

[6] See argument of counsel in *Tinsley v Lacy* (1863) 1 H & M 747, 749.

years later, in 1875, Benjamin Disraeli appointed a Royal Commission to look into the law of copyright and report to the Government. Before, however, we examine the Commission's investigations and conclusion, it is necessary to consider the state of the book trade at this time.

A. Markets and Monopolies: The Mid-Nineteenth Century Book Trade

In the middle of the century, the book market was changing again. Indeed, James Raven pinpoints the 1840s as marking a transition between the ancient and modern ages of bookselling.[7] In 1834, the printers Bradbury and Evans installed a steam-driven press, which needed to be kept running almost constantly to make the investment worthwhile.[8] Transformations in printing capacity, as well as the lowering of costs of printing, typesetting and paper manufacture all allowed publishers to satisfy new types of demand.[9] Transport developments and new distribution systems also played their role in changing the way the market operated, with trains being the major factor. The railway also created new readerships. In 1848 WH Smith set up his first railway station bookstall, stocked with cheap editions aimed at both long-distance travellers and those who took the train to work.[10]

As noted in chapter three, the early years of the nineteenth century had seen the emergence of cheap popular literature, aimed at the working classes. However, high prices were maintained in some parts of the market, and books continued to be considered 'luxury' items. One of the most distinctive features of the period was the reign of the three-decker novel. The three-volume format hailed from the days of Scott[11] and dominated the publishing landscape of literature until its collapse in 1894, a period of 73 years.[12] Despite the fact that the prices of other types of book were falling, throughout this entire period the price of three-deckers remained at the hefty sum of 31s 6d, or 10s 6d a volume—a price which kept such books out of the hands of all would-be purchasers except the wealthy.[13]

The longevity of the three-decker is generally attributed in large part to the influence of circulating libraries in the Victorian age. The best known of these was Mudie's 'Select Library', which began lending books in 1842.[14] It was an auspicious time as the 1840s witnessed a wave of high quality novels, such as *Barnaby Rudge, Martin Chuzzlewit, Jane Eyre, Vanity Fair, Wuthering Heights* and *David Copperfield*,

[7] J Raven, *The Business of Books* (New Haven, Yale University Press, 2007) 321.

[8] G Law and RL Patten, 'The Serial Revolution' in D McKitterick (ed), *The Cambridge History of the Book in Britain*, vol 6: *1830–1914* (Cambridge, Cambridge University Press, 2009) 145.

[9] Raven, *Business of Books* 324.

[10] ibid 331–32.

[11] Scott published *Waverley* in three volumes, as well as many others of his extraordinarily popular novels.

[12] JA Sutherland, *Victorian Novelists and Publishers* (London, Athlone Press, 1976) 13.

[13] ibid 19.

[14] GL Griest, *Mudie's Circulating Library and the Victorian Novel* (Newton Abbot, Devon, David & Charles (Publishers) Ltd, 1970) 17.

which laid the foundations of the Victorian golden age of fiction.[15] Mudie's influence and buying power were such that he not only served the growing demand for fiction; soon he was creating and shaping it.[16]

The three-decker novel suited the circulating libraries, because it conferred dignity and status on a novel. The high price also suited them, because it placed novels out of reach of all but the wealthy and thereby created demand for library copies. The system created wide margins between the price paid by the customer and that paid by the retailer and, although the three-decker format did not result in high profits for publishers, its generous margins made it a safe and stable commercial format.[17] Publishers were able to make ends meet even on small editions and the result was not unfavourable to the cause of literature in general. In fact, as Sutherland points out, one of the main causes of the golden age of English literature that occurred in the Victorian period was the 'sheer superabundance of the novel'.[18] This superabundance can be largely attributed to the structure of the book market, which charged high prices, but encouraged controlled risk-taking and, consequently, new writing.

Nevertheless, the high cost of books gave rise to discontent in the middle of the century. By this time, the retail side of the book trade was almost completely severed from the production, or publishing, side. The retail side was nominally subject to the Regulations of the Booksellers' Association.[19] The Regulations sought to control the discounts offered by the trade, but were only sporadically enforced.[20] For reasons which may only be speculated upon, the Booksellers' Association decided in 1850 to reaffirm the Regulations.[21] In January of 1852, John Chapman was expelled from the Association for offering books imported from America at cost price plus commission. In response, he launched an attack that was taken up by *The Times* exposing the discount system, as 'an anomalous interference with the free course of competition and the natural operations of trade'.[22]

Under the pressure of such adverse publicity, the Committee of the Booksellers' Association requested Lord Campbell to intervene by arbitration, pledging to resign if the decision went against them. Lord Campbell, assisted by the historian George Grote and Henry Hart Milman, Dean of St Paul's, first heard the case of those in support of the Regulations led by such publishing stalwarts as William Longman, the chairman of the Association, John Murray and Rivington and others.

The publishers argued that the Regulations of the Booksellers' Association served the interests of publishers and authors alike, as well as the interests of

[15] ibid 15.

[16] ibid 36.

[17] ibid 15–16.

[18] ibid 17.

[19] See above: ch 3.

[20] JJ Barnes, *Free Trade in Books: A Study of the London Book Trade since 1800* (Oxford, Clarendon Press, 1964) 20.

[21] ibid; NN Feltes, *Modes of Production of Victorian Novels* (Chicago, University of Chicago Press, 1986) 20–21.

[22] *The Times* (30 March 1852) 5d.

literature and the public in general.[23] They claimed that the principles of free trade were not applicable to the bookselling trade due to the nature of the article in question, which did not allow one book to be substituted for a different one. If the retail prices of books were not fixed, argued Longman, they would be sold at different prices from street to street, the public would suffer and the whole trade would be thrown into confusion. The Regulations maintained the system of multiple retail outlets, which many parts of the trade had long taken for granted as being the most efficient way to promote and distribute books. Longman asserted that if the power of restricting competition were taken away, the underselling that would ensue would inevitably lead to the establishment of large monopolies which would injure literature, cause inconvenience and destroy the business of hundreds of retailers all over the country.[24] The Association members also argued that high prices were necessary due to the custom of booksellers giving long credit to customers, as well as the fact that books were a luxury and were the first expense to be curtailed in times of economic crisis. These factors were claimed to justify large allowances between the sale price and the retail price.[25]

Although the high profit margins benefited the retail booksellers, much of the discontent regarding the Regulations had been generated by a group of them, led by Chapman and known as 'the undersellers'. The undersellers resented the restrictions which prevented them from lowering the price to customers at their discretion, which might result in more sales overall.[26] Chapman's supporters included the booksellers Bickers and Bush, and William Tegg, son of Thomas Tegg.[27] Others involved in opposing the Association were Bentley, a publisher and former prominent Committee member, Charles Knight, JW Parker, printer for the University of Cambridge and publisher of *Fraser's Magazine*, and Bradbury and Evans, publishers of *Punch*, *Daily News* and *Household Words*.[28] They were supported by William Gladstone, who spoke out against the Regulations in Parliament. Moreover, Chapman and his associate Parker had enlisted the support of numerous authors, including Charles Dickens, Wilkie Collins, Tom Taylor, Thomas Carlyle, John Stuart Mill and Leigh Hunt. Their opposition to retail price maintenance was extremely damaging for the Assocation.[29]

Like the Booksellers' Association, the undersellers and their supporters invoked the spectres of free trade, monopoly and public interest. In Parliament, Gladstone expostulated that the book trade in England was 'a disgrace to the present state of civilization'[30] and accused the trade of 'monopoly and combination',[31] which had reduced it to minimum levels of production. Speaking before Lord Campbell,

[23] *The Times* (15 April 1852) 5d.
[24] ibid.
[25] Letter from John Murray to Gladstone, quoted in Barnes, *Free Trade in Books* 79.
[26] Letter from Bickers and Bush to *The Times* (14 April 1852) 8a.
[27] See above: ch 4, text at n 106.
[28] Barnes, *Free Trade in Books* 32–35.
[29] ibid 26–27, 67.
[30] *The Times* (13 May 1852) 3a; Parl Deb HC vol 121 col 595 (12 May 1852).
[31] *The Times* (13 May 1852) 3a.

Bickers invoked the undersellers' right 'to dispose of their property in whatever manner they deemed most conducive to their own interests, unshackled by trade regulations, which they considered impracticable and impolitic, as well as unjust to themselves as traders and to the public as purchasers'.[32] He further claimed that by reducing prices the undersellers 'had greatly increased the sale of books, and through their instrumentality persons of small incomes were enabled to provide themselves with libraries, which otherwise they could not possess'.[33] Whether this was in fact the case, or whether the undersellers' main customers were middle-class people looking for a bargain, is debatable. In a letter to *The Times*, Bickers championed moderately priced literature for an increasingly educated population, and employed utilitarian rhetoric, arguing that the interests of bookseller, author and consumer were best served by selling the greatest number of books to the greatest number of people.[34]

On 19 May 1852, Lord Campbell delivered his opinion, stating that the regulations seemed '*prima facie* to be indefensible and contrary to the freedom which ought to prevail in commercial transactions'.[35] Although he recognised the advantages in having numerous respectable book dealers in cities and provincial towns, he considered that the existence of more retail establishments than were necessary to supply the commodity tended to raise prices. He advocated reliance on the principles of the free market, stating that the removal of restrictions might cause distress to the trade in the short term but that the 'wholesome principles of commerce' would soon bring a remedy.[36] Lord Campbell's application of economic principles was straightforwardly simple: a lowering of the price would lead to an increase in demand, and consequently large sales and profits to all.[37]

Sutherland sees the mid-nineteenth century as being characterised by a tension between innovation and conservatism in the book trade.[38] Feltes, on the other hand, identifies the Bookselling Question of 1852 as 'a moment in a larger historical struggle between two modes of literary production, the older, petty-commodity production of *books* being revolutionized by the capitalist production of *texts*'.[39] He characterises the pre-1852 book trade as a hegemonic structure of market control, formed and supported by high prices, circulating libraries and the three-decker format, which had been in place so long, and had come about so gradually, that it appeared natural.[40]

Another element underpinning this hegemonic market, which Feltes does not explicitly identify, was copyright law. In 1842, the duration of copyright protection had been extended, but the publishers, who had been so slow to support

32 *The Times* (18 May 1852) 8b.
33 ibid.
34 *The Times* (14 April 1852) 8a. See also Barnes, *Free Trade in Books* 97.
35 *The Times* (20 May 1852) 7a.
36 ibid.
37 ibid.
38 Feltes, *Modes of Production* 21; JA Sutherland, *Victorian Novelists* 72.
39 Feltes, *Modes of Production* 20.
40 ibid 23–24.

Talfourd's Bills, now showed little interest in the increased term. Their business practices were not reliant on long periods of protection; frequently, they purchased copyright from authors for only a limited number of years, demonstrating that the highest value was placed on a copyright while it was 'new'. Bentley, one of the most eminent fiction publishers, developed the custom of selling copyrights back to his authors, usually after he had made a considerable profit. There were, of course, exceptions, such as Routledge's purchase of 19 of Lytton's copyrights for ten years at the bargain price of £20,000. The other publishers had considered them to be worn out, but they were wrong and Routledge received a very nice return when he published the works in his 'Railway Library'.[41]

Other factors involved in keeping the prices of books high and maintaining the trade structure to support them were largely the result of Government-imposed duties, or the 'taxes on knowledge', as they came to be called. These were the paper duties, the newspaper stamp, the duty on advertisements and library deposit. All added to the production price of books, and were reflected in retail prices. The taxes were opposed in Parliament by radical free-traders led by Richard Cobden and John Bright. In 1851, a select committee had been appointed to look into the taxes, and over the following nine years all of them were repealed.[42]

Held in place by such a complex web of burdens and restraints, the book market structure was so entrenched that Lord Campbell's decision had little immediate impact on the trade. For some of the undersellers, it made no difference to their already struggling businesses. Chapman was insolvent in 1854 and sold his business a few years' later, but others were more fortunate.[43] The Booksellers' Association disbanded, but made some attempts to resuscitate the Regulations. Although these were unsuccessful, the publishers were still able to punish undersellers on an individual basis, by refusing to supply them with their own publications.[44] High prices, particularly for three-decker novels, remained the norm, but continued to attract protest.

In the 1830s and 1840s, there had been some experimental attempts to produce cheap literature. In 1833, Smith's 'Library of Romance' sold new fiction at 6s per volume, and in 1838 Bentley advertised new fiction at 8s a volume. Both these schemes had only short lives.[45] The hegemonic market structure militated against the success of such ventures, as it had been internalised by readers and purchasers to such an extent that a novel in three volumes represented quality and prestige, while cheaper novels, in fewer volumes, were considered inferior.[46]

[41] JA Sutherland, *Victorian Novelists* 34.

[42] J Black, *The English Press, 1621–1861* (Stroud, Sutton Publishing Limited, 2001), 183–6; Altick, *English Common Reader* 354.

[43] Barnes, *Free Trade in Books* 141. Bentley remained in business with some difficulty, as in 1854 he was particularly hard hit by the House of Lords decision in *Jefferys v Boosey*, which rendered his heavy investment in American literature worthless. See ibid 174–76.

[44] ibid 142.

[45] JA Sutherland, *Victorian Novelists* 18.

[46] ibid 29.

Although these projects foundered on the conservatism of the English reader, new marketing models began to have more success in circumventing high prices. Collective issues, part publication, magazine serialisation and the growth of the popular press were instrumental in opening up the book market to the literate but less wealthy consumer.[47] Magazine serialisation was particularly significant, as magazines from publishing houses became the conduits for high quality serialised publications. Frederick Marryat was first to issue instalments of fiction from 1832, but he stopped his first novel midway through, fearing completing the story would destroy the market for the entire volume. However, the method he pioneered came into its own with the runaway success of *The Posthumous Papers of the Pickwick Club*, and over the next three decades serialisation came to rival the three-decker.[48] Nor were Marryat's fears of impeding demand for the full novel realised. Wilkie Collins' *The Woman in White* was first published in 40 instalments in *All the Year Round* from November 1859 to August 1860. The high sales of the magazine in no way affected the sales of the novel, which appeared in August 1860 and sold the entire first three-volume edition of 1,000 copies on the day of publication.[49]

The latter half of the nineteenth century was a time of conflict between powerful, conservative forces within the book trade that sought to maintain its traditional and historically determined structure in every way available to them, including copyright law reform, and the emergence of new players and new modes of production that challenged the existing hegemony. This conflict continued into the debates over the aim and role of copyright law which were aired in the Royal Copyright Commission.

B. Abolition or Extension? A House Built upon the Sand

Disraeli agreed to appoint the Commission in response to urging from the Association to Protect the Rights of Authors.[50] The members of this ad hoc society included the novelist and dramatist Charles Reade; Edward Jenkins, the author and Liberal Member for Dundee; Charles Dickens the younger; and the journalist Blanchard Jerrold. The central concern of these men was colonial and international copyright. Charles Dickens the elder had suffered greatly at the hands of American pirates, and Edward Jenkins had had similar experiences in

[47] ibid 20–21. Sutherland also identifies the circulating library as one of the strategies developed to circumvent high prices. However, it should be seen as an element of the system itself, rather than a new and defensive strategy.

[48] G Law and RL Patten, 'The Serial Revolution' in D McKitterick (ed), *The Cambridge History of the Book in Britain*, vol 6: *1830–1914* (Cambridge, Cambridge University Press, 2009) 149–50.

[49] Three hundred and fifty copies of the second edition were sold within 5 days, and seven editions were sold in 6 months. By April 1861, 10,000 cheap copies (at 6s) were in production, with plans for 40,000 to follow. Altick, *English Common Reader* 42.

[50] In a letter to the *Pall Mall Gazette* (15 July 1872) Charles Reade explained that, despite their tendencies to disunity, authors had joined together to form the Association and make a public plea for protection. He then proceeded to set out his complaints over the course of 12 further letters: *Pall Mall Gazette* (July–September 1875).

relation to his satiric book *Ginx's Baby*. Indeed, Disraeli himself was only too aware of the problem, as his novel *Lothair* had also been extensively pirated in Canada. However, the deputation did not restrict itself to international and colonial issues, pointing to domestic problems such as the imperfections of the registration system, the dramatisation of novels without consent (an issue which had particularly affected Reade), the question of newspaper copyright and the unsatisfactory condition of the laws in general.[51]

Disraeli's Government responded to the concerns of the deputation by appointing a Royal Commission under the chairman of Lord Stanhope. Lord Stanhope (formerly Lord Mahon) had been a strong supporter of Talfourd's Copyright Bills and instrumental in the compromise which resulted in the passing of the Copyright Act of 1842. However, he died before the Commission began its work, and was replaced by Lord John Manners, who held the position of Postmaster-General.[52] The members of the Commission were drawn from a wide variety of backgrounds, and included the writer Anthony Trollope; JA Froude, the historian; FR Daldy, the publisher; Sir Louis Mallet, of the India Office and formerly of the Board of Trade; Sir Julius Benedict, the composer; and lawyers Sir James Fitzjames Stephen, Farrer Herschell and Sir John Rose.[53] Forty-nine witnesses appeared before the Commission and their evidence covered the length and breadth of copyright law as it related to books, magazines, artworks, music, plays and lectures.

The Commission's task was to consider all aspects of copyright law that arose before them. In effect, they were charged with assessing whether the boundaries of the law had been drawn correctly, whether any changes were required and, if so, what form they might take. Thus, the Commission considered issues ranging from registration, library deposit, the different subject matters of protection, the law of infringement and the question of duration. Although it was no part of their original remit, any assessment of copyright's scope would inevitably raise the issue of its underlying justifications.

The Commissioners identified the lack of a generally accepted foundation at the start of their Report, noting, 'The common law principles which lie at the root of the law have never been settled'.[54] They attempted to foreclose discussion on that issue by stating: 'we have arrived at the conclusion that copyright should continue to be treated by law as a proprietary right'.[55] However, the problem was not so easily circumvented. Matthew Arnold, commenting on the Report, noted that the

[51] *The Times* (11 May 1875) 10.

[52] Manners was the Conservative Member for North Leicestershire, an associate of Disraeli's and the Young England Party, and prominent in Lady Blessington's literary and artistic set.

[53] The other members were Robert Bourke (Under-Secretary of State for Foreign Affairs), Sir Charles Lawrence Young (barrister and dramatic author), Sir Henry Holland (Conservative MP), Sir Henry Drummond Wolff (Conservative MP and diplomat), Thomas Henry Farrer (Secretary of the Board of Trade), William Smith (Doctor of Civil Law) and the author Edward Jenkins.

[54] John James Robert (Lord) Manners, 'Royal Commission on Laws and Regulations relating to Home, Colonial and Foreign Copyrights' (C (2nd series) 2036, 1878) (hereinafter, Royal Copyright Commission) vii.

[55] ibid ix.

statement referred to a 'great battle', adding: 'here has been the point of conflict, as to the proprietary right of the author, as to his right of property in his production'.[56] The Commission's hearings thus became the site of considerable discourse on the nature of property, as well as the relationship between copyright law, the author and society. 'Battle' was engaged over the suggestion made by several witnesses before the Commission that the existing proprietary copyright system should be swept away and replaced with a royalty system. This system would remove the exclusive right of the author to publish his literary or artistic work; instead, the author would have a right to first publication but thereafter any person could copy or republish the work upon payment of a fixed sum to the author. The objective of such a system was the production of cheap books.

The high prices of books were the main factor leading several of the witnesses before the Copyright Commission to put forward the notion of replacing copyright with a royalty system. The very first witness to come before the Commission, Sir Charles Trevelyan, raised the issue. As literary executor of Lord Macaulay, Trevelyan's interest in copyright law was sparked by the poor returns he had received from Macaulay's works in Canada. As he had also spent time in India, he was particularly concerned about copyright law in relation to the colonies.[57] Trevelyan suggested that the recent legislative provision made for Canada, which allowed local publishers to reprint copyright books upon payment of a 12½ per cent royalty to the author,[58] ought to be adopted in the other colonies, as well as the United States.[59] He did, however, suggest that the Canadian solution would be more advantageous to authors if, instead of granting them control over republication, there were a general permission to reprint their works in all British possessions, from which they received a fair proportion of the proceeds.[60] Trevelyan went on to propose, rather tentatively, that such a system could be gradually introduced to England.[61] Trevelyan considered that the system would reconcile the interests of authors and the public, so that 'authors would, in a manner, be in a partnership with the public for the sale of their works, instead of holding a monopoly against them'.[62]

The second proponent of the royalty scheme was Robert Macfie. Macfie was a vocal patent abolitionist[63] and free-trader of the Cobdenite school who believed that allowing another publisher to print copies of a work, in the same way as inventors allowed other people to make and sell copies of their inventions, would introduce the 'panacea of competition' to the copyright system.[64] For Macfie

[56] M Arnold, 'Copyright' (1880) 49 *Fortnightly Review* 319, 321.

[57] Royal Copyright Commission 1.

[58] An Act to give effect to an Act of the Parliament of the Dominion of Canada respecting Copyright 1875 (38 & 39 Vict c 53). For more detail, see text to nn 216 ff below.

[59] Royal Copyright Commission 2. For more details on this system, see below: section I E.

[60] ibid 2

[61] ibid 3.

[62] ibid.

[63] F Machlup and E Penrose, 'The Patent Controversy of the Nineteenth Century' (1950) 10 *Journal of Economic History* 1, 14.

[64] RA Macfie, *Copyright and Patents for Inventions* (Edinburgh, T & T Clark, 1879) 37.

> copyright [was] an encroachment on the public domain which can only be justified on the plea that the public interest demands it or consists with it. Every author has unquestionably the fullest legal right to keep his manuscript from the world . . . but he has no natural right to prevent honest recipients from making other copies.[65]

Macfie proposed that any publisher ought to be able to print a new edition of any book after the first year of its original publication, or if the first edition was out of print, upon payment in advance to the author of 5 per cent of the retail price of the book.[66] Speaking before the Commission, he modified his proposal, suggesting that a person seeking to publish a book should be required to attend a Government office with an estimate of the cost he had incurred in printing the book. The publisher would then be permitted to sell the book at a reasonable price without competition until he had recouped that sum, after which others could publish the book.[67]

The final witness to support the royalty scheme was Thomas Farrer, Secretary to the Board of Trade and one of the most influential witnesses before the Commission. Although in favour of the system, Farrer was not prepared to advocate its immediate adoption, as he was of the view that 'whatever advantages a system of royalty might have, it would require new machinery of an elaborate kind, and it would disturb existing arrangements, and be opposed by existing interests'.[68] Farrer saw the aims of authors and the public as being inextricably linked. He stated:

> The ultimate object, I take it, of the law of copyright is, like that of every other law, the benefit of the public; but no doubt the more direct and immediate object is the benefit of the author, that is to induce and encourage the author to exert himself in a way beneficial to the public. You cannot separate the two objects.[69]

This approach was subjected to close analysis by Sir Louis Mallet, the only one of the Commissioners to endorse the royalty plan. Mallet, another radical free-trader and protégé of Cobden, applied neo-classical economic theory to ascertain whether copyright law did in fact operate in this way. He started by questioning the author's claim to a property right, stating it rested not on the usual reference to labour but was a result of the creation of artificial scarcity, which conferred upon copyright works their exchange value.[70] He stated that if the presumption upon which copyright law rested was that creating a limited monopoly encouraged literary production, and that without monopoly protection the literature of a country would suffer by deteriorating in supply or quality, then the question was the purely practical one of how to ensure the best possible literature at the cheapest possible price.

[65] ibid 34.
[66] Royal Copyright Commission, App A, 355.
[67] Royal Copyright Commission 139.
[68] ibid 210.
[69] ibid 150.
[70] ibid xlvii, xlviii.

Mallet considered that the present system of copyright had 'entirely failed in securing for the public an adequate supply of literature'[71] and that

> if the supply of literature could be largely increased, so as to bring the price within the reach of the masses of the people, it would react upon the demand to an extent which would afford possibilities of literary profit far exceeding anything which has hitherto been attained or imagined.[72]

The best way of attaining this increased supply, in Mallet's view, would be the royalty system because it would respond to the relationship between supply and demand, and it would also separate the profits of authorship from the profits of publication. While he conceded that legislation would be necessary to secure to authors the profits of their labours and that some sort of monopoly might be necessary to protect them, no monopoly was necessary to protect the profits of publication, which were of a normal commercial character. The royalty system would protect the former, but not the latter, and would benefit authors and the public by increasing circulation of books and by reducing their cost.[73]

The royalty scheme, however, was vehemently opposed by the authors and publishers who appeared before the Commission.[74] The publishers would never support a scheme which undermined the structure of the market with which they were familiar and which suited their business models. They also feared it would undermine the image of publisher as a gentleman, rather than a mere tradesman: the publisher Edward Marston, who was an active copyright campaigner, expanded upon his evidence before the Commission in a pamphlet, in which he stated that under such an 'unjust' scheme, publishers 'would be subjected to a miserable hole-and-corner warfare and the most unwholesome kind of underhand competition, such as no self-respecting publisher—no free-born Englishman—could submit to'.[75] Moreover, the publishers refused to admit that the production of cheap books should be an aim of copyright law. When Anthony Trollope asked William Longman, 'Have you considered whether the public is or is not entitled to extremely cheap editions of [Macaulay's] works?', he responded, 'I do not think the public are at all entitled to them'.[76]

A number of eminent academic authors appeared before the Commission and were also opposed to the scheme. The philosopher Herbert Spencer objected that the royalty scheme was not 'free trade' at all, but an 'artificial' cheapening of books. He preferred the 'natural' cheapening which would result from an increase in demand.[77] Professor Thomas Huxley, the distinguished Darwinian zoologist, also considered that authors should be left alone to make their own bargain with

[71] ibid xlviii.
[72] ibid xlviii.
[73] ibid xlviii–xlix.
[74] One exception was the publisher Thomas Boswell: Royal Copyright Commission 312.
[75] E Marston, *Copyright: National and International with Some Remarks on the Position of Authors and Publishers, by a Publisher* (London, Sampson Low, Marston, Searle & Rivington, 1887) 40–41.
[76] Royal Copyright Commission 20.
[77] ibid 282–83.

a publisher.[78] Another eminent scientist and proponent of Darwinism, Professor John Tyndall, also appeared before the Commission, and gave it as his opinion that the scheme would constitute a 'gross injustice' and 'might open a channel to interference of a still more serious and sweeping character, if the rights of an author over his hard-earned intellectual property were interfered with' in such a manner.[79]

Spencer further suggested that Macfie's proposal, as supported by Farrer, bore a greater similarity to Socialism or Communism than it did to free trade, noting: 'It is communistic practically; it is simply equalising the advantages of wealth and poverty'.[80] This accusation was picked up by Froude in an article he published commenting on the Commission, in which he asked

> Has the Board of Trade been converted to Socialism? Is it reverting to the exploded policy which punished 'regrating' and 'forestalling'? Is Government preparing again to fix the prices at which articles of necessary consumption are to be admitted to the market? . . . Are authors and publishers to be made use of to try the experiment of resuming the rejected methods of economic distribution? Why may not the author sell his wares at his own price like every other producer?[81]

The royalty debate therefore turned partly on different views of free trade principles, and their application to the law of copyright. It also involved contrasting views of the property right in issue. The authors before the Commission asserted that the rights of authors were natural rights. Professor Huxley stated:

> I should, however, be glad in the first place to express my belief that so far as a matter of right is concerned, if there be any foundation for rights of property, the right of an author in a book is as complete, and extends as far as the right of any person to any property whatever.[82]

These views were echoed by Professor Tyndall, who referred to the 'sacred right' of an author to his own intellectual work.[83]

Others took a different view. Sir Louis Mallet, as we have seen, characterised property as a function of scarcity and exchange value rather than the labour invested in the work, considering the latter 'a radical economic fallacy'.[84] Trevelyan, on the other hand, considered that all property was the 'creature of the law',[85] but that copyright was different from other property in that it was 'subject in a special manner to limitations having reference to the public interest'.[86] As Paul Saint-Amour has noted, this characterisation of property as subject to restric-

78 ibid 305.
79 ibid 314.
80 ibid 284.
81 JA Froude, 'Report of the Copyright Commission' (1878) 304 *Edinburgh Review* 295, 295–96.
82 Royal Copyright Commission 304.
83 ibid 316.
84 ibid xlviii.
85 ibid 7.
86 ibid.

tions based on public interest contradicted the plenary model of ownership favoured by the natural right proponents.[87]

The notion of copyright as a positive right created by legislation was shared by Edward Dicey, journalist and writer on the American Civil War. In an article commenting on the Commission's Report, Dicey contended that the 'fundamental error' of the disputants lay in their attempts to base their arguments on first principles.[88] Instead, he argued, property was created by law on the understanding that such property would not be used in a way detrimental to society.[89] Having noted that there was no abstract reason for copyright to exist at all, he conceded that it was 'most desirable, as a matter of expediency', and added:

> The object should be to give such protection as shall encourage individuals to give the toil and outlay requisite to the production of property, and at the same time to limit such protection sufficiently to secure this property, whatever its quality may be, being easily accessible to the general public.[90]

Matthew Arnold, poet, literary critic and Inspector of Schools, was in accord with Dicey. He exhorted: 'Let us beware of this metaphysical phantom of property in itself, which, like other metaphysical phantoms, is hollow and leads us to delusion. Property is the creation of the law'.[91] For Arnold, the instinct of ownership was a natural instinct but it was not a natural right, and society would comply with the instinct in a limited degree where there was some difficulty involved in giving effect to it.[92] Literary works were just such a case, because it was difficult to keep a work at one's own disposal and easy for others to appropriate it. Therefore, although the author's claim to some benefit of ownership was admitted, the ownership was limited in certain ways: copyright would not protect the spoken word and ideas, and it would last only for a set term of years.[93] Dicey and Arnold thus drew a middle course between those who asserted that copyright should be replaced by the royalty system and those who considered copyright to be a natural right of property based on labour.

Alongside the debate over the nature of the property right and the true aim of copyright law a subsidiary debate was occurring as to whether cheap books were, in fact, a benefit to society as a whole. The relationship between morality, books and society was still contentious. For the proponents of the royalty system, making books available to all classes of the community was considered an unalloyed social good. Trevelyan's faith in the educative power of books came across clearly in his evidence: 'I believe that the illiterate, semi-stolid character of our agricultural

[87] PK Saint-Amour, *The Copywrights: Intellectual Property and the Literary Imagination* (Ithaca, NY, Cornell University Press, 2003) 65.

[88] E Dicey, 'The Copyright Question' (1876) 19 *Fortnightly Review* 126, 126.

[89] ibid 128.

[90] ibid.

[91] Arnold, 'Copyright' 323.

[92] ibid.

[93] ibid 324–27.

labourers, and of the lower class of our work people in towns, is in considerable degree owing to the dearness and inaccessibility of books'.[94]

Objections, however, were made as to the quality of books which might be made available cheaply, particularly in light of the fact that the most expensive books were the three-decker novels. Sir James Fitzjames Stephen challenged Farrer as to whether the public had really been injured by not getting cheap copies of *Sketches by Boz* and *Pickwick Papers*, asking whether he considered 'that to cheapen all books indiscriminately as much as you possibly can is in itself a highly desirable object?' Farrer responded: 'Yes, I do; because on the whole we must trust to the public demand purifying itself; and reading almost any book is a better thing than most of the pleasures of our lower orders'.[95]

Froude, in his article on the Commission, took a similar attitude to Stephen, but with an even greater dose of patrician protectiveness towards the lower classes:

> Yet, in the name of education, a paternal government is called on to interfere, that the multitude may not be defrauded of their share in each prevailing and passing delirium. They must have each book as it comes out, or they are robbed of their spiritual nutriment . . . But that a paternal government should be expected to exert itself in such a cause is a new conception of its duties. The half-educated are the last to benefit by sensational imaginative literature . . . Better for the people, better for every one of us whose stomach is not seasoned by antidotes, to read books whose worth has been tested, than to devour every new dainty.[96]

Farrer contradicted this view in his article, arguing that it was the current system of copyright which produced so many poor-quality books:

> In fact the author, like the priest or the teacher whose place he is filling, ought to be above his audience. The tendency of the present commercial system is to degrade him to their level, and reward most munificently, not those who do the best service, but those who pander to the follies and vices of the greatest number.[97]

Arnold, unsurprisingly, also prized public education highly and, despite opposing the royalty scheme, was concerned by the high prices of books. He considered that in England there was a demand for cheaper books as well as dissatisfaction with the book trade and warned that if this were not recognised,

> there will be an explosion of discontent likely enough to sweep away copyright and to destroy the author's benefit from his work by reducing it to some such illusory benefit as that offered by the royalty plan of Mr Farrer.[98]

He added:

> As our nation grows more civilised, as a real love of reading comes to prevail more widely, the system which keeps up the present exorbitant prices of books in England, the

94 Royal Copyright Commission 8.
95 Royal Copyright Commission 262.
96 Froude, 'Report' 342–43.
97 TH Farrer, 'The Principle of Copyright' (1878) 24 *Fortnightly Review* 836, 845.
98 Arnold, 'Copyright' 327.

> system of lending libraries from which books are hired, will be seen to be, as it is, eccentric, artificial, and unsatisfactory in the highest degree.[99]

For Arnold, in fact, the real problem was not copyright law but the practices of the book trade in keeping prices high.

The Commission's Report, as previously noted, smoothed over the fundamental questions that had been raised over copyright's purpose and justification by recommending that the right 'continue to be treated by law as a proprietary right'.[100] Furthermore, it recommended that the duration of copyright be increased to the life of the author and 30 years thereafter,[101] and that this term be applied to all works which were the subject matter of protection, namely plays, lectures and works of fine art.[102] The extension of term had been supported by nearly all of the publishers and authors who appeared before the Commission, although they had differed as to the desired length. There was, however, some dissension among the Commissioners as to how the increase should operate.[103]

The Report of the Royal Copyright Commission seemed to present a united front on copyright law. However, on closer examination it is apparent that the underlying rationale of copyright law was heavily contested and its foundations fissured with cracks. Many of the Commissioners appended statements expressing reservations to the main Report, and Sir Louis Mallet dissented entirely. Although the royalty scheme was dismissed in half a page of the Report, it did not sink without a trace. In fact, the threat it presented to the view of copyright as a rational and just legal construct can be seen from the forcefulness of Scrutton and Birrell's subsequent rejections of it. In 1883, in a passage that owes a debt to Froude's article[104] and studiously ignores the majority view, Scrutton railed that:

> We have a commission, appointed by a Conservative Government and presided over by a Conservative Peer, recommending a form of legislation with regard to literary property which is denounced as the most pernicious communism when applied to land; and, while the measures of our earlier history concerning 'forestallers and regraters,' and fixing the price of bread and other material necessities, are considered as monuments of the obsolete errors of our less enlightened ancestors, we find the same commission in effect advising that the price of literary commodities should be fixed by the State.[105]

Sixteen years later, Birrell condemned it as a 'preposterous scheme, which reeks of our adorable "Civil Service"'.[106]

[99] ibid 327.

[100] Royal Copyright Commission ix.

[101] ibid xi.

[102] ibid xv, xvii, xviii.

[103] Sir Louis Mallet, with whom Sir Charles Young, Sir John Rose and Edward Jenkins agreed, recommended that the term be a fixed period from registration. Sir James Stephen considered that artworks should not be protected by copyright at all.

[104] See n 81 above.

[105] TE Scrutton, *The Laws of Copyright*, 1st edn (London, J Murray, 1883) 2.

[106] A Birrell, *Seven Lectures on the Law and History of Copyright in Books* (London, Cassell & Company Limited, 1899) 207.

Although little academic attention has been paid to the Commission,[107] it is significant as the site of considerable discursive activity regarding the justifications for copyright law, and the first real attack on their philosophic plausibility at the governmental level. It also gave rise to the first sustained economic criticism of copyright law, which sought to quantify or assess the objections to copyright based upon the public interest as opposed to relying on generalised assertions. However, neither the economic criticisms of copyright, nor the labour-based view of copyright as natural right was adopted wholeheartedly by the Commissioners in their final Report, which retreated to the vaguer proposition that 'we entertain no doubt that the interest of authors and the public alike requires that some specific provision should be afforded by legislation to owners of copyright'.[108]

C. Protection beyond the Printed Book: Lectures and Plays Again

The Report may have papered over the cracks in copyright's foundations, but they had not gone away. This can be clearly seen in the discussions that occurred before the Commission over the protection to be granted to artworks and works of architecture. Although engravings had been protected since the eighteenth century, copyright protection to paintings, drawing and photographs had only been granted in 1862.[109] Dissatisfaction with a number of aspects of artistic copyright were aired before the Commission, including the rules on copyright ownership after sale, the status of commissioned works, registration, subsequent uses of sketches and studies, and the desirability of consolidating all the statutes relating to artistic works into a single piece of legislation. The Royal Institute of British Architects argued strongly for copyright protection to apply to architecture, but the Commission's Report rejected their claims as 'impractical'.[110]

The witnesses appearing before the Commission also highlighted ongoing problems with the protection granted to lectures and dramatic and musical works. Lectures remained a contentious issue after the passing of the 1835 Lectures Act[111] because the protection related only to printing and not to redelivery, as well as being conditional upon the lecturer having given notice to two justices of the peace living within five miles of the place where the lecture were to be delivered.[112] In addition, exceptions operated in respect of universities, public schools and colleges and public foundations.[113] These limitations meant that the rights granted were frequently of little assistance to lecturers.

[107] One notable exception is Saint-Amour's excellent discussion in *The Copywrights* (above n 87) ch 2.
[108] Royal Copyright Commission ix.
[109] An Act for amending the Law relating to Copyright in Works of the Fine Arts, and for repressing the Commission of Fraud in the Production and Sale of such Works 1862 (25 & 26 Vict c 68).
[110] Royal Copyright Commission xxii. See also K Weatherall, 'Bringing Architecture into the Copyright System in the UK' (forthcoming).
[111] See above: ch 4, section I B.
[112] Lectures Act 1835 s 5.
[113] ibid.

Because lectures were delivered orally, they did not fit into the paradigm form of literary copyright, being protection of reproducing a physical entity, and thereby raised the question of whether the protection being sought related to ideas, or something more tangible. Professor Huxley was closely questioned on this point by the Commission:

> (Jenkins) But you admit that even if you give a lecture to a limited audience, your ideas are thereby distributed?
>
> (Huxley) I do not ask for any protection to ideas; it is the form of the thing that is mine.
>
> . . .
>
> (Jenkins) So that, really, to support the whole of your argument you would be obliged to fall back upon this: that a man has copyright in his ideas?
>
> (Huxley) No, in the form into which he puts them.[114]

Matthew Arnold dealt with this tension by refusing to accept the existence of a natural property right in literary creations, but he did not resolve it, likewise retreating to the argument that it would be impractical to protect ideas:

> There is no property, people often say, in ideas, in spoken words; and it is inferred that there ought to be no property in ideas and words when they are embodied in a book. But why is there no property in ideas and spoken words, while there is property in ideas and words when they come in a book? A brilliant talker may very well have the instinct of ownership in his good sayings, and all the more if he must and can only talk them and not write them. He might be glad of power to prevent the appropriation of them by other people, to fix the conditions on which alone the appropriation should be allowed, and to derive profit from allowing it. Society, again, may well feel sympathy with his instinct of ownership, and a disposition to assist and favour a production which gives it so much pleasure. But we are met by the difficulty, the insuperable difficulty, of giving effect to the producer's instinct of ownership in this case, of securing to him the disposal of his spoken ideas and words. Accordingly, effect is not given to it, and in such spoken ideas and words there is no property.[115]

The Commissioners were convinced by Huxley's arguments. Nevertheless, they wondered whether the public would accept such a property right, and how members of the public could be alerted to its existence. Farrer proposed as a solution that a notice be put up to warn the public that the lecture was claimed as property, adding that if the lecture was not published within a certain time the property right would cease.[116] These proposals attempted to replicate the registration requirement and to tie the protection to physical form. The Report of the Commissioners, however, recommended that the right to publish and redeliver a lecture be held by the lecturer and last for the same period as literary copyright, without the necessity of giving notice to two justices of the peace. At the same time, the Commissioners

[114] Royal Copyright Commission 306.
[115] Arnold, 'Copyright' 324.
[116] Royal Copyright Commission 161.

recognised the educational purpose of many lectures and recommended that exceptions continue to apply to lectures delivered in universities, as well as suggesting an exception to allow republication of lectures in newspapers.[117]

Dramatic and musical works proved to present even greater problems. The 1833 Dramatic Copyright Act appeared to bring dramatic authors and their assigns into the copyright fold, and its provisions were extended to apply to musical works in the 1842 Act.[118] However, the operation of these Acts was far from straightforward. One early question was how the new right was to be administered and enforced. In the case of printed books, there was physical evidence in existence to establish whether copyright was being observed, but a play was ephemeral, existing only at the time of its performance and leaving no trace once that was ended. A new body, the Dramatic Authors' Society, was set up to address this situation. Bulwer Lytton, who was responsible for the passing of the Dramatic Copyright Act, was a member, as were many of the other leading dramatists of the day, including JR Planché, Douglas Jerrold, James Sheridan Knowles, Edward Fitzball, Charles Dance and Richard Brinsley Peake.[119] The Society's main aim was to facilitate the dealings of dramatic authors with the provincial theatres. The usual practice in London was for dramatists to grant a theatre the right to perform a play for a certain amount of time, or forever, but it was far harder for the dramatists to deal with the theatres outside the capital. Giving evidence before a Select Committee on theatrical licences in 1866, the Society's then secretary, Joseph Stirling Coyle, explained that the Society had been established at the suggestion and wish of the provincial managers themselves.[120] Doubt is cast on this, however, by Planché's recollection that the managers raised an outcry at the Bill's introduction.[121]

The system operated by the Society changed several times throughout its fifty year life span. In the 1830s, the Society asked provincial managers to send a list of the plays they had performed, which were charged on a fixed scale according to how many acts the play had and the size and location of the theatre performing it.[122] This system of uniform pricing, however, was undermined by the preferential treatment given to Sheridan Knowles, the most famous playwright of the day. Sheridan Knowles was allowed to set prohibitively high prices for his plays, his objective being to earn greater profits by acting in them himself. By the 1840s, managers could negotiate with individual dramatists for reduced rates and in the Society's list of 1840 many plays appeared at different prices to the standard ones. By 1866, the system had changed yet again and, instead of provincial managers

[117] ibid xvii.

[118] Copyright Act 1842 s 20.

[119] JR Stevens, *Profession of the Playwright* 175; D Barratt, 'The Dramatic Authors' Society (1833–1883) and the Payment of English Dramatists' (1988) 7 *Essays in English Theatre* 19, 21–22.

[120] Select Committee to inquire into Working of Acts for Licensing and Regulating of Theatres and Places of Public Entertainment (1866) 373, 209–10.

[121] JR Planché, *The Reflections and Recollections of JR Planché*, 2 vols (London, Tinsley Brothers, 1872) vol 1, p 202.

[122] Barratt, 'Dramatic Authors' Society' 21.

submitting periodical lists of plays they had performed, they were required to pay a certain sum of money based upon the size of the theatre, and other factors, in return for which they could put on any play on the Society's list.[123] The London managers, however, continued to make arrangements on an individual basis.[124]

By the 1860s, however, the Society began to be affected by the growing status and prosperity of dramatic authors; ironically, the very change it had sought to achieve. A number of leading dramatists, such as Dion Boucicault, Francis Burnand, TW Robertson and WS Gilbert, all left the Society, as they could obtain better remuneration by negotiating individual prices with managers. In response, the Society revised its rules by allowing members to retain rights in popular plays for a certain period before they would enter the Society's list.[125]

Unfortunately, not all the parties involved understood the operations of the Society. One such example can be seen in a case that Planché brought against Hooper, the lessee of the Theatre Royal at Bath, for representing his play, 'White Cat', without permission. Counsel for Hooper argued that if he had committed an offence it was unintentional, and claimed that Hooper had 'been drawn into this present very disagreeable situation without any fault of his own by the conduct of the Society of Dramatic Authors'.[126] Apparently, Hooper had been under the impression that as long as he sent a monthly file of the plays performed to the Society he was entitled to represent a play even without the author's consent. The Court, however, instructed the jury that if they were satisfied that 'White Cat' was a dramatic entertainment, that Planché was the author, and the play was performed without his consent, then they must find for the plaintiff, which they accordingly did. The Dramatic Authors' Society was itself hampered by its inability to bring prosecutions to recover penalties. Simpson complained about this also before the Royal Copyright Commission, noting that the Society's application to register under the Friendly Societies Act 1875, which would allow them to sue as a body, had been rejected by the Treasury on the grounds that the Society's purposes appeared to amount to a restraint of trade.[127]

Another obstacle lay in the fact that the Act had not completely clarified the law on performances of dramatic works. Indeed, it had added new uncertainties. What was meant by a 'dramatic piece' and a 'place of dramatic entertainment'? What counted as a 'representation'? The latter question was tested in court by Planché, who brought an action against the manager John Braham. Braham had commissioned the libretto to Weber's opera *Oberon*, but the commissioned version used many of the same words that Planché had used in his libretto of the same piece, which had been performed at Covent Garden with Braham in the principal role. Tindal CJ held that the word 'represent' must be taken to mean 'the bringing forward on stage or place of dramatic representation' and included the singing

[123] ibid 21–24.

[124] Royal Copyright Commission 120.

[125] Barratt, 'Dramatic Authors' Society' 26–29; JR Stevens, *Profession of the Playwright* 179–80.

[126] *Planché v Hooper* (1844), *The Times* (19 January 1844) 7c.

[127] Royal Copyright Commission 121–22.

of one or more songs from a theatrical piece.[128] Planché was ashamed to have used the Dramatic Copyright Act against a respected colleague and referred to the incident as 'one of the most disagreeable recollections of my professional life'.[129] His excuse was that he was acting at the behest of the proprietors of Covent Garden.[130]

The question of what amounted to a 'dramatic piece' was considered in *Lee v Simpson*[131] and the Court held that the introduction to a pantomime easily fell within the meaning of the statute, despite not being mentioned specifically in the Act. More difficult issues arose in respect of musical works, which will be discussed below. The question of what was meant by 'place of dramatic entertainment' occupied the courts on several occasions. In *Russell v Smith*,[132] Lord Denman CJ held that a lecture room, Crosby Hall, became a place of dramatic entertainment for the purposes of the Act when it was used for the public representation for profit of a dramatic piece.[133]

Yet another problematic issue was the responsibility of the landlord, or manager, for such unauthorised performances. This was held to turn on the question of knowledge, or *mens rea*. In *Lee v Simpson*, the defendant argued that he had purchased the play in the bona fide belief that he was purchasing it from the author, which was not in fact the case. Wilde CJ held that the knowledge of the person actually representing the dramatic work as to ownership was irrelevant, because 'the object of the legislature was to protect authors against the piratical invasion of their rights'[134] and the statute would altogether fail in this object if it were necessary to show that the defendant had knowledge of the plaintiff's right of property.[135] However, in *Russell v Briant*, the same judge held that the landlord of the Horn Tavern in Kennington could not be held liable for the unauthorised performance of a dramatic piece, despite the fact that he had provided the venue, advertising and allowed tickets to be sold from the bar, on the basis that 'no one can be considered as an offender against the provisions of [the statute] . . . unless, by himself or his agent, he actually takes part in a representation which is a viola-

[128] *Planché v Braham* (1837) 2 Car & P 68, 74.
[129] Planché, *Reflections*, vol 1, p 272.
[130] ibid pp 270–71.
[131] *Lee v Simpson* (1847) 3 CB 871.
[132] *Russell v Smith* [1848] 2 QB 217.
[133] In *Wall v Taylor*; *Wall v Martin* (1882–23) 11 QBD 102 (see below at n 245 for more detail) Brett MR held that 'performing a dramatic piece makes the place where it is performed a place of dramatic entertainment' (at 108). He amended this view the following year, however, in *Duck v Bates* (1883–34) 13 QBD 843 which arose when an amateur dramatic club put on a free performance for the staff of St Guy's Hospital of a play called *Our Boys*. Brett MR stated that he may have been interpreted as going too far in the earlier case, as the statute clearly contemplated that there may be some place at which a piece is performed which would not breach the statute. He went on to find that domestic and private performances would not fall within the Act. It was necessary that the representation be 'public' by which was meant 'a representation to which any portion of the public are freely admitted with or without payment' (848).
[134] (1847) 3 CB 871, 883.
[135] ibid.

tion of copyright'.[136] By contrast, in the case of *Marsh v Conquest*,[137] the manager of a theatre who had no involvement in the performance of a play was found to be liable because he was the owner of the theatre and his son, who was in charge of the representation, was acting with his permission.

For the Dramatic Authors' Society an important related problem was non-compliance by the provincial managers, who had been accustomed to performing plays without payment and either avoided or did not understand the new system. Particularly problematic were travelling companies. In 1866, Stirling Coyle complained before the Select Committee of 'certain managers, disreputable and dishonest men, who go about from theatre to theatre, and do not pay'.[138] The same concerns were reiterated before the 1878 Copyright Commission by the current secretary, John Palgrave Simpson.[139] Both men complained that the means of recovering the penalties against such managers through the bringing of proceedings at common law was frequently ineffective, as well as expensive. The petition presented by Simpson also complained that the remedy of 40s was wholly inadequate to ensure compliance with the Act.[140]

Still more fundamental and confusing was the relationship between the copyright in the printed work and the right to perform that work. Once again, Planché was involved in dealing with this issue. However, this time he was defendant to an action brought by the publisher John Cumberland.[141] In 1828, Planché had made an assignment to Cumberland of 'all right, title and interest whatsoever in the copyright' of his farce *The Greeneyed Monster*. Prior to this assignment, Planché had granted the right to represent the piece to the Haymarket theatre and, after the passing of the Dramatic Copyright Act, Planché had allowed another theatre to perform the piece. Cumberland, however, claimed that Planché's assignment of the copyright to him meant that it was now Cumberland who had the sole liberty of representing the farce (subject to any rights of the Haymarket theatre), thereby making Planché's purported assignment an infringement of his right.

Cumberland retained Frederick Pollock as counsel, and he argued that Planché's assignment to Cumberland placed him in the same position as if he had been the author, following the Dramatic Copyright Act. Sir James Scarlett argued for Planché that the Act created a new right and could not have been assigned away by the defendant before he possessed it. He contended that the intention of the legislature was to encourage genius, and that any new privileges created must therefore have been intended to be conferred upon the author. Pollock countered that the Act's object was the protection of literary property and so an assignment of copyright must perforce carry with it the right of representation. Lord Denman

[136] *Russell v Briant* (1849) 8 CB 836 at 848. See also *Lyon v Knowles* (1863) 3 B & S 556; (1864) 5 B & S 751.

[137] *Marsh v Conquest* (1864) 17 CB (NS) 418.

[138] Select Committee to inquire into Working of Acts for Licensing and Regulating of Theatres and Places of Public Entertainment (1866) 373, 209.

[139] Royal Copyright Commission 121.

[140] ibid App VIII, 354.

[141] *Cumberland v Planché* (1834) 1 Ad & E 580; SC 3 N & M 537; LJ 3 KB 194.

CJ accepted Pollock's argument that the intention of the Act was to protect literary property and therefore an assignment of the copyright must carry with it the right of representation. He noted that this would not injure future authors, as they would merely sell their rights for a higher price.[142] This outcome was much resented by dramatic authors. In his autobiography, Edward Fitzball recalled:

> The act passed by parliament, in favour of dramatic authors, at this time, the better to allow them to meet with remuneration equal to their labour, proved highly beneficial to me; and would have been more so, had I not previously disposed of so many of my copyrights, to Mr Cumberland, who claimed upon his assignment the new privilege of nightly remuneration for dramatic pieces acted, either in town or country. This event, of course, was never contemplated by the legislature, whose intention was simply to assist literary (and too frequently necessitous) men, not publishers. However, the case was tried with Cumberland by the Authors' Society, and the judge gave it in favour of the forms. (Law but not justice).[143]

The unsatisfactory situation was amended by the 1842 Copyright Act which explicitly provided that assignment of the copyright of a book containing a dramatic piece or musical composition would not convey the right to represent that work unless entry was made in the Registry Book expressing the intention that the right of representation was conveyed.[144] That this provision acted to prevent an assignment of copyright from automatically conveying the right of representation, or acting, or stage right (as it was sometimes called), was confirmed in the cases of *Lacy v Rhys*[145] and *Marsh v Conquest*.[146]

The ongoing confusion over the relationship between the right of representation and printed copyright provided a continuing incentive for dramatic authors not to publish their plays. However, the status of unpublished works was even less clear. In 1865, Stirling Coyne brought an action against the publisher Maxwell for publishing and selling copies of Coyne's play, *The Woman in Red*.[147] Coyne had never published his works and alleged that he had a common law property in his play. The defendant argued that by giving copies of the play to the actors, Coyne had published the work and therefore, as he had not registered it, there was no copyright in it for Maxwell to infringe. Cockburn CJ appeared convinced by Coyne's argument that there was a common law right, but directed him to state the facts in the form of a special case to raise the question for the opinion of the Court.[148] In the event, it seems such a case was never brought.

It is clear that the relationship between copyright and the right of representation was not well understood in the theatrical world. However, it was not just publishers, dramatists and theatre managers who were confused. In the Digest of

142 *Cumberland v Planché* (1834) 1 Ad & E 580, 583–86.

143 E Fitzball, *Thirty-five Years of a Dramatic Authors' Life*, 2 vols (London, TC Newby, 1859) vol 1, pp 271–72.

144 Copyright Act 1842 s 22.

145 *Lacy v Rhys* (1864) 4 B & S 873.

146 *Marsh v Conquest* (1864) 17 CB (NS) 418. See also *Lacy v Toole* (1867) *The Times* (29 April 1867) 11c.

147 *Coyne v Maxwell* (1865), *The Times* (7 June 1865) 11a; *The Times* (10 June 1865) 11a.

148 *The Times* (10 June 1865) 11a.

Copyright Law which Sir James Fitzjames Stephen had prepared prior to the 1878 Commission and which was annexed to the Report, Stephen stated, 'The exclusive right of representing or performing a dramatic piece or musical composition cannot be gained if such dramatic piece or musical composition has been printed and published as a book before the first representation thereof'. He added: 'A dramatic piece or musical composition published as a book may (it seems probable) be publicly represented without the consent of the author or his assigns'.[149]

This was an odd interpretation of section 1 of the 1833 Dramatic Copyright Act which, after providing that the author of an unpublished work should have the sole liberty of representing it, extended the same liberty to 'the Author of any such Production, printed and published within Ten Years before the passing of this Act by the Author thereof or his Assignee, or which shall hereafter be so printed and published'.[150] Moreover Stephen's view was not shared by Lord Denman who, in the unreported case of *Morton v Shelders the Elder*, held that even though the plaintiff's play had been printed by the Dramatic Authors' Society, the plaintiff had not lost his right to consent to its performance.[151]

If the lawyers were unable to agree on the meaning of the statute, what chance did the general public stand, particularly given its operation was far from intuitive? Simpson explained his understanding of the law before the Commission to be that a club or society was liable to pay fees to the copyright owner for putting on an amateur dramatic performance even if they had not charged entry money, that there was no requirement to pay fees in cases where one man recited long passages from a play, but if two men recited passages together, even without costumes or scenery, they were liable to pay fees. If songs were also sung, composers could charge fees or claim the penalty.[152] Such subtle distinctions in the statutes' operation were not obvious and it is clear from the number of complaints and the amount of litigation generated that those involved were tripped up time and again.

The situation was still more complex in relation to musical works, which spawned controversies of their own. Although, as mentioned above, the 1842 Copyright Act extended the operation of the 1833 Dramatic Copyright Act to cover 'musical compositions', there remained uncertainty as to whether all music, or just certain types of song, would be covered. In *Russell v Smith*,[153] which involved

[149] Royal Copyright Commission lxxiii–lxxiv.

[150] Dramatic Copyright Act 1833 s 1.

[151] *Morton v Shelders the Elder* (1838) *The Times* (1 December 1838) 6d. Presumably, the distinction between this case and the earlier decision of *Cumberland v Planché* was that in the former case there had been an assignment of copyright and none such was in evidence here. The issue was also considered in *Chappell v Boosey* (1882) 21 Ch D 232 a case brought by Chappell against Boosey relating to the singing of a song in which Chappell owned the copyright, North J rejected Chappell's argument which relied on the statement of law in Stephen's *Digest*, stating he was unable to agree with that assessment of the law, and that it ignored the provisions of the 1833 Dramatic Copyright Act and the 1842 Copyright Act. Stephen's view was also not shared by Scrutton in his treatise on copyright law: Scrutton, *Laws of Copyright*, 1st edn, 134–35.

[152] Royal Copyright Commission 125. This interpretation seems to be largely based on *Russell v Smith* (1848) 12 QB 217. No reported cases held that it was irrelevant whether or not an entry fee was charged until 1883; see above: n 133.

[153] (1848) 12 QB 217.

the singing of a song called 'The Ship on Fire' in a lecture hall, the defendant argued that the only musical compositions intended to be protected were those composed for performance with dramatic pieces. Unfortunately, the Court did not decide on the point, as Lord Denman CJ found that the song in question was a dramatic piece because it had a dramatic subject matter and was sung with great expression. He held that the words 'dramatic piece' should be interpreted widely as any piece which 'would produce the emotions which are the purpose of the regular drama, and which constitute the entertainment of the audience'.[154]

Most music publishers were firmly of the view that only songs used in conjunction with dramatic works, or performed in theatres, music halls or as parts of operas were subject to the statutory penalties. Before the Royal Copyright Commission, John Boosey and Henry Littleton, of Novello's, argued that this was the case.[155] The composer, Arthur Sullivan was similarly of the view that the current law held that only songs sung as 'dramatic works' could be protected.[156] Thomas Chappell, however, was less sure, stating that although there had been no case on the matter, he believed that the singing of a song separately from an opera or dramatic piece would also be subject to the statute.[157]

The position of unpublished musical compositions was also unclear and, when it came before the Court, sparked debate as to whether music should be protected at all. In the case of *Clark v Bishop*,[158] the plaintiff, a comic vocalist, had purchased a song from a composer, Elton. He sang it in music halls, after which it became very popular, but he never published it. The defendant, Bishop, printed and published the song in a 1d book of songs, whereupon the plaintiff brought an action, alleging that the song was now valueless to him. On appeal, Martin B asked the plaintiff whether he relied on the common law or the statute, to which he responded that he relied on both. With respect to the common law right, he referred to *Millar v Taylor* and *Donaldson v Becket* as deciding that a right in unpublished works existed at common law. With respect to the statutes, he argued that the 1842 Copyright Act did not require registration of songs. The re-emergence of the common law right at this juncture is of interest and the plaintiff may have been influenced by the apparent success of the argument in *Coyne v Maxwell*.[159]

Kemp, who was counsel for the defendant, submitted that the song could not be protected by the 1842 Act, which was intended 'to afford greater encouragement to the production of literary works *of lasting benefit to the world*', adding, 'that cannot apply to such a wretchedly worthless production as the vulgar doggerel which is the subject of the present action'.[160] He argued that there was no infringement, because by singing the song, the plaintiff had given it to the public:

[154] ibid 236.
[155] Royal Copyright Commission 102, 118.
[156] ibid 114.
[157] ibid 109.
[158] *Clark v Bishop* (1872) 25 LT (NS) 908.
[159] See above: text to n 147.
[160] *Clark v Bishop* (1872) 25 LT (NS) 908, 910.

> It is similar to a speech by a demagogue at Blackheath or Primrose-Hill, or by a member of Parliament to his constituents; once uttered, it is published to the whole world, and it is no infringement in a newspaper to print it.[161]

Kemp relied on Pollock CB's opinion in *Jefferys v Boosey* that allowing copyright in non-physical objects could be easily taken too far. In that case, the Chief Baron had asked, rhetorically:

> And where is it, on principle, to stop? Why is it not to apply to a well-told anecdote or witty reply, so as to forbid the repetition without the permission of the author? And carried to its utmost extent, it would at length descend to lower and meaner objects, and include the tricks of a conjuror or the grimace of a clown.[162]

Kemp concluded by arguing that the mere singing of the song amounted to publication and because the song was unregistered there could be no action for infringement.

Martin B, dissenting, accepted the defendant's case, noting in the course of argument, 'A man writes a song and sings it in public, and another takes down the words and publishes it. It is new to me if that is actionable'.[163] In his judgment he added that there could be no infringement because printing the words of the song would only increase its reputation and popularity.[164] The rest of the Court, however, agreed with Kelly CB, who held that the singing of a song did amount to publication,[165] but that the song fell within the category of 'dramatic piece' and did not therefore require registration under the 1842 Copyright Act.[166] The judges refused to consider the common law question as it had only been raised in argument before them and was not raised at trial. They did not reject it out of hand, however, and its reappearance shows the enduring legacy of the eighteenth-century debates and the Lords' failure, in *Donaldson v Becket*, to address the issue of unpublished works.[167]

The music publishers' poor understanding of the right of representation was reflected in their contractual arrangements with composers. Chappell described how he had foreseen 15 years earlier that there might be a problem with the right of representation and began including an assignment of the performing right in his contracts. However, he noted that not all publishers had been so wise, noting 'Mr Boosey, who is a very clever man of business, and has as large a business as anybody, has not done so'.[168] Arthur Sullivan gave evidence that the performing right

161 ibid.
162 ibid 911.
163 ibid 910.
164 ibid 911.
165 The Court of Appeal similarly held in *Boucicault v Chatterton* (1877) 5 Ch D 267, following *Boucicault v Delafield* (1864) 33 LJ (NS) 38, that performance amounted to publication. In both cases, Dion Boucicault had first represented (but not printed) his plays in the United States of America but the operation of the International Copyright Act 1844 (7 Vict c 12) s 19) meant that works first published overseas could not be protected by copyright within the United Kingdom.
166 *Clark v Bishop* (1872) 25 LT (NS) 908, 911.
167 See above: ch 2, section IV.
168 Royal Copyright Commission 106.

had never been included in any of his publishing contracts[169] and the Rev Bennett referred to a conversation he had had with an employee of Novello's that they did not know which songs they owned the performing rights to.[170] When Littleton, of the same firm, was asked about the difficulties of assignments, he admitted 'I have that book on Copyright by Copinger but it is very difficult to follow it'.[171]

One person who had quickly understood the opportunities offered by the Dramatic Copyright Act and its extension to music in 1842 was the infamous Harry Wall, who set up a business which he called the Authors', Composers' and Artists' Copyright Protection Office, based upon the statutory penalties provided for in the 1833 and 1842 Acts. Wall's business consisted of collecting fees for unauthorised performances of songs, often by deceased composers whose assigns had given Wall power of attorney.[172] Thus, he takes his place in history as the world's first 'copyright troll'.[173]

The musical world was outraged by Wall's effrontery at exploiting the statutory penalties. From 1876, complaints about his activities appeared in the musical press. The first to complain was a T Backhouse who had received a letter from Wall demanding £2 after he held a concert at which one of the singers sang a song by Wallace.[174] The music publishers raised the matter before the Royal Copyright Commission. Thomas Chappell said he had refused to deal with Wall when approached because he 'did not like the character of the man or the character of the proceedings',[175] later adding that such things were done by 'people who do not care anything for the work or anything else, all they want is the money they can get'.[176] John Boosey said that 'no living composer cared to employ' him[177] and Anthony Trollope spoke of a 'mercenary, vulgar, and I may say, immoral person'.[178] Evidence was also given that ladies would be discouraged from singing songs in public for fear of receiving letters from agents such as Wall demanding money.[179] Wall was clearly of a class with which the publishers did not care to mix.[180]

Moreover, the composers and music publishers were not convinced that charging money for performances was to their advantage. Only two composers were

[169] ibid 114.

[170] ibid 116.

[171] Royal Copyright Commission, 119. The issue was litigated in *Re the Songs 'Kathleen Mavourneen' and 'Dermot Astore' ex parte Hutchins & Romer* [1878] LR 4 QB 90; [1878–79] LR 4 QB 483. The Court of Appeal found that *Cumberland v Planché* was no longer good law, but that the particular words used by the composer had been expansive enough to pass the right of representation as well as the copyright.

[172] Royal Copyright Commission 101, 105–06.

[173] I am indebted to Lionel Bently for this apposite description of Wall's activities.

[174] *Musical Times* (1 February 1876) 371. See also *Musical Times* (1 March 1876) 394–95, (1 May 1876) 471.

[175] Royal Copyright Commission 106.

[176] ibid 109.

[177] ibid 101.

[178] ibid 194.

[179] ibid 115.

[180] Born Henry Whiting, Wall had a criminal record, having been imprisoned in 1860 for eighteen months after being found guilty of unlawfully receiving property obtained under false pretences: *Old Bailey Proceedings Online*, May 1860, trial of Henry Whiting (t18600507–491) www.oldbaileyonline.

members of the Dramatic Authors' Society in 1876, and they had requested the Society not to enforce the penalties for the singing of single songs, but only in respect of selections from operas.[181] The market for composers and their publishers revolved around sales of sheet music. The music publisher John Boosey gave evidence that the collection of fees would interfere with a composer's profits, as performance was what made music popular and stimulated sales.[182] Charles Purday likewise thought that composers should be glad to have songs sung, to make them known, and that this was also the best arrangement for publishers.[183] The composer Arthur Sullivan suggested that there should be a small fee, which in most cases composers would not collect, and no penalty for non-payment. Again, he based his views on his belief that the sale of a work depended on the popularity it acquired through performance.[184] While Sullivan supported extending the right to collect such a small fee in respect of more than just 'dramatic performances', for him the real value would lie in obtaining the power to stop his songs being sung in undesirable contexts, such as burlesques, in the street or by people with bad voices.[185] The difference between the attitudes of music composers and publishers towards the right of performance and those of dramatic authors can probably be ascribed to the strength of the market for sheet music when compared to the comparatively weak market for printed dramatic works for much of the nineteenth century.[186]

The amount of money that ought to be collected for unauthorised performances was also contentious. The 1833 Act, it may be recalled, provided that every offender would be liable for not less than 40s for each representation.[187] Thomas Chappell pointed out that while this might be a reasonable sum for an opera, it was excessive for the singing of a single, or even several, songs on their own. In his view, 1s would be more appropriate.[188] This related to another objection made to Wall's mode of doing business. Rather than acting as soon as he discovered a song he owned, or for which he was the agent, was being performed, he would wait until the performance had run on for many nights, and then collect a much larger sum in respect of each performance.[189]

Related to this ongoing confusion about the different rights was a further concern. Even if the general public could be educated to accept that purchasing a printed copy of a play or piece of music did not automatically bring with it the right to perform it, how would they know to whom they should apply for

[181] Royal Copyright Commission 122, 125.
[182] ibid 102. See also the evidence of T Chappell, ibid 106.
[183] ibid 193.
[184] ibid 113.
[185] ibid 113–14.
[186] See JR Stevens, *Profession of the Playwright*, ch 5; MR Booth, 'Public Taste, the Playwright and the Law', in C Leech and TW Craik (eds), *The Revels History of Drama in English*, vol 6, (London, Methuen & Co, 1975) 52.
[187] Dramatic Copyright Act 1833 s 2.
[188] Royal Copyright Commission, 106–07.
[189] ibid 106.

permission? This question was raised before the 1878 Copyright Commission by several witnesses.[190]

Faced with these many difficulties, the Copyright Commissioners were brief in their Report on dramatic and musical works. They stated that 'in order to avoid the disunion between the literary and performing rights in musical compositions and dramatic pieces, that the printed publication of such works should give dramatic or performing rights, and that public performance should give literary copyright'.[191] The Commissioners, however, responded more strongly to the objection that it was impossible for a member of the public to know to whom they should apply for permission to perform a work. The Report recommended that 'every musical composition should bear on its title page a note stating whether the right of public performance is reserved, and the name and address of the person to whom application for performance should be made'.[192] Furthermore, it recommended that instead of the penalty being automatically assessed at 40s, the courts should award compensation by reference to the damages sustained.

Those who appeared to give evidence before the Royal Copyright Commission in relation to lectures and dramatic works were largely concerned with strengthening the ownership claims of lecturers, dramatists, composers and publishers. However, public interest considerations were also aired in various guises. One issue that arose in relation to both kinds of work was the question of how the public would be able to find out what it was allowed to do with the works—whether they could redeliver a lecture, publish an account in a newspaper, recite lines from a play, sing a song for friends and so on. The 'public' in such matters was made up of actors and singers (both amateur and professional) and theatre manaters, rather than the more passive 'reading public'. Although there remained at one end of the spectrum those who were sceptical as to whether copyright should subsist in such works at all, most of the other groups, whether classed as 'owners', 'public' or 'users', could agree that greater clarity in the law would benefit everyone.

D. Registration and Deposit

Registration was another of the aspects of copyright law with which the Association for the Protection of the Rights of Authors had expressed dissatisfaction during their meeting with Disraeli. This was to a large extent a practical issue, as many witnesses were unhappy with the procedures and staff of Stationers' Hall. Palgrave Simpson told the Commissioners that Stationers' Hall was 'in the most chaotic and ignorant state of any institution in England'.[193] However, registration also raised public interest issues through its function of providing evidence of copyright existence and ownership. In his evidence, Thomas Farrer noted that

190 ibid 116 (Rev JW Bennett); 119 (Henry Littleton).
191 ibid xvi.
192 ibid xxviii.
193 ibid 123.

registration of books was not so useful as in the case of stocks, shares, ships and lands, as it did not provide conclusive proof of ownership. Further, as it would be impossible for two people to write the same book, any person copying a book must know he is copying. The advantages Farrer identified were that registration provided notice of copyright to the world, fixed a publication date from which protection could run, and had the potential to provide evidence of transfer of ownership. However, Farrer conceded that these advantages were not sufficient to justify continuing with the present system unless it could be simplified and made compulsory. In addition, he recommended that it be combined with a single deposit of a copy of a book at the British Museum.[194]

Having heard evidence on deposit from numerous witnesses, the Commissioners noted that registration presented one of the most striking instances of the anomalies in copyright law, and considered that the present system was 'practically useless, if not deceptive'.[195] They noted Farrer's objections, as well as the fact that an owner can prove his right by extrinsic evidence just as well as by registration.[196] However, on the other hand, they accepted that a number of witnesses considered registration to be a useful system of giving visible evidence of existence to incorporeal property. They also noted the public utility in being able to ascertain to whom certain books belonged and whether copyright existed in a book.[197]

In the end, the Commissioners appeared convinced by the latter arguments, as they recommended continuing registration but reforming it in a number of significant ways. First, they suggested combining the two acts of deposit and registration by making registration complete on depositing a copy of the relevant book at the British Museum.[198] Second, they recommended making registration compulsory. However, they stopped short of recommending that registration on the date of publication should be a condition of an effective copyright, choosing instead that a copyright owner should not be entitled to maintain proceedings until registration. In addition, he should not be able to recover in respect of any acts of piracy that preceded registration.[199]

A number of publishers appeared before the Committee to complain about the legal deposit requirements. As William Longman reported, the publishers still considered it to be 'a great hardship, and an unnecessary hardship, and . . . a mischievous hardship'.[200] Daldy suggested combining registration and deposit through depositing a single copy at the British Museum, and being provided with a receipt as evidence of registration.[201] Many publishers were still failing to deposit books in the various libraries and the witnesses from the British Museum revealed that the Museum had taken proceedings to enforce penalties for non-delivery in

194 ibid 151.
195 ibid xxii–xxiii.
196 ibid xxiii.
197 ibid xxiii.
198 ibid xxiv.
199 ibid xxv–xxvi.
200 ibid 21. See also 11 (E Marston), 33 (SG Turner), 196 (CH Purday).
201 ibid 50.

158 cases since May 1850.[202] No witnesses appeared from any of the university libraries, and when Farrer was questioned on whether he thought the libraries of Cambridge and Oxford would agree with his view that deposit should be abolished, he argued they were quite rich enough to buy the books they wanted.[203]

With respect to legal deposit, the Commissioners were sympathetic to the claims of witnesses that deposit to five separate libraries represented a 'heavy and unjust tax'. Only the British Museum had given evidence, and had pointed out that their collections were of considerable use to the public. The Commissioners recommended that the provisions relating to deposit at all libraries other than the British Museum be repealed.[204] Without the university libraries present to argue their case in terms of the public service they provided, the claims of copyright owners proved the more persuasive.

E. International and Colonial Copyright

Another significant aspect of the Commission's inquiries had related to international issues. As noted above, the lack of copyright control over the colonies and the United States had been the main concern of the Association for the Protection of Authors, whose deputation had pushed for the Commission's establishment. As mentioned above, another major issue for British publishers during the first part of the century was the growing number of foreign reprints which appeared on the British market, undercutting local prices.[205]

In the second half of the century, copyright in Europe became caught up in a complex web of bilateral agreements. France had protected the copyright of all works which were published in France, including those by foreigners, since 1793.[206] In 1852, a decree was passed which fully recognised the rights of foreign authors on the same basis as French authors, even for works published in other countries.[207] This universalist approach was far from matched by Great Britain which, from 1844, protected only those works published in countries other than Britain with which it had concluded treaties, and which gave the same protection to British authors.[208] As noted in chapter four, Britain concluded a convention with France in 1851[209] and this treaty provided protection for French authors against translations of their works published in the British dominions for a period

[202] ibid 83.

[203] ibid 154.

[204] ibid xxvii.

[205] For more detail on all that is discussed below regarding European copyright, see Seville, *Internationalisation*, esp ch 3.

[206] French Literary and Artistic Copyright Act 1793 art 1, see L Bently and M Kretschmer (eds), *Primary Sources on Copyright (1450–1900)* www.copyrighthistory.org.

[207] French International Copyright Act 1853, see L Bently and M Kretschmer (eds), *Primary Sources on Copyright (1450–1900)* www.copyrighthistory.org.

[208] An Act to amend the Law relating to International Copyright (1844) See above: ch 4, n 160.

[209] See above: ch 4, n 206.

of not more than five years after the first publication.[210] In order to gain such protection, the translation had to appear in part within a year and in full within three years.[211] Similar provision was made for dramatic authors, but the period in which a translation had to be produced in order to gain protection was reduced to three months.[212] The 1844 International Copyright Act had, however, explicitly excluded translations from its provisions and in 1852 a further Act was passed to bring the French treaty into effect.[213]

The French, however, remained dissatisfied with the requirement that French authors had to deposit and register their books before they could take advantage of British copyright law, as well as the protection given to translations and dramatic works. Charles Gavard from the French Embassy appeared before the Commission to complain about these matters.[214] The Commission's Report recommended that the requirement for registration in Britain be abandoned, and that production of a copy of the foreign register should be treated in legal proceedings as prima facie evidence of title.[215]

Colonial copyright raised different issues.[216] The 1842 Copyright Act applied throughout the British Dominions, meaning that no books published in Britain could be printed in the colonies. However, prices for such books were beyond what the colonists could afford and they were compelled to wait until cheap editions were printed and exported. As they had been accustomed to cheap American reprints of British works, this was an extremely unpopular measure and nowhere more so than in Canada whose proximity to the United States had hitherto allowed books to enter the country faster and more cheaply than those shipped from Britain. In 1845, the Novia Scotia House of Assembly wrote to Her Majesty, claiming that the Imperial copyright laws had 'a most injurious effect in British North America the circulation and influence of modern English literature, in affecting the tone of sound feeling, and impeding the advancement and refinement of the provincial mind'.[217] In an attempt to address these concerns, the Foreign Reprints Act[218] was passed in 1847. It suspended the 1842 Act to the extent that it allowed the colonies to import foreign reprints (usually from America), on condition that they 'made due provision for securing or protecting the rights of British

[210] Convention between Her Majesty and the French Republic for the Establishment of International Copyright (signed 3 November 1851, Paris) art 3.

[211] ibid art 3.3.

[212] ibid art 4.

[213] An Act to enable Her Majesty to carry into effect a Convention with France on the Subject of Copyright; to extend and explain the International Copyright Acts; and to explain the Acts relating to Copyright in Engravings 1852 (15 Vict c 12) ss 2, 8.

[214] Royal Copyright Commission, 86 ff, 95 ff, 190 ff. This is discussed in more detail in ch 6 below.

[215] ibid xl. For the Commission's recommendations on translations, see below: ch 6, text to nn 535 ff.

[216] For more on colonial copyright, see Seville, *Internationalisation*, esp ch 4.

[217] Copies or Extracts of Correspondence between the Colonial Office, the Board of Trade, and the Government of Canada (1872) 339, 1. (hereinafter, Colonial Correspondence (1872)).

[218] An Act to amend the Law relating to the Protection in the Colonies of Works entitled to Copyright in the United Kingdon 1847 (10 & 11 Vict c 95).

authors'.[219] 'Due provision' meant import duties.[220] Canada passed an Act immediately, claiming that it protected British authors, but the Board of Trade refused to endorse an Order in Council which would suspend the 1842 Act, as it made no provision for import duties.[221] The other North American provinces also passed acts, which were approved and a second attempt by Canada was approved by the Board, on the basis that a duty of 12½ per cent duty be levied on imported imprints and the 1842 Act was accordingly suspended.[222]

Other colonies also took advantage of the Foreign Reprints Act, but by 1876 it was considered an abject failure by British publishers, as very little duty was ever collected.[223] Canadian publishers too were unhappy with the system, as it prohibited local reprinting of British books.[224] The decision in *Routledge v Low*[225] led to further dissatisfaction, by highlighting the unfairness of a system in which publication in the United Kingdom gave copyright protection throughout the empire, while publication in a colony gave only local protection.[226]

Continuing negotiations between Canada and the United Kingdom made no headway and in 1872, Canada took matters into its own hands, passing an Act which allowed British books to be reprinted in Canada, on payment of a 12½ per cent duty.[227] Britain's assent was required as the Act was repugnant to Imperial legislation, and it was refused.[228] In 1875, a more limited scheme was finally approved, giving Canadian copyright to books published in Canada, even where such books had been first published elsewhere.[229] British authors and publishers were generally opposed to the Foreign Reprints Act and such licensing schemes as they objected to losing their copyright monopoly in the colonies, and frustration at the failure of the Act and opposition to Canada's response were some of the driving forces behind the establishment of the Copyright Association in 1872. The publishers complained before the Commission that colonial reprints would find their way back into the British market, where they could undersell local books.[230]

219 ibid s 1.

220 W Briggs, *The Law of International Copyright (with Special Sections on the Colonies and The United States of America)* (London, Stevens & Haynes, 1906) 667.

221 Barnes, *Authors, Publishers and Politicians* 149. Seville, *Internationalisation* 87.

222 Barnes, *Authors, Publishers and Politicians* 150–51; Seville, *Internationalisation* 87.

223 According to the Royal Copyright Commission Report, from 1866–1876 the amount received from the 19 colonies which took advantage of the Act was £1,155 13s 2½d, of which £1,088 13s 3½d was received from Canada, 7 paid nothing at all, and 6 paid sums of a few shillings. Royal Copyright Commission xxxi.

224 Colonial Correspondence 27–28.

225 See above: ch 4, text to n 210.

226 Colonial Correspondence 36.

227 S Nowell-Smith, *International Copyright Law and the Publisher in the Reign of Queen Victoria* (Oxford, Oxford University Press, 1968) 89; Seville, *Internationalisation* 103.

228 Copies of or Extracts from Correspondence between the Colonial Office and any of the Colonial Governments on the subject of Copyright; and of Colonial Acts relating to Copyright which have been sanctioned by Her Majesty (1875) 144, 3–19.

229 Nowell-Smith, *International Copyright Law* 89; Seville, *Internationalisation* 106–08.

230 Royal Copyright Commission xxxiv. See A Fraser, 'John Murray's Colonial and Home Library' (1997) 91 *Papers of the Bibliographical Society of America* 339.

A number of complaints regarding these aspects of the colonial situation were aired before the Commission. In its report, the Commission recommended that a book first published in any of the colonies should receive the same protection as if it were first published in the United Kingdom. Further, it recommended that a British author who published a work outside the British dominions, ought not to be prevented from obtaining copyright within the dominions by republishing there, but that such republication must occur within three years of the first publication. The Commissioners did recognise the grievances of colonial readers in not being able to obtain cheap books, and outlined a proposal for a licensing scheme that would allow books to be republished in a colony if supplies were not made available there within a reasonable time. Accepting that such provisions would only be possible in the larger colonies, they recommended continuing the Foreign Reprints Act, with alterations facilitating remuneration under it.[231]

A still more unsatisfactory situation was created by America's continuing refusal to recognise the copyright of British authors. The efforts of respected authors such as Charles Dickens and Edward Bulwer Lytton in the 1840s and 1850s to convince the Americans of the virtues of international copyright had come to nothing, and the 1868 decision in *Routledge v Low* removed any further incentives, by providing a simple mechanism for American authors to obtain copyright in the United Kingdom and its dominions.[232] Numerous authors and publishers appeared before the Copyright Commission to complain that their books were reprinted in the United States with impunity. The Commission was acutely aware of the difficulties, stating in its Report: 'the United States is of all nations the one in which British authors are most concerned—the nation in regard to which the absence of a copyright convention gives rise to the greatest hardships'.[233]

The Commission sought to ascertain the opinion of Americans on the question, and concluded that while American authors would welcome a convention with the United Kingdom, publishers would be less amenable unless provision could be made for local manufacture. Thus, the Commission was prepared to contemplate entering into a convention which allowed British authors to get copyright protection in the United States if they republished and reprinted their books there. It further recommended that a mixed commission be set up to inquire into the conditions which would be acceptable for entering into an agreement with the United States.[234]

The discussions that took place before the Commission on international and colonial copyright were largely concerned with shoring up the position of British authors and publishers, and ways in which their rights could be enforced beyond the United Kingdom's borders. However, in relation to colonial copyright, the broader interests of colonial readers also needed to be considered, and the Commission's decision to retain the Foreign Reprints Act, while making it easier

[231] Royal Copyright Commission xiii–xiv, xxxiii.
[232] See above: ch 4, text to nn 210 ff.
[233] Royal Copyright Commission xxxvi.
[234] ibid xxxvii–xxxix.

to obtain the royalties payable under it, reveals that it appreciated the need to balance both sets of interests.

F. Outcome of the Commission

As noted above, the central concern of those authors who had urged Disraeli to establish the Commission had been international and colonial copyright. Although much evidence had been gathered on the problems in this area, the Commission had also given considerable attention to reform of domestic law. This was the area in which immediate action could be taken by the legislature. However, while the Commissioners' Report might have given the impression of a certain level of consensus regarding the desirability of reform of copyright law, and the shape such reform should take, the reality was quite different. This was reflected in the attempts to reproduce the Commission's recommendations in legislation. In 1878, Edward Jenkins introduced a private Bill into Parliament,[235] but withdrew it upon being told the Government intended to introduce one.[236] Lord John Manners introduced the Government's Bill the following year,[237] but with the intention of circulating it at home and in the colonies, rather than passing it and it quickly vanished from sight.[238] In 1881, George Hastings, a barrister and magistrate, introduced another private Bill into Parliament but it did not progress beyond the first reading.[239]

Following these failures, copyright reformers decided to address the most pressing issues. In 1882, Hastings introduced a Bill relating solely to fine arts.[240] Sir Henry Drummond Wolff argued against the Fine Arts Bill in Parliament, objecting to making special provision for art works while not addressing the 'great question' of literary copyright and before an arrangement could be made with foreign countries, namely the United States.[241] The Bill was dropped, as it did not have the support of the Board of Trade, but Hastings introduced further Fine Arts Bills in 1883, 1884, 1885 and 1886.[242] All of these Bills were either withdrawn or dropped.

The only statutes based on the Commission's Report to be successfully enacted were the Copyright (Musical Compositions) Acts of 1882[243] and 1888.[244] The

[235] A Bill to Codify and Amend the Law of Copyright HC (1878) [53].

[236] Parl Deb HC vol 243 col 1308 (17 February 1879).

[237] Copyright [No 2] HC Bill (1879) [265].

[238] Parl Deb HC vol 246 col 1706 (12 June 1879).

[239] Copyright HC Bill (1881) [121].

[240] Copyright HC Bill (1882) [119].

[241] Parl Deb HC vol 269 col 948 (18 May 1882).

[242] Copyright HC Bill (1883) [141]; Copyright (Photographs) HC Bill (1883) [294]; Copyright (Works of Fine Art) HC Bill (1884) [183]; Copyright (Works of Fine Art) HC Bill (1884–85) [84]; Copyright (Works of Fine Art) HC Bill (1886) [125].

[243] An Act to amend the law of Copyright relating to Musical Compositions 1882 (45 & 46 Vict c 40).

[244] An Act to amend the Law relating to the Recovery of Penalties for the unauthorized Performance of Copyright Musical Compositions 1888 (51 & 52 Vict c 17).

impetus was the growing number of complaints about the collection practices of Harry Wall.[245] These complaints reached the ear of Parliament when John Eldon Gorst, MP for Chatham, drew the House's attention to recent prosecutions for singing songs at penny readings and introduced a Bill to deal with the issue.[246] The Bill, which became the 1882 Act, required the owner of the copyright in a musical work who wished to assert his right of performance to print a notice on the title page of every published work stating that he reserved the right of publication or representation.[247] The aim of the Act was 'to protect the public from vexatious proceedings'.[248] The 1888 Act clarified the earlier Act to provide that a sum of less than 40s could be awarded for infringement of the Act, and to codify the common law decisions that a landlord or proprietor of premises would not be liable for performances unless he 'wilfully caused or permitted' the performance.[249]

That these Acts were considered necessary demonstrates the unsettled status of performances; the law might be clear but many people still found it difficult to appreciate that copyright protection could, or should, extend beyond the printed page, and the legislators had some sympathy with this position. Clarifying this issue was obviously in the interests of all of those involved with copyright law, public and owners alike. Its relatively simple appeal to the public interest and its uncontroversial nature meant that legislation on this topic was able to be enacted relatively promptly. However, despite the efforts directed towards more wide-ranging copyright reform by the Copyright Commissioners and many of the witnesses who appeared before it, consolidation of the proliferation of copyright laws into a single statute with a coherent foundation was simply not possible at this stage.

II. THE RISE OF INTEREST GROUPS AND THE INTERPLAY OF DOMESTIC AND INTERNATIONAL COPYRIGHT

The hearings held by the Royal Copyright Commission and its Reports, both majority and minority, may have uncovered the lack of certainty and consensus regarding copyright's purpose and appropriate scope. However, they also revealed the existence of powerful expansionist urges on the part of authors and publishers towards greater control and coverage. In the last three decades of the century these urges were expressed in the emergence of collective organisations which had copyright reform as their major goal. The impetus towards international copyright also gathered steam at this time, culminating in the Berne Convention in 1887, and the

[245] Wall had brought two legal actions to recover penalties for unauthorised musical performances in 1882. The Queen's Bench reluctantly found in his favour, and the decision was upheld on appeal, although no costs were ordered. *Wall v Taylor*; *Wall v Martin* (1881–82) 9 QBD 727; (1882–83) 11 QBD 102 (CA). See also G McFarlane, *Copyright: the Development and Exercise of the Performing Right* (Eastbourne, John Offord (Publications) Ltd, 1980) 88.

[246] Parl Deb HC vol 269, col 354 (9 May 1882).

[247] Copyright (Musical Compositions) Act 1882 s 2.

[248] ibid, Preamble.

[249] Musical Copyright Act 1888 ss 1, 3.

role played by such interest groups was not insignificant. The area of international copyright is one of considerable complexity and the summary provided in this chapter does not do it justice. The aim is merely to place the domestic developments in context and to demonstrate the interplay between domestic and international copyright in this period.[250]

The formation of the Dramatic Authors' Society following the passing of the Dramatic Copyright Act has already been described, but literary authors were slower to form organisations that could advocate their interests collectively. The co-operation that was finally generated in response to Talfourd's campaign for copyright reform in the 1830s combined in the 1840s with growing resentment at the treatment of British authors at the hands of American publishers. This led, in 1843, to the establishment of a short-lived body calling itself the Society of British Authors.[251] Another organisation had been formed the previous year under the name The Association for the Protection of Literature, and included among its members authors, printers and publishers. The Association, however, was troubled from the beginning by friction between the author and publisher members, and probably split over a proposal by the prominent Leipzig publisher Tauchnitz to pay British authors a modest sum for reprinting their works on the Continent.[252] Authors such as Dickens and Bulwer Lytton were in favour of the proposal, but several of the publishers opposed it, on the basis that 'for publishers as a body to give up all chance of selling their editions abroad or in the colonies would be perfect folly'.[253]

A second attempt to unite the two groups came in 1872, when the Copyright Association was formed under the chairmanship of Lord Stanhope.[254] The Association was formed in response to the Canadian troubles and its stated objectives were 'To watch over the general interests of the Owners of Copyright Property' and 'To obtain early information of all measures affecting Copyright property, and, as opportunity offers, to suggest and promote improvement in existing Copyright laws'.[255] Author members of the Committee were Charles Reade, Wilkie Collins, Anthony Trollope, Robert Browning and JA Froude. However, in reality the Copyright Association was the creature of the publishers, led by Murray and Longman, and counting among its members the prominent publishers MacMillan and Daldy. Trollope, Froude and Daldy were to become members of the Royal Copyright Commission three years later.

The publishers in this group engaged in a public campaign against the Foreign Reprints Act, employing the language of public interest in their favour. Thomas

250 For a much more detailed account, see Seville, *Internationalisation.*

251 See W Besant, *Essays and Historiettes* (London, Chatto and Windus, 1903) and Barnes, *Authors, Publishers and Politicians* 128.

252 Barnes, *Authors, Publishers and Politicians* 133–34.

253 ibid 134.

254 As Lord Mahon he had played an important role in bringing about the 1842 Act after Talfourd left Parliament (see above: ch 4, section II).

255 Copyright Association, *Report of the Copyright Association for the year 1874–5* (London, Longmans, Green & Co, 1875) 7.

Longman not only wrote to *The Times*,[256] but also published a pamphlet protesting against the Act. The pamphlet commenced by endorsing Lord Macaulay's speech in 1841 as providing information on a matter of 'some importance affecting the interests of the public'[257] and went on to set out the reasons why the copyright monopoly acted in the best interests of the public. Since this was so, strong protection was justified: 'A system by which learned and able writers are induced to supply the public with valuable information and intellectual entertainment having been fairly established, the supply of their writings at the most moderate cost should in every way by facilitated and encouraged'.[258]

Despite the claims of publishers that their interests coincided with those of authors, this was not always the view of authors. During the nineteenth century, the gap between the two groups was becoming more visible, as authors became increasingly vocal in their complaints about their publishing contracts. The major bone of contention was the half-profits arrangement preferred by the majority of publishers for their authorial contracts. This method of publication took over in the middle of the nineteenth century from the old practice of buying copyrights for a lump sum, and involved sharing the expenses of production between publisher and author, and profits were shared between them once expenses had been met.[259] This was a particularly popular model for the publication of first novels by unknown authors and other cases where not much was expected from a book.[260] However, in practice it often led to abuses, because the publishers were responsible for making up the accounts of costs which made invisible surcharging possible.[261]

Some very successful authors, such as Dickens, had the bargaining strength to drive a publisher down to a quarter or third of the profits, as well as making other beneficial deals. In the 1840s, Bulwer Lytton had employed a lawyer to look over his publishing contracts, and liked to arrange deals that would give him a steady income at half yearly intervals.[262] Wilkie Collins was another such author who took an informed legal approach to his publication deals, leasing his copyrights for seven-year periods and retaining control of his syndication rights with newspapers.[263] In November 1874, he made an agreement with his publisher Chatto to issue new editions of all the novels he bought within twelve months and that no edition would be sold for under 2s.[264] However, authors who could strike such bargains were rare, and even those who did have such power frequently only retained it for a short period in their careers.[265]

[256] Letter of 26 March 1872, reproduced in T Longman, *Some Observations on Copyright and our Colonies* (London, Longmans, Green & Co, 1872) 6.
[257] Longman, *Some Observations on Copyright* 5.
[258] ibid 7.
[259] JA Sutherland, *Victorian Novelists* 88.
[260] ibid.
[261] ibid 88–89.
[262] ibid 59.
[263] A Weedon, 'From Three-Deckers to Film Rights: A Turn in British Publishing Strategies, 1870–1930' (1999) 2 *Book History* 188, 195.
[264] ibid.
[265] JA Sutherland, *Victorian Novelists* 93.

It was partly to assist the cause of authors who were not in such strong bargaining positions that an effective organisation for authors was finally established. On 30 June 1884, the Society of Authors was incorporated. Walter Besant (later Sir Walter Besant), a popular novelist of the period, was the chairman and Lord Tennyson was the first president. Other prominent literary figures involved in the Society from its early days included Charles Reade, Charlotte M Yonge, George Augustus Sala, H Rider Haggard, William Frederick Pollock, RD Blackmore,[266] Sir Henry Thompson,[267] as well as those with more peripheral literary interests, such as Cardinal Manning. The year before the establishment of the Society of Authors had seen the demise of the Dramatic Authors' Society, which formally ceased to exist on 25 March 1883.[268] Dramatic authors such as Charles Reade, Herman Merivale and WS Gilbert played roles in the Society, and a dramatic subcommittee was set up in 1884, but the copyright issues facing dramatists largely became subsumed into more general issues of copyright reform after this time.[269] The chief aim of the Society of Authors was

> to promote recognition of the fact, hitherto most imperfectly understood, that literary property is as real a thing as property in every other kind of business: that it should be safeguarded in the same manner, and regarded with the same jealousy.[270]

Two aims that supported the first were the consolidation and amendment of domestic copyright law and the promotion of international copyright.[271] A complementary but separate object was the Society's determination to ensure that all authors received from publishers 'just and honourable treatment, fair and open agreements, and honourable observance of those agreements'.[272] In pursuit of this latter objective, the Society published a number of technical works, informing authors of the actual costs of production and methods of publication, in an attempt to reveal to authors where any hidden costs in half-profit agreements might be found.[273] It also provided information about business and legal matters to authors, as well as receiving complaints about publishers with unfair practices.[274] Both the Copyright Association and the Society of Authors played important roles in the promotion of international copyright protection in Europe, the colonies and the United States of America.

As noted in the previous section, achieving an agreement for recognition of copyright in the United States was seen as the most important of the three. The Royal Copyright Commission had recommended setting up a 'mixed commission' to look into the matter and, although no such committee was set up, the Board of

[266] The author of Lorna Doone.

[267] A prominent surgeon who was interested in astronomy, as well as being an amateur painter and author of numerous works on medicine and two novels published under the name 'Pen Oliver'.

[268] JR Stevens, *Profession of the Playwright* 180.

[269] ibid 181.

[270] *The Author* (15 May 1890) 1.

[271] ibid 24.

[272] ibid 2.

[273] *The Author* (1 June 1901) 6.

[274] ibid 6–7.

Trade also recognised the importance of reaching a copyright agreement with the United States. In 1884, Thomas Farrer noted that 'to our authors the US are of far more consequence than all the nations of Europe'.[275]

Notwithstanding Britain's dismissive attitude towards its nearest neighbours, the cause of international copyright in Europe was advancing apace. In 1883, the International Literary Association[276] met in Berne, and produced a scheme for forming an international copyright union. The following year, a Diplomatic Conference was held in Berne, and delegates from 10 countries attended. Several documents were produced which provided the basis of a multilateral convention. Britain remained distant and its delegate, FO Adams,[277] attended in a consultative capacity only. Adams was a founding member of the Society of Authors, and kept it informed of progress.

However, between 1884 and 1885, Britain's attitude changed.[278] At a second Conference in 1885, Adams was accompanied by John Henry Gibbs Bergne and given greater powers.[279] The Copyright Association, which had played an important role in urging the British Government to become involved in the negotiations, assisted the delegates, largely through the intermediary of its indefatigable secretary Daldy.[280] Some changes were made to the 1884 draft, largely in order to retain the involvement of the British,[281] and the resulting draft was adopted by the Convention. The draft was presented to the British Government and found acceptable.

Before the Government could proceed to ratify any convention based on the draft, some changes had to be made to British copyright legislation. This gave rise to the hope in some quarters that the opportunity could be taken for general codification. The Board of Trade considered that

> it is of such importance that foreign countries should be enabled clearly to understand what the Law of Copyright is in this country, that they think it will be most desirable, if the circumstances of the Session admit of it, to take the opportunity of codifying the present Copyright Law in the bill which they hope to introduce into Parliament at an early date.[282]

[275] Quoted in L Bently and B Sherman, 'Great Britain and the Signing of the Berne Convention in 1886' (2001) 48 *Journal of the Copyright Society of the USA* 311, 327.

[276] The International Literary Association (later, *ALAI, L'Association littéraire et artistique internationale*) was formed in 1878, under the presidency of Victor Hugo. It was to be open to writers and literary societies from anywhere in the world, and its objects included the protection of the principles of literary property. See S Ricketson and J Ginsburg, *International Copyright and Neighbouring Rights: The Berne Convention and Beyond*, 2nd edn, 2 vols (Oxford, Oxford University Press, 2006) vol 1, p 49.

[277] Francis Ottiwell Adams was Britain's Envoy in Berne in 1881, and the author of two books, *The History of Japan* and *The Swiss Confederation*.

[278] For discussion of the possible reasons for this *volte-face*, see Bently and Sherman, 'Signing of the Berne Convention' 329–40.

[279] Bergne, 'International Copyright Union' 24.

[280] For more on Daldy's role in the Copyright Assocation, see the article by John Murray in *The Author*, (1 April 1905) 202–04.

[281] Ricketson and Ginsburg, *International Copyright* vol 1, p 79.

[282] Mr Calcraft to Sir J Pauncefote, 18 December 1885, quoted in EM Underdown, 'The Copyright Question' (1886) 2 *Law Quarterly Review* 213, 215–16.

However, it seemed the circumstances of the Session did not admit of it. Bergne noted that the Government of the day was well-disposed towards codification, but that it was felt it would require too much discussion and take too long; in the meantime it would be better to focus on what was immediately necessary for conforming with the Berne Draft.[283]

A Departmental Committee, including agents of the major self-governing colonies, was appointed to consider the necessary changes and, in June 1886, an Act to amend the law of International and Colonial Copyright was passed by Parliament.[284] This new Act made little substantive change to the domestic law. The problem of duration had been avoided in the Berne Draft by making it a matter to be determined by the author's country of origin. With respect to translation, a compromise giving authors an absolute right of translation for a minimum of 10 years[285] had been reached between Britain, who wanted the matter to remain one of domestic law, and those countries such as France which sought to make protection against unauthorised translation absolute and co-terminous with copyright duration.[286]

The Diplomatic Conference met once more in Berne on 6 September 1886, and the Convention came into force on 5 December 1887, creating a 'Union for the protection fo the rights of authors over their literary and artistic works'. Britain acceded on its own behalf and on behalf of its principal self-governing dominions.[287] The other countries which acceded and later ratified the Convention were Germany, Belgium, Spain, France, Haiti, Italy, Switzerland and Tunisia. Liberia had signed the *procès-verbal de signature*, but did not ratify the Convention for another 20 years. Japan attended as an observer and adhered to the Convention in 1899.[288]

The United States had also attended the Berne Conference of 1886 as an observer, but did not join the Union. This was extremely disappointing to the British, and the Society of Authors became heavily involved in seeking to arrive at an agreement with the United States which would recognise the copyright of British authors. However, it was to be Americans who played the crucial roles by forming new and effective organisations to lobby for international copyright. The American Copyright League (later the Authors' Copyright League) was formed in 1883 with the aim of bringing about international copyright, and in 1887 it joined forces with the newly formed American Publishers' Copyright League.[289] One significant factor that was proving divisive, and to which the British were implacably

[283] Bergne, 'International Copyright Union' 25.

[284] Ricketson and Ginsburg, An Act to amend the Law respecting International and Colonial Copyright 1886 (49 & 50 Vict c 33).

[285] Ricketson and Ginsburg, *International Copyright* vol 1, p 77. See International Copyright Act 1886 s 5.

[286] Ricketson and Ginsburg, *International Copyright* vol 1, p 77.

[287] ibid p 82. This was a matter of considerable delicacy, especially in relation to Canada. For details, see Seville, *Internationalisation* 114–18.

[288] Ricketson and Ginsburg, *International Copyright*, vol 1, p 82.

[289] Seville, *Internationalisation* 217–18, 227.

opposed (despite the Royal Commission's willingness to contemplate it), was the question of whether international copyright should be reliant on the inclusion of a 'manufacturing clause', that is, that protection would only be granted for books printed on type set in the United States of America. Most publishers were in favour of a manufacturing clause, and the powerful typographical unions also lobbied extremely vigorously in its favour. Ultimately compromise was reached on the point. Several Bills, adopting differing schemes for protection were presented in the 1880s, including Senator Chace's Bill in 1886. After considerable opposition, much amending and re-amending, the Chace Act, as it was known, became law in 1891.[290]

The pleasure felt by the British at the prospect of copyright protection in the United States was tempered by some of the conditions set by the Act, in particular the need for works to be manufactured in the United States and the prohibition on the importation of other editions. A second matter of uncertainty was that the Act would only apply to foreigners who gave protection to US authors on 'substantially the same basis as its own citizens' or if their state was party to an international agreement that gave reciprocal protection in granting copyright.[291] It was not clear whether British law would be considered to be reciprocal. In the end, it was decided that simultaneous publication in both countries would not prevent the acquisition of British copyright, and so British authors would be able to obtain copyright protection under the Act.[292] At long last, British authors were eligible for copyright protection in the United States of America.

III. CONCLUSION

By the final decade of the nineteenth century, copyright law had been subjected to extremely detailed examination, in the form of the Royal Copyright Commission, and it had also expanded in almost every direction. Not only did it fill a larger space, in the sense of many more pages, on the statute books, its boundaries had also widened to include the spoken word, in the form of lectures and plays, and performances of musical works.[293] It spanned the Channel as well as the Atlantic and Pacific Oceans, both through common law decisions giving protection to foreign authors first publishing in the United Kingdom, and through international treaties. Furthermore, copyright had extended in length, first through the 1814 Act[294] and then the 1842 Copyright Act.

[290] For more detail on the events of these years, see ibid 206–45.

[291] An Act to amend title sixty, chapter three, of the Revised Statutes of the United States, relating to Copyrights (1891) c 565 s 13.

[292] Seville, *Internationalisation* 246–47.

[293] From 1798 it covered sculptures (38 Geo 3 c 71) and from 1862 it covered paintings, drawings and photographs (25 & 26 Vict c 68). However, discussion of these additions is beyond the scope of the present book.

[294] See above: ch 3, section II.

In some senses, this extension was the result of pressure from individuals and groups. Talfourd and his supporters worked long and hard to achieve their small measure of copyright reform, pushing the Act through against a large and vocal opposition both inside and outside Parliament. Other measures, like the Lectures Act of 1835, the recognition of foreign authors' copyright and copyright protection for British authors in the United States, took place against a background of significant resistance. However, in many ways this expansion fell considerably short of the ideals of many of those seeking it. Talfourd's original objective of a term of the life of the author plus 60 years had been severely circumscribed and his attempts to strengthen the remedies available to authors had been rejected. The achievement of reciprocal protection with the United States was also subject to an undesirable manufacturing clause. There were, moreover, some contractions in the rights. The Dramatic Copyright Act had provided for a penalty of no less than 40s in respect of unauthorised performances; the 1888 Act provided that less than this, including a nominal amount, could be awarded at the discretion of the court. Most importantly, however, from the point of view of those in favour of expansion, a serious proposal to abolish copyright altogether had been successfully headed off. Overall, copyright at the end of the century had a markedly increased scope compared to one hundred years previously.

In all these different areas of expansion, rhetoric of authors' rights and the public interest had played their roles. Common law copyright and the ideology of romantic authorship were pressed into service to justify claims for a greater scope of protection. Meanwhile, the rhetoric of public interest appeared at every point, marshalled into service to support arguments in favour of increased protection, as well as arguments against it. Sometimes, it was used to argue that copyright should not exist at all. The interests of authors and the public were presented at times as complementary and, at other times, as being in opposition to each other. The 'public' itself was far from being a constant or coherent construct. At times, it was the British public; at other times the imperial public. Frequently, it comprised readers or attendees at performances or lectures, but on other occasions it was made up of actors, singers and managers. Sometimes it was an elite public; sometimes it was a popular public. Moroever, the 'interests' of this ever-shifting public also varied, from being the interest in being able to ascertain whether a work was copyright and who owned it, to being the interest in being able to purchase cheap books, or good books, or to access other educational materials. In the case of traders, the interest might lie in the ability to reprint books; for performers, it might lie in the ability to perform. Thus, while the rhetoric of 'public interest' remained constant, its content did not. At this critical period of copyright's expansion the ideology of romantic authorship cannot be held fully accountable, but nor can the concept of public interest be seen solely as a counterweight to such an ideology. On the contrary, the rhetoric of public interest, in its multitude of forms, was used both to resist and to support the expansion of copyright law.

6

Infringement at Common Law

Drawing Copyright's Boundaries

MOST HISTORIES OF copyright, including this one so far, tend to concentrate on the broader, more accessible (at least to non-lawyers) aspects of the law, such as duration or its general legislative scheme. This chapter, by contrast, looks at the legal doctrine of infringement and its development from the Statute of Anne to the end of the nineteenth century. The law of infringement is clearly a crucial aspect of copyright law because it determines its boundaries just as much as the term of copyright: what is protected determines what will infringe. As in the previous chapter, the story of copyright told here is one of expansion. At the beginning of the eighteenth century, copyright was a right to print and reprint books. By the end of the nineteenth century it extended much more widely, covering non-verbatim reprints, such as abridgments, and translations, and preventing the copying of anything more than an 'insubstantial' part, unless for a specific purpose deemed to be acceptable.

In a recent article, Oren Bracha departs from the general tendency referred to above and considers the doctrinal law of copyright in the nineteenth century in detail. He persuasively argues that the nineteenth century was a time of transformation for the American law of infringement, in which a 'new concept of copyright as general control of an intellectual work' emerged.[1] This 'work' could be controlled irrespective of form and was identified in terms of its market value.[2] Bracha's main concern is to examine the role of romantic authorship ideology in bringing about this transformation, concluding that copyright, as it evolved in the nineteenth century, has many features that are 'diametrically opposed to the fundamental tenets of original authorship, but at the same time it is saturated with concepts that are directly traceable to those tenets'.[3]

Bracha is not the first to identify copyright's shift from being a limited right to print, reprint and sell *books* to a more expansive right to control uses of an abstract

[1] O Bracha, 'The Ideology of Authorship Revisited: Authors, Markets, and Liberal Values in Early American Copyright' (2009) 118 *Yale Law Journal* 186, 190, 226. See also his unpublished doctoral dissertation, O Bracha, 'Owning Ideas: A History of Anglo-American Intellectual Property' (unpublished SJD Dissertation Harvard Law School, June 2005).

[2] Bracha, 'The Ideology of Authorship Revisited' 226–27.

[3] ibid 265.

'work'. In 1988, L Ray Patterson and Craig Joyce argued that in the twentieth century copyright was transformed from a monopoly for competitive, market place purposes only ('monopoly for the market') to a monopoly for the work per se or for all purposes ('monopoly of the work').[4] In 1999, Peter Jaszi identified the emergence of the 'work' as a 'free-standing abstraction'[5] but placed its birth in the mid-eighteenth century. Bracha's work offers a corrective to Jaszi's claim that the ideology of authorship was 'essentially complete'[6] by the early nineteenth century.

This chapter shows that the history of infringement in the United Kingdom shares some of the features identified by Bracha in the American context. As the publishers sought to capture new markets for their products, they generated case law testing their claims. In some cases their claims were recognised by the courts, resulting in expansion of the rights of copyright owners. However, there was also some resistance on the part of the judiciary to an all-encompassing copyright and, contrary to Jaszi's claims, it cannot be said that the transformation from the concrete 'book' to a more abstract 'work' took place before the courts. While such a transformation did ultimately occur, it was not until later, and the legislature, not the courts, was responsible.[7] The increase of owners' territory that did occur cannot be chalked up as a victory for romantic authorship, but rather to the characterisation of copyright law as adjudicating between competitors in the market. Moreover, this was far from being unique to the nineteenth century. The dominant forces shaping copyright law, dating back to the Statute of Anne and earlier, had long been commercial.

This chapter traces the development of the law of infringement through the courts and the legislature over the two hundred years between the Statute of Anne and the Imperial Copyright Act. In particular, it investigates the extent to which the shape of the law was influenced by concerns for the public interest or the claims of authorship. The fair-dealing exceptions are frequently said to represent the public interest by curtailing the copyright owner's exclusive rights in favour of certain specified uses. Laddie et al characterise the permitted acts as 'the rights of the public',[8] while Paul Torremans states that 'These defences exist in order to restore the balance between the rights of the owner of copyright and the rights of society at large'.[9] Numerous other scholars, as well as judges, have situated the fair-dealing exceptions at the heart of copyright's balancing act.[10] In recent years,

[4] LR Patterson and C Joyce, 'Monopolizing the Law: The Scope of Copyright Protection for Law Reports and Statutory Compilations' (1988–89) 36 *University of California at Los Angeles Law Review* 719, 798.

[5] P Jaszi, 'Toward a Theory of Copyright: The Metamorphoses of "Authorship"' (1991) *Duke Law Journal* 455, 473

[6] ibid 471.

[7] See below: ch 7.

[8] H Laddie et al, *Modern Law of Copyright and Designs* (London, Butterworths, 2000) 737.

[9] P Torremans, *Holyoak and Torremans Intellectual Property Law*, 4th edn (Oxford, Oxford University Press, 2005) 248.

[10] See, eg, Gibson LJ who described s 30(2) of the Copyright, Designs and Patents Act 1988 as aiming to strike 'a proper balance between protection of the rights of a creative author [and] the wider public interest, of which free speech is a very important ingredient' in *Newspaper Licensing Agency v Marks*

use of the word 'rights' has begun to take over from the word 'interest'.[11] This shift has significant implications for the status of the public in copyright law, as a right is clearly of a higher order than a mere 'interest'.[12]

A number of claims have been made about the history of fair dealing. Puri contends that the concept of fair dealing 'has been applied from times immemorial' and is 'perhaps as old as copyright protection itself'.[13] Patry, in his tome on the American law of fair dealing, states that between 1740 and 1839 the judges had developed 'a relatively cohesive set of principles governing the uses of a first author's work by a subsequent author without the former's consent'.[14] Robert Burrell has pointed out that the dominant history of the fair-dealing exceptions places the judiciary in the role of protector of the public interest, reining in the overly broad protection given by Parliament in the Statute of Anne.[15] Burrell, however, considers that the early cases are better seen as placing limits on judicial expansion of a restricted right granted by Parliament.[16] Melissa de Zwart agrees with Burrell's assessment, but discerns one 'certain principle' emerging from the cases:

> [G]radually, any use of material protected by copyright came to be seen as an incursion upon the rights of the owner and such incursions would only be justified where there was an overwhelming interest in the public interest in freedom of communication.[17]

The central argument of this chapter is that no such 'certain principles' can be uncovered, particularly not ones with human rights overtones. That is not to say

& Spencer [2001] Ch 257, 271. See also J Griffiths, 'Preserving Judicial Freedom of Movement: Interpreting Fair Dealing in Copyright Law' (2000) *Intellectual Property Quarterly* 240; K Garnett, G Davies, G Harbottle, *Copinger and Skone James on Copyright*, 15th edn, 2 vols (London, Sweet & Maxwell, 2005) vol 1, p 469 and K Puri 'Fair Dealing with Copyright Material in Australia and New Zealand' (1983) *Victoria University of Wellington Law Review* 277, 290.

[11] *CCH Canadian Ltd v Law Society of Upper Canada* (2004) 30 CPR. (4th) 1, [48]: 'The fair dealing exception, like other exceptions in the *Copyright Act*, is a user's right. In order to maintain the proper balance between the rights of a copyright owner and users' interests, it must not be interpreted restrictively'. See also D Vaver, *Copyright Law* (Toronto, Irwin Law, 2000) ch. 7; R Burrell, 'The Future of the Copyright Exceptions' in D McClean and K Schubert (eds), *Dear Images* (London, ICA, 2002) 455; and M de Zwart, 'Seriously Entertaining: *The Panel* and the Future of Fair Dealing' (2003) 8 *Media and Arts Law Review* 1, 4 and 17.

[12] It has also been criticised for shifting the emphasis of copyright law away from authors and creativity, re-imaging it as a law to facilitate consumption, see, eg: J Ginsburg 'Authors and Users in Copyright' (1997) 45 *Journal of the Copyright Society of the USA* 1.

[13] Puri 'Fair Dealing with Copyright Material' 278.

[14] WF Patry, *The Fair Use Privilege in Copyright Law*, 2nd edn (Washington DC, BNA Books, 1995) 3.

[15] R Burrell, 'Reining in Copyright Law: Is Fair Use the Answer?' (2001) *Intellectual Property Quarterly* 361, 365–66. See also Patry, *The Fair Use Privilege*; Puri 'Fair Dealing with Copyright Material' 277; D Bradshaw, '"Fair Dealing" as a Defence to Copyright Infringement in UK Law: An Historical Excursion from 1802 to the *Clockwork Orange* Case 1993' (1995) *Denning Law Journal* 67; JL Oakes, 'Copyrights and Copyremedies: Unfair Use and Injunctions' (1990) 18 *Hofstra Law Review* 983, 988; and D Vaver, 'Abridgements and Abstracts: Copyright Implications' (1995) 5 *European Intellectual Property Review* 225.

[16] Burrell, 'Reining in Copyright Law' 367.

[17] M de Zwart, 'An Historical Analysis of the Birth of Fair Dealing and Fair Use: Lessons for the Digital Age' [2007] *Intellectual Property Quarterly* 60, 90.

that notions of public interest did not have any role in the development of the law of infringement, just that there was no *single* public interest consideration, and that other factors also played their parts. The existing historical work in this area generally takes as its starting point the current fair-dealing provisions and then looks backwards to find their antecedents in the case law of the last two centuries. The problem with such an approach is that it tends to give the impression of having reached a fixed end-state towards which previous generations, consciously or unconsciously, were heading.[18] This is the case even where the argument is that the law's passage in a particular direction was somehow blown off course during the course of its development.[19]

By contrast, this chapter highlights the contingency of the development of the law of infringement. It is important to emphasise the perhaps obvious point that jurists of the past were not addressing the specific issue of how to carve out exceptions in favour of copyright users or the public in general. Nor were they *deliberately* setting out to expand the rights of copyright owners.[20] The central question that faced judges, lawyers and their clients was: what kinds of uses of copyright works would amount to infringement? The reason the question was couched in such general terms is that the Statute of Anne referred only to the printing, reprinting and importing of books, and made no mention of the far from uncommon situation where something other than a *verbatim* copy of a book was reprinted by a competitor. What would happen if only part of a book were copied? Or a translation of the book were printed? Or an abridged version of it? Each of these actions, resulting in what would today be known as a derivative work, might interfere with the original bookseller's market for the book, depending on how that market is characterised. Consequently, it is not surprising that the courts were called upon to adjudicate disputes in relation to them. It was in the process of answering this more general question, as well as the subsidiary questions it threw up, that the foundations of the fair-dealing provisions were laid, as well as the law relating to two other important principles of infringement: the copying must be of a 'substantial part' of the work and it must relate to expression rather than ideas. This question also had the effect of bringing the focus of the inquiry onto the attributes of the work that justified protection, such as the labour expended upon it.

Kathy Bowrey has recently argued that, in the nineteenth century, 'Deciding what was to be protected, and what use of another's work was permitted, involved

[18] Peter Jaszi performs a similar sleight of hand in his discussions of the emergence of the 'work', describing it as 'still incomplete' (471), 'essentially complete' (471), coming 'fully into its own' (475 and 'mature' (477), while those who fail to accept this are labelled 'retrogressive' (477). Jaszi, 'Toward a Theory of Copyright'.

[19] See, eg: Robert Burrell's (in my view, correct) argument that Parliament in 1911 did not intend the fair-dealing provisions in the Imperial Copyright Act to represent a full codification of permissible uses of works; R Burrell, 'Reining in Copyright Law: Is Fair Use the Answer?' (2001) *Intellectual Property Quarterly* 361, 368.

[20] Cp R Burrell and A Coleman, *Copyright Exceptions: The Digital Impact* (Cambridge, Cambridge University Press, 2005) 256.

broad considerations into the social purpose served by copyright'.[21] In this chapter, it is contended that, on some occasions, the courts did consider the social purpose, or public interest, of copyright. However, this was by no means a consistent or even dominant approach to the law of infringement. In fact, a number of different and competing lines of authority can be distinguished. In order to draw out these different approaches, it is necessary to consider a large number of cases in detail. While this makes for a long and detailed chapter, to do otherwise would result in ironing out the complexity and contingency of the law of infringement during its first two hundred years of development.

This chapter begins by considering the law of infringement in the eighteenth century, before moving its focus to the nineteenth century. The eighteenth century saw a small but steadily growing number of cases come before the courts, and the emergence of the doctrine that an abridgment would not amount to an infringement. Around the turn of the century, this doctrine extended to include any work that could be characterised as 'new'. However, over the course of the nineteenth century, this doctrine was to be eclipsed by a growing focus on the damage suffered by the plaintiff and, or alternatively, a focus on the labour expended by the original author and annexed by the secondary author. At the same time, a number of different tests for identifying infringement were developed by the courts, but no single, authoritative approach crystallised during this period.[22] This chapter also considers the attempts by Serjeant Talfourd to introduce a legislative infringement clause into what became the 1842 Copyright Act, and the views of the Royal Copyright Commission on infringement. The discussions of policy-makers, and those who sought to influence the legislative form of copyright law, may have placed infringement into a broader context of public and private interests than did the judicial decisions, but they likewise reveal the lack of a generally accepted foundation or principle upon which to develop the law.

I. INFRINGEMENT IN THE EIGHTEENTH CENTURY

A. Partial and Altered Copying and the Booksellers

As discussed in chapter two, the new legal order ushered in by the Statute of Anne by no means provided a detailed, regulatory structure for the book trade. In particular, it gave no guidance relating to a key concern of eighteenth-century booksellers—partial or altered copying of books. A series of skirmishes were fought on this front from the third decade of the century. In the Court of Chancery, Lord Hardwicke's response was to develop a principle of 'fair abridgment'. However,

[21] K Bowrey, 'On Clarifying the Role of Originality and Fair Use in 19th Century UK Jurisprudence: Appreciating the "Humble Grey Which Emerges as a Result of Long Controversy"' in L Bently, G D'Agostino, C Ng, *The Common Law of Intellectual Property: Essays in Honour of Professor David Vaver* (Oxford, Hart Publishing, forthcoming) 16.

[22] Cp ibid.

before turning to examine this line of cases, it is worth briefly considering the situation prior to 1710 and noting that, while the Statute of Anne may have made several significant changes to the legal character of printing and publishing rights, there was as much continuity as there was discontinuity in the early years of the century.

Abridgments and adaptations had long been popular with booksellers and printers trying to gain or retain a foothold in the trade because, like piratical reprints, they were an easier and cheaper way of riding on the established success and initial financial outlay of others. By the end of the sixteenth century, the Stationers' Company was allowing separate entries in the register for ballad versions of histories, romances and plays, but this suddenly stopped in the seventeenth century.[23]

The Stationers' Company and others were conscious that such works could have an adverse effect on the sales of the original version. In 1580, Thomas Man was fined 5s for printing 'The Holy Fast' without licence, as it was a close imitation of one of the books within John Day's privilege.[24] In 1615, Thomas Snowden paid 20s to be allowed to print a book of 'sacrid himmes by Joyce Taylor taken out of the psalmes which belong to the Company'.[25] The same year the Court of the Stationers' Assistants recorded that John Budge was fined 40s for printing a book called 'The Mirror of Martyrs', which was taken from the 'Book of Martyrs' owned by the Company.[26] In 1631, Archbishop Laud refused a licence to Robert Young to publish an abridgment of Foxe's *Book of Martyrs* on the grounds that 'abridgments, by their brevity and their cheapness, in short time work out the authors themselves'.[27]

Although a patent would not be granted for a book which had already received one, an enterprising way of circumventing the controls of the Stationers' Company was to apply for a patent for an abridgment of an existing book.[28] Moreover, some royal patents were expressly drafted to cover the right to print abridgments of the works applied for.[29]

[23] W St Clair *The Reading Nation in the Romantic Period* (Cambridge, Cambridge University Press, 2004) 72, App 3, 496–98.

[24] C Blagden, *The Stationers' Company: A History 1403–1959* (London, George Allen & Unwin Ltd, 1960) 83–85.

[25] WA Jackson, *Records of the Court of the Stationers' Company 1602–1640* (London, The Bibliographical Society, 1957) 456. This may represent one of the earliest examples of compulsory licensing.

[26] ibid 76, 456. Budge made no secret of the fact he was aiming his book at a different audience, including a preface as follows:

> Dear Christian Reader, who either wantest leisure to read or ability to buy that rich and plentiful storehouse of Storie, Doctrine, and Comfort, the Acts and Monuments: penned by that most innocent hearted man of God, and true Nathanaell, M. Iohn Foxe . . . Accept then (good Reader pray thee instead of the greater) this little Institution of a Christian Martyr (J Foxe, *The Mirror of Martyrs* (London, Budge, 1615)).

[27] A Hunt, 'Book Trade Patents' in A Hunt, G Mandelbrote and A Shell (eds), *The Book Trade and its Customers, 1450–1900* (Winchester, St Paul's Bibliographies, 1997) 33.

[28] eg, in 1624 Gilbert Diglen was granted a 21-year patent for an abridgment of Camden's *Britannia*. See also Hunt, 'Book Trade Patents' 33.

[29] eg, on 19 May 1607 a patent was granted to Thomas Wilson and Percival Golding to print the 'manie works of great volume and importance' translated by Arthur Golding and Thomas Wilson,

Abridgments and other kinds of partial taking were forbidden by a Company ordinance of 1678, which forbade the printing of any book 'or any part of any Book' without the consent of the owner. Any person who did so was penalised by being refused admittance as a Pensioner of the Society.[30] In 1681, a second ordinance was passed which strengthened this prohibition both by making it more explicit that 'any part of any such Copy or Copies, Book or Books' could not be printed, imported, sold, bound, stitched or exposed without the owner's consent and by introducing a penalty of 12s for every contravening copy.[31] The prohibition was extended to apply to books printed under Letters Patent owned by the Company as well as those held by individuals.[32]

However, it was beyond the power of the Stationers' Company, and later the bookselling congers, to stamp out completely such common and lucrative practices, particularly following the lapse of the last Licensing Act in 1695. A large part of the work of 'garetteers', or hired writers consisted of identifying the works that were or would become popular, and reproducing them in altered forms. Richard Savage, insolvent poet and friend of Johnson, described his career as one of Edmund Curl's hired writers thus:

> Sometimes I was Mr John Gay, at other times Burnet or Addison; I abridged histories and travels, translated from the French what they never wrote, and was expert in finding new titles for old books. I was the Plutarch of the notorious thief.[33]

The eighteenth century was a time of great commercial change or, in McKendrick's phrase, a 'consumer revolution'.[34] It was also a time of growing urbanisation and there was considerable expansion in the book trade during this period. The Licensing Act of 1662 had limited the number of master printers to 20, and the number of presses they could own to one or two, although these limits had never been successfully enforced.[35] In 1723, there were 80 printing presses in London alone, and by 1764 the printer William Strahan estimated that the number had risen to between 150 and 200. In 1801, 210 master printers were recorded.[36] This expansion occurred despite the fact that there were no significant technological advances in printing during the century.[37]

together with any other works which Wilson might in future translate, and any abridgments of the said works: Hunt, 'Book Trade Patents' 42, see also 43, 44, 47.

30 E Arber, *A Transcript of the Registers of the Company of Stationers of London, 1554–1640*, (London, privately printed, 1875–94) vol 1, p I16.

31 ibid I23.

32 ibid I23–I24.

33 AS Collins, *Authorship in the Days of Johnson: Being a Study of the Relationship Between Author, Patron, Publisher and the Public, 1726–1780* (London, Robert Holden & Co, 1927) 2.

34 N McKendrick, J Brewer and JH Plumb, *The Birth of a Consumer Society: The Commercialisation of Eighteenth-century England* (London, Hutchinson & Co, 1983) 1.

35 Licensing Act (1662) s 11. C Blagden, *The Stationers' Company* 173.

36 D McKitterick, *Print, Manuscript and the Search for Order, 1450–1830* (Cambridge, Cambridge University Press, 2003) 188.

37 J Raven, 'The Book Trades' in I Rivers (ed), *Books and their Readers in Eighteenth Century England: New Essays* (London, Leicester University Press, 2001) 5.

Change was also encroaching in other ways. From the start of the century there was growing activity in producing new types of books for new types of markets. Literary periodicals, such as the *Spectator* and the *Tatler* had popularised the periodical essay, and were soon joined in the market by magazines which incorporated news of the day, literature and poetry, such as the *Gentleman's Magazine*. Although such magazines were not printed in large editions, their circulation and readership was far larger than the edition size suggests, due to the popularity of coffee houses where a single issue might find many readers.[38] Books issued in parts on a weekly or monthly basis made large works more affordable and accessible and newspaper circulation was also increasing. The first successful daily newspaper, the *Daily Courant*, appeared in 1702, and was soon followed by other papers.

Another important agent of change was the circulating library. London had its first circulating library in 1740[39] and between 1740 and 1770 the number of establishments calling themselves circulating libraries increased in number, flourishing outside London as well as within.[40] The main attraction of circulating libraries was a new literary form, the novel, and the period between 1740 and 1753 saw the emergence of the first 'best-sellers', such as Richardson's *Pamela*,[41] and Fielding's *Amelia*.[42] The rapid growth of these libraries in the mid-seventeenth century suggests that there was a growing class of new readers emerging, and that economic factors had played an important role in restricting the book-buying public.[43]

The emergence of new markets for different, and cheaper, books put increased pressure on the booksellers to clamp down on derivative works. Even before the final lapse of the Licensing Act and the decline in the power of the Stationers' Company, the Court of Chancery had sometimes been used as an alternative venue to the Court of Assistants for dispute resoluation.[44] Following the Statute of Anne, the courts of law and equity became the appropriate fora for such disputes, but the Statute gave no guidance on how works which did not amount to direct reprints were to be treated. Although John How had suggested in 1709 that legislation should prohibit the printing of 'any Part, or Epitome' of any book that was the property of another man,[45] the Statute made no mention of partial or altered copying. Once again, therefore, the Court was compelled to interpret the statutory text in order to make a decision in such cases.

[38] RD Altick, *The English Common Reader: A Social History of the Mass reading Public 1800–1900* (Chicago, University of Chicago Press, 1957) 47.

[39] CA Stewart-Murphy, *A History of British Circulating Libraries* (Newtown, Bird & Bull Press, 1992) 14.

[40] HM Hamlyn, 'Eighteenth-century Circulating Libraries in England' (1946–7) 1 *The Library* 197, 198.

[41] Richardson, a printer himself, was surprised by its success and sold two-thirds of his copyright for £20. I Watt, *The Rise of the Novel: Studies in Defoe, Richardson and Fielding* (London, Penguin, 1963) 57.

[42] RD Altick, *The English Common Reader: A Social History of the Mass Reading Public 1800–1900* (Chicago, Chicago University Press, 1957) 49.

[43] Watt, *The Rise of the Novel* 44.

[44] For a full discussion of the fora in which copyright issues were adjudicated prior to the Statute of Anne, see T Gomez-Arostegui, 'What History Teaches Us about Copyright Injunctions and the Inadequate-Remedy-at-Law Requirement' (2008) 81 *Southern California Law Review* 1197.

[45] J How, *Some Thoughts on the Present State of Printing and Bookselling* (London, 1709) 14.

However, in the early years of the Statute's operation there was little litigation on the point. In 1719, it seems that Thomas Cox published an abridgment of *Robinson Crusoe*, and its proprietor, William Taylor, printed a notice in the *St James Gazette* threatening legal action.[46] The suit does not appear to have progressed far, as there is no further evidence of it. Taylor was a conger member and Cox was not, although he later became one, and perhaps the threat of legal action, backed by the economic power of the conger, was enough to deter Cox, or to persuade him to come to an extra-judicial arrangement.

The following year a case was brought before the Court of Chancery which raised the issue of whether the Statute of Anne should be read narrowly, so as to apply only to verbatim reprints of books. This was the case of *Burnett v Chetwood*,[47] discussed above in chapter three, in which an injunction was granted on the basis that the work was damaging to religion and morality. However, the defendant's argument was to set out two approaches that were to become significant in later cases. First, he argued before the Court that:

> A translation of a book was not within the intent of the act, which being intended to encourage learning by giving the advantage of the book to the author, could be intended only to restrain the mechanical art of printing, and that others should not pirate the copy and gain an advantage to themselves by reprinting it; but not to hinder a translation of a book into another language, which in some respects might be called a different book.[48]

The first limb of the argument was thus that the Act applied only to exact reprints. The second limb was that a translation could be seen to be a new work, on the basis that the translator was a new author. The argument continued:

> and the translator may be said to be an author, in as much as some skill in language is requisite thereto, and not barely a mechanic art, as in the case of reprinting in the same language; and that the translator dresses it up and clothes the sense in his own style and expression, and at least puts it into a different form from the original, and *forma dat esse rei*; and therefore should rather seem to be within the encouragement than the prohibition of the act.[49]

Lord Chancellor Macclesfield accepted the defendant's contention, stating that:

> [A] translation might not be the same with the reprinting the original, on account that the translator has bestowed his care and pains upon it, and so not within the prohibition of the act.[50]

The Lord Chancellor's reference to 'care and pains' as conferring authorship status on the translator and, in consequence, a finding of non-infringement is interesting as labour would become a key concept for the law of copyright as the century progressed.

46 P Rogers, *Robinson Crusoe* (London, G Allen & Unwin, 1979) 7–9.

47 *Burnett v Chetwood* (1720) 2 Mer 441. This case was not reported until 1817, attached to *Southey v Sherwood* (1817) 2 Mer 435.

48 ibid 441.

49 ibid.

50 ibid 442.

The argument that the book was a different book to the one it was alleged to have copied was consistent with the approach taken in pre-Statute of Anne cases in Chancery. In the 1681 case of *Chiswell v Lee*, the Court ordered that the author, again Dr Burnett, should read the book complained of and ascertain whether or not it was the same book as his book, *History of the Reformation of the Church of England*.[51] Similarly, in the 1709 case *Wellington v Levi*, the defendant argued that his book 'differed in substance as well as title' from the plaintiff's book.[52] The court ordered a Master to compare the two books in question to see if they were the same book, or whether they differed materially.[53]

Following *Burnett v Chetwood*, no cases before the Court of Chancery involving partial taking have been identified until 1739, when there began a spate of legal action. This surge of activity may represent the fading power of the congers in the middle of the century.[54] The increase in judicial activity may also be explained by the failure of the London booksellers to achieve their objectives in another forum: the legislature. As mentioned in chapter two, the London booksellers began to petition Parliament for new legislation in the 1730s. The Bill of 1737 was the first to address the problems of both partial copying and altered copying. Part taking was included in the definition of the right as applying to 'any book, pamphlet or writing or any *sheet* of such book pamphlet or writing'. A second clause prohibited any person from printing an abridgment or translation of a book within three years of its publication without the consent of the author or proprietor.[55] This clause suggests, first, that the drafter of the Bill considered that abridgments and translations were currently permitted by law; and, second, that they should be prevented for long enough to give the author or owner some 'lead time' in the market, which, in turn, suggests they were perceived as economically damaging to the booksellers' interests. However, the draftsman did not go so far as to ban them completely.

A third clause of the Bill addressed another problem experienced by the booksellers. This clause was explicitly aimed at:

> [A] frequent Practice among Authors and Publishers of Books of Value, as soon as an Impression has been sold, to publish another Edition thereof with Alterations, Additions or Notes, whereby the Purchasers of the former Edition have been much injured, and the Value of their Books greatly diminished.[56]

[51] *Chiswell v Lee* (1681) C33/257/112.

[52] *Wellington v Levi* (1709) C33/314/54–55.

[53] I am indebted to Tomas Gomez-Arostegui for locating and transcribing these cases.

[54] Blagden ascribes the congers' mid-century demise to several factors including the apparent success of the Chancery injunction as a means of dealing with the pirates, the death of key members, and, after 1753, the growth of subscription publishing, which shared the risk by passing it on to subscribers. See N Hodgson and C Blagden, *The Notebook of Thomas Bennet and Henry Clements* (Oxford, Oxford University Press, 1956) 99–100.

[55] A Bill for the better Encouragement of Learning by the more effectual Securing the Copies of printed Books to the Authors or Purchasers of such Copies, during the Times therein to be mentioned (British Library, BS 68/16(1), 1737) or (House of Lords Parchment Collection, 1714–1718, 1737).

[56] ibid.

The remedy provided in the Bill was to provide that, in the case of books sold in sheets for a price exceeding 5s, authors, assigns or anyone else who published a subsequent edition with correction or alterations within 21 years[57] of the original edition, had to publish, at the same time or within six months, separate sheets containing the additions and alterations, with the pages to which they referred at a proportionate price. Any person who failed to do this would lose the protection of the Act and forfeit £50 to any person who sued for it. Furthermore, in the case of books sold in sheets for a price exceeding 3s, a new edition of which was printed with corrections and alterations, 14 copies must be delivered to the Stationers' Company to be distributed to the libraries set out in the Act.[58]

This provision could be interpreted in two ways. On the one hand, it could be interpreted in accordance with the values it professed, namely protecting readers who had paid considerable sums for books, only to find that they had become obsolete. However, the clause also protected booksellers against competition from those who sought to ride on the coat-tails of successful and popular works by reprinting them with notes. The legal proceedings over the notes added to Milton's *Paradise Lost*, discussed below,[59] reveal that this was a real issue for the copy-owning booksellers. However, the Bill was unsuccessful in the House of Lords[60] and the booksellers turned back to the Court of Chancery.

B. Lord Hardwicke in the Court of Chancery

The first two cases to deal with the problem of partial or altered taking to come before the Lord Chancellor, Lord Hardwicke, were heard on 7 August 1739 and may have been part of an organised strategy, as both groups of plaintiffs used the same legal counsel.[61] The first case was brought by Stephen Austen, Lawton Gilliver and John Clark against Edward Cave.[62] Austen, Gilliver and Clark were conger members, well-connected and powerful booksellers.[63] Edward Cave was the proprietor of the ground-breaking *Gentleman's Magazine*, and was not involved in the London booksellers' complex network of book shares. His magazine, although operating in the well-worn footsteps of the traditional historical and literary miscellanies, was the first magazine that also sought to cover current events, and drew its material from a broad range of sources. It was successful from the first, and immediately drew a host of imitators. In fact, Cave's accuser Clark was

57 Twenty-one years was the new maximum period of copyright duration under the Bill.

58 This clause is summarised from the version of the Bill that was sent to the House of Lords. The Bill also increased the number of deposit libraries from 9 to 14.

59 *Tonson v Walker* (1752) 3 Swans 672: see below: text at n 104.

60 Pope, writing contemporaneously, claimed that the Bill failed because it was prejudicial to the 'True Intention of Encouraging Learning'. Deazley, however, points out its failure was more probably due to the fact that the bill was prejudicial to the interests of booksellers: Deazley, *On the Origin* 107–08.

61 The procedure for bringing an action in the Court of Chancery is discussed above in ch 3, section III B.

62 *Austen v Cave* (1739) c 11 1552/3, c.33 371/493, 535, 373/41, 224, 415, 535, 540.

63 Hodgson and Blagden, *The Notebook* Apps 13, 14.

one of the proprietors of Cave's closest rival, *The London Magazine; or Gentleman's Monthly Intelligencer*.[64]

The work at issue in the litigation was a book of four sermons by Dr Joseph Trapp, entitled, *The Nature, Folly, and Danger of Being Righteous Overmuch*, extracts from which Cave had printed in the *Magazine*. The plaintiffs claimed that Cave had printed Trapp's sermons and sold 'great part thereof'. Crucially, they also claimed that Cave had stated he would soon be printing the remainder. Cave entered a demurrer, first questioning the plaintiffs' title to their work. He then admitted he had frequently published short extracts from new writings, but added that he did so:

> Not with an Intent to prejudice the Proprietors of such Books or Pamphlets in the Sale of them on the Contrary this Defendant believes his Publishing such Extracts have many times if not mostly been agreeable to the Proprietors of the Books and the same hath never been Complained of by them as being contrary to the Said Act of Parliament or detrimental to them.[65]

Cave went on to emphasise the smallness of the amount taken, stating that he had condensed 30 pages out of 69 into three and a half pages in the *Magazine*. He argued he had been carrying out similar exercises for several years without complaint. Finally, he appealed to the legislator's intention, stating he

> humbly apprehends it was not in the meaning or intention of the said Act of Parliament to restrain any Person from Extracting any Passage or Passages out of the Works of any Author and submits it to the Judgment of this Honourable Court whether such a Construction would not be greatly prejudicial to the spreading of knowledge and learning and therefore this Defendant hopes that by his Publishing such Extract as aforesaid he hath not acted contrary to the meaning and intent of the said Act of Parliament.[66]

The second case was brought by another group of powerful, copy-owning conger members, against the architectural writer Batty Langley.[67] Langley was accused of printing parts from two books on architecture and, again, the plaintiffs claimed he had stated he would soon publish the whole works. Like that of Cave, Langley's response began with an attack on the plaintiffs' title.[68] He then admitted he had taken some of the prints from their books, but, again like Cave, emphasised the small number taken, noting that he had taken around 14 prints, which made up less than four pages, and were interspersed throughout the book. Langley also claimed that he had made improvements to the work, and emphasised the public benefit of his book, which was aimed at the education of builders. He claimed that compilations such as his were not in breach of the Statute of

[64] CL Clarkson, *The First Magazine: A History of the Gentleman's Magazine* (Providence, RI, Brown University, 1938) 63.

[65] *Austen v Cave* (1739) c 11 1552/3.

[66] ibid.

[67] *Hitch v Langley* (1739) c 11 1559/23, c 33 371/493, 541, 591.

[68] c 11 1559/23.

Anne, 'most Especially as Compiling all Kinds of Learning have been Deemed Lawfull and Advantagious to the Community'.[69]

Cave was not successful in his answer to the complaints and the injunction obtained by the plaintiffs against Cave was ordered to continue.[70] Langley's case proceeded no further after his answer was drawn up.[71] A possible explanation for Cave's failure is found in a remaining fragment of Lord Hardwicke's reasoning which quotes him as stating: 'It is not material what Title you give the Book, nor whether you print it all at once or not'.[72] The meaning of this is not entirely clear, but it seems to respond to the plaintiffs' claim that Cave would print the rest of the book in future editions of the *Magazine*; thus, it does not address the reality of the situation, which was that Cave had not printed the entire work and, moreover, was extremely unlikely to do so given the nature of the *Magazine*.

Although Cave (unlike Langley) did not use the word 'abridgment' in his answer, the word was picked up by Samuel Johnson, who wrote an article championing Cave.[73] Johnson characterised Cave's publication as an abridgment rather than an extract, and argued such abridgments should be allowed. He began by claiming that the purchaser of the copy of a book has the sole right of printing and selling it, but no right to add to it or take from it without the consent of the author, which followed from the author's right to protect his reputation.[74] Once sold, the book became the property of the buyer 'who purchases with the book the right of making such use of it as he shall think most convenient, either for his own improvement or amusement, or the benefit and entertainment of mankind'.[75] The reader could use this right to the disadvantage of the author and the proprietor, who had no ground of complaint as they knew or ought to have known that there was a danger of such treatment at the time of making the sale. 'Thus' concluded Johnson, 'every book, when it falls into the hands of the reader, is liable to be examined, confuted, censured, translated and *abridged*; any of which may destroy the credit of the author, or hinder the sale of the book'.[76]

Johnson continued by arguing that the existence of countless abridgments, and the lack of complaint prior to *Austen v Cave* showed that they had always been considered legal. As well as trade custom, reason dictated that abridgments should be allowed, as the aim of an abridgment was

> to benefit mankind by facilitating the attainment of knowledge, and by contracting arguments, relations or descriptions, into a narrow compass; to convey instruction in the

[69] ibid.
[70] c 33 373/224.
[71] c 33 371/591.
[72] *Austen v Cave* (1739) 2 Eq Ca Abr 522.
[73] S Johnson, 'Considerations [by the late Dr Samuel Johnson] on the Case of Dr T[rapp']s Sermons, abridged by Mr Cave, 1739' (1787) *The Gentleman's Magazine* 555. Although it does not appear to have been published until 1787, the editor of the magazine at the time, John Nichols, assured the reader that the article was written upon the occasion of the law suit, as 'on all difficult occasions, Johnson was Cave's oracle': 555 fn.
[74] ibid 555.
[75] ibid.
[76] ibid 556.

> easiest method, without fatiguing the attention, burdening the memory, or impairing the health of the student.[77]

He added that although abridgments may diminish the original author's value and the profits of the publisher, these considerations should give way to the 'advantage received to mankind from the easier propagation of knowledge'.[78]

Johnson's eloquent defence was of little use to Cave but it may have influenced subsequent defendants in emphasising that their works were 'abridgments'.[79] The first to do so was James Hodges, against whom James Read brought an action in April 1740 for printing a book called *The Life and Reign of Czar Peter the Great Emperor of all Russia and Father of his Country*. Read claimed this book was 'almost wholly taken and copied' from his own book, entitled *The History of the Life of Peter the First Emperor of Russia*.[80] Unlike the previous two cases, which had involved conger members taking on outsiders, both Read and Hodges were prominent members of the book trade. Hodges was a bookseller who had made his fortune in chapbooks. He was one of the Court Assistants to the Stationers' Company, and was knighted in 1758.[81] Read was a well-connected London printer.[82] The book itself had been sold to many well-known London booksellers and may have been a conger book.[83]

Read claimed that Hodges' aim was to undercut his market by selling the work more cheaply.[84] Hodges countered by claiming that his book was an 'abridgment', that only a small amount had been taken and that not one page appeared without variation. Hodges also sought to separate the parts of the work that might belong to Read from that to which he could not lay claim, pointing out that much of the book consisted of tracts, manifestos and public papers which had been in print before the plaintiff's book was compiled. He claimed that his book targeted a different audience, 'of more ordinary and mean readers'.[85] Finally, he argued that his book was not a piracy because, 'it is not the same as the Plaintiff's book on History but it is of a different Nature and humbly insists that it is in the Nature of an Abridgment'.[86] The case was referred to a Master, who considered Hodges' answer sufficient, and the initial injunction was dissolved. Read, however, immediately sought a further injunction from Chancery, disputing Hodge's claim that his book was an abridgment. This injunction was granted and continued until the

[77] ibid.

[78] ibid.

[79] Although this would depend on the extent to which Johnson's article was circulated at the time of its writing.

[80] *Read v Hodges* (1740) c 11 583/36, c 33 374/153, 250, 255, 275, 276.

[81] J Nichols, *Literary Anecdotes of the Eighteenth Century* (London, Nichols, 1812) vol.3, p 246.

[82] Power struggles between printers and booksellers had long been a feature of the internal book trade politics.

[83] Hodges stated in his answer that he sold the book for 2s 6d to those who bought a number of copies at once, and 3s for retail. Those who had bought the book included Charles Hitch, Thomas Longman, John Brotherton, the Knaptons and Stephen Austen: *Read v Hodges* (1740) c 11 583/36.

[84] ibid.

[85] ibid.

[86] ibid.

hearing of the cause.[87] The case continued through several more phases, before finally coming to rest in Read's favour.[88]

The following year, another case came before Lord Hardwicke.[89] Fletcher Gyles and two other booksellers sought an injunction against Wilcox, the bookseller, Barlow, the compiler and Nutt, the printer, in respect of Sir Matthew Hale's *Pleas of the Crown*, or *Historia Placitorum Coronae*. Barlow's counsel conceded that the plaintiff would be entitled to claim property in Hale's book if he had made a 'transcript' of the whole or 'great part' of it. However, he claimed that he had not made a transcription, but rather an abridgment which contained new material.[90] Wilcox also claimed that the book, in which the French and Latin quotations were translated into English, was an abridgment, stating: 'The Defendant never understood such Abridgments or Translations were within the words and meaning of the Act or were understood or construed to be'.[91]

In this case, at last, we have a recorded judgment of Lord Hardwicke applying the Statute of Anne to an alleged infringement. He apparently gave the matter fresh consideration, for, when counsel for the plaintiff (who had also acted for Read) referred him to *Read v Hodges*, he stated that he had given his thoughts upon that case without much consideration and would therefore not lay any weight upon them.[92] There are two reports of Lord Hardwicke's decision in *Gyles v Wilcox*, each with a slightly different emphasis on Lord Hardwicke's interpretation of the Statute of Anne. In Barnardiston's report, Lord Hardwicke seems to emphasise that the object of the Act was for the encouragement of learning, and public benefit and advantage.[93] However, according to Atkyns' report, Lord Hardwicke started from a construction of the Statute of Anne as having the purpose of securing books to authors, 'as some recompense for their pains and labour in such works as may be of use to the learned world'.[94] The difference between the two reporters' approach to the underlying justification for the Statute of Anne is striking. Where Barnardiston's version of Lord Hardwicke's approach is essentially the utilitarian aim of encouraging learning in the public interest, Atkyns saw him as taking a view of the Act that prioritised rewarding authors for their 'pains and labour' or investment.

Despite differing in their views of the interpretation of the Act's intent, the reporters agreed that Lord Hardwicke's approach was to interpret the Act in a purposive manner. Following the words of the Act, he differentiated between a colourable copy, which was effectively the same book in disguise, and a 'fair'

87 c 12 1796/41, c 33 374/299.

88 Hodges was served with a subpoena, but Read died before the matter could progress further, and the cause abated. Read's widow, Mary, having been granted probate, then brought a bill to Chancery requesting that the injunction be revived, pending hearing of the cause: c 12 1796/41. When Hodges made no answer, the Master of the Rolls revived the injunction, and the matter does not appear to have been continued: c 33 374/379.

89 *Gyles v Wilcox* (1740) c 33 375/274, 275; 2 Atk 141; Barn C 368; 2 Eq Ca Abr 697.

90 c 33 375/274.

91 c 33 375/274, 275.

92 2 Atk 141, 141.

93 Barn C 368, 368.

94 2 Atk 141, 143.

abridgment, which was a different book and thus outside the Act's scope. According to Atkyns' report, the Lord Chancellor appreciated that the interests of authors might be prejudiced by allowing derivative works to be made, 'by mistaking and curtailing the sense of the author',[95] but that fair abridgments should nonetheless be allowed, being not only a new book in physical form but also in content. Lord Hardwicke stated: 'abridgments might with some propriety be called a new book, because not only the paper and print, but the invention, learning and judgment of the author is shown in them, and in many cases are extremely useful'.[96] He further noted that suppression of such works would have 'mischievous consequences' if it prevented the publication of scholarly journals.[97] Lord Hardwicke's own opinion seemed to favour the plaintiffs. However, as he considered that the work was not so flagrant a copy as in *Read v Hodges*, he directed that Master, attended by two persons skilled in the law, to read both books and make an award. They found that Wilcox's book was a fair abridgment and no injunction was awarded.[98]

In 1743, Edward Cave was once again enjoined in Chancery.[99] Francis Cogan, a bookseller, alleged that Cave had begun to print a book with the edifying title of *Memoirs of an Unfortunate Young Nobleman, returned from a thirteen years slavery in America, where he had been sent by the wicked contrivance of his cruel Uncle, a story founded on Truth and addressed equally to head and heart.*[100] This time, Cave was careful to portray his actions as an 'abridgment', making the (wholly credible) claim that, having read the book, he found it 'prolix' and so had removed a great deal of material as well as altering some phraseology.[101] Changing his argument somewhat from the one he had made four years earlier, he claimed he had a right to print the abridgment as he was its author.[102] It appears that his arguments were successful and the injunction was dissolved.[103]

The next and final case to come before Lord Hardwicke was *Tonson v Walker*[104] in 1752. This case concerned Walker's attempts to publish Milton's *Paradise Lost* with notes by Dr Newton. William Murray, later Lord Mansfield, was acting for Tonson, and he moved for an injunction to restrain Walker, basing his argument on common law copyright. Lord Hardwicke cautiously refused to address the common law copyright issue, as the notes remained within the statutory periods. Walker's counsel argued that the now-established abridgment principle applied to the current situation. Lord Hardwicke, however, was not prepared to accept this, stating that 'a fair abridgment would be entitled to protection'[105] but that this was

95 ibid.
96 ibid.
97 ibid.
98 See *Tonson v Walker* (1752) 3 Swans 672, 679.
99 *Cogan v Cave* (1743) c 12 2204/24.
100 ibid.
101 ibid.
102 ibid.
103 See *Tonson v Walker* (1752) 3 Swans 672, 678.
104 ibid.
105 ibid 681.

'a mere evasion'.[106] Lord Hardwicke appeared to consider that the reason for allowing an abridgment was that it was a 'new work'.[107]

A new development in Lord Hardwicke's reasoning, however, was the emphasis he placed on the amount taken. Comparing the case before him with *Gyles v Wilcox*, he noted that, in the former case, the original contained 275 sheets, while the abridgment contained only 35. In the present case, however, it appeared that the whole work had been taken, or 'colourably abridged', with only 28 notes added.[108] It seems that Lord Hardwicke considered either that the amount taken (the whole work) was too large or that the amount added was too small for the work to qualify as a new work, or perhaps based his decision on a combination of the two.

In 1761, Sir Thomas Clarke MR, who had been counsel for Walker in *Tonson v Walker*, heard the case of *Dodsley v Kinnersley*[109] which, ironically, involved Samuel Johnson's book *Rasselas*. Dodsley, as assignee of Johnson's copyright, complained that part of the book's narrative had been printed in the *Grand Magazine of Magazines*. Clarke MR appeared to treat it as settled that a 'fair abridgment' would not be considered a piracy, stating that 'no certain line can be drawn to distinguish a fair abridgment; but every case must depend on its circumstances'.[110] However, he did identify two factors that should be considered: the amount taken and the prejudice caused to the plaintiff.[111] On the question of amount, he found that less than one-tenth had been abstracted. On the question of prejudice, several booksellers, including Jacob Tonson, had appeared to give evidence of the damage caused by abridgments. However, Clarke MR accepted Kinnersley's evidence that it was also usual in the trade to publish extracts in magazines. Ultimately, he rejected the plaintiff's arguments as to prejudice because they themselves had already published an extract of the work in the *London Chronicle*[112] and refused the injunction.[113]

Sir Thomas Clarke's emphasis on the amount taken was followed eight years later in *Macklin v Richardson*.[114] This case presented a new issue, as it involved the printing of a dramatic work that had only ever been performed. The defendants argued that in the case of plays, 'the audience had a right to carry away what they could, and make any use of it'.[115] Lord Commissioner Smythe, who was hearing the case, dismissed this argument and granted the injunction, stating that the plaintiff had a right to be protected in respect of any profit he might obtain from printing and publishing the play as a book. He considered that as one half of the

106 ibid.
107 ibid 678.
108 ibid 680.
109 *Dodsley v Kinnersley* (1761) Amb 403.
110 ibid 405.
111 ibid.
112 ibid 405–06.
113 ibid 406.
114 *Macklin v Richardson* (1770) Amb 694.
115 ibid 696.

play had been printed, it could not be considered an abridgment. He also distinguished *Dodsley v Kinnersley* on the basis that 'only an extract' had been copied in that case.[116] This appears to be a reference to the small amount taken, rather than including extracts per se in the rule regarding abridgments.

Over the course of his years as Lord Chancellor, Lord Hardwicke's views on infringement evolved to the point of developing the principle that a 'fair abridgment' would not be considered to fall foul of the Statute of Anne. By 1761, Clarke MR, following Lord Hardwicke, could confidently state that all that was required in the case of *Dodsley v Kinnersley* was to see whether it was 'adapted to the rules and principles laid down'.[117] The fair-abridgment rule was the seed from which the fair-dealing defences would grow but, in recent years, different views have been expressed as to whether it was a victory for copyright owners or the public more generally. Ronan Deazley argues that Lord Hardwicke's decisions were 'insightful and well-intentioned' because they were guided by the central policy underlying the Statute of Anne, namely, a 'social bargain struck between the author, the bookseller and the reading public'.[118] Robert Burrell, however, contends that the abridgment principle expanded the rights of the copyright owner by limiting the uses that could be made of a work. This went beyond the intention of Parliament, because the correct reading of the Statute of Anne should have been that there would be no infringement unless it could be shown that the defendant *reprinted* the plaintiff's book.[119] Thus, he considers that the abridgment rule favoured copyright owners over copyright users and the public in general. Jane Ginsburg emphasises Lord Hardwicke's focus on the abridger as having his own claims to authorship,[120] a concern which can be traced back to *Burnett v Chetwood*.

In assessing whether Lord Hardwicke was most influenced by the claims of owners, authors or the public, it is helpful to begin by remembering that the nature of litigation places certain constraints and formulae upon the parties as well as the judges. Milsom reminds us that:

> Lawyers have always been preoccupied with today's details, and have worked with their eyes down. The historian, if he is lucky, can see why a rule came into existence, what change left it working injustice, how it came to be evaded, how the evasion produced a new rule, and sometimes how that new rule in its turn came to be overtaken by change. But he misunderstands it all if he endows the lawyers who took part with any vision on any comparable scale, or attributes to them any intention beyond getting today's client out of difficulty.[121]

In the absence of specific guidance in the Statute as to what would amount to piracy, the question before the Court was whether the defendant's book was, as a

[116] ibid.
[117] (1761) Amb 403, 404.
[118] Deazley, *On the Origin* 85.
[119] Burrell and Coleman, *Copyright Exceptions* 255.
[120] J Ginsburg, '"Une Chose Publique"? The Author's Domain and the Public Domain in Early British, French and US Copyright Law [2006] *Cambridge Law Journal* 636.
[121] SFC Milsom, *Historical Foundations of the Common Law*, 2nd edn (London, Butterworths, 1981) 7.

matter of fact, *the same* as the plaintiff's book. If so, reprinting would have occurred; if not, then it would fall outside the scope of the Statute. Indeed, this approach pre-dated the Act by many years. It was easy to argue that a translation was a different book, but more difficult when there was no change in language. The defendants experimented with several arguments that might explain why a book that borrowed some of the language of another book should be seen to be a different work, including the amount taken, the lack of prejudice caused, and the public interest in the spread of learning. It was not until these arguments were brought within the specific category of abridgment that they were found acceptable to the Court. Categorising a book as 'an abridgment' automatically conferred on it the status of a new book, which was therefore a different book to that of the plaintiff. Moreover, it emphasises how limited was the market to which the plaintiff could lay claim. This is particularly apparent in *Dodsley v Kinnersley* when Clarke MR held that the plaintiffs could not argue they had been prejudiced by the defendant's abridgment since they had published an abridgment themselves (in a newspaper of which they were part-proprietors).[122]

Both reports of Lord Hardwicke's judgment in *Gyles v Wilcox* suggest that he was sympathetic to public interest arguments, as he referred to the encouragement of learning as well as to the dissemination and multiplication of knowledge as desirable outcomes. He also recognised that these interests could conflict with the interests of authors, noting that they might be prejudiced by poor abridgments. However, it is also likely that Lord Hardwicke recognised that the parties before him were involved in a commercial dispute with significant ramifications for the whole trade. Moreover, he was aware that reference to the public interest was a powerful rhetorical tool, as can be seen in his statement in *Tonson v Walker* that 'Arguments from public utility may be urged on both sides'.[123]

It is also apparent that Lord Hardwicke strongly favoured an interpretation of the Statute of Anne which would have predictive value for future litigants. Whereas, as Milsom explains, the lawyers' main concern was to get their client out of trouble, judges could take a longer term view of the Statute and the consequences of their decisions. Lord Campbell, in what is close to a hagiography, described Lord Hardwicke thus: 'Two objects seem entirely to absorb the attention of the Judge: 1. Properly to adjust the disputed rights of the parties. 2. To establish a rule by which similar questions may be solved in future'.[124] Lord Campbell added that 'He never resorted, however, to forced interpretations or fanciful analogies . . . Nor was he betrayed into the seductive and dangerous practice of laying down rules in loose and sweeping terms'.[125]

The construction of a specific category of work that would not be considered a piracy satisfied Lord Hardwicke's demand for certainty and precision, by providing a method for determining whether the second work was a new work or the

[122] Today, this would clearly be one of the copyright owner's rights.
[123] (1752) 3 Swans 672, 680.
[124] J Campbell, *Lives of the Lord Chancellors*, vol 6 (London, John Murray, 1868) 195.
[125] ibid 196.

same work in disguise. It also recognised that there was a social benefit in allowing new works to be produced and made available to greater numbers of people, while avoiding the uncertainty and rhetorical seduction of appeals made solely to the public interest. Therefore, although Burrell is correct in noting that the abridgment principle was not a judicial limitation on an unlimited right granted by Parliament to prevent all forms of copying, it was not simply a judicial expansion of a very limited right either. From the outset, litigants and judges accepted that the Act's prohibition would have to extend beyond exact reprints, in order to catch books that were reprints in disguise. This meant that evidence had to be led in order to establish whether the defendant's book was, or was not, the same as the plaintiff's and one way of showing this was to prove that the second book was an abridgment of the first.

Although the doctrine of precedent had yet to take its modern shape in the middle of the eighteenth century, the nature of the common law encouraged litigants to adopt arguments that had been successful in the past. A simple test that both followed the words of the Statute and could be linked to a public interest rationale was attractive to suitors as well as judges. The processes of the common law meant that the favourable treatment of abridgments hardened into a rule, but at no stage was it suggested that this was the only permissible use of a work. As Willes J noted in *Millar v Taylor*, '[c]ertainly bona fide imitations, translations and abridgments are different; and, in respect of the property may be considered as new works: but colourable and fraudulent variations will not do'.[126] The abridgment rule may have presaged the judicial preference for categories over broad principles of infringement, but cannot by itself be claimed to herald the start of a judicial programme of expansion of copyright owners' rights. Moreover, the abridgment approach continued to sit alongside a more ad hoc approach, in which the Court of Chancery simply referred the parties to a Master for a report as to whether the books in question were the same or different.[127]

C. Testing the Limits of the Text

The cases involving partial taking and abridgments required judges and litigants to scrutinise the text of the Statute of Anne. However, they also implicitly raised the question of what, precisely, the Statute was protecting, and why. This question was debated at considerable length in the common law copyright cases of the latter part of the century. As Sherman and Bently have argued, the most interesting discussion of the literary property debates which culminated in the case of *Donaldson v Becket* was 'whether or not and, if so, in what circumstances the subject matter of a book—ideas, sentiments, words, letters and style by which it was

[126] *Millar v Taylor* (1769) 4 Burr 2303, 2310.

[127] See *Trusler v Cummings* (1773) c 33/440; *Jefferys v Bowles* (1770) c 33/433. Cp *Strahan v Newbury* (1774) c 33/442 in which the Lord Chancellor refers the works to the Master, asking him whether the book in question was a 'fair abridgment'.

composed—could be conceived as a distinct species of property'.[128] Questions of partial and altered copying were relevant to the arguments surrounding the common law copyright because, as De Grey J[129] noted in *Donaldson v Becket*, 'Abridgments of Books, . . . Translations, Notes, as effectually deprive the original Author of the Fruits of his Labours as direct particular Copies, yet they are allowable'.[130]

Others who, like De Grey J, were opposed to perpetual copyright argued that its effect would be to inhibit *any* use of a book. Addressing the House in *Donaldson v Becket*, Lord Camden rhetorically asked:

> Then what Part of the Work is exempt from this desultory Claim? Does it lie in the Sentiments, the Language, and Style, or the Paper? If in the Sentiments, or Language, no one can translate or abridge them. Locke's Essays might perhaps be put into other Expressions, or newly methodised, and all the original System and Ideas be retained. These Questions shew how the Argument counter-acts itself, how the Subject of it shifts, and become public in one Sense and private in another: and they are all new to the Common Law, which leaves us perfectly in the Dark about their Solution?[131]

One pamphleteer warned that the courts would be overrun with cases brought by authors: 'Poet would commence Action against Poet, and Historian against Historian, complaining of Literary Trespass'.[132] Similarly, in *Millar v Taylor*, Yates J considered that disputes might arise between authors

> whether the works of one author were or were not the same with those of another author; or whether there were only colourable differences . . . [or] whether those who should compile notes on a publication, and should insert the text, should be liable to an action for it.[133]

Those in favour of common law copyright responded to such fears by distinguishing at one level between the physical work and the ideas it contained. In *Millar v Taylor*, Willes J explained:

> [S]o all the knowledge, which can be acquired from the contents of a book, is free for every man's use; if it teaches mathematics, physic, husbandry; if it teaches to write in verse or prose; if, by reading an epic poem, a man learns how to make an epic poem of his own; he is at liberty.

[128] B Sherman and L Bently, *The Making of Modern Intellectual Property Law* (Cambridge, Cambridge University Press, 1999).

[129] Who rejected the common law copyright, see R Deazley, 'Re-reading Donaldson (1774) in the Twenty-First Century and Why it Matters' (2003) *European Intellectual Property Review* 270, 273.

[130] 'The Cases of the Appellants and Respondents in the Cause of Literary Property wherein the Decree of Lord Chancellor Apsley was Reversed, &c, by a Gentleman of the Inner Temple' in S Parks (ed), *The Literary Property Debate: Six Tracts 1764–1774* (New York, Garland Publishing Inc, 1975) 46.

[131] ibid 52.

[132] W Warburton, 'An Enquiry into the Nature and Origin of Literary Property' (London, 1762) in S Parks (ed), *Horace Walpole's Political Tracts (1747–1748)* (New York, Garland Publishing Inc, 1974) 12–13. Note that Parks attributes the pamphlet to William Warburton, but Ross claims this attribution is erroneous: T Ross, 'Copyright and the Invention of Tradition (1992) 26 *Eighteenth Century Studies* 1, 23 fn.

[133] (1769) 4 Burr 2303, 2394.

> But printing is a trade or manufacture. The types and the press are the mechanical instruments: the literary composition is as the material; which always is property. The book conveys knowledge, instruction, or entertainment; but multiplying copies in print is a quite distinct thing from all the book communicates. And there is no incongruity, to reserve that right; and yet convey the free use of all the book teaches.[134]

However, as the cases involving partial and altered copying demonstrate, it was not enough for the booksellers to limit the Act's operation to multiplying exact copies; they required broader protection. As Sherman and Bently have shown, this resulted in the formulation of the notion that what was protected was not the ideas in the work, as such, but the way in which they were expressed.[135]

Blackstone had first considered the problem of ascertaining what it was that gave rise to property rights in books, and which elements of them could therefore be protected as counsel in *Tonson v Collins*.[136] He expanded his ideas in his *Commentaries*, stating:

> Now the identity of a literary composition consists intirely in the sentiment and language; the same conceptions clothed in the same words, must necessarily be the same composition: and whatever method be taken of conveying the composition to the ear or eye of another, by recital, by writing, or by printing, in any number of copies or at any period of time, it is always the identical work of the author which is so conveyed; and no other man can have a right to convey or transfer it without his consent, either tacitly or expressly given.[137]

While Blackstone's use of the word 'sentiment' might be taken to mean 'ideas', thereby extending protection beyond the language of the text itself, a case decided shortly after *Donaldson v Becket* reveals that this is not so. In this case, the publisher Strahan sought an injunction against Newbery for publishing a book which Newbery claimed was an abridgment of *Dr Hawkesworth's Voyages*.[138] Lord Apsley LC consulted Blackstone J before delivering his judgment. After several hours of discussion, they concluded that

> an abridgment where the understanding is employed in retrenching unnecessary and uninteresting circumstances, which rather deaden the narration, is not an act of plagiarism upon the original work, nor against the property of the author in it, but an allowable and meritorious work.[139]

The case was referred to a master to ascertain whether the book was, in fact, a 'fair abridgment'[140] and injunction was subsequently refused.

[134] ibid 2331.

[135] Sherman and Bently, Making of Modern IP Law 33.

[136] *Tonson v Collins* (1761) 1 Black W 321, 343.

[137] W Blackstone, *Commentaries on the Laws of England*, 4 vols, 1st edn (Oxford, Clarendon Press, 1765–69) Bk 2, p 406 (c 26 s 8).

[138] *Strahan v Newbery* (1774) Lofft 775. For a fascinating account of the history Hawksworth's *Voyages*, see M Leeming, 'Hawkworth's *Voyages*: The First 'Australian' Copyright Litigation' (2004) 9 *Australian Journal of Legal History* 159. The case is reported without a name by Lofft, but Leeming points out that the publisher of Lofft's Reports was Strahan himself, who may have wished to conceal his loss.

[139] (1774) Lofft 775, 775.

[140] c 33/442.

The proponents of common law copyright were thus arguing for a redrawing of copyright's boundaries. Aiming to push them out in one direction, length, they sought to reassure their opposition by insisting on a restricted 'depth' of protection which, if not wholly limited to the physical form, was at least tethered to it very closely. While they may have failed to convince the House of Lords of their position, their formulation of an approach that distinguished between the language and expression of a work, and the ideas it contained was to prove more enduring. Moreover, as the law of copyright did expand and move away from a limited right to print and reprint books, the fears expressed by Yates and the anonymous pamphleteer as to the difficulty of deciding cases that turned on more subtle distinctions were also realised.

D. Labour and Originality at the Turn of the Century

These difficulties were demonstrated in the years following *Donaldson* in a series of legal disputes involving works of fact and information. In 1899, Augustine Birrell complained:

> In reading the cases in the Reports for the last hundred years, you cannot overlook the literary insignificance of the contending volumes. The big authors and the big books stand majestically on one side—the combatants are all small fry. The question of literary larceny is chiefly illustrated by disputes between rival book-makers and rival proprietors of works of reference, sea charts, Patterson's 'Roads', the antiquities of *Magna Graecia*, rival encyclopaedias, gazetteers, guide books, cookery books, law reports, post office and trade directories, illustrated catalogues of furniture, statistical returns, Poole's farce, 'Who's Who?', Brewer's 'Guide to Science.' This is not by any means an exhaustive list but it accurately shows the nature of the proceedings.[141]

The disdain in Birrell's tone obscures the fact that the reason such works repeatedly came before the courts is that works of fact and information were big business in the eighteenth and nineteenth centuries. Riding on the tide of the Enlightenment thirst for knowledge, educational and informative books were safe investments for the booksellers. It was important, therefore, for the composers, producers and sellers of these books that they were recognised as literary property by the courts. On the other hand, it would be a significant victory for those booksellers seeking quick and sure profits by riding on the coat-tails of others if they could establish that there was no prohibition on copying such books.

Lord Mansfield was presented with a case that allowed him to put the arguments of the proponents of common law copyright into practice in the 1785 case of *Sayre v Moore*.[142] The work in issue, a sea chart, was protected by the Engraving Act,[143] but

[141] A Birrell, *Seven Lectures on the Law and History of Copyright in Books* (London, Cassell & Company Ltd, 1899) 170–71.

[142] *Sayre v Moore* (1785) 1 East 361 fn; 102 ER 139 fn.

[143] An Act for more effectually securing the Property of Prints to Inventors and Engravers by enabling them to sue for and recover penalties in certain Cases 1777 (17 Geo 3 c 57).

Lord Mansfield considered that the law of literary copyright supplied the principles necessary to decide the case. In language that echoed that of Blackstone in his *Commentaries*, Lord Mansfield instructed the jury that 'The Act that secures copyright to authors guards against the piracy of the words and the sentiments; but it does not prohibit writing on the same subject'.[144] The jury found for the defendant.

Implicit in such a statement is the idea that the 'subject' itself remained free for the use of later authors. The following year a similar issue arose in the case of *Carnan v Bowles*.[145] This was the first of several cases involving the popular road book compiled by Captain Daniel Paterson.[146] The two books in question were referred to the Master for a determination as to whether they were 'the same book'. The Master found that they were not, but his order was challenged and came before Lord Thurlow LC. As Solicitor-General and Attorney-General, Edward Thurlow had argued against the common law right in *Tonson v Collins*, *Millar v Taylor* and *Donaldson v Becket*. However, the approach that he took in *Carnan v Bowles*, although differently worded, was similar to that of Lord Mansfield. Lord Thurlow stated:

> [A]s the roads of *Great Britain* were open to the inspection and observation of all mankind, every one was at liberty to publish the result of such observation: the subject-matters of these books were therefore *in medio*: but the question will be, whether the author has exhibited any new and distinct idea in the exposition of them; and then, whether the subsequent editor has, in substance, adopted the same.[147]

The Latin phrase '*in medio*' can be translated as 'in the community' or 'for the common good', and thus provides what may be the earliest reference to the public domain in copyright law. For the Lord Chancellor, the touchstone for deciding what would not be protected turned upon the public interest in preventing monopolisation of knowledge and learning. Such an approach is consistent with the arguments made by those opposed to common law copyright.[148] For Lord Thurlow, property rights would arise only through the exhibition of a 'new and distinct idea'. Further, infringement would only be established where this idea, and not the common material, was copied. In the end, Lord Thurlow dissolved the Master's injunction on the basis that the second work was original in itself.[149] Thus, the case is also significant in that the Lord Chancellor considered that a work which was 'original' would not amount to infringement.

Similar issues arose three years later in 1789 when the publisher John Murray (later to become one of the wealthiest and most conservative of London publishers) argued that in a book of chronology 'there was no originality, and that it was

[144] 1 East 361 fn, 362 fn.

[145] *Carnan v Bowles* (1786) 2 Bro CC 80 and 1 Cox 283.

[146] For background on Paterson and his road books, see SGH Fordham, 'Paterson's Roads: Daniel Paterson, His Maps and Itineraries' (1925) 5 *The Library*, 4th series, 333.

[147] 2 Bro CC 80, 85.

[148] Bently and Sherman, *Intellectual Property Law* 28–30.

[149] 2 Bro CC 80, 85.

not on the whole, such a kind of work as merited the protection of the court'.[150] However, according to Trusler, the author of the allegedly infringed chronology, Sir Thomas Sewell MR 'admitted that every man might publish a Chronology, but made the following distinction; that a chronology, like other subject-matter of books, was a work of labour, of course, it came under the denomination of property, and merited protection'.[151] Labour thus provided the rationale for protection. Three years later Lord Kenyon CJ heard the case at common law and similarly used labour as the foundation for finding infringement, stating: 'Any man might look into universal history, and might make a chronology, but no man had a right to avail himself of the industry and Labour of another'.[152]

The two judgments in this case illustrate the emergence of four important and interlinked themes: first, the idea that facts and information are not property and that anyone might use them to create a work that could be the subject of protection; second, the notion that copyright would subsist in the industry and labour expended upon that information; third, infringement was related to the labour expended on the materials rather than the materials themselves; and, fourth, that the underlying rationale for a finding of infringement could be traced back to 'reaping without sowing'[153] or what we would today call unjust enrichment or unfair competition.

These three cases demonstrate that the eighteenth-century courts had little difficulty protecting works of information against copying. They were also able to engage in the difficult task of separating the raw materials on which the book was based from the form that they took in the text. Nevertheless, the way that the respective judges approached this notion differed somewhat. Lord Mansfield located protection in the 'words' and 'sentiments', Lord Thurlow considered a 'new idea' to be necessary for protection, and Lord Kenyon seemed to think that only labour and industry was required. None of the three, however, referred to any kind of literary skill as being necessary, and this was also the approach taken by Lord Eldon in the1802 case of *Hogg v Kirby*.[154] In this case it was argued that a monthly magazine was not a literary property but a commercial venture, and that for copyright to subsist 'there must be a new arrangement of ideas and a new expression of them'.[155] Lord Eldon, however, had little time for this argument, stating

[150] J Trusler, *An Essay on Literary Property containing comments on the Statute of Queen Anne and Animadversion on that Statute* (London, 1798) 16.

[151] ibid.

[152] *Trusler v Murray* (1789) *The Times* (2 December 1789) 3c. The case was actually a fabricated controversy, designed to gain free publicity for the publications; W Zachs, *The First John Murray and the Late Eighteenth-Century London Book Trade* (Oxford, Oxford University Press, 1998) 198.

[153] It is worth noting that St Paul's message in Galatians (6:7–10) is that a man will reap what he sows. It is to take this message a step further to suggest that a person has a *right* to reap what he sows and to warn that a person must not expect rewards unless he has first put in the effort necessary for deserving them.

[154] *Hogg v Kirby* (1803) 8 Ves Jun 215.

[155] ibid 220.

I do not see, why, if a person collects an account of natural curiosities, and such articles, and employs the labour of his mind by giving a description of them, that is not as much a literary work as many others.[156]

In 1806, Lord Erskine LC expressed some dissatisfaction with conferring copyright so easily on works of information. In *Matthewson v Stockdale,*[157] which involved an East India Calendar, or Directory,[158] he stated:

Thinking it dangerous to carry this doctrine of copyright too far, the turn of my mind would lead me to a different decision of this case from that, which, following what I find to be the established law, I mean to give.[159]

His hesitation, however, did not stem from any concern to protect literary originality or any attributes of the romantic author. In particular, he was unhappy about the cases involving maps, on the basis that if two maps were accurate then they would be identical. The only way that he could reconcile the authorities was by locating the copyright in the labour and industry involved in creating the work. Although he believed there could be no copyright in an East India Calendar generally, he held that where a man had

by considerable expense and labour procured with correctness all the names and appointments on the Indian Establishment, he has a copyright in that individual work; which has cost him considerable expense and labour; and employed him at a loss in other respects.[160]

Thus, Lord Erskine followed Sewell MR in *Trusler v Murray* by locating copyright subsistence in the labour or industry invested in the work, further adding the criterion of expenditure. In the Court of Chancery, Lord Eldon took a similar approach in a case involving a court calendar, stating:

I have said nothing that has a tendency to prevent any person from giving to the public a work of this kind; if it is the fair fruit of original labour: the subject being open to all the world: but if it is a mere copy of an original work, this Court will interpose against that invasion of copyright.[161]

In Lord Eldon's formulation, originality was relevant also to infringement, because a 'mere copy' would not be an original work and therefore an infringement. Essentially, it seems, the law would protect works produced by fair labour.

During the literary property debates of the late eighteenth century, the proponents of common law copyright had developed the Lockean conception of property arising from labour to apply to rights in printing and publishing books.

[156] ibid 221–22.

[157] *Matthewson v Stockdale* (1806) 12 Ves 270.

[158] Up until 1775, almanacs had been the subject of an extremely valuable patent owned by the Stationers' Company, which formed part of the English Stock. For the story of Carnan's challenge to the monopoly, see C Blagden, 'Thomas Carnan and the Almanack Monopoly' (1961) 14 *Studies in Bibliography* 23.

[159] (1806) 12 Ves 270, 273.

[160] ibid 276.

[161] *Longman v Winchester* (1809) 16 Ves 269, 272.

In these debates, the touchstone of protection came to be the author and the focus was on his labour. The key player in forming this theoretical approach to copyright was William Blackstone, and he became the most influential, with many of the earliest writers on copyright law commenced their works by quoting Blackstone's statements on copyright in his *Commentaries*.[162] According to Jaszi, by this time, the ideology of authorship was 'essentially complete'.[163] It might, therefore, seem surprising that the ideology of romantic authorship played such a negligible role in the infringement cases. What an examination of these cases does reveal is that the references to labour did not begin with the literary property debates, but earlier in the century, and it was far from being the labour of a creative, inspired genius that was crucial to the courts' determinations.

As noted above, Lord Macclesfield first considered 'pains and care' to be relevant in *Burnett v Chetwood* and references to 'labour' can also be found in the later bills of complaint and responses, where it was further linked to cost or expense. In *Hitch v Langley*,[164] for example, the Complainants claimed that the author, the distinguished architect James Gibbs, had expended much 'labour' on them, and that they had paid £300 for the right to print them. Langley's defence alleged that Gibbs was not the author at all, but rather that it was a Mr Burlock or Burlow who had been lodging with Gibbs (presumably his draughsman John Borlack). Likewise, in *Read v Hodges,* Read's bill of complaint had emphasised the labour and expense incurred in collecting and compiling the materials, as well as arranging for the book to be written by John Mottley, while Hodges's Answer challenged Read's claim to have gone to 'very Great Industry Pains and Labour', claiming the book was itself copied from other sources.

While the literary property debates gave philosophical weight to the notion of labour and linked it to the claims of authorial rights, in the context of infringement cases the role of labour was subtly different. Here it was combined with the matter of expense, thereby focusing attention on copyright as a commercial investment and infringement as a question of trade competition. The language of 'originality' was also introduced at this time, as a standard that derived from the labour invested, and the focus of the courts' protection. It was thus also relevant to infringement because a new and original work would be protected also against allegations of infringement. The complex relationship between subsistence, infringement, labour and originality was to develop further in the second half of the century.

162 See above: ch 2. J Montefiore, *The Law of Copyright* (London, James Wallis, 1802) 1. See also R Maugham, *A Treatise on the Laws of Literary Property* (London, Longman et al, 1828) 2, 126. Copinger, however, footnoted directly to Locke in his opening sentences: WA Copinger, *The Law of Copyright in Works of Literature and Art*, 1st edn (London, Stevens & Haynes, 1870) 1.

163 Jaszi, 'Toward a Theory of Copyright' 471. See also Mark Rose, who considers it to have occurred even earlier, in 1774: M Rose, *Authors and Owners: The Invention of Copyright* (Cambridge, MA, Harvard University Press, 1993) 132.

164 (1739) c 11 1559/23, c 33 371/493.

II. THE NINETEENTH CENTURY

A. The Common Law to 1842

The first part of the nineteenth century saw the emergence of various principles that would become intrinsic to the law of copyright infringement. The language used is familiar to twenty-first century copyright lawyers: 'fairness', 'exception', 'defence', 'fair quotation', 'criticism' and 'review' are all words which form the linguistic currency of the law of fair dealing today. This should not, however, lead us to the mistaken assumption that the law of the nineteenth century was the same as it is today, just in an earlier stage of development, nor to overlook its instability and internal tensions.

Two approaches to infringement can be discerned during this period. The first represented a broadening of the fair-abridgment rule, which developed into the principle that any 'new work' would not be considered an infringement. The second approach focused on the damage suffered by the copyright owner. The two approaches were not necessarily in conflict; whether they were or not depended on the extent of the market that the copyright owner could claim. This section traces the development of these two approaches through an examination of the case law in the period up to the 1842 Copyright Act. It also looks at the emergence of certain categories of use that would not be considered infringements, and the move away from considering solely the amount taken, to looking at the nature of what was copied.

It was argued above that the abridgment rule came into existence because an abridgment was demonstrably a different work from the one allegedly infringed, and allowing such works could also be underpinned by reasoning which emphasised the public benefits of such works, as well as claims of 'labour' invested by the abridger. In the years after *Donaldson* the abridgment rule continued to be an accepted doctrine, being referred to favourably in *Bell v Walker*[165] (1785) and *Murray v Elliston*[166] (1822). However, the elements that justified its existence were not restricted to abridgments; they could be applied to other kinds of works and it was not long before this began to occur. In the 1785 case of *Sayre v Moore*[167] Lord Mansfield applied similar reasoning to that employed by Lord Hardwicke in *Gyles v Wilcox*,[168] stating: 'If an erroneous chart be made, God forbid it should not be corrected even in a small degree, if it thereby becomes more serviceable and useful for the purposes to which it is applied'.[169]

Lord Mansfield was also aware that allowing such new works to be made could conflict with the interests of copyright owners, noting that

[165] *Bell v Walker* (1785) 1 Bro CC 451.

[166] *Murray v Ellison* (1822) 5 B & Ald 657. Although note that the case involved the performance of an abridged version of a poem by Lord Byron.

[167] (1785) 1 East 361 fn.

[168] See above: text to n 89.

[169] (1785) 1 East 361 fn, 362 fn.

> we must take care to guard against two extremes equally prejudicial; the one, that men of ability, who have employed their time for the service of the community, may not be deprived of their just merits, and the reward of ingenuity and labour; the other, that the world may not be deprived of improvements, nor the progress of the arts be retarded.[170]

Lord Mansfield directed the jury that if they found that the defendant had been correcting errors, rather than 'servilely copying', they should find in his favour.[171] The jury so found and a verdict was entered for the defendant.[172]

Copying with alterations that would enhance a map's accuracy gave an obvious advantage to the sea-faring community. The reasoning applied in this case was soon applied in another case relating to maps. This time, however, the advantage was less a matter of life and death and more a matter of making better information available to the public. In 1802, Paterson's Road Book was again the subject of litigation in the case of *Cary v Kearsley*.[173] This time Lord Ellenborough took a broader view of the issues involved in cases of partial copying, noting that the question in cases of partial taking was whether the material taken was 'taken colourably, merely with a view to steal the copy-right of the plaintiff or 'fairly done with a view of compiling a useful book, for the benefit of the public'.[174] Thus, the crucial matter was the intention of the defendant: did he copy in order to compete in an unfair way or to benefit the public?

Lord Ellenborough was also sensitive to the potential conflict between the interest of the copyright owner in being able to protect his market, and the interests of the public in having new books. He stated:

> That part of the work of one author is found in another, is not of itself piracy, or sufficient to support an action; a man may fairly adopt part of the work of another: he may so make use of another's labours for the promotion of science, and the benefit of the public: but having done so, the question will be, Was the matter so taken used fairly with that view, and without what I may term the *animus furandi*.[175]

Later, he added 'while I shall think myself bound to secure every man in the enjoyment of his copy-right, one must not put manacles on science'.[176]

In the Court of Chancery, Lord Eldon was also prepared to refuse injunctions where a book could be characterised as a new work, despite the fact that it copied some material from the plaintiff's book. The 1810 case of *Wilkins v Aikin*[177] arose when Wilkins complained that his book, entitled *The Antiquities of Magna Graecia*, was infringed by the defendant's book, *An Essay on the Doric Order of Architecture*. Consistent with his approach in *Longman v Winchester*,[178] Lord Eldon asserted that

[170] ibid.
[171] ibid.
[172] ibid.
[173] *Cary v Kearsley* (1802) 4 Esp 168.
[174] ibid 171.
[175] ibid 170.
[176] ibid.
[177] *Wilkins v Aikin* (1810) 17 Ves Jun 422.
[178] See above: text to n 161.

'The question upon the whole is whether this is a legitimate use of the Plaintiff's publication in the fair exercise of a mental operation, deserving the character of an original work'.[179] He added: 'The effect, I have no doubt is prejudicial: it does not follow, that therefore there is a breach of the legal right'.[180]

Abinger CB in the Court of Exchequer also discussed the principle that a new work would be no infringement if it could not be said to be the same as the plaintiff's work in *D'Almaine v Boosey*.[181] He similarly employed reasoning based on the public interest, noting:

> It is a nice question what shall be deemed such a modification of an original work as shall absorb the merit of the original in the new composition. No doubt such a modification may be allowed in some cases, as in that of an abridgment or a digest. Such publications are in their nature original. Their compiler intends to make of them a new use; not that which the author proposed. Digests are of great use to practical men . . . The same may be said of an abridgment of any study[182].

However, he went on to state that it must be 'a bonâ fide abridgment, because if it contains many chapters of the original work, or such as made that work most saleable, the maker of the abridgment commits a piracy'.[183] In this case, although the music in question was an 'adaptation' of an opera, Lord Abinger considered that it was still 'the same' work, finding that the 'mere adaptation of the air . . . does not, even to common apprehensions, alter the original subject. The ear tells you that it is the same'.[184]

Yet, when he referred to taking what made a work most 'saleable', Lord Abinger alluded to a second approach to infringement that was also emerging at this time. Contrary to Lord Eldon's statement above that prejudice to the plaintiff was to be discounted if a new work were produced, this approach emphasised the marketplace effects of copying and prioritised the impact on the plaintiff's work. Five years after his decision in *Cary v Kearsley*, Lord Ellenborough heard the case of *Roworth v Wilkes*.[185] In this case, the plaintiff complained that 75 pages from his treatise on fencing had been copied by the defendant, the editor of the *Encyclopaedia Londinensis*. This time, Lord Ellenborough held that 'the question is, whether the defendant's publication would serve as a substitute for [the plaintiff's publication]'.[186] Although he had placed emphasis on the question of '*animus furandi*' in *Cary v Kearsley*, in this case he went on to add: 'The intention to pirate is not

[179] *Wilkins v Aikin* (1810) 17 Ves Jun 422, 426.

[180] ibid. Lord Eldon refused to grant the injunction, but ordered the defendant to account pending the action. No action appears to have been brought. In 1833, Shadwell V-C followed this lead, stating in a case involving engravings, 'Any person may copy and publish the whole of a literary composition, provided he writes notes upon it, so as to present it to the public, connected with matter of his own'. *Martin v Wright* (1833) 6 Sim 297, 298.

[181] *D'Almaine v Boosey* (1835) 1 Y & C Ex 288.

[182] ibid 301.

[183] ibid.

[184] ibid 302.

[185] *Roworth v Wilkes* (1807) 1 Camp 94

[186] ibid 98.

necessary in an action of this sort; it is enough that the publication complained of is in substance a copy, whereby a work vested in another is prejudiced'.[187] The competition justification for allowing or refusing extracts was also applied by the Vice-Chancellor in 1839, in the case of *Sweet v Shaw*.[188] The Vice-Chancellor found against the defendants on the grounds that their book, which had copied 11 law cases from the plaintiff's book, would 'manifestly operate to prevent the sale by the plaintiffs of their work'[189] and that it was a 'work of supererogation'.[190]

The emphasis on competition-based reasoning in turn affected the attitude of the courts to the question of the amount copied. It was common for plaintiffs to specify the amount they alleged had been copied. Indeed, if they did not they ran the risk of having their claims for equitable relief denied, as in *Mawman v Tegg*,[191] when Lord Eldon found it difficult to grant the injunction in the absence of credible evidence as to how much was copied. In *Lewis v Fullarton*,[192] Lord Langdale MR stated, 'The piracy proved may be so inconsiderable, and so little likely to injure the Plaintiff, that the Court may decline to interfere at all, and may leave the Plaintiff to his remedy at law'.[193] However, he found for the plaintiff on the basis that 'piracy had been committed to an extent which [was] likely to be seriously prejudicial to the Plaintiff'.[194]

The Court of Chancery's focus on amount in these cases combined the *de minimis* principle and an assessment of the effect of the taking on the original work. In the early cases, the inquiry as to amount was straightforward and mechanistic. However, an element of subjectivity was added in *Bramwell v Halcomb*[195] when Lord Cottenham LC took a broader view, stating:

> When it comes to a question of quantity, it must be very vague. One writer might take all the vital part of another's book, though it might be but a small proportion of the book in quantity. It is not only quantity but value that is always looked to. It is useless to refer to any particular cases as to quantity.[196]

This echoed Lord Abinger CB's point made a year earlier in *D'Almaine v Boosey*,[197] when he had noted that an abridgment would not be bona fide if 'it contains many chapters of the original work, or such as made that work most saleable'.[198]

The other major development in relation to infringement in the first part of the nineteenth century was the emergence of accepted categories of use which would

[187] ibid.
[188] *Sweet and Others v Shaw* (1839) 3 Jur 217.
[189] ibid 219.
[190] ibid.
[191] *Mawman v Tegg* (1826) 2 Russ 385.
[192] *Lewis v Fullarton* (1839) 2 Beav 6.
[193] ibid 11.
[194] ibid 12. Sir Lancelot Shadwell V-C applied similar reasoning in the 1841 case of *Sweet v Cater* (1841) 11 Sim 572.
[195] *Bramwell v Halcomb* (1836) 3 My & Cr 737.
[196] ibid 738. Lord Cottenham reiterated this principle two years later in *Saunders v Smith* (1838) 3 My & Cr 711.
[197] (1835) 1 Y& C Ex 288.
[198] ibid 301.

not amount to infringement. In some cases this was the result of attending to the effect of the defendant's work on the plaintiff's market. For example, in *Roworth v Wilkes*, the defendant had alleged that publishing extracts for the purpose of criticism in a review would not constitute a piracy. Lord Ellenborough accepted this argument, linking it back to the rationale that a review would not normally serve as a substitute for the book itself.[199] However, in *Wilkins v Aikin* Lord Eldon, as noted above,[200] placed emphasis on the labour invested by the defendants when deciding the case. The defendants argued specifically that, although there had been copying from the plaintiff, this amounted to 'fair quotation, compilation and abridgment'.[201] Lord Eldon agreed with this construction, stating, 'There is no doubt, that a man cannot under pretence of quotation, publish either the whole or part of another's work; though he may use, what is in all cases very difficult to define, fair quotation'.[202] He went on to give another example involving copying maps to make an 'illustration' of history, which would be acceptable. However, he added that 'if a jury could perceive the object to make a profit by publishing the map of another man that would require a different consideration'.[203]

Lord Eldon also played down the significance of the effect that the defendant's work would have on the plaintiff's market if the defendant's work were 'legitimate'.[204] Furthermore, he continued the use of the term 'fair' but added to it the word 'quotation', thereby approving another example of permissible copying to sit alongside fair abridgments. Fifteen years later, in *Mawman v Tegg*,[205] Lord Eldon again referred to quotation as being permissible. In obiter dicta, he noted, 'Quotation, for instance, is necessary for the purpose of reviewing; and quotation for such a purpose is not to have the appellation of piracy affixed to it; but quotation may be carried to the extent of manifesting piratical intention'.[206] From the reports of Lord Eldon's decisions in these cases, then, it seems that the most relevant consideration was whether the defendant had employed his own labour to produce a work with a different object or merely attempted to 'free-ride' on the labour of others. Quotations and illustrations were examples of the former and therefore allowable. However, public interest considerations were not entirely absent from his reasoning. While Lord Eldon made no mention of them in *Wilkins v Aikin*, in *Mawman v Tegg* he did refer to Lord Mansfield and Lord Ellenborough's reasoning (presumably in *Sayre v Moore* and *Cary v Kearsley* respectively) in relation to new works.[207]

By the 1820s, then, the courts of law and equity were accepting litigants' claims that quotation, criticism, review, compilation and abridgment were the kinds of

[199] (1807) 1 Camp 94, 98.
[200] See above: text to n 177.
[201] (1810) 17 Ves Jun 422, 423.
[202] ibid 424.
[203] ibid 425.
[204] See above: text to n 179.
[205] *Mawman v Tegg* (1826) 2 Russ 385.
[206] ibid 393.
[207] See above: text to nn 167, 173.

uses that would not amount to infringement. However, there was no real consensus on the justifications for allowing such uses. The lack of agreement on the approach to be taken and the reasons for allowing certain uses, is highlighted in the different reports of *Bell v Whitehead*.[208] This case related to the copying of an extract from the *Monthly Chronicle* into a weekly periodical, the *Railway Times*, on a controversial subject concerning railways. According to the *Law Journal*, Lord Cottenham LC explained that extracts for the purpose of criticism did not interfere with the sales of the works reviewed, but in fact tended to extend their sales.[209] The Lord Chancellor distinguished this situation from cases where a work is published in a cheaper form, and acknowledged that it had long been a custom of the newspaper trade to print extracts of articles that appeared in other papers.[210] While the *Law Journal* linked the criticism principle to trade and competition concerns, the *Jurist* reported that Lord Cottenham stated that an extract made for the purpose of criticism was a 'fair extract'[211] on the basis that it 'would be injurious to the public to limit the right of discussing questions of this kind, and for that purpose to make necessary extracts'.[212] Thus, on the basis of the *Jurist*'s report, extracts for criticism were allowed because they performed the public purpose of enabling the free circulation of information.

The defendants in the 1842 case of *Campbell v Scott*[213] focused on competition, arguing that they had made 'fair and legitimate extracts'[214] for the purposes of illustration,[215] and that the plaintiff could sustain no injury because their work was not a substitute and was sold at a higher price.[216] Indeed, they claimed that sales of the plaintiff's work would be benefited by their edition.[217] The defendants in this case had produced a book that comprised a collection of poetry accompanied by biographical essays of various poets. They had copied six entire poems by the plaintiff and taken extracts from others. The Vice-Chacellor, Sir Lancelot Shadwell, while accepting criticism to be a permissible use of the plaintiff's book, did not consider that the defendant's work fell into that category as a matter of fact, stating, 'I cannot think that it can be considered as a book of criticism, when you observe the way in which it is composed'.[218] Nor did he accept their argument as to lack of intention, stating that 'if A takes the property of B, the *animus furandi* is inferred from the act'.[219]

In the early part of the nineteenth century, therefore, courts continued to approach infringement questions in an ad hoc manner. It appears that judges

208 *Bell v Whitehead* (1839) 8 LJ (Ch) 141; 3 Jur 68.
209 8 LJ (Ch) 141, 142.
210 ibid 142.
211 3 Jur 68, 68.
212 ibid.
213 *Campbell v Scott* (1842) 11 Sim 31; 6 Jur 186.
214 11 Sim 31, 35.
215 ibid 37.
216 ibid.
217 ibid.
218 ibid 38.
219 ibid.

decided the handful of cases that came before them based largely on their subjective impression of the conduct of the parties. The legal tests were developed to fit the facts, rather than being objectively applied to them. Matters were not helped when different reporters provided different reasons for decisions. This was not a climate that favoured the development of a consistent, reasoned approach to copyright infringement.

Several general trends can, however, be identified. The principle emerged that a 'new work' would not amount to infringement and was justified either on the basis that taking a liberal approach to the use of extracts from existing works was beneficial to society in general, or upon the basis of labour invested by the alleged infringer. The former justification prioritised the reading public over the rights of copyright owners, while the latter adjudicated between competing claims of authorship. Alongside the 'new work' principle sat a different approach, which focused on the damage suffered by the copyright owner. While the market of the copyright owner remained limited, the two approaches did not conflict and could even be combined, as in *D'Almaine v Boosey*,[220] but it was more common for the courts to choose one approach over the other. Meanwhile, the word 'fair' became the touchstone for deciding whether infringement had occurred, but, while the word became crucial, its meaning remained opaque. At times it was used to mean lacking *animus furandi*,[221] while on other occasions it referred to the defendant's use of his own mental labour.[222] In other cases it seemed to refer to the fact that the new work would not compete with the old.

The treatise writers of the period supported the new-work principle and combined the public interest and labour justifications in so doing. In his 1823 treatise on copyright and patents, Richard Godson wrote, 'Many valuable works are so voluminous that abridgments of them are extremely useful. To make them, some judgment must be exercised, and some labour employed; and therefore the authors of them ought certainly to be encouraged'.[223] He added that, 'The inquiry whether the work is *prejudiced* by the *manner* of making the abridgment cannot be entertained'.[224] Five years later, in his copyright treatise, Robert Maugham similarly proposed:

> Where labor, judgment and learning, however, have been applied in adapting existing works into a new method, and the composition has evidently been made with a fair and honest intention to produce a new and improved work, it seems that the law will justify the publication, although the abridgment or compilation should injure the sale of the former works.[225]

[220] See above: text to n 181.

[221] See above: text to n 175.

[222] See above: text to n179.

[223] R Godson, *A Practical Treatise on the Law of Patents for Inventions and of Copyright, with an Introduction Book on Monopolies*, 1st edn (London, Butterworth & Sons, 1823) 238.

[224] ibid.

[225] R Maugham, *A Treatise on the Laws of Literary Property* (London, Longman et al, 1828) 126.

In other respects, however, these contemporary treatises highlight the unsettled state of the law during this period. In explaining the law of infringement, Godson was reduced to quoting from the various cases, and attempted to reconcile Lord Ellenborough's decisions in *Cary v Kearsley* and *Roworth v Wilkes* on the basis that it was only necessary to establish intention if a small portion of a work had been copied.[226] Robert Maugham openly acknowledged the difficulties in his treatise, beginning his discussion of piracy by noting:

> It would, perhaps, be unreasonable to expect, that any full and precise definition should have been made of the extent to which a writer may lawfully quote or extract from the works of his predecessors. The courts have generally confined themselves to the mere point in litigation.[227]

He went on to note:

> The general principle, however, may be collected to be, that extracts made in a bona fide manner, are justifiable. According to some authorities, however, they must not be so extensive as to injure the sale of the original work, even though made with no intention to invade the previous author; nor must they be speciously or colorably adapted from the original into a form differing only in appearance and manner of composition.[228]

This is probably the best exposition of the law at this juncture. It is not possible to state with certainty that the emergent new categories of permissible use, such as criticism and quotation, owed their acceptance solely to the recognition of the public interests that such exceptions or defences might serve. With the exception of the *Jurist*'s report of *Bell v Whitehead*, the dominant consideration appeared to be that such uses would not compete with the existing book in an unfair manner. In fact, the development of specific categories of acceptable uses began to exert a more general pressure on the law of infringement that was unlikely to have been foreseen by those who advanced such arguments. This can be seen in the case of *Campbell v Scott* where the plaintiff characterised the defendant's argument thus:

> The taking is not denied; but the defence set up is that the case comes within the exception in favour of criticism and fair quotation; or, if not, that no injury has been done to the Plaintiff. In order to bring a case within the exception in favour of criticism, the critique must not be colourable.[229]

Shadwell V-C followed this formulation in his decision, noting first that the defendants had admitted copying and then asking whether 'the work complained of [is] anything like an abridgment of the Plaintiff's work, or a critique upon it?'[230] As it was a collection of poems accompanied by some biographical material, he concluded it was not. He also considered the amount taken, concluded that there had been injury and damage to the plaintiff and granted an injunction.[231]

[226] R Godson, *A Practical Treatise* 214–17. Godson actually misattributes one of his quotes, citing it as being from *Roworth v Wilkes* when in fact it was from *Cary v Kearsley* 216.

[227] R Maugham, *A Treatise on the Laws of Literary Property* (London, Longman et al, 1828) 126.

[228] ibid.

[229] (1842) 11 Sim 31, 36.

[230] ibid 38.

[231] ibid 40; 6 Jur. 186, 187.

The statement made by Campbell's counsel in this case is the first reported description of use for the purpose of criticism or quotation as a 'defence' and an 'exception'. It is interesting that both words should be used, for the taxonomical uncertainty as to the precise status of the fair-dealing provisions persists to the present day. However, it also heralds a subtle, but significant, shift in legal approach. The abridgment rule was essentially an argument of lack of *actus reus*—there was no infringement because the defendant's book was not the same as the plaintiff's book. However, shifting the permissible uses to the status of defence or exception presupposed that there was a prima facie infringement through any act of copying, subject only to the quality and quantity of the extracts copied. This case, then, marks a significant turning point in the characterisation of infringement, although it would not be reflected in legislation until 1911.

B. Infringement and the 1842 Copyright Act

The cases that came before the courts offered only limited opportunities to make rhetorical appeals to concepts such as authorship and the public interest. Matters were different in the political sphere. As the nineteenth century progressed, the number of disputes involving partial copying of books to come before the courts was steadily increasing. Thus, it is not surprising that Serjeant Talfourd sought to codify the law of infringement in his project for the reform of copyright law. However, the entrenched positions that emerged in relation to the matter of duration were repeated in relation to infringement and between 1837 and 1842 Talfourd's proposed infringement clause was frequently revised.

Talfourd's first bill provided that infringement would occur where any person shouldin any part of the British dominions, after the passing of this Act, print or cause to be printed any Book in which there shall be subsisting Copyright or any Book containing *any portion* of a Book in which there shall be such Copyright.[232] (emphasis added). This Bill also provided that it would be an infringement to import unlawfully printed books, to sell, publish or expose to sale any book knowing it had been unlawfully printed or imported, or to cause any such book to be sold, published or exposed to sale or to be in possession for sale of any such book. Any person found to be committing one of these acts would be liable to a special action on the case, brought by the proprietor of the copyright of the book.[233] This clause itself made no great change to the law; it merely made explicit the principle that partial copying could also infringe. What was new was that it was subject to the exception that:

> Provided always, that nothing herein contained shall be construed to extend to the publication of any extracts fairly and bona fide made from any Book for the purposes of

[232] A Bill to consolidate and amend the Laws relating to Copyright in Printed Books, Music, Plays and Engravings (1837) [380] s 13.

[233] ibid.

> criticism, observation or argument, or to any translation into another language, or abridgment fairly made of any Book.[234]

Talfourd thus continued the nascent approach of specifying categories of non-infringement. The content of these categories, however, was more controversial. When drafting his second Bill, introduced to Parliament in February 1838, Talfourd altered the infringement clause so as to treat abridgments of books in which copyright subsisted as constituting infringement. There was also an addition in respect of translations into another language, providing that

> the Copyright in every translation shall be deemed to be the property of the Translator thereof and his assignees as though it were an original work.[235]

In his second reading speech on this Bill, Talfourd referred to the infringement clause as a 'matter of detail', adding that the prohibition on extracts 'made merely for the compiler's gain' was declaratory of the common law.[236] He admitted, however, that the inclusion of unauthorised abridgments as a prohibited act was new.

The change in Talfourd's position on abridgments between the 1837 and 1838 Bills reflected the lack of legal certainty about whether or not abridgments should be considered part of the author's copyright and the inclusion of abridgments with other prohibited acts met with considerable resistance. The Select Committee removed abridgments from the category of acts forbidden without consent and the 1838 Bill provided that they were to be allowed as long as they were 'fairly and bona fide made'.[237] By the fifth version of the Bill, introduced on 11 February 1840, all references to abridgments had been removed.[238]

The provision as to extracts changed little until the 1839 Bill, which prohibited printing or causing to be printed without consent any

> [b]ook containing any portion of a Book, in which there shall be such Copyright, to such an extent as shall be injurious to the property therein.[239]

The infringement clause, without any reference to abridgments, remained in the Bill more or less unchanged through numerous Commons committees in 1841 and 1842, until it was removed in the House of Lords. No records survive that explain why the Lords made this decision but it is likely that its contentious nature meant that removal assisted the Lords to reach a final agreement on the Bill.

Although most of the opponents of the Copyright Bills focused on the extension of term, there were some who also directly opposed the infringement provisions. In 1838, the Operative Letterpress Printers of Carlisle protested that

> the present liberty enjoyed of extracting from books is not prejudicial to the authors of such books, inasmuch as those books which have been most liberally extracted from have

234 ibid.
235 A Bill to amend the Law of Copyright HC (1837–38) [164] s 19.
236 Parl Deb HC vol 42 cols 556–57 (25 April 1838).
237 A Bill to amend the Law of Copyright HC (1837–38) [461] s 19.
238 A Bill to amend the Law of Copyright HC (1840) [61] s 15.
239 A Bill to amend the Law of Copyright HC (1839) [19] s 17.

> enjoyed the greatest sales; and that to forbid such extracts being made would be productive of great injury to the community, who, from their generally impoverished condition, are unable to purchase original and expensive works.[240]

The petitioners added that the legislation would 'destroy all those useful and hitherto considered necessary compilations for the instruction of the young which have been so eminently useful in exciting in the youthful mind a taste for literature and science'.[241] The petition finished by asserting that the proposed legislative changes would be 'injurious to the public interest'.[242]

A second petition, introduced two days later, came from the Company of Stationers of Glasgow.[243] Like the Printers of Carlisle, the Stationers of Glasgow claimed to view the proposed legislation with alarm. With respect to the prohibition on publication of any portion or any abridgment of a book, the Stationers objected

> upon the ground that such provisions will prevent the publication of all cheap editions of works which may endure beyond the present statutory period of Copyright, of all compilations of extracts, of all compendiums of science, and of all abridgments, which several classes of works form a large proportion of books that are commonly used in schools, and of those which constitute the libraries of the middle ranks and common people.[244]

The Stationers wove together three separate arguments: the interests of the trade, the interest of the public in dissemination of learning and the interests of authors, claiming:

> A considerable proportion indeed of the trade of your Petitioners consists in the manufacture or in the sale of books that may be ranged under one or other of these heads; and the suppression of such works will be highly injurious to the interests of your Petitioners, and also, in their humble opinion, to the best interests of society, by destroying the kind of books which alone the common people have the means to purchase or the leisure to read; these provisions would almost wholly suppress the general diffusion of literature and science; and there would be soon effected such a diminution in the number of readers, that your Petitioners are of opinion that the proposed arrangement would in the end be highly detrimental even to authors themselves.[245]

The Glasgow Stationers also pointed out that compendiums and abridgments were 'at present authorized and protected by Law, as being useful to the public and not hurtful to original authors'.[246] They added that the clause which allowed copyright of portions of works published in parts to be calculated from the date of publication of the most recent part, could result in perpetual copyright for works

240 Petition 4,629. See ch 4 n 113.
241 ibid.
242 ibid.
243 It appears from the petition that this organisation was involved in publishing and book-selling.
244 Petition 4,631. See ch 4 n 114.
245 ibid.
246 ibid.

published under a running title. The combination of this clause and the prohibition on extracts and abridgments would then 'prohibit every possible mode of announcing scientific discoveries to all those who have not access to those peculiar works in which the discoveries and inventions of scientific men are originally recorded'.[247]

The third petition of that year to consider the infringement provisions of the Bill came not from the printing or publishing trades, but from 'persons interested in the general diffusion of literature and science'.[248] The signatory to this petition was Dr George Birkbeck, and it was presented by Joseph Hume. As noted in Chapter three, Birkbeck had a long-standing involvement in educational issues and had also participated in the debates for repeal of the newspaper stamp. Birkbeck's petition, which was the product of a public meeting, began by criticising the term extension on the grounds that 'the interests of society require that the results of those labours [of authors] should be enjoyed by the public at as early a period as is consistent with justice to the authors'.[249]

With respect to the infringement clause, Birkbeck claimed that it,

> would prevent the compilation of many instructive selections and useful schoolbooks, which have been found to be of great value in creating a taste for modern literature in young persons, and which, so far from injuring the property of those authors from whose works the selections have been made, have actually promoted their sale and increased their circulation, by making them more generally known.[250]

Birkbeck's petition ended by urging the House not to allow the Bill, as it would only 'increase the profits of a few monopolising capitalists in the publishing trade'[251] and injure the public by restricting the diffusion of cheap literature.[252]

A letter to *The Times* also focused on the problems caused by the prohibition on extracts. This letter, from 'CHW', noted that this was an important feature of the Bill which had been 'overlooked, or very slightly noticed'.[253] The writer's complaint was the clause's lack of specificity:

> If nothing short of a review be included in this definition, the far greater proportion of those periodicals which send the streams of knowledge throughout all our provinces, and open to the humbler classes a channel of enjoyment of which no friend to his species would deprive them, will be instantly stopped, while the wording of the clause is such that every lawyer in England might differently interpret; a series of harassing and absurd litigations must ensue, till authors confess their impotence to enforce a statute which nothing but ignorance at first suggested.[254]

247 ibid.
248 Appendix to the Twenty-Fourth Report of Public Petitions, Petition 5,953, presented on 9 May 1838, App 455 (1 signature).
249 ibid.
250 ibid.
251 ibid.
252 ibid.
253 *The Times* (30 April 1838) 6.
254 ibid.

The writer concluded by adding that the clause is

> so great an innovation, so destructive to the interests of general literature, so opposed to the welfare of those who manufacture, circulate, or read the majority of works which come from the press, that it not only justifies but demands, the opposition of all who would preserve the intelligence and greatness of Britain.[255]

After 1838, public opposition to the infringement clause dried up. It is possible that the removal of the reference to abridgments in 1839 may have assuaged some of the concerns of the printing and publishing trades and led them to focus less on this clause as an issue. However, it is equally likely that those opposed to the Bill merely set aside concerns as to detail to concentrate greater resources on what Talfourd had referred to as the 'main object of the bill'[256]—the increase in term.

In 1842, when the latest version of the infringement clause was being debated in Parliament, objections arose again. Thomas Wakley objected to the prohibition on extracts on educational grounds, stating that it would 'prevent elegant extracts being put into school-books'[257] and claimed that it was stricter than the present law. Wakley was supported by Alglionby, who also opposed the clause on the ground that its effect would be to remove cheap books on important subjects from the reach of the public.[258] He was also supported by Dr Bowring, author and editor of Bentham's *Westminster Review,* who objected to the clause as an 'impediment to the general diffusion of literature'.[259]

Godson, who had so struggled to find a coherent line on infringement in his treatise on monopolies, pointed out that the clause allowed extracts for purposes of criticism, judgment or argument, and claimed that this merely reflected the practice of equity judges in making decisions on extracts.[260] He argued that if the words 'or school-books' were added, then entire books would be able to be reproduced. Lord Mahon agreed that the clause merely enacted the existing law, and added that the clause was necessary to prevent the artifices resorted to by those who sought to profit by making extracts from important works.[261]

The question of infringement fell on the same intersection of trade interest and public interest as the question of duration. An infringement clause would impact most heavily on books such as encyclopaedias, compilations, abridgments and school books, which represented extremely valuable commodities for publishers, booksellers and printers.[262] Those of an educational nature had a ready market in schools and libraries, while other kinds were able to supply demand for cheaper

255 ibid.
256 Parl Deb HC vol 38 col 872 (18 May 1837).
257 Parl Deb HC vol 62 col 890 (20 April 1842).
258 ibid.
259 ibid 892.
260 ibid 890–91.
261 ibid.
262 A petition to Parliament adopted by a meeting of the booksellers and publishers of London, which included such leading figures as Murray, Butterworth and Rivington, made this clear: 'Many of the most valuable copyrights exist in books and works on geography and history, in scientific and legal works, and in school books' (*The Times* (2 April 1838) 5a).

books. Such books were cheap and quick to produce, as the material was already to hand, and publishers could identify a fashion for a certain type of knowledge or book, and easily and quickly produce a book to compete in that market. However, these works were also primarily educational and informational, and therefore attracted the attention of social reformers, such as Birkbeck, who were concerned that placing limits on the way such books were produced would lead to fewer of them being published, or an increase in price, which would in turn impact upon the diffusion of learning.

The debates surrounding Talfourd's Copyright Bills provided the opportunity to consider some of the ways in which either allowing or preventing partial copying and transformative uses of works could impact on the public more generally. Such an opportunity was lacking in litigation, where the focus was necessarily on the parties before the court. In the petitions and parliamentary debates, the public interest was employed in different ways. At times it was introduced as a rhetorical device by traders, such as printers, who had a vested interest in making it as easy as possible to produce derivative works, on the basis that this would allow more books to be printed. More disinterested participants in the debates, such as Birkbeck, were also opposed to tightening the law on infringement on the basis of the perceived public interest in the educative value of books of compilations and selections. Thus, while public interest arguments were employed to resist expansion of the law, such arguments complemented and, at times masked, private interests. And, as had been the case when it came to duration, appeals to the ideal of romantic authorship provided an ineffective counter. In the end, the infringement clause was one controversy too far for the proponents of copyright law reform, and infringement was to remain a matter for the common law for another 69 years.

C. Infringement to 1911

With the 1842 Copyright Act leaving the law of infringement untouched, it continued to develop through the courts of law and equity. As discussed in chapter five, in the second half of the century the large and established publishers continued their efforts to maintain control over competition in the book trade, while others sought to break into the market for cheaper publications. As time went on, publishers also began to experiment with different forms of literary production, such as serialisation and issuing books in different formats. Their attempts to capture different markets in the trade inevitably spilled over into litigation and corresponding attempts to persuade the courts to expand their protection. As noted above, Oren Bracha and others have argued in the American context that copyright law was increasingly concerned with allowing copyright owners to capture the full market value of their products.[263] However, it is important to remember

[263] See text to nn 1–5 above. Bracha, 'Owning Ideas' 319.

that protecting commercial value had always been the key concern of copyright law, as well as the book market regulation of the Stationers that preceded it. What was changing was the extent of the market that a copyright owner could hope to capture, that is, what '*full* market value' actually covered. No longer was this merely the market for the particular book, play or musical work in question, but multiple markets for multiple forms of the work.

During the latter half of the century, concepts such as substantial taking also became accepted as key elements of copyright doctrine. The notion, based on Locke's theory of property, that labour gave rise to property rights continued to hold considerable sway over the courts and the position of copyright owners was strengthened as the courts were increasingly prepared to grant them protection from competition in different ways. However, overall, the law remained characterised by competing strands of authority and the lack of a concrete basis for further development.

i. Extracts, Amounts and Permissible Uses

The success of the publishers in convincing the courts to widen the scope of protection conferred by copyright can be seen in the decline of the abridgment principle and the reconfiguring of the new-work principle in the second half of the century. The wane of the abridgment rule was apparent as early as the 1844 case of *Dickens v Lee*,[264] when Knight Bruce V-C stated he was 'not aware that one man has the right to abridge the works of another'.[265] He considered that property rights were paramount, believing that he must consider the question 'merely and solely as a question of property'[266] and finding that 'It is a valuable property, and he is entitled to be protected from the unauthorized use of it by another'.[267]

On the other side of the Atlantic, dissatisfaction with the abridgment rule was also creeping in. Story J had begun the process in the 1839 case of *Gray v Russell* when he noted, 'although the doctrine is often laid down in the books, that an abridgment is not a piracy of the original copyright; yet this proposition must be received with many qualifications'.[268]

The real question, according to Story J, was whether the abridgment would 'prejudice or supersede' the original work.[269] In the 1841 case of *Folsom v Marsh*, he noted that a 'fair and bona fide abridgment' was no piracy, but added that deciding what constituted a bona fide abridgment was 'one of the most difficult points . . . which can well arise for judicial discussion'.[270] Six years later, in a case that happened to involve Story's *Commentaries on Equity Jurisprudence*, McLean J also expressed dissatisfaction with the rule, considering that:

264 *Dickens v Lee* (1844) 8 Jur 183.
265 ibid 184.
266 ibid.
267 ibid.
268 *Gray v Russell* (1839) 10 F Cas 1035 (CCD Mass 1839) 1038.
269 ibid.
270 *Folsom v Marsh* (1841) 9 F Cas 342 (CCD Mass 1841) 345.

> The argument that the abridgment is suited to a different class of readers, by its cheapness, and will be purchased on that account by persons unable and unwilling to purchase the work at large, is not satisfactory. This to some extent may be true; but are there not many who are able to buy the original work, that will be satisfied with the abridgment . . . The reasoning on which the right to abridge is founded, therefore, seems to me to be false in fact. It does, to some extent in all cases, and not unfrequently to a great extent, impair the rights of the author—a right secured by law.[271]

Abridgments were clearly falling out of favour. In *Sweet v Benning*,[272] which involved the copying of head-notes and marginal notes from law reports in the *Jurist* and other publications, the defendants argued that digests and abridgments should not be treated as piracies. Maule J commented on this argument: 'You cannot justify the pirated use of another man's book, by merely calling the result an abridgment or a digest'.[273] And in 1863, Wood V-C commented in the course of a case involving dramatic works:

> The Court has gone far enough in that direction [of endorsing abridgements]; and it is difficult to acquiesce in the reason sometimes given, that the compiler of an abridgment is a benefactor to mankind, by assisting in the diffusion of knowledge.[274]

The public interest justifications for allowing new works also appeared to be losing their persuasive power in the case of the new-work principle. This can be also be seen in *Sweet v Benning*, in which the leading judgment of Jervis CJ held that a digest of published reports need not necessarily infringe those reports, so long as the maker of the digest applied 'the exertion and skill of his own brain in extracting the principle or the substance of the decisions before him, dressing it up in his own language, so as to produce an original work'.[275] However, in the present case

> there is no thought or skill brought to bear upon the work that is complained of; it is a mere mechanical stringing together of marginal or side-notes which the labour and intelligence of the authors had fashioned ready to the compiler's hand.[276]

Crowder J took a similar approach. While he accepted that the two publications would not compete, and that the defendants did not intend that they should do so, he believed that the language of the statute dictated that this should be considered a piracy, noting that the defendants had availed themselves 'of the labour, skill and capital of the plaintiffs, and have appropriated to their own use that which is substantially the property of the plaintiffs'.[277] He added that 'however useful and meritorious the defendants' work may be, they were not justified in making the use they did of the plaintiffs' work'.[278]

271 *Story v Halcombe* (1847) 23 F Cas 171 (CCDOh 1847) 172–73.
272 *Sweet v Benning* (1855) 16 CB 459.
273 ibid 478.
274 *Tinsley v Lacy* (1862) 1 H & M 747, 754.
275 ibid 482.
276 ibid.
277 ibid 490.
278 ibid.

These two judgments demonstrate that although the new-work principle was still accepted as part of the law, the reason for allowing new works was shifting away from considerations of the advantages such works brought to the public, and favouring the rationale that prioritised the authorship claims of the alleged infringer. Thus, where the copier could be seen to have employed his own labour, he would not infringe copyright. The following year, Wood V-C also focused on labour in *Spiers v Brown*.[279] The case involved copying from French-English dictionaries, and Wood V-C noted 'the mere striking out of a certain quantity of the plaintiff's words would not entitle the defendant to publish such an abridgment'[280] and later commented that the defendant's work 'went beyond a mere abridgment'.[281] Noting that it was very difficult to decide 'how far this very considerable use of the work of another might be taken to be legitimate', in the end he found for the defendant on the basis that 'a good deal had been taken here from the plaintiff, yet a good deal of labour had been bestowed on what had been taken'.[282] Moreover, the defendant had produced a 'different work from that of the plaintiff'.[283] Wood V-C also focused on the lack of independent labour by the defendant as a crucial factor in finding infringement in *Kelly v Morris*.[284]

In the 1867 case of *Wood v Boosey*,[285] Kelly CB of the Exchequer Chamber, explicitly held for the first time that a work could be both a new work *and* an infringement. Distinguishing between the question of whether an arrangement of an opera should be considered to be a new work and the question of infringement, he stated:

> I have no hesitation in saying that if Brissler had published this arrangement for the pianoforte during Nicolai's lifetime without his authority, or since his death without the authority of Bote and Bock, his representatives, he would have pirated the work . . . But although the work of Brissler, if published without the authority of the composer, would be the piracy of that work, yet it may be a new and substantive work in itself, and be the subject of a copyright at Berlin.[286]

This was a significant shift; previously, courts had proceeded on the basis that if an otherwise infringing work could be characterised as 'new', by reason of the labour and judgment expended upon it, it would not be found to be an infringement. However, as Kelly CB's statement was mere obiter dictum, its significance was slow to seep into legal discourse. In a case of 1892, North J referred to the older approach, stating:

> In the present case what the Defendants have had recourse to is not a mental operation involving thought and labour and producing some original result, but a mechanical

[279] *Spiers v Brown* (1857–58) 6 WR 352.
[280] ibid 353.
[281] ibid 354.
[282] ibid.
[283] ibid.
[284] *Kelly v Morris* (1866) LR 1 Eq 697. See below: text to n 332.
[285] *Wood v Boosey* (1866–67) LR 2 QB 340; 15 LT (NS) 530.
[286] *Wood v Boosey* (1867–68) LR 3 QB 223, 228–29.

> operation with scissors and paste, without the slightest pretension to an original result of any kind.[287]

Just as the courts began to circumscribe the operation of the rule that abridgments and other new works should not amount to infringement, so too did criticism of it grow amongst the treatise writers. Again, the process began across the Atlantic, with the influential copyright treatise written by George Ticknor Curtis. Writing in 1847, Curtis complained that allowing abridgments was 'contrary to principle'[288] because 'the very form in which this matter is reproduced, of necessity tends to the injury of the true proprietor. The real object of most abridgments is to undersell the original work'.[289] He was just as sceptical of the 'new work' principle, noting 'this doctrine may be very convenient in some of its aspects; but it admits of great doubt, whether it is consistent with the rights of original authors'.[290]

Curtis's work is significant for the British law of copyright not just because he was the first writer to attempt to locate in the case law a coherent and systematic approach to the law of infringement, but also because of his influence on Walter Copinger, who, in 1870, published the first edition of what would become the longest running and best known treatise on copyright law. However, Copinger's treatise on copyright was heavily reliant on Curtis and adopted many of his views without alteration. Copinger followed Curtis's lead on abridgments, noting that the rule

> appears to be very unreasonable, and has been the subject of much criticism by late writers. Why should an abridgment, tending to injure the reputation, and to lessen the profits of the author, not be considered an invasion of his property?[291]

By contrast, Charles Palmer Phillips, writing seven years before Copinger, had no criticism of the abridgment rule or the 'new work' principle, and in fact discerned that

> [t]he cases and dicta on this point seem to warrant the conclusion that any unauthorised use of a copyright book in a later publication is an infringement of the earlier, unless that use involves a fair amount of thought and judgment.[292]

However, he did point out that Wood V-C had recently been critical of the abridgment rule in *Tinsley v Lacy*.[293]

Another way in which the public interest element of the new-work principle was curtailed was by subsuming it into a more general inquiry as to the impact that the allegedly infringing work would have on the original. This approach is demonstrated in the dissenting judgment of Maule J in *Sweet v Benning*. He stated:

287 *Walter v Steinkopf* [1892] 3 Ch 489, 495.

288 GT Curtis, *A Treatise on the Law of Copyright* (London, Maxwell & Son, 1847) vii.

289 ibid 276.

290 ibid 163.

291 Copinger, *The Law of Copyright*, 1st edn 36.

292 CP Phillips, *The Law of Copyright in Works of Literature and Art and in the Application of Designs* (London, V & R Stevens, Sons & Haynes, 1863) 110–11.

293 ibid 131. See above: n 274.

> It is difficult to draw the line, where the question is whether the use that is made of a work is fair and reasonable, or is substantially what is unlawful and forbidden, and only colourably and evasively different from it. It is a different work, having a different object in view, and being totally different in its result, from the work published by the plaintiffs.[294]

He noted that it was unlikely that people would buy the defendants' work in preference to the plaintiffs'. Even if they did refrain from buying the reports and relied upon accessing them in libraries, that just demonstrated that the defendants' work was 'useful for a different purpose from that of the plaintiffs' and not intended as a substitute.[295] In such terms, a new work was no infringement because it did not compete with the original work.

Although this was a dissenting judgment, in other cases the courts were similarly prepared to look at the effect on the original book's market. Copyright owners could object to a reprint, including a merely 'colourable' reprint, on the basis it would act as a 'substitute' in the original work. However, increasingly in this context, some judges began to expand the kinds of unacceptable effects beyond this limited ground. In 1847, in *Bohn v Bogue*, Shadwell V-C held that it was not necessary to establish that a book would act as a substitute, but that infringement would occur where a book would have 'a very material effect in diminishing the price of the first book'.[296] In *Scott v Stanford*, Wood V-C held that infringement would occur where the plaintiff's copyright was 'injured', and to establish this he looked at the difference in price between the publications.[297] The Court of Exchequer also took an expansive approach to infringement in *Bradbury v Hotten*.[298] The case arose when the defendant copied from *Punch* a number of cartoons depicting Napoleon III into a book about the Emperor. The defendant argued that his publication had a different purpose to the plaintiffs' magazine, and was aimed at a different class of readers, but the Court did not accept this as exculpating him. Kelly CB held that a piracy would occur where 'one man for his own profit puts into his work an essential part of another man's work, from which that other may still derive profit or from which, but for the act of the first, he might have derived profit'.[299] Bramwell B also found for the plaintiffs, but on the basis of a broader understanding of the 'purpose' of publication. He held that both publications had the same purpose, which was to 'excite the amusement of [their] readers'.[300]

Another approach that was sometimes taken to infringement was to look at the defendant's intention, first considered by Lord Ellenborough in 1802 in *Cary v*

[294] (1855) 16 CB 459, 485.

[295] ibid.

[296] *Bohn v Bogue* (1847) 10 Jur 420, 421. Note, however, that some judges did continue to refer to the test as being whether the work would act as a substitute. See, eg, *Johnson v Lister* (1872), *The Times* (30 May 1872) 11b.

[297] *Scott v Stanford* (1866–67) LR 3 Eq 718, 723. In *Black v Murray* (1870) 9 Court Sess Cas 3s 341, Lord Kinloch also referred to the test for infringement as being whether the alleged infringing work would 'injure the sale' of the original.

[298] *Bradbury v Hotten* (1872) LR 8 Exch 1.

[299] ibid 6.

[300] ibid 7.

Kearsley. In *Smith v Chatto*,[301] Hall V-C considered that the test was based not on the injury done to the plaintiff but on the intention of the defendant in taking the extracts. In that case, he found that the defendants had used the extracts to enhance the value of their own book, and therefore were guilty of infringement.[302] Lord Ellenborough's test of '*animus furandi*'[303] was adopted as one test among several by Wood V-C in *Jarrold v Houlston*[304] and also considered relevant by Kekewich J and the Court of Appeal in *Moffatt v Gill*[305] and by Romer J in *Cooper v Stephens*.[306]

However, in *Oxford and Cambridge Universities v Gilli*[307] a case involving extracts from the New Testament, Cozens-Hardy J considered both intention and competition to be irrelevant to the question of infringement, stating:

> The motive of the defendants in printing and publishing seems to me to be wholly immaterial. It makes no difference that their object was not commercial or to compete with the plaintiffs in the way of trade, but to disseminate, it may be, gratuitously, information among the persons mentioned. The only question is whether there has been an infringement.[308]

Other cases contributed to broadening the kinds of activity to which a copyright owner could object. Despite the fact that section 15 of the 1842 Copyright Act limited the availability of the action on the case to being brought against those who had printed 'for sale or exploitation', in *Novello v Sudlow*, Talfourd J found the Liverpool Philharmonic Society (a society whose members were unpaid but who did charge small entrance fees for concerts to non-members) had infringed the defendant's musical copyright by making copies which it distributed for free amongst its members.[309] Similarly, in 1844, Kay J found infringement had occurred when the defendants made copies of the plaintiffs' collection of words used in telegraphy and distributed them privately to their own agents, on the basis that this interfered with sales that the plaintiffs might otherwise have made.[310]

Yet another approach was to focus on the nature of what had been taken. Here the language tended towards opacity, giving the impression that judges were proceeding largely on gut instinct. In *Bohn v Bogue*,[311] Shadwell V-C considered that an injunction could be granted on the basis that the defendant had taken a 'materially valuable part'.[312] Similarly, in *Murray v Bogue*,[313] Kindersley V-C looked at

301 *Smith v Chatto* (1875) 31 LT 775.
302 ibid 777.
303 *Cary v Kearsley* (1802) 4 Esp 168, 170 Lord Langdale had also employed the expression in *Lewis v Fullarton*, (1839) 2 Beav 6, 8.
304 *Jarrold v Houlston* (1857) 3 K & J 708.
305 *Moffatt v Gill* (1901) 84 LT 452; (1902) 86 LT 465.
306 *Cooper v Stephens* [1895] 1 Ch 567.
307 *Oxford and Cambridge Universities v Gill* (1899) 43 Sol J 570.
308 ibid.
309 *Novello v Sudlow* (1852) 12 CB 177.
310 *Ager v Peninsular and Oriental Steam Navigation Company* (1884) LR 26 Ch 637.
311 *Bohn v Bogue* (1847) 10 Jur 420.
312 ibid 421.
313 *Murray v Bogue* (1852) 1 Drewry 353.

the amount taken, questioning whether the use made of the plaintiff's work 'amounts to such an extraction from it as comes up to an extraction of the *vital* part; whether it comes up to an unfair use, or is only a fair use of it'.[314]

The expression 'substantial part' was used by Pigott B in *Bradbury v Hotten*[315] and the issue of partial copying was considered in some detail in *Chatterton v Cave*.[316] In this case, the plaintiffs had adapted a French novel into a play, the novel having also been adapted previously into a French play. The plaintiffs accused the defendant of having copied some scenes from their play, and at trial Lord Coleridge CJ held that two 'scenes or points' had been copied, but found in favour of the defendant. When the plaintiffs appealed, Lord Coleridge explained his finding on the basis that

> the extent to which the one was taken from the other was so slight, and the effect upon the total composition was so small, that there was no substantial and material taking of any one portion of the Defendant's drama from any portion of the Plaintiffs'.[317]

The plaintiffs appealed, arguing that copying *any* part should amount to infringement. All of the judges in the Court of Common Pleas were of the view that the authorities had established the rule that unless the taking were material and substantial, infringement would not be made out.[318] The House of Lords dismissed the appeal, thereby giving the seal of approval to the notion that a taking had to be material and substantial for both dramas and books. This did not, of course, solve the problem of what would be considered to be substantial and material. Lord O'Hagan referred to *Bramwell v Halcomb*,[319] emphasising that both quantity and quality of the part taken must be taken into consideration.[320] Lord Hatherley, on the other hand, had considered it an application of the principle of *de minimis non curat lex*,[321] while Lord Blackburn merely noted that a jury would need to look at the nature of the points that were copied, the 'general character' of the dramas and the effect of the taking on the total composition.[322]

A related approach that can be identified in this period was to continue the tendency to consider certain types of use as being permissible. Criticism, review, quotation, comment, illustration were all referred to at different times and almost interchangeably by different judges and courts as being legitimate purposes for copying.[323] In *Sweet v Benning*, Maule J (dissenting) considered that a number of

314 ibid 369.

315 *Bradbury v Hotten* (1872) LR 8 Ex 1, 7.

316 *Chatterton v Cave* (1874–75) LR 10 CP 572; (1877–78) 3 App Cas 483.

317 *Chatterton v Cave* (1878) LR 3 HL (E) 483, 485.

318 (1874–75) LR 10 CP 572, 575–76 per Brett J, 578 per Grove J, 580 per Lindley J, 581–2 per Coleridge CJ.

319 *Bramwell v Halcomb* (1836) 3 My & Cr 737.

320 (1878) LR 3 HL (E) 483, 498.

321 ibid 492.

322 ibid 503.

323 In *Maxwell v Somerton* (1874) 30 LT (NS) 11, for example, the Vice-Chancellor referred to extracts for the purpose of criticising or reviewing. In *Walter v Steinkopf* [1892] 3 Ch 489, North J noted legitimate extracts might have been made to criticise the article in question (at 494). In *Sweet v Benning* (1855) 16 CB 459, Jervis CJ referred to 'the fair right of extract which the law allows for the purpose of

factors must be considered in order to decide whether a work is a piracy, including 'the length of the extract, the purpose for which it was made, and other circumstances'.[324] The notion that infringement should be assessed by reference to a combination of factors had been expressed on the other side of the Atlantic in the 1841 case of *Folsom v Marsh*.[325] However, the case does not appear to have been noticed judicially in England until 1867 when Wood V-C stated in *Scott v Stanford*[326] that the general principles of the law of infringement could 'hardly be better stated'[327] than by Story J in *Folsom v Marsh*.

The work complained of in *Folsom v Marsh* was an abridgment of the *Writings of President Washington*. Story J commenced his judgment by noting the difficulties inherent in deciding cases where only a part of a work had been taken:

> This is one of those intricate and embarrassing questions arising in the administration of civil justice, in which it is not, from the peculiar nature and character of the controversy, easy to arrive at any satisfactory conclusion, or to lay down any general principles applicable to all cases. Patents and copyrights approach, nearer than any other class of cases belonging to forensic discussions, to what may be called the metaphysics of the law, where the distinctions are, or at least may be, very subtile and refined, and, sometimes, almost evanescent.[328]

The test he proposed was to

> look to the nature and objects of the selection made, the quantity and value of the materials used, and the degree in which the use may prejudice the sale, or diminish the profits, or supersede the objects of the original work.[329]

Story J noted that on an application of this test a reviewer making extracts for the purpose of criticism would not be guilty of infringement.

The test set out by Story J brought together the different justifications for finding infringement in a far more coherent way than any British court had done and provided the foundation for the American doctrine of fair use.[330] By contrast, the British courts continued to pick and choose between the different approaches adopted in the cases depending on the particular facts before them.

ii. Labour and Originality at the End of the Century

It has been agued that Story J's judgment in *Folsom v Marsh* had the effect of significantly expanding the scope of copyright protection in the United States[331] but

comment, criticism or illustration' (at 481), while Cresswell J referred to 'a fair and legitimate use of an author's work for the purpose of extract, or comment, or illustration' (at 488). See also *Black v Murray* (1870) 9 Court Sess Cas 3s 341, 348, 356.

[324] (1855) 16 CB 459, 487.
[325] (1841) 9 Fed Cas 342.
[326] (1866–67) LR 3 Eq 718.
[327] ibid 722.
[328] (1841) 9 Fed Cas 342, 344.
[329] ibid 348.
[330] Bracha, 'Ideology of Authorship Revisited' 230.
[331] ibid 229–30.

in Britain a still more expansive approach was emerging. This arose in the case of *Kelly v Morris*,[332] which was the first of a series of cases dealing with postal directories. In this case, Wood V-C held that:

> In the case of a dictionary, map, guide-book, or directory, when there are certain common objects of information which must, if described correctly, be described in the same words, a subsequent compiler is bound to set about doing for himself that which the first compiler has done. In case of a road-book, he must count the milestones for himself. In the case of a map of a newly-discovered island . . . he must go through the same process of triangulation just as if he had never seen any former map, and, generally he is not entitled to take *one word* of the information previously published without independently working out the matter for himself, so as to arrive at the same result from the same common sources of information, and the only use that he can legitimately make of a previous publication is to verify his own calculations and results when obtained. So in the present case the Defendant could not take *a single line* of the Plaintiff's Directory for the purpose of saving himself labour and trouble in getting his information.[333] (emphasis added)

By prohibiting even the smallest taking, Wood V-C's decision went much further than previous cases, and made Story J's test look flexible by comparison. The fact that it was Wood V-C who adopted Story J's test the following year demonstrates that judges continued to select the test that they would apply in infringement cases based on their assessment of the facts. It seems, however, that works of information were deemed to require stronger protection.[334] In *Morris v Wright*,[335] Giffard LJ questioned whether Wood's test did not go too far,[336] but some courts continued to apply it in cases involving infringement of factual works.[337] The crucial concept in such cases was the labour that was expended in creating the work. It was even given a rhetorical link to public interest considerations by Wood V-C in *Spiers v Brown*,[338] where he stated:

> Copyright was considered for the highest purposes of society in every country as necessary to be secured to those who contributed to the civilization, refinement, or instruction of mankind, and extended in this country, if not elsewhere, to every description of work, however humble it might be, even to the mere collection of the abodes of persons and to streets and places; and labour having been employed upon subjects of that class, no one had a right to avail himself of it.[339]

In the years following *Spiers v Brown*, many cases involving compilations of various kinds came before the courts. Although some uncertainties arose at the peripheries, the core principle applied in each case was that copyright arose due to the labour invested in the material. However, this was far from being the

[332] *Kelly v Morris* (1865–66) LR 1 Eq 697.

[333] ibid 701–02.

[334] The case was followed in *Morris v Ashbee* (1868–69) LR 7 Eq 34 which also involved directories.

[335] *Morris v Wright* (1869–70) LR 5 Ch App 279.

[336] ibid 285.

[337] *Hogg v Scott* (1874) LR 18 Eq 444; *Ager v Peninsular and Oriental Steam Navigation Company* (1884) 26 ChD 637.

[338] (1857–58) 6 WR 352. See also *Cornish v Upton* (1861) 4 LT (NS) 862, 863.

[339] (1857–58) 6 WR 352, 352.

romantic version of authorial labour, manifesting itself in creative expression. More often than not it was the labour of collection, editing and organisation, and in some cases the reference to labour was supplemented by references to time and expense. In *Cornish v Upton*,[340] for example, a case involving a trades list and a street list, Wood V-C held that the plaintiff acquired copyright in 'matters patent to all the world, when he employed his own time, labour and expense upon the subject-matter'.[341]

The same Vice-Chancellor retreated somewhat from this position two years later in *Hotten v Arthur*.[342] In this case, he suggested in obiter dicta that copyright would *not* subsist in a 'mere dry list of names'.[343] In *Kelly v Morris*, as mentioned above, Wood V-C appeared simply to assume that copyright subsisted in the Directory before applying his stringent test of infringement to it. However, in *Morris v Ashbee*,[344] when the defendant in *Kelly v Morris* complained of someone else copying his *Business Directory of London*, Giffard V-C appeared to make his finding that copyright both subsisted and had been infringed on the basis that the plaintiff 'incurred the labour and expense first of getting the necessary information for the arrangement and complicate of the names as they stood in the directory, and then of making the actual compilation and arrangement'.[345] In subsequent cases, labour, sometimes in combination with time and expense, was the key for finding (or not finding) copyright in a list of bills of sale,[346] a trade catalogue and price list,[347] railway timetables[348] and a list of articles for sale by a chemist.[349]

Focusing on labour in the law of infringement had a number of different effects. In some cases, it might allow a second party to make use of a book and escape a charge of piracy, as in the new-work principle discussed above. In other cases, it was used to justify granting copyright protection to factual works. And in yet another line of cases, labour was employed in a manner which made the law of infringement appear more like a general claim of unjust enrichment. In *Hogg v Scott*,[350] for example, Hall V-C held that

> the true principle in all these cases is, that the Defendant is not at liberty to use or avail himself of the labour which the Plaintiff has been at for the purpose of protecting his work—that is, in fact, merely to take away the result of another man's labour, or, in other words, his property.[351]

[340] *Cornish v Upton* (1861) 4 LT (NS) 862.
[341] ibid 863.
[342] *Hotten v Arthur* (1863) 1 H & M 603
[343] ibid 607.
[344] *Morris v Ashbee* (1868) LR 7 Eq 34.
[345] ibid 40.
[346] *Trade Auxiliary Company v Middlesborough and District Tradesmen's Protection Association* (1889) 40 Ch D 425.
[347] *Harpers, Limited v Barry, Henry and Company, Limited* (1892) 20 R 133.
[348] *Leslie v J Young & Sons* [1894] AC 335. Note that in this case the timetables were found not to be copyright works as no independent labour had gone into their compilation.
[349] *Collis v Cater, Stoffell and Fortt Limited* (1898) 78 LT 613.
[350] *Hogg v Scott* (1874) 18 LR (Eq) 444.
[351] ibid 458.

In *Maple & Co v Junior Army and Navy*,[352] Jessel MR referred to the defendants as 'appropriat[ing] the result of other men's labours'.[353] Two years later, in *Ager v Peninsular and Oriental Steam Navigation Company*,[354] Kay J observed that 'what the Defendants are doing is to avail themselves unnecessarily of the labour and research of the Plaintiff without adequately recompensing him'[355] in a way that would seriously interfere with the Plaintiff's sales.

The emphasis on labour also came to be used to justify stronger proprietary rights for copyright owners, moving even beyond the scope of the legislative text. In *Cox v Land and Water Journal Company*,[356] which concerned the copying of hunting lists from a newspaper, Malins V-C found that even though newspapers were not protected under the 1842 Copyright Act, newspaper proprietors were able to assert a property right, even if not a copyright, in newspaper articles.[357] The Vice-Chancellor was somewhat vague about the nature of this right, stating it arose either under section 18 of the 1842 Copyright Act or 'by the general rules of property'.[358] He made no mention of *Donaldson v Becket*[359] and it does not appear to have been mentioned in argument before him. To support the existence of such a right he employed the same labour-based reasoning referred to above, stating:

> It is clear that in this case the getting the names of masters of hunts, the numbers of hounds, the huntsmen, and whips, and so forth, is information open to all who seek to obtain it; but it is information they must get at their own expense, as the result of their own labour, and they are not entitled to the results of the labours undergone by others.[360]

Towards the end of the century, the existence of a common law property right was referred to in other cases involving collections of information.[361] Moreover, in *Weatherby v International Horse Agency*,[362] the emphasis on property and misappropriation allowed the court to dispense with evidence of injury to the original work. The case involved published lists of breeding racehorses, which the defendants were alleged to have copied. Parker J noted:

> [I]n my opinion, an unfair use may be made of a book in the preparation of another, even if there is no likelihood of competition between the former and the latter. After all

[352] *Maple & Co v Junior Army and Navy Stores* (1882) 21 Ch D 369.
[353] ibid 379.
[354] *Ager v Peninsular and Oriental Steam Navigation Company* (1884) LR 26 Ch 637.
[355] ibid 642.
[356] *Cox v Land and Water Journal Company* (1869–70) LR 9 Eq 324.
[357] The non-protection of newspapers was reversed in *Walter v Howe* (1881) 17 Ch D 708.
[358] (1869–70) LR 9 Eq 324, 331.
[359] *Donaldson v Becket* (1774) 2 Bro PC 129.
[360] (1869–70) LR 9 Eq 324, 332.
[361] *Exchange Telegraph Company Limited v Gregory & Co* [1896] 1 QB 147, 153, 155, 157; *The Exchange Telegraph Company (Ltd) v Howard and the London and Manchester Press Agency* (1906) *The Times* (22 March 1906) 3a. Two Australian cases of the 1870s also posited the existence of a more expansive property right in relation to news; see *Wilson v Rowcroft* (1873) 4 Aust Jurist Reps 57; *Wilson v Luke* (1875) 1 VLR (Eq) 127. In the latter case, Molesworth J explicitly stated that he was not dealing with a common law copyright.
[362] *Weatherby v International Horse Agency* [1910] 2 Ch 297.

> copyright is property, and an action to restrain the infringement of a right of property will lie even if no damage be shewn. In the present case there may not be much probability that any one will buy the defendants' book instead of vol 21 of the Stud Book, but the fact remains that in preparing this book the defendants have utilized, wholesale and without permission, lists prepared by the plaintiffs at much trouble and expense. In so doing they have appropriated the result of this labour and expense to their own use.[363]

These cases show that in the second half of the nineteenth century labour continued to be the touchstone for questions of both copyright subsistence and infringement in a way that focused attention on commercial considerations, such as competition and commercial morality or fair trading.[364] The concept of labour, often combined with time or expense, was sometimes used to provide a rationale for conferring copyright on factual works. However, it was not always felt that such a rationale was needed. In many cases, copyright subsistence was not raised as a contentious issue, but in such cases the plaintiff's labour was discussed in the context of whether it had been unfairly appropriated by the defendant. In such instances the law of copyright began to shade into a more general law of unfair competition, unjust enrichment or simple misappropriation.

There was, however, some resistance to an ever-expanding law of copyright by reference to the concept of labour. In several cases, litigants sought to limit the labour relevant to subsistence to creative or authorial labour using the contested concept of originality. As early as 1798, John Murray had unsuccessfully argued in *Trusler v Murray* that Trusler's book was not 'original'.[365] Although this case was a fabrication aimed at garnering publicity for Trusler,[366] future defendants picked up on this argument and continued to attack the originality of works they were allegedly infringing, seeking to link copyright to notions of creativity. Such attempts were, however, rarely successful. In 1847, in the Scottish case of *Alexander v Mackenzie*,[367] the respondent argued that there was no copyright in a book of legal precedents or styles to be employed in relation to a new statute. The argument was rejected by the Lord Ordinary, who held that such a work could be the subject of copyright, despite the fact that it was not 'a treatise of high original genius', because it was the 'fair result of skill, experience and intelligent labour'.[368] On appeal, Lord Fullerton likewise considered that copyright did not require 'original and creative genius', but rather 'industry and knowledge'.[369]

[363] ibid 305.

[364] It is noteworthy that the nineteenth-century courts were often reluctant to deal in questions of unfair competition in a positive way. In a non-copyright case of 1899, Fry LJ noted, 'to draw the line between fair and unfair competition, between what is reasonable and unreasonable, passes the power of the courts'. *Mogul S.S. v McGregor Gow* (1889) 23 QBD 598, 625–26. But cp *Helmore v Smith* (1885) 35 Ch D 449 per Cotton LJ at 454.

[365] J Trusler, *An Essay on Literary Property* 16.

[366] See above n 152.

[367] *Alexander v Mackenzie* (1847) 9 Sc Ct Sess 748.

[368] ibid 754 fn.

[369] ibid 755. See also 758, per Lord Jeffery.

Wood V-C responded in a similar way in the 1857 case of *Jarrold v Houlston*,[370] which involved a book entitled 'The Guide to Science'. In response to the argument that there was no originality in the scientific principles contained in it, Wood V-C held that the question of copyright was beyond doubt, as the material in the book had been collected by 'pains and labour'.[371] However, this low standard of originality was challenged once again in another Scottish case of 1858,[372] which related to bills of entry and shipping lists. One of the respondents' grounds of defence was that the complainers had no copyright in the bills of entry because they had hired clerks to compile the materials, and therefore were not to be considered 'authors' within the meaning of the statute. They contended that

> copyright is ultimately founded upon authorship. Mental labour of some kind, if not of original invention, at least, of altering, arranging, or preparing, is to be implied in authorship; and a proprietor of copyright must either be the author or one deriving right from him.[373]

On appeal, Lord Deas, with Lords Ivory and Curriehill concurring, gave his opinion that the respondents' argument, 'although ingenious, is unsound. The Act does not confine the privilege to works of literary merit'.[374] Although the respondents had specifically distinguished their claim for authorship from that of literary merit, Lord Deas clearly considered that the latter implied the former, and refused to accept that the scope of copyright protection could be so limited.

Another Scottish case, 12 years later, did place more emphasis on authorship and literary skill. In *Black v Murray*,[375] a case involving annotated editions of Sir Walter Scott's works in which the Defenders alleged there could be no copyright as it had expired, Lord Kinloch stated:

> There is involved in such annotation, and often in a very eminent degree, an exercise of intellect, and an application of learning, which place the annotator in the position and character of author, in the most proper sense of the word. The skill and labour of such an annotator have often been procured at a price which cries shame on the miserable dole which formed to the author of the text his only remuneration.[376]

The Lord President observed that 'the selection and application of such quotations from other books may exercise as high literary faculties as the composition of original matter. They may be the result of great skill and of labour and of great literary taste'.[377] This, however, was a case in which literary merit could be dis-

[370] *Jarrold v Houlston* (1857) 3 K & J 708.
[371] ibid 713.
[372] *Maclean v Moody* (1858) 20 Sc Ct Sess 1154.
[373] ibid 1157 fn. The Lord Ordinary found that the complainers did have a copyright in the bills of entry and shipping lists, but considered that the question of infringement should be laid before a jury: ibid 1156–57.
[374] ibid 1163.
[375] *Black v Murray* (1870) 9 Court Sess Cas (3s) 341.
[376] ibid 355.
[377] ibid 345.

cerned, and so the question of whether much lower amounts of authorial input were acceptable was not raised.

A more restricted view of originality appeared to be adopted by Lord Romilly MR in the case of *Cobbett v Woodward*.[378] The Master of the Rolls held that no copyright could subsist in a advertising catalogue but added that a different rule applied to the letterpress, which would be protected wherever it 'bears the trace of original composition, but not where it simply describes the contents of a warehouse, the exertions of the proprietor, or the common mode of using familiar articles'.[379] This case was applied by the Lord Ordinary in *White v Briggs*[380] but it had already been overruled in England by the Court of Appeal in *Maple & Co v Junior Army and Navy Stores*.[381] In this case, Lindley LJ noted:

> The Plaintiffs' works is original in this sense, that they employed artists to make original drawings from pieces of furniture and from these drawing engravings were made which the Plaintiffs made into a book with descriptions and prices . . . That the work was original in the sense I have mentioned is clearly proved: and originality, not skill or merit, is the test whether a work is the subject of copyright.[382]

A year earlier, Jessel MR had considered the question of originality in relation to the title 'Splendid Misery' and had suggested that what was necessary was some kind of invention.[383] Lush LJ agreed, stating:

> I take it to be established law that to be the subject of copyright the matter must be original, it must be a composition of the author, something which has grown up in his mind, the product of something which if it were applied to patent rights would be called invention. Nothing short of that would entitle a man to copyright.[384]

The meaning of originality was considered in much greater detail in the case of *Walter v Lane*,[385] which involved newspaper reports of speeches. The case for the defendant was argued by the TE Scrutton and Augustine Birrell. In his Yorke Prize-winning essay, Scrutton had contended that copyright works should be original[386] and have literary value[387] (although, as counsel, he had argued in favour of granting property rights to a list of stocks and shares in *Exchange Telegraph v Gregory*[388] and advised Reuters that information and news could be protected by copyright[389]). In his treatise on copyright law, Birrell also indicated his preference for the 'old lofty conception of copyright as being something intended to promote

378 *Cobbett v Woodward* (1872) LR 14 Eq 407.
379 ibid 414.
380 *White v Briggs* (1890) 13 R 223, 225 fn.
381 *Maple & Co v Junior Army and Navy Stores* (1882) 21 Ch D 369.
382 ibid 380.
383 *Dicks v Yates* (1881) 18 Ch D 76, 88.
384 ibid 92.
385 *Walter v Lane* (1899) 2 Ch 749; [1900] AC 539.
386 TE Scrutton, *The Laws of Copyright* 1st edn (London, J Murray, 1883) 173.
387 ibid 168.
388 *Exchange Telegraph v Gregory* [1895] 1 QB 147.
389 Reuters Archive 1/867515. See also below: ch 7 text accompanying n 101 and following. My thanks to Lionel Bently for providing me with copies of this correspondence.

the production of literary works of a lasting benefit to mankind', further adding that the promoters of the 1842 Act 'certainly never contemplated that its provisions should afford protection to the contents of a telegram to a newspaper stating the results of a cricket match at the Antipodes'.[390] Before the Court of Appeal, Scrutton and Birrell argued for a slightly broader view, but still maintained that a reporter could not be an author because 'There must be some originality and this may be difficult to define. But the decided cases shew that independent labour, research, originality is necessary'.[391] They noted that all that the reporter had done was to perform the mechanical operation of taking down the speaker's words[392] and complained that the case was an attempt to reduce the amount of originality necessary to secure copyright to little or nothing.[393]

The Court of Appeal's judgment was delivered by Lindley MR, who expanded upon his definition of originality in *Maple & Co*, and accepted Scrutton and Birrell's emphasis on the definition of 'author' as pivotal. Lindley MR stated that

> [t]o hold that every reporter of a speech has copyright in his own report would be to stretch the Copyright Act to an extent which its language will not bear, and which the Legislature obviously never contemplated. The Act was passed to protect authors not reporters.[394]

The Court also accepted the argument that the labour required involved an element of originality, stating that although it required education and ability to make a good report of a speech, 'an accurate report is not an original composition'.[395]

The Times appealed the decision to the House of Lords which overturned the Court of Appeal's decision, stating that it was based upon too narrow and misleading a use of the word 'author'.[396] The Earl of Halsbury LC rejected the use of the word 'original' completely, stating that it should not be read into the statute. For the Lord Chancellor, it was the *book* that was the locus of protection, and any person who produced a book was to be considered an 'author'.[397] Lord Davey likewise considered that the key to protection was the fact that the reporter 'brought into existence in the form of a writing the piece of letterpress which the respondent has copied'.[398] However, he would have allowed slightly more scope for setting a threshold for protection, referring to the reporter's 'memory and trained judgment' as relevant.[399] Lord James of Hereford also referred to the 'degree of skill' exercised by certain reporters as relevant to claims for authorship, while Lord Brampton considered the 'brain and handiwork' of the reporter to be

[390] Birrell, *Seven Lectures* 145.
[391] *Walter v Lane* [1899] 2 Ch 749, 763.
[392] ibid 769.
[393] ibid 766.
[394] ibid 771.
[395] ibid 772.
[396] *Walter v Lane* [1900] AC 539, 545 per Earl of Halsbury LC.
[397] ibid 545–46.
[398] ibid 551.
[399] ibid.

significant.[400] Lord Halsbury, Lord Davey and Lord Brampton all held that literary merit had nothing to do with copyright law,[401] and Lord James of Hereford considered that an 'author' might come into existence without producing any original matter at all.[402]

Lord Robertson, dissenting, agreed with the Court of Appeal, noting he found it 'difficult to understand what attribute of an author belongs in [a shorthand reporter]'.[403] Although he noted that previous decisions relating to timetables and furniture catalogues had applied the Act to 'very pedestrian efforts of the mind', he could reconcile those decisions with the present, by focusing on the 'structure and arrangement' expended upon them.[404] For Lord Robertson the word 'author' presented 'a criterion consistent with the widest application of the Act to all who can claim as embodying their own thought, whether humble or lofty, the letterpress of which they assert the authorship'.[405]

The judges' rejection of literary merit as a criterion for copyright protection was a distortion of Scrutton and Birrell's case, as they had explicitly distinguished originality from literary quality before the House of Lords, emphasising that novelty and composition were the key to conferring protection.[406] Scrutton complained in the preface to the 1903 edition of his book, the House of Lords' decision meant that 'this so-called author shares his authorship with the mechanical phonograph'.[407] This was, however, precisely the point. By giving the most minimal content to the word 'author' and rejecting any attempts to elevate the concept of 'originality' to a significant criterion in granting copyright subsistence, the House of Lords confirmed that copyright was a commercial right, the main function of which was to regulate trade and competition. Some of the Lords said so explicitly. Lord Halsbury commenced his speech thus:

> My Lords, I should very much regret it if I were compelled to come to the conclusion that the state of the law permitted one man to make profit and appropriate to himself the labour, skill, and capital of another. And it is not denied that in this case the defendant seeks to appropriate to himself what has been produced by the skill, labour and capital of others. In the view I take of this case I think the law is strong enough to restrain what to my mind would be a grievous injustice.[408]

This approach to the statute, however, could also be justified on public interest grounds, as Lord Halsbury did later in his speech, when he observed:

> An importer of a foreign invention is for the purpose of the patent laws an inventor, and, as Lord Brougham said in *Re Berry's Patent*, there were 'two species of public benefactors—

[400] ibid 559.
[401] ibid 548, 552, 558.
[402] ibid 554.
[403] ibid 561.
[404] ibid.
[405] ibid 562.
[406] ibid 542–43.
[407] TE Scrutton, *The Law of Copyright*, 4th edn (London, William Cloves & Sons, 1903) vi.
[408] *Walter v Lane* [1900] AC 539, 545.

> the one, those who benefit the public by their ingenuity, industry and science and invention and personal capability; the other, those who benefit the public without any ingenuity or invention of their own, by the appropriation of the results of foreign inventions. Now the latter is a benefit to the public incontestably and therefore they render themselves entitled to be put upon somewhat, if not entirely, the same footing as inventors' . . . I might paraphrase Lord Brougham's language by asking whether those who preserve the memory of spoken words, which are assumed to be of value to the public, are not entitled to a merit analogous to that which Lord Brougham attributes to the importer of foreign inventions.[409]

Lord Davey likewise appeared to be approaching the case from the point of unfair competition, noting:

> It is a sound principle that a man shall not avail himself of another's skill, labour and expense by copying the written product thereof. To quote the language of North J in another case: 'For the purposes of their own profit they desire to reap where they have not sown, and to take advantage of the labour and expenditure of the plaintiffs in procuring news for the purpose of saving labour and expense to themselves'.[410]

Others, however, referred to the public interest in interpreting the statute broadly. Lord James mentioned giving speeches to the public[411] and Lord Brampton noted that the publication by *The Times* meant that 'the thousands of readers of that journal might be truthfully and accurately informed of those intellectual and interesting utterance of Lord Rosebery which they had not been privileged to hear'.[412]

The result of *Walter v Lane* was that the notion of originality remained firmly linked to labour, and labour was to be determined by reference to investment in commercial, rather than creative, terms. Moreover, such an approach *could* be justified in terms of the public interest in encouraging wide dissemination of information, even if such justifications were not always mentioned or prioritised. The emphasis on commercial aspects represented an unbroken line of continuity from the pre-Statute of Anne book trade regulation. Locating the protection in the physical form of the 'book', as the Lord Chancellor did, might seem out of step with the emerging judicial antipathy to abridgments and 'new works', but it was consistent with the line of cases emphasising competition and unjust enrichment. For example, in *Maple & Co v Junior Army and Navy Stores*, Hall V-C held that a catalogue could be protected because it was a 'book' and 'a book is a thing which the statute protects'.[413]

However, in other cases reliance on the categories of physical form in the 1842 Copyright Act acted as a brake on expansionist claims. In *Hollinrake v Truswell*, protection was denied to a sleeve chart on the basis it was neither a book, map, chart nor plan.[414] Similarly, in *Chilton v Progress Printing and Publishing Company*, the announcement of horse names which the plaintiff predicted to be winners was

409 ibid 549.
410 ibid 552. The case in which North J made that statement was *Walter v Steinkopf* [1892] 3 Ch 489.
411 ibid 553.
412 ibid 559.
413 (1882) 21 Ch D 369, 373.
414 *Hollinrake v Truswell* (1894) 3 Ch 420.

found not to be a subject matter for protection.[415] In that case, Lindley LJ held that even if the meaning of literary composition were extended as wide as possible, adding that it had been extended very widely by Wood V-C in *Kelly v Morris*, an opinion could not be a literary composition.[416]

There was also resistance to extending copyright protection to cover titles and on this matter the courts' views oscillated over time. In 1865, Wood V-C first suggested that copyright would not extend to titles, and a similar finding was made in cases in the subsequent three years.[417] Some doubt was cast on this proposition by Lord Romilly MR in *Mack v Petter*[418] and Malins V-C in *Weldon v Dicks*[419] but in *Dicks v Yates*,[420] the Court of Appeal found that there could be no copyright in the title *Splendid Misery*, effectively overruling *Weldon* on the basis that case was really a case of fraud or deception. In *Schove v Schminke*,[421] Chitty J stated shortly that 'there mere taking of a title consisting simply of two ordinary words of the English language would not be an infringement of copyright'.[422] By contrast, in *Lamb v Evans*,[423] the Court of Appeal considered that headings denoting different trades appearing in a trades directory could be the subject of copyright. Bowen LJ stated that the headings 'are the result of literary labour'.[424]

The flip-side of a broad test of originality which drew its protection from labour rather than creativity was that the unlaboured-upon materials would not be the subject of property. The courts in some cases made reference to this distinction and, in doing so, prepared further groundwork for the development of the idea/expression dichotomy. Although this principle would not come to be referred to in such a manner until the following century, the reasoning that informs it can be detected in the cases relating to factual works. In the Scottish case of *Alexander v Mackenzie*, which (as noted above[425]) related to a book containing statutory forms or styles, the Court of Session harked back to the language used in *Carnan v Bowles*,[426] observing

> while there is no doubt that it would be dangerous to encroach on the liberty of all who are disposed to make a selection from materials '*in medio*' with a view similar to that of any person who has previously made a selection from these materials, still the question comes to be whether any party making such selection has gone into the matter '*in medio*' for himself, and has not merely followed in his predecessor's traces.[427]

[415] *Chilton v Progress Printing and Publishing Company* (1895) 2 Ch 29, 33.
[416] ibid 34.
[417] *Correspondent Newspaper Company Limited v Saunders* (1865) 11 Jur (NS) 540; *Maxwell v Hogg; Hogg v Maxwell* (1867) 2 LR (Ch) 307; *Kelly v Hutton* (1868) 3 LR (Ch) 703.
[418] *Mack v Petter* (1872) LR 14 Eq 431.
[419] *Weldon v Dicks* (1878) 10 Ch D 247.
[420] *Dick v Yates* (1881) 18 Ch D 76.
[421] *Schove v Schminke* (1886) 33 Ch D 546.
[422] ibid 550.
[423] *Lamb v Evans* [1892] 1 Ch 219.
[424] ibid 227; see also ibid 232 (per Kay LJ).
[425] See above: text to n 367.
[426] *Carnan v Bowles* (1786) 2 Bro CC 80 and 1 Cox 283.
[427] (1847) 9 Sc Ct Sess 748, 758.

Similarly, in *Pike v Nicholas*,[428] which related to two books on the same historical subject, the court emphasised that the defendant was entitled to make use of the plaintiff's book, but that he had worked up the material in his own style and language. The court disapproved of the defendant's failure to acknowledge the assistance he had obtained from the plaintiff's book, explicitly stating that 'common fairness and justice' suggested he should have expressed his 'obligations to him in giving [him] the idea'.[429] However, as he had not copied the plaintiff's language, there was no infringement. Another example of this reasoning can be found in *Bradbury v Hotten*,[430] where the Court of Exchequer noted the defendant had 'not availed himself of the knowledge acquired from *Punch*, but he has actually reproduced the very pictures'.[431] The former would have been no infringement.

In these cases, as well as the directory cases which referred to the need for a subsequent author to make his own calculations, the notion of keeping information and facts free for subsequent compilers can be discerned. This aligns with the current notion of the idea/expression dichotomy, which holds that ideas should be kept free for use and only the way in which they are expressed is protected. However, several other cases of the mid-nineteenth century appear to suggest that some sort of protection was extended to ideas. In *Jarrold v Houlston*, the defendant denied taking 'any idea or language'[432] from the book he was alleged to have copied. Likewise, in *Chatterton v Cave*, the court stated that taking the 'idea or language' would amount to an infringement.

While these two cases might appear to give more expansive protection to 'ideas', as Lord Hailsham has since famously observed, 'it all depends what you mean by ideas'.[433] Examining the former case more closely, it emerges that what the courts referred to as 'ideas' is what would today be referred to as 'expression'. In *Jarrold v Houlston*, Wood V-C explained that it would have been acceptable to read books in order to check he had not forgotten some words, as well as to make use of the same material, but that it would be an infringement to 'adopt [the] arrangements' of his predecessor.[434] Although it is not explicitly stated, it seems that Wood V-C considered the 'arrangement' to be a protectable 'idea'.

By contrast, in *Chatterton v Cave*, both parties had made adaptations of a French play (which was no infringement) but the Lord Chief Justice found that two of the plaintiffs' scenes had been copied by the defendant. On appeal, Brett J observed that the defendant had copied the idea from the French play and the mode of representing it from the plaintiffs' play, but went on to say 'not having copied the idea or the language from the plaintiffs' drama, but only the dramatic situation' there was no infringement.[435] Grove J agreed, suggesting that a very striking stage

[428] *Pike v Nichlas* (1869–70) LR 5 Ch App 251.
[429] ibid 252–53.
[430] *Bradbury v Hotten* (1872) LR 8 Ex 1.
[431] ibid 7.
[432] (1857) 3 K&J 708, 715
[433] *LB Plastics v Swish* [1979] FSR 145, 160 (quoting Professor Joad).
[434] (1857) 3 K&J 708, 716–17.
[435] (1874–75) LR 10 CP 572, 577.

situation or important novel scenic effect might be the subject of copyright, but that in the present case 'this was an ordinary stage effect, such as everyone familiar with melodramatic pieces normally sees'.[436] Lord Coleridge CJ thought that an 'idea' had been copied, but that it was too slight to amount to a substantial taking.[437] In this case, then, it seems that the Court of the Exchequer Chamber was not quite clear whether the copying of ideas would amount to infringement. However, again, this does not seem so much to be an acceptance that copying ideas as such could infringe, but a difficulty in ascertaining whether a substantial enough part had been copied.

By the final decade of the century the views of the courts were beginning to take a more definite shape. In *Kenrick v Lawrence,* which related to the alleged copying of a voting card which depicted a hand pencilling a cross in a square, Wills J held definitively that 'there is no copyright in the subject [of his drawing]'.[438] Four years later, in *Hollinrake v Truswell*, Lindley J observed in the Court of Appeal that 'Copyright does not extend to ideas, or schemes, or systems, or methods; it is confined to their expression; and if their expression is not copied the copyright is not infringed'.[439] The other judges made similar remarks but Lindley LJ's statement is of interest as he points to the 1879 American case of *Baker v Selden* as providing an illustration of this point.[440] Oren Bracha considers that *Baker v Selden* is important as it 'expressed the *new version* of the principle that copyright does not extend to knowledge' (emphasis added).[441] However, as shown above, this was not a new principle in Britain. Despite some decisions which seemed to suggest that protection might extend to ideas, the general tendency was to tether protection to labour and to leave the raw materials free for general use. What was new was the certainty with which the principle was expressed, making *Hollinrake v Truswell* the point at which the principle that copyright protects only expression and not ideas definitively crystallised as a central doctrine of copyright law. It is also significant that the main factor motivating the Court of Appeal in reaching its decision that the plaintiff's sleeve chart could not be protected, and that even if it could be it was not infringed, was fear of monopolies.[442] Thus, while the reach of copyright expanded in terms of the amount taken and the use made of it, the idea/expression dichotomy could be seen as placing at least one kind of limit on this expansion which was informed by concerns for the public interest in free competition.

In the second half of the nineteenth century, an ever-increasing number of cases relating to copyright infringement came before the courts. While much of the language used by the litigants and judges is familiar to copyright lawyers of the twenty-first century, it could not be said that coherent or consistent doctrines were developed during this period. Different courts and judges (and sometimes even the same court

[436] ibid 579.
[437] ibid 582.
[438] *Kenrick v Lawrence* (1890) 25 QBD 99, 103.
[439] *Hollinrake v Truswell* [1894] 3 Ch 420, 427.
[440] ibid 427; *Baker v Selden* (1879) 101 US 99.
[441] Bracha, 'Ideology of Authorship Revisited' 235.
[442] [1894] 3 Ch 420, 423, 426, 428.

or judge, at different times) would apply one or a combination of different approaches in order to decide whether infringement had occurred. While some of these approaches could potentially be reconciled in a coherent manner by reference to some underlying rationale such as the public interest, there is only sporadic evidence of the courts actually doing so. This does not mean that no conclusions can be drawn from a study of this period; it does, however, mean that recourse to the nineteenth century 'precedents' should be an exercise undertaken with extreme caution.

What we can see from this period is a continued expansion of the rights of copyright owners, as the abridgment and new-work principles began to be overtaken by a growing concern to protect the copyright owner's market, and a corresponding expansion of that market's potential scope. Where the new-work principle prioritised the labour of the alleged infringer, as the century progressed it was the initial owner's labour that came to be the more significant factor for a finding of infringement.

The treatise writers of the second half of the century sought to extrapolate general principles from the morass of cases before them. George Ticknor Curtis, in 1847, began his discussion of infringement by setting out what he saw as the underlying premise of the law:

> In endeavouring to trace the just scope of these principles and doctrines, we must bear in mind that while the primary object of the law of copyright is protection to the product of all literary labour, the interests of knowledge demand a reasonable freedom in the use of all antecedent literature. To administer the law in such a way as to not curtail the fair use of existing materials, in any department of letters, is one of the great tasks of jurisprudence. It proposes to itself, first, the vindication of rights acquired by genius, discovery, invention and labor, in the productions of the mind; secondly, the acknowledgment upon motives of public policy, of the right to a fair use by any writer of all that has been recorded by previous authors.[443]

Although he conceded a 'right to a fair use', for Curtis the primary concern of copyright law was the right of the author 'to take all the profits of publication which the book can, in any form, produce'.[444] He went on to set out four ways in which the right could be invaded:

> 1. By reprinting the whole work, verbatim; 2. By reprinting, verbatim, a part of it, either with or without acknowledgment of the source from which the extract or passage is taken; 3. By imitating the whole or a part, or by reproducing the whole or a part with colorable alterations and disguises, intending to give to it the character of a new work; 4. By reproducing the whole or a part under an abridged form.[445]

He went on to add that the intention of the infringer did not enter into the determination of infringement.[446] Instead, he suggested that the main question should be whether the author had sustained any injury, or was likely to do so.[447]

443 GT Curtis, *Treatise on the Law of Copyright* 236–37.
444 ibid 238.
445 ibid.
446 ibid.
447 ibid 240.

Curtis's loyal follower Copinger was far from consistent in his approach and, like those authors on copyright before him, became very bogged down in the courts' conflicting decisions. In his first edition, he noted:

> [Y]et to be a piracy it is not necessary that the latter work should be a substitute for the original composition. It can seldom if ever be the requirement . . . The inquiry in most cases, is not, whether the defendant has used the thoughts, conceptions, information and discoveries promulgated by the original, but whether his composition may be considered a *new work*, requiring invention, learning, and judgment, or only a mere transcript of the whole or parts of the original, with mere colourable alterations.[448]

In his second edition, Copinger retained this statement, but noted on the previous page:

> But the question of piracy cannot properly depend on the intention of the pirate. The main point must always be what effect will the extracts have upon the original work—how far will they supply its place or injure its sale. If the extracts are such as to render the protected work less valuable, by superseding its use in any degree, the right of the author is infringed, and it can be of no importance to inquire with what intent this was done.[449]

Writing seven years before Copinger's first edition, Charles Palmer Phillips had similarly been reduced to quoting from a series of decisions, and made even less of an attempt to draw out coherent principles from them. In a rare moment of editorial intervention, he identified a public interest rationale in the rule about extracts for the purposes of criticism, stating that to find such extracts piratical would 'fetter public discussion, and such discussion is in this country considered beneficial to the public'.[450] He added that such extracts did not injure the author but often extended the sale of a book.[451]

Three influential copyright works appeared in the final decades of the century. First amongst them was TE Scrutton's Yorke Prize-winning essay on copyright. Unlike Phillips, Scrutton did attempt to construct an organising principle for the law of infringement. He identified four different varieties:

1. Open reproductions of the whole or a part of a work *simpliciter*, without extraneous matter.
2. Open reproductions of the whole or a part of a work together with other matter.
3. Disguised or altered reproductions of the whole or a part of the work, as abridgments, plagiarisms and the like.
4. Reproductions of the whole or part of the work through another channel than that chosen by the author, as dramatisations of novels.[452]

Scrutton merged the descriptive and the normative in some of these categories. He admitted that abridgments had sometimes been allowed by English courts but

448 Copinger, *The Law of Copyright*, 1st edn, 86–87.

449 WA Copinger, *The Law of Copyright in Works of Literature and Art*, 2nd edn (London, Stevens & Haynes, 1881) 174–75.

450 CP Phillips, *The Law of Copyright* 125

451 ibid 125.

452 TE Scrutton, *The Laws of Copyright*, 1st edn (London, J Murray, 1883) 42.

submitted this was wrong on principle, for the same reason that the new-work principle was wrong:

> That fresh matter has been added to the part appropriated does not alter the fact of its appropriation without payment, and appropriation without payment defeats the end of protection. The question should not be whether 'work and labour' has been bestowed on the portion appropriated, but whether a substantial portion of original and protected work has been taken without payment and without authority.[453]

For Scrutton, the principle underlying infringement ought to be:

> Whenever a substantial part of an author's copyright work is reproduced without his authority, whether alone or in conjunction with new matter, whether by the same or a different channel to the original, so as to tend to damage the sale of such original work, and thus to lessen the original author's return for his work, such reproduction is an infringement of copyright.[454]

However, when it came to practical application of these principles, he noted that it was difficult to draw the line between what was and was not infringement:

> [W]e can only say that any direct reproduction of the author's material which tends to supersede, or act as a substitute for, the original work, is an infringement of his copyright, but that moderate quotation for the purpose of fair review or criticism is not such a reproduction.[455]

The second influential work was by Augustine Birrell, and based on his popular lectures on copyright.[456] Birrell harked back to the 1810 case of *Wilkins v Aikin* when defining infringement, and focused therefore on the infringer's intention. He summarised the position as follows: 'The intent to steal, the unscrupulous determination to benefit by another's labours (that other being a 'protected' author) without independent work of one's own, this is to be a pirate at law'.[457] Birrell was not overly interested in the question of abridgments as he believed they had 'gone out of fashion'.[458] However, he was attuned to the direction in which things were moving and noted, 'there can be little doubt that the next time the law is taken in hand the too seldom exercised right of cutting themselves short will be reserved to authors during their periods of protection'.[459]

Introducing the language of theft into copyright discourse, Birrell referred to infringement as 'literary larceny', a practice also adopted by EJ Macgillivray in his treatise of 1902. Macgillivray, a barrister of the Inner Temple, was heavily involved in the Society of Authors and the legislative reform of copyright law, and he published a treatise on copyright which he dedicated to Scrutton 'in gratitude

[453] ibid 46–47.
[454] ibid 52–53.
[455] ibid 43.
[456] Birrell, *Seven Lectures.*
[457] ibid 172.
[458] ibid 158.
[459] ibid 158–59.

of much instruction and kindness'.[460] The structure Macgillivray adopted for discussing the law of infringement was closer to that employed today than those of his predecessors, his first seven chapter sub-headings being as follows:

What is a Copy?
A Substantial Part must be Taken
No *Animus Furandi* need be Proved
Taking not necessarily for Profit
Copying may be Indirect and Unintentional
Custom of Trade
Fair Use[461]

With the exception of 'Custom of Trade', which Macgillivray dismissed as a feasible ground of defence[462], this would not look out of place today as a list of principles to be applied to the question of infringement.

Like his mentor Scrutton, Macgillivray considered that a piratical copy would be 'that which will provide a substitute for the whole or for a substantial part of the original book'.[463] His section headed 'Fair Use,' however, was a novel departure. Under this heading he listed various types of non-infringing uses. Unsurprisingly, extracts for the purpose of criticism[464] came under this heading, but his list extended more widely, including the principle that 'No one can monopolize a Field of Labour'.[465] Macgillivray also included the idea/expression dichotomy in his discussion of fair use, stating that it was no infringement to take facts,[466] nor to take the general scheme or idea of another book or the theories therein.[467] Discussing the new-work principle, as found in the cases of *Sayre v Moore* and *Cary v Kearsley*, he noted:

> The theory of these early cases on infringement seems to have been—colourable alteration is not to be allowed, but no check is to be put on the taking of material when it is taken *bona fide* in the interests of scientific or literary knowledge. Gradually, however, the Courts in questions of infringement came to look more to the interests of the author than to those of the public, and regarded the law of copyright more as a means of securing rights of property to the individual than as an unnatural monopoly created for the purpose of encouraging and developing literary effort.[468]

He went on to note that the rule allowing abridgments had been founded on the same basis as the new-work principle and suggested that abridgments would now

[460] EJ Macgillivray, *A Treatise upon the Law of Copyright* (London, John Murrary, 1902).
[461] ibid x–xi.
[462] ibid 103.
[463] ibid 97.
[464] ibid 111.
[465] ibid 103.
[466] ibid 104.
[467] ibid 104–05.
[468] ibid 113.

be seen as infringements.[469] He also asserted that translations should likewise amount to infringement.[470]

Recourse to the treatise writers of the nineteenth century provides little more consistency than the case law on infringement. Different writers emphasised different tests and standards for infringement; some focused on intention, some on competition and some on property rights. There was an emerging consensus that some types of use would not amount to infringement, and general agreement that quotation for the purpose of criticism was amongst these, but what the other kinds of use might be remained unclear. Moreover, there was no single view on *why* these uses were permissible; some, like Scrutton, ascribed it to lack of competition, while others, like Phillips, gave more weight to public interest considerations.

The difficulties experienced by the treatise writers in beating a clear path through the ever-growing mass of judicial decisions might have suggested this was an area ripe for codification, but the Royal Copyright Commission of 1875–78 was reluctant to get overly involved in such matters. It characterised the question of extracts as one of 'what is a fair use of the works of other authors in the compilation of books'[471] and considered that it would not be possible to lay down a rule that could govern all the cases that might arise and that such matters were best left to the courts.[472] More attention was paid to the question of abridgments, and several witnesses raised this issue before the Commission. On being asked his view of the law regarding abridgments, the publisher John Murray commented that it was 'ticklish'[473] and unclear, but submitted that an author should have the same right regarding abridgments as to the rest of the copyright. Lord John Manners inquired as to whether he did not think that 'some relaxation of the proposed law should be made so as to enable the community to have the advantage of the substance of a work of that kind'.[474] Murray responded that such a relaxation would interfere with 'a man's right of property'.[475] In their final report, the Commissioners recommended that the right to abridge should be one of the rights of the copyright owner.

iii. Transformative Works and Market Limits

Copyright owners might have begun to taste success in their quest to annex the market for abridgments and other derivative works in a literary format. However, they met with more resistance in their attempts to expand their control over works into different media or different languages. When works were not just altered but transformed into a new kind of work, claims of secondary users and the public in general were met with more sympathy.

[469] ibid 115–16.
[470] ibid 116–18.
[471] Royal Copyright Commission xv.
[472] ibid xv.
[473] ibid 59.
[474] ibid 60.
[475] ibid.

One significant kind of transformation that copyright owners sought to control was the popular practice of turning novels into plays. It was, however, an author, Charles Reade, rather than a publisher who led the charge on this issue.[476] In 1861, Reade unsuccessfully brought an action against George Conquest of the Grecian Theatre in the Court of Common Pleas, complaining he had dramatised Reade's novel, *It is Never Too Late to Mend*, itself based on a play Reade had written earlier.[477] Reade's counsel resurrected the spectre of common law copyright in his argument that although the statute did not apply to dramatising plays, the common law would prevent it, and he quoted Lord Mansfield at great length. The Court, however, rejected this claim, noting that although 'much might be urged in favour of the common law right' the time had long passed when it was open for discussion.[478]

Three months later, however, Reade was successful in obtaining an injunction against Lacy, who had *published* a drama based on Reade's novel.[479] The injunction related only to the passages that were copied verbatim in Lacy's book, but Wood V-C also expressed scepticism as to the correctness of the defendant's argument that a novel could be adapted into a play without permission.[480] Armed with this favourable obiter dictum, Reade returned to the Court of Common Pleas to resume his action against Conquest.[481] Here the Court upheld his claim that Conquest had infringed copyright in the play upon which the novel was based.

Despite Reade's success, the precedent he set was narrow. The first decision had turned on the printing of the play and the second on the fact that dramatising the novel was an indirect infringement of the dramatic copyright in the play on which the novel had been based. The principle that it was no infringement to dramatise a novel was upheld several years later in *Toole v Young*,[482] despite the fact that the plaintiff in that case had produced an unpublished dramatisation of his own novel. Cockburn CJ noted:

> When an author has once given his novel to the world, he cannot take away from other persons the right to dramatize it by himself transforming it into a drama, subject to this, that they must not borrow from his drama but only from his novel.[483]

In this case, the Court was clearly of the view that dramatising a novel came within the prohibition of neither the 1842 Copyright Act, nor the 1833 Dramatic Copyright

[476] Reade's championship of the right of an author to prevent dramatisation of his works was revealed to be more self-serving than principled. In 1872, he was himself guilty of dramatising a book by his friend Anthony Trollope. Trollope was furious, particularly when the media reported that the play contained obscene language. The incident led to a four-year rift between the two authors. For detail of their acrimonious epistolary exchanges, see BA Booth, 'Trollope, Reade and "Shilly-Shally" (Part I)' (1947) 1 *The Trollopian* 45 and BA Booth, 'Trollope, Reade and "Shilly-Shally" (Part II)' (1947) 2 *The Trollopian* 43.

[477] *Reade v Conquest (No1)* (1861) 9 CB (NS) 755.

[478] ibid 767.

[479] *Reade v Lacy* (1861) 1 J & H 524.

[480] ibid 656.

[481] *Reade v Conquest (No 2)* (1862) 11 CB (NS) 479.

[482] *Toole v Young* (1874) LR 9 QB 523.

[483] ibid 527.

Act. By contrast, the assignee of the popular novelist Miss Braddon successfully obtained an injunction against the publisher Lacy, for publishing dramatisations of two of Miss Braddon's books.[484] The key to preventing dramatisations under the Copyright Act was, therefore, to establish the dramatisation had been *printed*.

Outside the courts, authors had been agitating for protection against unauthorised dramatisation for some time. In 1866, Lord Lyttelton had introduced a Bill into the House of Lords which provided that the right of dramatising a work should be held by its author.[485] The Bill was supported by Earl Stanhope but opposed by Lord Taunton, Earl Granville and the Lord Chancellor, Lord Cranworth. Lyttelton and Stanhope both emphasised that dramatisation was injurious to authors in terms of money and reputation, as they would lose potential profits and the dramatisations may be of poor quality. Those in opposition argued that the Bill would cause greater injury to authors, because a dramatisation might stimulate sales.[486] Moreover, the Bill would be against the interests of the public. As Earl Granville noted, 'it would be a great hardship upon the play going public if play writers were to be precluded from founding dramas upon successful works of fiction'.[487] Lord Cranworth's objections took their lead from the new-work principle; he argued:

> The argument in support of the existing law had always been that, though it gave an author a copyright in his work, it did not prohibit anything founded upon that work which was new and original in its character. Now, nothing could be more different from a novel than a drama founded upon it.[488]

He went on to add that an author might forbid all dramatisations.[489]

These objections prevailed and the Bill vanished from sight. However, dissatisfaction amongst dramatists resurfaced again before the Royal Copyright Commission. The theatre manager John Hollingshead submitted a number of letters from leading novelists, including Charles Reade, Wilkie Collins, Mrs Braddon and George Eliot, complaining of the current law. Several witnesses suggested that the right of dramatisation should be included in the definition of copyright law,[490] and the dramatist AW Dubourg argued:

> I contend that an author, if there be a law of copyright, is entitled to the full fruits of his creation, and that he ought to have the right of shaping his ideas either into the narrative or book form of expression or into the dramatic form.[491]

[484] *Tinsley v Lacy* (1862) 32 LJ (Ch) 537; 1 H & M 747.

[485] Parl Deb HL vol 184 col 360 (14 June 1866). The right to dramatise a novel had in fact appeared two years earlier in a codifying bill prepared and introduced to the House of Commons by Adam Black MP: Copyright (No 2) A Bill to consolidate and amend the Acts relating to Copyright in Works of Literature and the Fine Arts (1864) 59 s 6.

[486] Parl Deb HL vol 184 col 362 (14 June 1866).

[487] ibid.

[488] ibid 363.

[489] ibid.

[490] See the evidence of Sharon Grote Turner, Royal Copyright Commission 79; of John Palgrave Simpson, ibid 124–25; of Tom Taylor, ibid 134–35; and of Hollingshead, ibid 131–33.

[491] Royal Copyright Commission 130.

Even Thomas Farrer agreed that it was anomalous that copyright in a novel should not extend to its dramatisation. Noting that one of the reasons that the 1866 Bill was defeated was that it was considered to be bad for authors and the public and, drawing on the treatment of translations under the International Copyright Act,[492] he suggested the compromise of allowing an author a specified period of time to abridge or dramatise the work himself, after which time it should be thrown open to the public.[493]

The majority of the Commissioners, however, favoured the arguments of the authors to those of Farrer, stating that the benefits that the public would gain by Farrer's suggestions were outweighed by the desirability of a uniform term of protection. They were convinced by the authors' proprietary claims. However, the Report combined property reasoning with the language of unfair competition and unjust enrichment, stating it was

> only just that an author should be entitled to the full amount of profit which he can derive from his own creation;—that the product of a man's brain ought to be his own for all purposes;—and that it is unjust, when he has expended his invention and labour in the composition of a story, that another man should be able to reap part of his harvest.[494]

Although the Commission's recommendations fell on stony ground, in 1888 *Toole v Young* was applied in the case of *Warne & Co v Seebohm*,[495] which related to a dramatisation of Frances Hodgson Burnett's popular novel, *Little Lord Fauntleroy* Counsel for the plaintiff took a new approach, focusing on the fact that four copies had been made of the play, one of which was required to be deposited with the Lord Chamberlain. Counsel argued that the defendant had therefore infringed the 1842 Copyright Act by multiplying copies. Relying in part on *Novello v Sudlow*,[496] Stirling J accepted this argument, and granted a perpetual injunction.[497] However, he emphasised that printing was 'the only restriction . . . and, subject to it, every person is free to make such use of the book as he pleases'.[498] Despite Stirling J's emphasis on the limited nature of the property right, in practice his judgment expanded the rights of the novel's copyright owner, as it would be impossible for a novel to be dramatised without any written copy being produced, particularly in light of the requirement that a copy of every play be sent to the Lord Chamberlain.[499]

Edward Cutler QC, a lawyer who was deeply involved in legislative copyright reform, wrote in 1890, that 'Novelists will no doubt welcome this decision',[500] but added that

[492] See below: nn 522 ff.

[493] Royal Copyright Commission 156–57.

[494] ibid xvi.

[495] *Warne & Co v Seebohm* (1888) 39 ChD 73.

[496] (1852) 12 CB 177. See above: text to n 309.

[497] (1888) 39 ChD 73, 82.

[498] ibid 81.

[499] An Act for regulating Theatres 1843 (6 & 7 Vict c 68) s 12. This duty of the Lord Chamberlain was only abolished in 1968.

[500] E Cutler et al, *The Law of Musical and Dramatic Compositions* (London, Cassell & Co, 1890) 16.

> the decision only serves to show that a logical and liberal interpretation of the law may often be opposed to common sense: If the representation of a play constructed from the novel of another is no legal wrong to the novelist (and that is admitted) how can it be seriously said that the making of a few copies for stage purposes interferes with the sale of the book?[501]

Cutler's criticism drew out the lack of a clear justification underlying the courts' approach in such cases. He suggested that lack of competition between the works could not be the true standard, as there could be no competition between the novel and a small number of stage copies. However, Stirling J could hardly be said to be gesturing towards an expansive proprietary right for authors. Instead, he side-stepped all such issues by a narrow focus on the wording of the Act—a literal approach that continued to be applied until reform of the law in 1911.[502]

Another kind of derivative work that raised similar issues was translations. However, surprisingly, no cases came before the United Kingdom courts that squarely raised the issue. As noted above, Lord Macclesfield in 1720 had stated that a translation would not be an infringement,[503] and the same point had been made, obiter dicta, by several judges in *Millar v Taylor*. Willes J, for example, had commented, 'Certainly bona fide imitations, translations, and abridgments are different, and in respect of the property, may be considered as new works'.[504] Aston J had likewise noted that a book's purchaser 'may improve upon it, imitate it, translate it, oppose its statements, but he buys no right to publish the identical works'.[505] In the 1814 case of *Wyatt v Barnard*,[506] Lord Eldon had considered a translation to be an original work.[507]

Cases raising the issue directly did arise, however, in other jurisdictions. In the United States, Harriet Beecher Stowe brought an action against the defendant who had translated her book *Uncle Tom's Cabin* into German.[508] Grier J held that the translation did not infringe on the basis that

> those only can be called infringers of her rights, or pirates of her property, who are guilty of printing, publishing, importing, or vending without her license 'copies of her *book*.' A translation may, in loose phraseology, be called a transcript or copy of her thoughts or conceptions; but in no correct sense can it be called a copy of her book.[509]

501 ibid 17.

502 Two subsequent cases were brought before Kekewich J in Chancery in 1890, both of which related to works by Wilkie Collins. In both of these cases Kekewich J upheld the authority of *Toole v Young* and *Reade v Conquest*. In the former, the plaintiff was unsuccessful, as copying could not be proven; *Schlesinger v Bedford* (1890) 63 LT 762. In the latter, the plaintiff was successful, as it was established that the defendant had copied from a drama written before the novel; *Schlesinger v Turner* (1890) 63 LT 764.

503 In *Burnett v Chetwood*, n 47 above.

504 (1769) 4 Burr 2303, 2310

505 ibid 2349.

506 *Wyatt v Barnard* (1814) 3 V & B 77.

507 The case related to foreign works, which were not protected, and so the issue of infringement by translation did not arise.

508 *Stowe v Thomas* 23 F Cas 201 (CCED Pa 1853) (No 13, 514); 2 Am L Reg 210 (1854).

509 23 Fed Cas 201, 208.

For Grier J, the key was to focus on the book and its language as providing the locus of protection, and he took a limited view of the legislature's scope.

In the final decade of the nineteenth century, two cases involving translations came before the High Court of Bombay. The first arose when the defendant translated the plaintiff's book from Urdu to Persian, and the finding of no infringement was made on the basis of the Indian copyright law.[510] However, Parsons J, when giving judgment, observed that the same situation would prevail under the United Kingdom law.[511] In addition to mentioning *Wyatt v Barnard* and *Burnett v Chetwood*, the judge also referred to the case of *Prince Albert v Strange*,[512] which had involved unpublished works. In that case, Knight Bruce V-C had stated, obiter dicta, 'A work lawfully published . . . may be liable to be translated, abridged, analysed, exhibited, complimented'.[513]

Five years later a second case came before the High Court of Bombay. This case involved the London publishing firm of Macmillan's complaint that several of their works had been translated into Urdu for local readers.[514] This time, the case was decided on the basis of the 1842 Copyright Act which, by section 29, extended to all parts of the British dominions. However, Ferran J made the same finding as Parsons J had in the prior case. In a passage that merits being quoted in full, he stated:

> The current of judicial *dicta* since the passing of Act 5 and 6 Vict cap 45, has not, I think, changed from its previous direction. If we read the words of the statute in their ordinary, natural meaning, they do not, I think, cover translation. It would be a strained and unnatural use of language to say that translations are 'copies'. To my understanding they are essentially different productions—one is intellectual, the other mechanical. It may be—doubtless is—desirable to afford to authors protection in respect of translation of their works if they desire it; but, I think, that it must be conceded that such translations stand on a different footing from copies. They are rarely, if ever, made by the author of the original work: they circulate, as a rule, among a different class of readers, a class to which the original works are as completely sealed as if they had not been written. There is here a conflict of rights and interests; a conflict between the intellectual interests of the persons for whom the translations are intended, and the caprice or possible pecuniary interest of the proprietor of the copyright, if he shall not, or shall, intend to translate the work himself or cause it to be translated. There is no hardship on him; he can always protect himself by being first in the field with a translation. In matters of copyright, the Legislature has always kept the interest of the public before it. Section 5 of the original Act, ch 5 and 6 Victoria, shows this; and when the Legislature provided in the later International Copyright Acts 15 and 16 Vict cap 12, for translations, it took care (section 2) that the public should not be neglected by being left without them; and translations in this Act are dealt with in an entirely different manner from copies.[515]

[510] *Munshi Shaik Abdurruhma'n (and Another) v Mirza' Mahomed Shira'zi* (1890) 14 ILR (Bombay) 586.
[511] ibid 589
[512] *Prince Albert v Strange* (1848–49) De G & Sm 652.
[513] ibid 693.
[514] *Macmillan and others v Khàn Bhàdur Shamsul Ulama M Zaka* (1895) 19 ILR (Bombay) 557.
[515] ibid 570.

The issue of translations was especially thorny in the context of India, as Lionel Bently has discussed elsewhere.[516] However, this passage of Ferran J is remarkable for its attention to the different issues raised by translations. Contrasting the type of production (intellectual versus mechanical) he alludes to the type of labour involved in creating works, and explicitly recognises that conflicting claims of readers and owners, favouring the former and demonstrating little sympathy for the attempts of owners to expand the market for their works.

Commentators on the law, however, were firmly of the view that the translation right should form part of the copyright owner's property. Scrutton argued that the US Court's approach in *Stowe v Beecher* was 'opposed to all correct principles'[517] and Birrell thought it 'unreasonable to permit [a book] to be translated without the consent of the owner of the copyright'[518] Macgillivray took the same view in his treatise.[519] Policy-makers also paid attention to the issue which, as noted in chapter five, had been raised before the Royal Copyright Commission by a French representative, Charles Gavard.[520] Britain's relations with France on the matter were governed by a treaty concluded in 1851,[521] and corresponding domestic legislation[522] which gave French authors protection against translations for five years.[523] However, certain requirements had to be fulfilled, in particular, an authorised translation had to appear in part within one year and in full within three years.[524] The protection against unauthorised translations applied in similar terms to dramatic works, but with the rider that 'fair imitations or adaptations to the English stage' were permitted.[525] In order to gain protection, an authorised translation of a dramatic work had to appear within three months of registration of the original.[526] It was also necessary for the author to place a notice on his work stating his intention to reserve the right of translation.[527]

Translation of plays was a particularly sensitive issue due to the heavy reliance of the English stage on works adapted from the French in the mid-nineteenth century. The low prices paid to dramatic authors meant that they needed to produce great quantities of material very quickly, and the easiest way of doing this was to

[516] Lionel Bently, 'Copyright, Translations, and Relations Between Britain and India in the Nineteenth and Early Twentieth Centuries' (2007) 82 *Chicago-Kent Law Review* 1181

[517] Scrutton, *Laws of Copyright*, 1st edn, 49.

[518] Birrell, *Seven Lectures* 154.

[519] Macgillivray, *A Treatise* 116–18.

[520] See above: ch 5, n 214.

[521] Convention between Her Majesty and the French Republic for the establishment of international copyright (signed 3 November 1851, Paris) art 3.

[522] An Act to enable her Majesty to carry into effect a Convention with France on the Subject of Copyright; to extend and explain the International Copyright Acts; and to explain the Acts relating to Copyright in Engravings 1852 (15 Vict c 12).

[523] ibid *s* 2.

[524] 1852 International Copyright Act s 8.

[525] ibid ss 4, 6.

[526] ibid s 8(6).

[527] ibid s 8(1).

adapt either novels or French plays.[528] Charles Reade had complained at length about the reliance of English authors on French material before the Select Committee on Theatrical Licenses of 1866.[529] The provisions of the International Copyright Act relating to dramatic works meant that an adaptation altered to suit English conditions, such as changing the names of the characters, would not amount to an infringement, and nor would it receive protection against any other translation or adaptation of the same play.[530] This particular exception was removed by a declaration of Her Majesty in Council in 1875.[531] However, this did not assuage all the French concerns and Charles Gavard appeared before the Royal Copyright Commission on behalf of the French Government to complain that the period of five years for preventing translations, as well as the periods within which translations had to be made in order to gain their own copyright protection were too short, particularly in relation to dramatic works.[532]

Some attention was paid to considerations of public interest with respect to translations. While Gavard advocated that the period in which a full authorised translation had to appear should be nine years, stating that it was a question of private contractual arrangements between owner and translator, Sir Henry Holland argued that the interests of the public must be taken into account. He considered that if someone published a very interesting book it would be hard on the public if it were not to be translated for nine years.[533] In relation to the period during which an owner could prevent translations, Gavard proposed extending it to 10 years.[534] In their Report, the Commissioners took a compromising line. They accepted that the current periods were insufficiently long and recommended that there should be an unconditional right to prevent publication of translations for three years after the original work's publication. If an author did publish an authorised translation within three years, his work should be protected against unauthorised translations for a further ten years.[535] They made the same recommendation for unauthorised translations of plays and, although the French had not complained about the position regarding adaptations following the Order in Council of 1875, the Comissioners further recommended that the translation need not be a literal translation and the right to translate and adapt to the English stage should be reserved to the author for three years.[536]

528 MR Booth, 'Public Taste, the Playwright and the Law' in C Leech and TW Craik (eds), *The Revels History of Drama in English*, vol 6: *1750–1880* (London, Methuen & Co Ltd, 1975) 50.

529 Reade's complaints are somewhat surprising, given that he was not averse to adapting French plays and plundering them for material himself. For Reade's schizophrenic attitudes towards plagiarism and originality, see R Macfarlane, *Original Copy* (Oxford, Oxford University Press, 2007) ch 4.

530 International Copyright Act 1852 s 6. See *Wood v Chart* (1870) LR 10 Eq 193.

531 Declaration cancelling section 3 of article IV of the Copyright Convention between Great Britain and France of November 3, 1851 (C (2nd series) 1358, 1875).

532 Royal Copyright Commission 87, 95–97.

533 ibid 88.

534 ibid.

535 ibid xlii.

536 ibid xliii.

The Commission's recommendations came to nothing but, following the Berne Convention, another Act was introduced to deal with various issues relating to international copyright.[537] Under this new Act, a foreign copyright owner was given the same right to prevent translations as he was to prevent importation into the United Kingdom. However, if an authorised English translation had not appeared within 10 years, the right to prevent translation ceased.[538]

The third kind of transformative work copyright owners wished to control arose when new technology emerged to challenge the limits of the copyright acts in relation to music. Mechanical musical instruments found themselves at the forefront of copyright litigation at the turn of the nineteenth century, when the music publisher Boosey, with the support of the Music Publishers' Association, brought an action against the sellers of perforated rolls of paper for use in Aeolians. In *Boosey v Whight*,[539] Scrutton appeared for the plaintiffs with a Queen's Counsel, Butcher, and argued that the Aeolian producers were falling foul of the Act's intention, which was to 'prevent one man from appropriating another's labour without paying for it'.[540] Edward Cutler was among those appearing for the other side who argued that the Act extended only to sheets of music.[541] Stirling J found that the rolls were not copies of the musical works, but part of the machinery for the production of musical sounds.[542] He also emphasised that the copyright protection conferred by the 1842 Act related to multiplying copies in the nature of a book. The rolls could not be considered this way:

> They are used as a means of appealing to the mind directly through the ear; not, as in the case of a book, through the eye of the ordinary reader, or through the sense of touch in the case of a blind person.[543]

Stirling J's judgment was affirmed in the Court of Appeal.[544] Lindley MR, with whom Sir FH Jeune concurred, found that a sheet of perforated music could not be considered a copy of a sheet of music under the 1842 Copyright Act: 'The fundamental ideas underlying the two are different and the uses to be made of them are fundamentally different. Music appeals to the ear, but a sheet of music appeals to the eye'.[545] He also considered that competition was not necessarily conclusive, stating:

> It may be true that the manufacture and sale of the perforated sheets diminish the sale of the plaintiffs' sheet music. But it does not follow that the plaintiffs' copyright has been infringed; and I am of the opinion that it has not.[546]

537 An Act to amend the Law respecting International and Colonial Copyright 1886 (49 & 50 Vict c 33).

538 ibid s 5.

539 *Boosey v Whight* [1899] 1 Ch 836.

540 ibid 838.

541 ibid 839.

542 ibid 842.

543 ibid.

544 *Boosey v Whight* [1900] 1 Ch 122.

545 ibid 124.

546 [1900] 1 Ch 122, 124.

Romer LJ gave a separate, concurring judgment, also emphasising the different purposes of the two types of work.[547] The judgments of both courts illustrate the continued reliance placed on physical form in relation to copyright law. Lindley MR noted that while the plaintiffs had the right to print or otherwise multiply copies of sheet music, they had

> no exclusive right to the production of the sounds indicated by or on those sheets of music; nor to the performance in private of the music indicated by such sheets; nor to any mechanism for the production of such sounds or music.[548]

Boosey v Whight was relied upon as authority governing another new type of musical technology: the gramophone, or phonograph. In *Newmark v The National Phonograph Company*,[549] Sutton J focused on the point that a music roll could not be read like a book, stating that

> there was no evidence before him that even a skilled person would read a phonographic record, and he could not, therefore, hold that a record was a sheet of music as understood at the date of the Copyright Act, 1842.[550]

A similar result was reached in *Monckton v The Gramophone Company*,[551] but in this case the composer Monckton relied not on the statute, which would not avail him following *Boosey v Whight*, but a common law right of proprietorship which would reserve to him the right to make gramophone records. Joyce J dismissed the case, stating that Monckton had published his song to the world and could only claim copyright under the statute. The decision was upheld on appeal.[552]

Interestingly, it seems that the same reasoning was not applied to cases involving reproductions of dramatic works on cinematographic film. In *Karno v Pathé Frères*,[553] Jelf J said in obiter dicta that a sketch protected as a dramatic work would be infringed by cinematographic reproduction because the reproduction would be a representation within the meaning of the Dramatic Copyright Act.[554] Similarly, in *Glenville and Another v The Selig Polyscope Company and Another*,[555] Channell J held that the plaintiffs' case of infringement by cinematograph representation failed only because the place in which the film was shown was not a place of dramatic entertainment with the Dramatic Copyright Act.[556] He added that 'he could not help thinking that some day or other it would be decided that a copying of that portion in a cinematographic exhibition, which was undoubtedly a place of dramatic entertainment for payment, would come within the statute'.[557]

547 ibid 127.
548 ibid 123.
549 *Newmark v The National Phonograph Company* (1907) 23 TLR 439.
550 ibid.
551 *Monckton v The Gramophone Company, The Times* (6 December 1910) 3c; (7 December 1910) 3c.
552 *Monckton v The Gramaphone Company (Limited)* (1912) 28 TLR 205.
553 *Karno v Pathé Frères* (1908) 99 LT 114.
554 ibid 119.
555 *Glenville and Another v The Selig Polyscope Company and Another, The Times* (20 July 1911) 3g.
556 ibid.
557 ibid.

The cases described in this section reveal that, despite the expansion of copyright to cover new markets and different uses of works, the courts were not prepared to let owners annex every market to which they laid claim. Boundaries were drawn in respect of some, transformative, types of work and the potential markets for copyright works were not considered to be infinite. Sometimes in making these decisions the courts explicitly recognised that interpreting the copyright acts too broadly would impinge upon the interests of the public, largely in their role as secondary users. However, when the decisions are examined in detail it becomes clear that it would be overstating matters to say that it was purely public interest considerations driving courts and judges. In an uncertain and evolving area of law, some judges retreated to literalism, while others focused on the physical form of the work, as well as the lack of competition between the two works and their respective markets.

This aspect of the cases has not always been recognised. For example, in their treatise on modern copyright law, Laddie et al explain the dramatisation cases by reference to the width of the conceptual separation between printing and performance, noting that 'the dramatic virtue of the novel had, so to speak, escaped down the gulf separating the two regimes'.[558] This approach suggests that the cases resulted from a lack of vision on the part of the nineteenth-century courts, and a failure to understand the connection between the two regimes. The statement takes for granted that there *is* a necessary connection between the two and overlooks the fact that there is no overwhelming or inevitable reason why a person who owns the copyright in one type of item of commerce should necessarily be able to control its more abstract forms into every conceivable marketplace.

The cases involving attempts by copyright owners to control their works into different formats or languages raised the issue of how much value could and should be captured from a copyright work. While this was not explicitly considered by the courts, restricted by procedure and convention to considering the narrow issues brought before them, the Royal Copyright Commission had the opportunity of taking a wider view. The Commissioners' Report was, as has been pointed out already, a compromise on a number of levels. But a crucial compromise can be seen regarding the law of infringement: abridgments and dramatisations would form part of the bundle of rights making up copyright; translations would receive a lower level of partial protection; while other types of derivative uses would be left to the courts to negotiate. None of the Commission's recommendations on infringement were enacted until 1911, despite many attempts,[559] but the record of proceedings exhibits the same tensions as the case law. Considerations of public interest might have been more explicit but the real question remained one of markets and commerce.

The views of two of the Commissioners exemplify the tension the question of transformative works generated. Appearing as a witness, the publisher FR Daldy,

[558] Laddie et al, *Modern Law of Copyright and Designs* 56.

[559] These attempts are discussed in chs 5 and 7.

who was also a Commissioner, proposed an expansive definition of copyright as 'an exclusive right to copy, print, engrave, photograph or in any way multiply copies, dramatize, abridge, translate, represent, perform or deliver'.[560] By contrast, Sir James Fitzjames Stephen dissented on the recommendations as to abridgments and dramatisations. He wrote:

> All these proposals appear to me to be founded on a mistaken view of the principle on which the law of copyright ought to be based. They assume that the author of a work of art ought to be considered to have a right to every advantage which can possibly be derived from that work of art, even indirectly and by the exercise of independent ability. A dramatic author is not to use a novel as material for a drama, a painter is not to copy the painting of another painter, although in the one case the adaptation and in the other the copy may required great labour and skill. Casts are not to be made of statuary, nor is a statue to be photographed, drawn or engraved without the leave of the owner of the copyright. It is admitted that in many cases these acts inflict no money loss on the author of the work of art, but it is said that they may hurt his reputation, and it is assumed that he is entitled to appropriate to himself every indirect advantage which may be obtained from his work.
>
> I think artistic reputation is too delicate a matter to be made the subject of legal protection. The law of copyright ought, in my opinion, to protect money interests only; and I think that the only money interests which it should protect are those which it creates; that is to say, the money interest of the author of a work of literature or art capable of being reproduced by mechanical means in such a manner that every copy is as valuable as the original.[561]

Where Daldy conceived of copyright as a broad right to control a work through various abstractions and manifestations, Stephen wished to circumscribe copyright's scope and resisted its expansion beyond the immediate market for the particular form and format of the work in question. With the benefit of hindsight, we know that Daldy's view would prevail, but this should not lead us to discount Stephen and others who thought like him, nor to brand them as reactionary or behind the times. To do so would be to iron out the instabilities and conflicting views of copyright during the nineteenth century, and portray its ultimate format as inevitable.

III. INFRINGEMENT AT THE CENTURY'S END

Two centuries of litigation, growing at an exponential rate, had changed the law of copyright almost beyond recognition. In the middle of the eighteenth century, copyright was a limited right to control reprints of books; by the final decades of the nineteenth century, the physical artefact of the 'book' as locus of protection had begun (although the process was far from complete) to be replaced by the more abstract, and economically constructed, 'work', allowing copyright owners

560 ibid 47.
561 ibid lvii.

to control their investment into different markets and through different manifestations. However, although many of the doctrines and principles and much of the language, of modern copyright law can be traced to the nineteenth century, by its final decade copyright law was far from having crystallised as a coherent and stable body of law.

At the start of the eighteenth century, the question upon which infringement turned was: is the defendant's book the same as the plaintiff's book? By the end of the nineteenth century, the question could be put in a number of different ways: Has there been a fair use? Does it compete in an unfair manner? Has a substantial part been taken? Has the alleged infringer sought to annex the labour of the owner for his own profit? In developing and answering these questions, many competing views and arguments had emerged involving such contentious, and ultimately unresolved, issues as the role played by labour and the meaning of words like 'original', 'substantial' and 'fair'. One striking consequence of the emergence of so many competing and co-existing strands of reasoning is that the nineteenth-century cases in relation to infringement and subsistence can supply precedents for widely divergent views.

Melissa de Zwart argues that the early cases reveal that 'the law of fair dealing was developed by the common law judges to accommodate a range of uses that promoted values which may, it is submitted, be classified as promoting freedom of communication' and that fair dealing builds 'important public space' into copyright.[562] However, when the law of infringement is looked at as a whole, it is difficult to see any overarching public interest principle guiding the development of the law of infringement, or even of specific elements such as the law of fair dealing. Refusing protection against quotation and criticism was sometimes ascribed to a desire for free communication, but at other times it was justified on the basis that it did not compete with the original work, and frequently such uses were simply stated to be acceptable without providing any reasons at all. It is also true that broader concerns for society's interests in the continued production of books and being protected against monopolies inform some of the judicial reasoning and played a role in some of the resistance to expansion. Kathy Bowrey has recently demonstrated that nineteenth-century jurisprudence did not separate the questions of infringement and originality, but that both questions were considered together and the originality of both parties was compared in the light of the public interest.[563] While this can certainly be seen in some of the cases, particularly those early in the period, in the latter part of the nineteenth century this approach was already being eclipsed by the growing emphasis being placed on competition and the plaintiffs claims to an expanding market. Thus, despite the more fluid approach that was taken to infringement in the period before the 1911 Act, it was far from being a halcyon time when the interests of the public were prioritised or even consistently 'weighed up' against those of authors or owners.

[562] De Zwart, 'Historical Analysis of the Birth of Fair Dealing' 11.

[563] Bowrey, 'On Clarifying the Role of Originality and Fair Use' 22.

Nor does the ideology of romantic authorship play a key role in expanding copyright. In the context of infringement law, the author was very much an economic actor, whose labour was not necessarily creative or 'literary', except in the very broadest sense. The frequent appeals to 'labour' as providing the basis for subsistence and, in the case of the new-work principle, a finding of non-infringement, might have echoed the appeals to Lockean natural rights in the common law copyright cases of the late eighteenth century but the labour envisaged was far from being the outpourings of creative genius. Anything falling on a spectrum beginning with the investment of time or money through collection, compilation and arrangement, and ending with ingenuity and literary skill could be counted as acceptable 'individual labour' for the purposes of copyright law. This is hardly surprising, given the limited scope for policy-based arguments before the courts of law and equity. What emerges instead from a study of the cases in this period is that copyright law continued to take as its central concern and guiding principle the interests of commerce and trade: this is what the Stationers had been concerned with in the years prior to the Statute of Anne, and this is what kept on bringing parties to court over the next two centuries.

7

The Making of the 1911 Imperial Copyright Act

I. THE *FIN-DE-SIECLE* YEARS: LAYING THE FOUNDATIONS

A. The Book Trade

THE FINAL DECADE of the nineteenth century was a transitional period in social and political terms. Many of the changes which would accelerate in the next century had their roots in the 1890s. Technological developments included the bicycle, the automobile, the motion picture, the telephone and radio. In politics, the labour movement emerged, the seeds of the decline of empire were planted and they began to reap their harvest when the Boer War began in 1899. The book trade was not immune to these *fin-de-siècle* currents and the 1890s saw the demise of the three-decker and circulating libraries,[1] as well as the onset of modern publishing practices.

The three-decker novel and the circulating library died together, victims of an inadvertent suicide pact. Two of the largest libraries, Mudie's and WH Smith, were unhappy with the increasing speed with which cheap editions were appearing on the market and, in 1894, instructed publishers that they would pay no more than 4s per volume for novels, and that the publishers must wait a year before issuing cheaper editions.[2] After a show of resistance in the pages of the *Publishers' Circular* and elsewhere, the major publishers conceded defeat and began to issue novels in single volumes, for 5s or 6s.[3] The end of the three-decker also spelled the end of the circulating libraries' influence over pricing, and particularly the power and influence of Mudie's Select Library. Although Mudie's and Smith's libraries lingered until 1937 and 1961 respectively, they were shadows of their former selves.

A second sign of transformation was the arrival on the scene of Frederick Macmillan's Net Book Agreement. In 1890, Frederick Macmillan introduced to the trade his plan to address the ongoing problem of underselling in the retail trade. Macmillan proposed that certain books, 'net books', would be sold at the full

[1] See above: ch 5, text to nn 14–18.

[2] GL Griest, *Mudie's Circulating Library and the Victorian Novel* (Newton Abbot, Devon, David & Charles (Publishers) Ltd, 1970) 171.

[3] ibid 176–202.

retail price, set by the publisher, from which there would be no discount to the public. The system differed from the practices of the 1850s in two ways: first, it was voluntary, and did not involve the coercion that had so alienated the retail booksellers in 1852; second, in order to enforce the net price, Macmillan proposed to reduce the trade allowance to give such a narrow margin of profit that retailers would not be able to afford to reduce the price any further.[4] Furthermore, these trade terms would only be given to booksellers who undertook not to engage in underselling.[5]

Although most of the early public and trade reactions to Macmillan's plan were hostile, it slowly gained acceptance and finally became trade-wide through the involvement of a new body: the Publishers' Association of Great Britain and Ireland, founded in 1896 under the presidency of CJ Longman. Other members included John Murray, Frederick Macmillan, RB Marston, Richard Bentley and William Heinemann.[6] Longman had initially rejected the suggestion of establishing 'a ring of publishers to raise prices and to maintain them by application of coercion to those who did not obey its regulations'.[7] However, following consultation with the Society of Authors, the Publishers' Association eventually agreed to adopt the net book system.

The Agreement faced an early challenge from *The Times* when its editor, Charles Frederic Moberly Bell, attempted to compete with the booksellers by expanding the the *Times* Book Club, a kind of circulating library, into a second-hand bookshop. The bookshop obtained books from the publishers at discounted prices and then sold them on within a few months of publication at very low prices on the grounds they were second hand. This practice fell within a strict interpretation of the Net Book Agreement, which *The Times* had signed, but was definitely outside its spirit. The Publishers' Association re-drafted the Agreement, but *The Times* refused to sign it and battle was joined. *The Times* published articles condemning the publishers, and the publishers withdrew advertising from the paper, as well as restricting their book supplies.

The arguments employed by *The Times*, and its correspondents, bore a marked resemblance to those of 1852. The Manager of the *Times* Book Club claimed that the publishing trade was fostered by 'the most vicious and irrational form of protection'.[8] Someone signing himself 'Copyright Reformer' wrote that the conditions under which books were sold were 'contrary to public interest, unfavourable to authors, and of very doubtful benefit to publishers'.[9] The writer finished by advocating the replacement of copyright by a royalty system, on the basis that it

[4] JJ Barnes, *Free Trade in Books: A Study of the London Book Trade since 1800* (Oxford, Clarendon Press, 1964) 143.

[5] F Macmillan, *The Net Book Agreement 1899 and the Book War 1906–8* (Glasgow, MacLehone & Co., 1924) 16.

[6] *The Times* (23 April 1896) 14c.

[7] ibid.

[8] *The Times* (11 October 1906) 6b.

[9] ibid.

was copyright which allowed publishers to form such monopolies.[10] Arthur Shadwell, in one of a series of articles on the net book controversy, pleaded with newspapers who were concerned with public welfare to consider whether the bookselling system did not 'rivet the shackles of restriction tighter round the book trade and raise higher the barrier between the people and the better sort of current literature'.[11]

The publisher Edward Bell feared that 'many well-meaning people took the managers of the Club at their own valuation, and were heartily persuaded that they were fighting the cause of cheap literature against a selfish trade combination'.[12] Macmillan, however, maintained that his object was the preservation of the book trade. At a meeting of the Publishers' Association in 1898, he stated:

> What we have to decide today, is whether it is wise or possible to take such steps as shall make it unprofitable for any bookseller to conduct his business in a manner which seems likely to be injurious to the large majority of his fellow-traders.[13]

In the end, the controversy ended with a whimper when the Walter family sold the newspaper to Lord Northcliffe in 1908, and he agreed to abide by the terms of the Agreement.

Macmillan's object of preserving the book trade meant he was not so different to the booksellers of 1852, who had also seen the trade as threatened by retail underselling. The Net Book Agreement, however, came about in remarkably different circumstances. Cheap books were now more readily available, and Britain was well on the way to developing a mass reading market. This meant that the old forms of trade organisation, which invoked the guild system of the previous century, were no longer appropriate methods of preserving trade structures. By introducing his system as exemplary, rather than compulsory, and seeking consultation between publishers, retailers and authors, Macmillan moved the book trade towards a more associative model of trade organisation, albeit one that was similarly protective.[14]

[10] ibid 6c.

[11] *The Times* (31 October 1906) 15c.

[12] E Bell, '*The Times* Book Club and the Publishers' Association' in F Macmillan, *The Net Book Agreement* 48–49.

[13] Macmillan, *Net Book Agreement* 23.

[14] The Net Book Agreement (NBA) continued in force until 1957, when it was re-written to comply with the new restrictive trade practices legislation, the Restrictive Practices Act, 1956. The Restrictive Practices Court held that the agreement was not contrary to public interest. (*Net Book Agreement 1957* [1962] 1 WLR 1347 and *Net Book Agreement (No. 2)*[1964] LR 4 RP 484) In 1973, the Publishers' Association was required to seek exemption from art 85(3) of the EEC Treaty and, in 1986, the Commission initiated proceedings. In 1989, the Commission of the European Communities refused the exemption (89/44/EC [1989] 4 CMLR 825). The decision was upheld by the Court of First Instance (T66/89 ([1992] 5 CMLR 120). The Publishers' Association appealed to the ECJ, which set aside the CFI's decision ([1995] 5 CMLR 33). Meanwhile, a number of major publishing houses withdrew from the NBA, which subsequently collapsed. Prior to the collapse, however, the Director General of Fair Trading had made an application to the Restrictive Practices Court regarding the NBA. The Publishers' Association did not oppose the application, but several parties were joined as respondents in its place. The Court found that due to material changes in the circumstances of the book trade since the last orders were made, the NBA was not in the public interest and the previous orders were discharged. (*Re The Net Book Agreement 1957* [1997] EMLR 647).

The changes brought about by the death of the three-decker, the erosion of the influence of circulating libraries and the Net Book Agreement were accompanied by other changes in publishing practice. When the certainty provided by the circulating library and fixed prices vanished, publishers began to develop innovative strategies and new forms of market exploitation in order to survive. One such tactic was the use of publication in different formats at structured intervals, which enabled the publisher and bookseller to access different market sectors, as well as keeping the market for the novel fresh.[15] A second new exploitation strategy was the practice of dividing copyright into subsidiary rights. In this less structured market serialisation took on a new importance as a safe way of gauging demand, as well as serving yet another market sector with the same work in a different format. The owner of the serialisation rights might be a different publisher to the one who had the right to publish the entire book, and contractual divisions of copyright became more common and more complex.[16] In this way, publishing practice mirrored the common law developments discussed in chapter six. Indeed, the law and reality of publishing appear to have formed a mutually reinforcing cycle, wherein copyright owners sought to derive revenue from books in innovative ways and the courts developed the law in directions which made this possible. As Alexis Weedon has pointed out, when the 'financially cosy relationship between the libraries and publishers began to fail, publishers had to develop a sharper economic edge to survive'.[17] Part of this strategy was to seek to reform the law of copyright in their favour.

B. Agitation for Legislation

In the 1880s, domestic reform of copyright law had largely taken a back-seat to the negotiations regarding American copyright. As Henry Calcraft had written to the under-Secretary to the Board of Trade, Sir Julian Pauncefote, in 1884, the Board of Trade had considered the issue of amending domestic copyright law with a view to putting the country into a position to enter into an international treaty. However, Calcraft noted that:

> The Board of Trade are therefore disposed to think it very unadvisable in view of the extreme importance of American copyright to English authors, and the negotiations still pending with the United States' Government, *that any steps should at this time be taken to alter the English Law,* and they would certainly at present advise the avoidance of any course which would commit Her Majesty's Government to any legislation with regard to copyright.[18]

[15] A Weedon, 'From Three-Deckers to Film Rights: A Turn in British Publishing Strategies, 1870–1930' (1999) *Book History* 188, 192.

[16] ibid 189.

[17] A Weedon, *Victorian Publishing: The Economics of Book Publishing for a Mass Market, 1836–1914* (Ashgate, Aldershot, 2003) 143.

[18] Quoted in EM Underdown, 'The Copyright Question' (1886) 2 *Law Quarterly Review* 213, 215.

Following the passing of the US Chace Act in 1891, agitation for domestic copyright reform recommenced. The last four years of the century saw copyright bills introduced into every session of Parliament, accompanied by hearings in select committees, and commentary in the media. Yet none of these attempts proved successful. As a result, this period of activity has been largely overlooked by copyright historians.[19] However, notwithstanding the lack of legislative progress, this was a significant era in the history of copyright law, as it provided the opportunity for experimentation with different forms of legislation and for the groups in favour of reform to advance their agendas. As a result, by the time that the Government was forced to take action in response to the Berlin Revision of the Berne Convention, they were able to build upon the foundations laid down at the end of the nineteenth century.

A number of organizations formed at end of the century were to play significant roles in copyright reform. As was noted in chapter four, the Society of Authors was established in 1883, and in 1886 the barrister EM Underdown had drafted a Bill on behalf of the Society, which was closely based on the recommendations of the Royal Copyright Commission.[20] It was not presented at that time, but was redrafted and introduced into the House of Lords by Lord Monkswell in 1890. By the second reading in the Lords, the Chace Act had been passed in the United States, but the Bill was opposed by Lord Halsbury and Lord Balfour and proceeded no further.[21]

In 1896, the Society set up a sub-Committee to consider the question of consolidating copyright law; however, in the end it decided to focus only on those points of law which most urgently needed clarification.[22] Meetings were also set up with the newly formed Publishers' Association, as well as the Copyright Association and, having agreed upon the points to be addressed, Basil Field was instructed to draft a Bill which dealt solely with the matters of magazine copyright, dramatisation of novels, lectures and abridgment.[23] This Bill was also introduced into the House of Lords by Lord Monkswell and sent to a Select Committee.[24] It was subsequently passed by the Lords and sent to the House of Commons, but it did not progress before the recess.

While the proponents of the Bill waited for Parliament to re-convene so the Bill could be re-introduced, co-operation between the three societies began to break down. Edward Cutler, barrister and author of several books on copyright law, was engaged to draft a codifying Bill on behalf of the Copyright Association. The Society of Authors did not support the Bill, believing such an ambitious project

[19] Recently, however, Catherine Seville has described the period in the context of the interplay between domestic and international law, see C Seville, *Internationalisation* 279–87.

[20] GH Thring, 'Recent Attempts at Copyright Legislation' (1898) 63 *Fortnightly Review* 461, 462; *The Author* (1 December 1893) 256.

[21] Thring, 'Recent Attempts' 462; *The Author* (1 June 1891) 11–12.

[22] Thring, 'Recent Attempts' 463–64.

[23] ibid. Copyright (Amendment) HL Bill (1897) 79.

[24] Report from the Select Committee of the House of Lords on the Copyright (Amendment) HL Bill (1897) 385.

would have no chance of success in the hands of private individuals. It was also pointed out by the Society's Secretary that a consolidating Bill should be the work of producers of copyright as well as holders of copyright because their interests did not always coincide.[25]

In 1898, the Copyright Association's Bill was introduced to Parliament at the same time as the earlier one and both Bills were sent to a Select Committee for consideration.[26] This Committee adjourned before it could come to a conclusion, and Lord Thring, an eminent and innovative parliamentary draftsman who had been one of the Committee members,[27] undertook to draft two separate Bills himself: one dealing with literary copyright and the other with artistic copyright.[28] These Bills were also referred to a Select Committee, but no conclusions were reached after two months.[29] In March 1900, Lord Monkswell re-introduced the two Bills into the House of Lords.[30] The Literary Copyright Bill had been subject to some alterations relating to international and colonial copyright,[31] and the Artistic Copyright Bill had been re-drafted entirely.[32] The Artistic Copyright Bill was dropped by Lord Monkswell in July 1900, although he did note it would be printed for circulation over the holidays. The Literary Copyright Bill was passed by the House of Lords and read for the first time the House of Commons, but in August it too was withdrawn.[33]

Until Lord Thring took over, the Bills before Parliament were produced by copyright creators and owners. Members of these two groups were also called before the Select Committees to give evidence about the state of copyright law and the need for legislation. Moreover, many of the Committee members were also involved with various interested parties. Lord Tennyson, Lord Monkswell and Lord Pirbright were members of the 1897 Select Committee and were also closely involved with the Society of Authors. Other members were Viscount Knutsford (Henry Holland), who had been a Commissioner on the 1878 Royal Commission and Lord Farrer (formerly Thomas Farrer), who had been one of its key witnesses.[34] The Committee heard evidence from the publisher FR Daldy, another former Copyright Royal Commissioner, and now secretary to the Copyright Association; the publisher Longman, president of the Publishers' Association;

[25] Thring, 'Recent Attempts' 467; *The Author* (1 April 1898) 282–83.

[26] Copyright HL Bill (1898) 21. Report from the Select Committee of the House of Lords on the Copyright HL Bill and the Copyright (Amendment) HL Bill (1898) 393.

[27] He was also the uncle of GH Thring, Secretary to the Society of Authors, and his involvement must have pleased the Society.

[28] Copyright HL Bill (1899) 44; Copyright (Artistic) HL Bill (1899); Report from the Select Committee of the House of Lords on the Copyright HL Bill and the Copyright (Artistic) HL Bill (1899) 362.

[29] Select Committee of the House of Lords on the Copyright Bill and Copyright (Artistic) HL Bill (1900) 377; Parl Deb HL vol 70 col 361 (24 April 1899).

[30] Copyright HL Bill (1900) 18; Copyright (Artistic) HL Bill (1900) 19.

[31] Parl Deb HL vol 81 col 606 (29 March 1900).

[32] Copyright (Artistic) HL Bill (1900) 19.

[33] Copyright HL Bill (1900) 295.

[34] The other members, Lord Hatherton, Lord Hobhouse and Lord Welby, were newer to the copyright debates.

GH Thring, secretary to the Society of Authors; and Bram Stoker, Acting Manager of the Lyceum Theatre.

In the subsequent Select Committee hearings, evidence was also given by the publisher John Murray, and lawyers Edward Cutler, who had drafted the Copyright Association's Act of 1898, and TE Scrutton. Representatives from the art world and music publishing also appeared, as did the editor of *The Times*. The star witness of the 1900 Select Committee was Samuel L Clemens (Mark Twain), who made an impassioned plea for perpetual copyright. Although the Committees were heavily stacked with copyright owners and creators, there were a few instances where other opinions were solicited. EM Thompson, principal librarian of the British Museum, and EWB Nicholson of the Bodleian Library appeared before the 1898 Committee to complain about the deposit clauses[35] and Thompson appeared again before the 1900 Committee. One witness appeared before the 1900 Committee to discuss the case of extracts in educational texts.

The Committees themselves continued to be made up of a mix of those with long-standing interests in the copyright question and those who were new to the debate. Lord Herschell, another former Copyright Commissioner, was a member of the 1898 Committee, but died the following year. The Board of Trade also continued its involvement, with Gerald Balfour, its new President, replacing Lord Pirbright in 1900. The Lord Chancellor, Lord Halsbury, joined the Committee in 1898 and continued to sit until 1900.

The composition of the Committees and the allegiances of the witnesses appearing before them invariably shaped the issues that arose. Some issues were uncontentious. After 1897, each Bill provided that the first owner of copyright in a literary work[36] was the author of the book first published in Her Majesty's dominions, or simultaneously there and elsewhere, whether or not he was a British subject.[37] Moreover, all the post-1897 Bills provided for copyright to subsist for the life of the author and 30 years thereafter, when the work was published during the author's lifetime.[38]

There were, however, a number of differences between the various Bills, reflecting different attitudes towards the shape that copyright law should take. Most fundamental among these was the question of whether all of the various copyright statutes should be gathered up into a single, consolidating measure. The Society of Authors' opposition to this project was merely a matter of practicality; whilst the

[35] Report from the Select Committee of the House of Lords on the Copyright HL Bill and the Copyright (Amendment) HL Bill (1898) 393, 207–15.

[36] The Copyright HL Bill (1898) 21 s 1, extended this to artistic works, but added the additional criteria of an '*original* literary or artistic work' (emphasis added).

[37] Copyright HL Bill (1898) 21 s 1; Copyright HL Bill (1899) 44 s 4; Copyright HL Bill (1900) 295 s 4.

[38] Copyright HL Bill (1898) 21 s 2(i); Copyright Bill (1899) 44 s 4(3); Copyright HL Bill (1900) 295 s 4(3). Each bill also included provisions similar to those in the 1842 Copyright Act dealing with retrospectivity by compelling assignees of copyright for valuable consideration to enter into agreements with the original author of the work. They also provided for the inclusion of a statutory licence to prevent suppression of books by publishers. Copyright HL Bill (1898) 21 ss 10, 45(2); Copyright HL Bill (1899) 44 ss 35, 40; Copyright HL Bill (1900) 295 ss 50, 37. See Copyright Act 1842 ss 4, 5.

Society was generally in favour of a uniform copyright law, it believed that only the Government could achieve such an outcome. Lord Thring, on the other hand, based his decision to separate literary and artistic copyright on his belief that 'there is not the slightest resemblance between the inchoate process by which an artistic work is brought into operation and a book; there is not the slightest resemblance between a sculpture and a book, and so on'.[39]

i. The Law of Infringement

Each of the Bills brought before Parliament in these years made some attempt to codify the law of infringement, and the various different approaches taken are instructive. GH Thring had noted in 1898 that the interests of producers and owners of copyright, while similar in some respects, were dissimilar in others, and the truth of this observation was apparent in the discussions over the law of abridgment. The Berne Convention had stopped short of outlawing abridgments, with Article 10 providing that unauthorised indirect appropriations which did *not* present the character of a new work would be considered as illicit reproductions, thereby making it possible for Member States to provide that new works should not be infringements. Although, as observed in the previous chapter, some of the treatise writers had considered abridgments a dead issue, this was apparently not the view of the publishers. The Publishers Association was particularly concerned by the actions of WT Stead in abridging numerous popular novels. Having taken the opinion of Cozens Hardy QC, in 1896 the firm of Smith Elder brought a test case against Stead in respect of a book by Mrs Humphrey Ward. An injunction was awarded and Stead ceased his abridgment series.[40]

It is not surprising, then, that despite Berne leaving open the possibility that new works would not infringe, all four Bills included the right to abridge a work as one of the exclusive rights of the copyright owner. However, the ways in which they constructed the right reveal the different interests at work. The 1897 Bill, which had been drafted by the Society of Authors in consultation with the Publishers Association and the Copyright Association, attempted to recognise an entitlement on the part of the author to control later transformations of his or her work as well as the economic significance of abridgments to both author and publisher. Thus, the Bill gave the right to abridge to the copyright owner, but provided that where an author had sold the copyright, but retained an economic interest in the book by royalty, profit share or other interest, the purchaser of the copyright could not abridge the book without the consent of the author.[41] However, if the author had sold the exclusive right of publication but retained the copyright, the author was not at liberty to publish an abridgment without the consent of the publisher.[42]

[39] Select Committee Report (1898) 84.

[40] RJL Kingsford, *The Publishers Association 1896–1946* (Cambridge, Cambridge University Press, 1970) 11.

[41] Copyright Bill (1897) 79 s 8(ii), amended in House of Lords as s 7(ii).

[42] Copyright HL Bill (1897) 79 s 8(iii), later s 7(iii).

Moreover, even where no pecuniary interest was retained by the author after selling his copyright, a copyright owner who intended to publish an abridgment should give notice of his intention and, if required by the author, print a notice on the title page that the abridgment was not by the original author.[43] The author was given the right to claim damages in the event of contravention of these sections.[44]

This formulation sought to recognise the concerns of authors that abridgments made by others could harm their reputation, as well as the concerns of publishers that if the author made an abridgment after having assigned the copyright or a licence to publish, sales of the original book might be undermined. The Copyright Association's Bill of 1898 altered the author's entitlement slightly, reducing it to a power to withhold consent to an abridgment.[45] Lord Thring, however, objected to such provisions, on the basis that this was an area more appropriately regulated by contracts between parties.[46] He did not include such a provision in his 1899 Bill, but a revised version appeared in the 1900 Bill. It provided that where the author had parted with the copyright in a book, and an abridgment or translation were made with the consent of the copyright owner, notice must be given on the title page that the abridgment or translation was by someone other than the author.[47]

This clause, like the Society of Authors' Bill's provisions, can be seen as an early gesture in the direction of recognising the moral rights of paternity and integrity. However, it is noteworthy that the abridgment question was now treated solely as a question of balancing the claims of copyright creators and owners, and the notion that abridgments might offer advantages to the public seemed to have been forgotten. Only Lord Farrer expressed concern that including abridgment among the copyright owner's rights might have some general adverse effects, and he limited his objections to the question of whether this would prevent indexes being made of books.[48]

All four Bills also included the right to dramatise a book as one of the exclusive rights of copyright owners. The dramatisation right had been the subject of some disagreement during the negotiations in Berne. The French had proposed in 1886 that dramatisations be considered unauthorised reproductions in the Berne Convention; however, the matter was not dealt with until the Paris Revision in 1896 when the French raised the matter again.[49] Britain opposed including dramatisations as an 'unauthorized indirect appropriation' under Article 10, and

[43] Copyright HL Bill (1897) 79 s 8(iv), later s 7(iv).

[44] ibid s 8(ii), (iii), (iv). This provision reflected in statutory form the decision in *Archbold v Sweet* (1832) 1 M & Rob 162; 5 Car & P 219. This case arose when Archbold objected to erroneous additions and alterations made to his book on criminal law by the publisher to whom he had sold his copyright.

[45] Copyright HL Bill (1898) 21 s 5.

[46] Select Committee Report (1898) 102.

[47] Copyright HL Bill (1900) 295 s 4(6).

[48] Lord Farrer had expressed similar concerns before the Royal Copyright Commission, suggesting he had had unfortunate experiences with German books, published without index or notes, 'so that it is wearisome to the flesh': Select Committee Report (1897) 12.

[49] W Briggs, *The Law of International Copyright (with Special Sections on the Colonies and The United States of America)* (London, Stevens & Haynes, 1906) 393.

a compromise was reached in the form of an Interpretative Declaration, stating that the transformation of a novel into a play, or of a play into a novel, came within the stipulations of Article 10. Britain was the only member of the Union which did not sign the Declaration.[50]

The discussions of the dramatisation right before the Select Committees demonstrate the continuing lack of consensus as to where the line of protection should be drawn, as well as the interpretative difficulties inherent in such opaque terms as 'idea' and 'expression'. Daldy suggested that authors should be protected against someone taking the plot of a novel, which he considered was 'expression' rather than 'idea', taking a broad view of authors' rights based on natural law principles: 'The idea of copyright, I maintain, is that we should protect original brain labour, and if it is given forth in the form of literature for the benefit of the public we should protect it'.[51] Daldy also asserted that the law should protect authors against any economic loss, and considered that an author would sustain economic damage if the plot of their novel was turned into a play.[52]

Although Daldy did not believe that protecting the plot was the same as protecting ideas, the media of the day took a different view. The *Daily News* reported approvingly that the Society of Authors' 1897 Bill 'proposed to make a statutory copyright in ideas, and to make the unauthorised dramatisation of a novel an infringement of it'.[53] An article in the *Birmingham Daily News*[54] complained that the law was unable to protect 'the labour of the brain' and described the novelist who turns a play into a novel as 'the man who has no ideas walks about like a hungry jackal, ready to devour without leave and without reward, the ideas of the man more favoured in that respect than himself'.[55] Edward Cutler considered protection should extend *beyond* expression, arguing before the 1898 Committee that 'copyright is not confined to the expression, but to the plot, the incidents, the delineation of character'.[56]

Alongside the debates over what uses of work should be included as falling within the copyright owner's exclusive property right were discussions over what uses, if any, should be carved out of the right, and upon what basis. The question of exceptions had arisen at the conferences preceding the Berne Convention. The matter was first raised by the German delegates in 1884, who suggested that extracts should be allowed, on condition that the author's name or source were indicated.[57] The proposal was rejected by France, Italy and Great Britain at the 1885 Conference, and it was decided that a new article be inserted which would leave the question to the domestic law of Union members.[58] The article agreed upon stated:

[50] ibid 394.
[51] Select Committee Report (1897) 12.
[52] ibid 12–13.
[53] Extracted in *The Author* (2 August 1897) 62.
[54] July 10, reproduced in *The Author* (1 September 1897) 91–92.
[55] ibid 91.
[56] Select Committee Report (1898) 100.
[57] Briggs, *Law of International Copyright* 396.
[58] ibid 397–98.

> As regards the liberty of lawfully making extracts from literary and artistic works for publications destined for education, or having a scientific character, or for chrestomathies, this matter is reserved to the law of the countries of the Union, and to particular arrangements existing or to be concluded between them.[59]

The Berne Convention, therefore, did not require any change in British law. However, the Publishers' Association identified extracts as an interference with their rights that required addressing. In 1896, the Council of the Association agreed to send a letter to the press, and to literary periodicals in particular, warning them against unauthorised quotation of excessive extracts in articles purporting to be reviews. The President CJ Longman wrote, 'It is believed that articles of this nature satisfy the desire of the public for information and enable them to learn the essential points in a book without buying it'.[60]

As a result, it is unsurprising that the Bills of 1898, 1899 and 1900 sought to address this issue. While there were some differences between the Bills, overall the approach tracked that of the common law by characterising extracts as an exception to a broad right preventing copying. In addition, the Bills set out specific purposes for which extracts would be allowed. For example, the Copyright Association's Bill of 1898 provided that 'the making of fair and moderate extracts from a book which is the subject of copyright and the publication thereof for the purpose of a review shall not be an infringement'.[61] In respect of musical works it gave an exception for 'a fair extract from any musical composition for the purposes of an analytical or other programme, or for fair quotation in a history, biography or review'.[62]

During discussion before the Select Committee, different viewpoints on these provisions emerged. The publishers Daldy and Murray were in favour of a stronger and more specific infringement clause. However, some Committee members appeared concerned that the reference to 'review' was too restrictive. Lord Thring noted that any writer must be aware of the difficulty of writing a book, not just a review, that did not take a part of another book, adding that the real issue was honest acknowledgement.[63] He suggested adding the words 'or criticism'.[64] Lord Herschell proposed adding 'for the purpose of controverting the statements or view of the author',[65] or 'all such extracts as are reasonably necessary for the purpose of review, criticism, discussion, comment or controversy'.[66]

Murray conceded that there was a difficulty in defining the limits of 'fair', and accepted that the intention of the section was to act as a deterrent to would-be infringers.[67] This led Lord Thring to express concern that a strict rule on the

[59] Berne Convention 1886, art 8.
[60] Kingsford, *The Publishers Association* 11.
[61] Copyright HL Bill (1898) 21 s 5 (fourth indent).
[62] ibid s 16.
[63] Select Committee Report (1898) 9.
[64] ibid 10.
[65] ibid.
[66] ibid 12.
[67] ibid 11.

matter might frighten authors and publishers, and therefore be disadvantageous to authors.[68] Daldy suggested as an alternative formulation of the proviso:

> Provided that the making of fair and moderate extracts, such as shall not injure by their extent the commercial value thereof, from a book which is the subject of copyright, and the publication thereof for the purpose of review, criticism, comment or controversy, shall not be an infringement of the copyright therein.[69]

Both Lord Herschell and Viscount Knutsford demurred as to the words 'commercial value', but Daldy opined that the courts based their judgments in such cases on pecuniary injury.[70]

There was also discussion as to whether private uses of works should be allowed. The 1898 Bill provided that copyright included the exclusive rights to '*make*, print or otherwise multiply' (emphasis added) an abridgment, translation or dramatisation.[71] While some members of the Committee were concerned that this would prevent people from making abridgments for their own use, Cutler considered it would be

> much better to depend upon the benevolence of the judge in a case where there was absolutely no *damnum* to anybody; it is much better to err on the side of severity, and to leave it to a judge to mitigate, than to have a Bill that anybody could drive a coach and four through.[72]

Nonetheless, the 1899 Committee inserted a clause providing that copyright would not be infringed

> by a person making a copy, abridgment or translation of a book for his private use, or by a person making fair extracts from or otherwise fairly dealing with the contents of a book for the purpose of a new work, or for the purposes of criticism, review or refutation.[73]

The music publisher Henry Reginald Clayton objected strongly to the private copying right as it applied to music. However, he had no objection to letting the private use exception stand in relation to abridgments and translations, which did not affect music publishers.[74] The clause that was adopted in the 1900 Bill therefore limited the private use exception to apply to abridgments and translations only, providing that copyright would not be infringed

> by a person making an abridgement or translation for his private use (unless he uses or allows it to be used by some other person for a public purpose), or by a person making fair extracts from or otherwise fairly dealing with the contents of a book for the purpose of a new work, or for the purposes of criticism, review or refutation, or in the ordinary course of reporting scientific information.[75]

[68] ibid 9, 37.
[69] ibid 36.
[70] ibid.
[71] Copyright HL Bill (1898) 21 s 5(i), (ii), (iii).
[72] Select Committee Report (1898) 98.
[73] Select Committee Report (1899) vii.
[74] ibid 28.
[75] Copyright HL Bill (1900) 295 s 4(5).

The reference to 'scientific information' responded to a representation made to the 1900 Select Committee by certain scientific societies, expressing concern that the Bill would affect publication of their reports.[76] Less sympathy was shown to Edward Arnold's request on behalf of school book publishers for a clause which allowed the use of extracts, as well as short stories and poems, in school books.[77] In fact, Lord Thring was generally of the view that with respect to extracts 'much greater discretion ought to be left to the courts and much less to statutory definition of what in my opinion is quite undefinable'.[78] Scrutton was similarly minded, and considered that the specific provisions on extracts had no place in legislation.[79]

Special pleading was also engaged in by the music publishers, regarding the situation of pianolas and musical rolls for mechanical instruments. The matter had been dealt with in the Berne Convention of 1886, which provided in the Closing Protocol that 'the manufacture and sale of instruments serving to reproduce mechanically musical airs in which copyright subsists shall not be considered as constituting musical infringement'.[80] Similar provisions were contained in the laws of France and Switzerland,[81] and the article was said to represent a concession to Switzerland, as the major manufacturer of musical boxes.[82] This was also the position of the British law, following *Boosey v Whight*.[83] Several music publishers argued that the musical rolls represented a threat to the industry, but the issue proved too difficult for the Committees and no provisions were drafted to deal with the situation.

Two important observations may be made of the approach to infringement during this period. First, the shape of the right and the exceptions to it were heavily influenced by the role taken by interest groups in drafting the Bills. Secondly, the characterization of copyright as a broad right out of which certain exceptions could be carved had begun to take hold in terms of legislative drafting. It is also hard to discern any strong or consistent argument that the interests of the public should be considered when defining infringement, something which is hardly surprising, given the nature of the witnesses giving evidence. One commentator who did consider such issues was Williams Briggs, in his 1906 book on international copyright. Briggs considered that the argument that a book which copied extracts did not infringe because it had a different purpose or appealed to a different public was utterly spurious and no express provision was required in an Act to make such behaviour illegitimate. However, in certain situations the author's interest could be 'over-ridden' and express statutory provision should be made for such situations.[84] In his opinion:

[76] Parl Deb HL vol 85 col 932 (9 July 1900).
[77] Select Committee Report (1900) 13, 19, App B.
[78] Select Committee Report (1898) 8.
[79] Select Committee Report (1899) 4.
[80] Berne Convention 1886, Closing Protocol s 3.
[81] S Ricketson and J Ginsburg, *International Copyright and Neighbouring Rights: The Berne Convention and Beyond*, 2nd edn, 2 vols (Oxford, Oxford University Press, 2006) vol 1, p 72.
[82] Briggs, *Law of International Copyright* 403.
[83] *Boosey v Whight* (1899) 1 Ch 836; [1900] 1 Ch 122. See above: ch 4.
[84] Briggs, *Law of International Copyright* 390.

> The liberty of abstracting fragments of literary and artistic works, without the consent of the author, which is conceded by some systems of law in respect of works designed for education, or having a scientific character, and chrestomathies, is in the nature of an exceptional privilege, derogating from the ordinary rights included in copyright.[85]

Briggs noted that this 'nullification' of the author's right was justified on the grounds of public interest:

> It is not that the State wishes to deprive the author of part of his copyright, but that it wishes to free the hands of educationists and others whose work is desirable to facilitate for the sake of the public good.[86]

For his part, Briggs did not approve of such reasoning, stating that

> in strict justice to the author, no plea of 'different purpose' or 'public benefit' should extend to legalize the unauthorized appropriation of any part of his work and if any part of a work be taken for any purpose, the consent of the author ought to be required and if necessary accompanied by monetary payment.[87]

In Briggs' view, 'public benefit' could only justify the taking of news, and in all other cases overriding individual rights would, in the long term, result in detriment to the public.[88] Interestingly, however, Briggs did refer to the 'Right of Quotation' as being separate to the question of extracts for educational and scientific purposes[89] and his characterization of quotation as a 'right' rather than an exception suggests that the boundary between rights and infringement remained fluid.

ii. *New Subject Matters of Copyright*

At the same time as the copyright owners and creators were seeking to define and expand the scope of the rights covered by copyright, there were also moves to expand the types of works covered by copyright. The question of lectures re-emerged, as two cases in the 1880s had once again raised the issue of their protection. In *Nicols v Pitman*[90] Kay J found in favour of the lecturer on the basis of *Abernethy v Hutchinson.* Noting that it was not clear whether Lord Eldon had found for Abernethy on the basis of implied contract or on the ground of property, he interpreted the decision as laying down the principle that, where a lecture is delivered to a limited audience, the audience may make their own notes but may not publish them for profit. He added that the case did not come with the Lectures Copyright Act of 1835 because the lecture was delivered in a public college, which was exempted from the Act's operation.[91]

[85] ibid 395.
[86] ibid.
[87] ibid 399.
[88] ibid 400.
[89] ibid 399.
[90] *Nicols v Pitman* (1894) 26 Ch D 374.
[91] Lectures Copyright Act 1835 s 5.

Four years later, the House of Lords had to decide a case which arose when Caird, a professor of moral philosophy at the University of Glasgow brought an action against Sime, who sought to publish pamphlets reproducing his lectures.[92] A majority again found in favour of the lecturer, but on different grounds. Lord Halsbury LC found for Caird on the basis that an author has a proprietary right in unpublished literary productions and that right continued notwithstanding some kind of communication.[93] He considered the Lectures Act to be too opaque to apply to the current case.[94] Lord Watson gave a more detailed judgment, noting first that it was decided in *Jefferys v Boosey* that authors retained a right of property in a work until it was communicated to the public.[95] Considering *Abernethy v Hutchinson* to be analogous, he found that in the case before him there had been no such communication to the public. Lord FitzGerald dissented, believing that there had been a public communication, and justified his decision with reference to the public interest, quoting Lord Young in the Court below: 'It is obviously expedient in the public interest that such teaching should be public, and open to public comment and criticism'.[96] Lord Watson, however, also referred to public interest considerations, stating:

> I am afraid that I do not estimate so highly as some of the learned judges the advantage of having the professor's lectures printed and subjected to the criticism of public opinion . . . I certainly do not appreciate the advantage to the public of furnishing (which is the professed object of the respondent) the appellant's students with a 'crib'; an aid to knowledge forbidden in well-regulated institutions.[97]

The 1897 and 1898 Bills sought to give effect to the recommendations of the Royal Commission with respect to lectures[98] but, again, appeals to the public interest were raised in opposition. Lord Thring was not prepared to protect lecturers against re-delivery after publication, expressing concern that giving full copyright would prevent the dissemination of useful ideas in lectures, and particularly sermons.[99] Canon Newbolt also gave evidence before the 1899 Committee, and supported the view that copyright should not be granted, as the further a sermon spread the greater the public benefit.[100] The 1899 and 1900 Bills did not, therefore, include lectures as a subject of copyright; instead, they provided for a separate 'lecturing right' which did not extend to publication.

The 1898 Bill included another new subject matter for protection: news. The question of whether a newspaper was protected by copyright had arisen several

[92] *Caird v Sime* (1887) 12 AC 326.
[93] ibid 337.
[94] ibid 339.
[95] ibid 343.
[96] ibid 354–55.
[97] ibid 345–46.
[98] See above: ch 5 section I B.
[99] Select Committee Report (1899) 12.
[100] ibid 42.

times since *Cox v Land and Water Journal Company*.[101] In *Walter v Howe*[102] in 1881, Jessel MR disagreed with the decision in *Cox* and held that the proprietor of a newspaper could not sue unless he had registered under the 1842 Act. Several years earlier, the Royal Copyright Commission had considered the matter and recommended that future legislation should define the parts of a newspaper that may be considered copyright 'by distinguishing between announcements of facts and communications of a literary character'.[103] The difficulties entailed by this subtle distinction became apparent following the 1892 case of *Walter v Steinkopf*.[104] In this case *The Times* brought an action against the *St James' Gazette* regarding the reproduction of several items, including an article by Rudyard Kipling. When delivering judgment, North J stated:

> It is said that there is no copyright in news. But there is or may be copyright in the particular forms of language or modes of expression by which the information is conveyed, and not the less so because the information may be with respect to the current events of the day.[105]

North J found that infringement had occurred in respect of the short passages, but he refused to grant an injunction or damages in respect of those items, as they were ephemeral items, whose interest had since passed away.[106] However, he continued the interlocutory injunction in respect of the Kipling article.[107] *The Times* hailed the decision as a great victory, stating: 'It has now been authoritatively laid down that the protection of literary products by copyright law extends fully over articles and news published in a newspaper'.[108] The *Law Quarterly Review* also approved, calling the judgment 'as near perfection both in law and literary common sense as any deliverance of a human and therefore fallible judge can be'.[109]

Even if the case *had* established that news could be the subject of copyright, the decision left newspapers which employed large numbers of foreign correspondents at considerable expense, such as *The Times*, without recourse to injunctive relief in respect of ephemeral items. Reuter's Telegraph Company was seeking advice in the late 1880s from various counsel, including TE Scrutton, about the copying of its telegrams by newspapers which did not subscribe to its service, in particular the *Evening News*. Scrutton advised them in 1895 that the news or information could be protected by copyright, but other advice was more equivocal, and the problem of registration (whether of a newspaper or the individual telegrams) remained as a practical barrier.[110] Consequently, the newspapers began to take an interest in the

[101] *Cox v Land and Water Journal Company* (1869–70) LR 9 Eq 324. See above: ch 6 text to n 356.
[102] *Walter v Howe* (1881) 17 Ch D 708.
[103] Royal Copyright Commission xvii.
[104] *Walter v Steinkopf* [1892] 3 Ch 489.
[105] ibid 495.
[106] ibid 500.
[107] ibid.
[108] *The Times* (3 June 1892) 9b.
[109] 'Notes' (1893) 9 *Law Quarterly Review* 16.
[110] Reuters Archive 1/867515.

Bills before Parliament. The 1898 Bill included a section on newspaper copyright that went beyond the recommendations of the Royal Copyright Commission:

> Copyright in respect of a newspaper shall apply only to such parts of the newspaper as are compositions of an original literary character, to original illustrations therein, and to such news and information as have been specially and independently obtained.[111]

This clause recognised both the literary nature of newspaper articles, as well as the economic value of news. It also sought to improve North J's finding in *Walter v Steinkopf* that news would be protected only to the extent of its literary expression by extending protection to the news itself.

Moberly Bell, manager of *The Times*, who was a member of the 1898 Committee and a witness before it, had clearly been influenced by the experience of protecting news in Australia.[112] He proposed the adoption of a system similar to that set out in the Tasmanian Newspaper Copyright Act of 1891, that 'specially and independently obtained' news be protected for a period of 24 or 48 hours.[113] Other members of the Committee, however, struggled with how such a proposal could be implemented, with the following exchange demonstrating the problem:

> (Lord Herschell) But on what principle would you rest the copyright in news? I am speaking not of the literary expression or mode of conveying it, but of the fact itself?—
>
> (Bell) It is not the fact itself, my Lord; I venture to think that there is an enormous difference between the fact and news of the fact.[114]

The subtlety of this semantic distinction was the crux of the problem: how was it possible to protect one and not the other in the real world of briefly worded telegrams and publication deadlines? Indeed, as Lord Herschell pointed out, 'Why should not the person who makes the fact have at least equal or superior protection to the press after it is published'.[115]

The prospect of extending copyright to news also raised public interest concerns. Lord Welby pointed out that the effect of granting such protection would be to keep the people of Edinburgh, Manchester or Liverpool waiting for the arrival of *The Times* each evening, in order to find out important pieces of news. Bell responded that other newspapers would therefore be compelled to have correspondents of their own, rather than relying on *The Times*. This, he contended, would be far more beneficial to the public, as it would lead to competition amongst the newspapers and agencies, allow reported news to be assessed by other newspapers, and result in a higher quality news service to the public.[116] However, he also conceded that the real effect of the Act would be to give *The Times* a right that

[111] Copyright HL Bill (1898) 21 s 11.

[112] For the story of the protection of telegraphic news in Australia, see L Bently, 'Copyright and the Victorian Internet: Telegraphic Property Laws in Colonial Australia' (2004) 38 *Loyola Law Review of Los Angeles* 71.

[113] Select Committee Report (1898) 53–54.

[114] ibid 53.

[115] ibid 54.

[116] ibid 55–56, 62.

it could transfer for payment. In Bell's words, 'the moment you pass the thing you would have an arrangement to which every paper in the kingdom would be a party, by which they had a right to its [the news'] use'.[117] This statement suggests that what Bell was really seeking was a right that *The Times* could transfer or license for value.

The issue of protecting news lay on the intersection of public and private interests. The 1899 Bill varied the provision to give protection to specially and independently obtained news for a period of 12 hours.[118] Although the provincial publishers expressed their opposition before the 1899 Committee, Lord Thring retained the clause in his Bill of 1900 and increased the period of protection to 18 hours.[119] Thus, it seemed that the interests of news-gathering newspapers were prevailing over those of newspapers which were accustomed to sourcing their news from other papers. The interests of the public in general had once more been subsumed into arguments between rival publishers. Writing in 1902, Bell demonstrated the way in which public interest rhetoric could be enlisted to his newspaper's service:

> Protection to the contents of a newspaper, whether it be news, reports, articles, or paragraphs, means more value to the newspaper, therefore better pay to the journalist; therefore better work and encouragement to the careful, painstaking, accurate journalist; therefore a better service to the public, better journals, and a higher class of journalist.[120]

Thus, Moberly Bell employed the argument of private rights leading to public benefit which publishers and authors had been developing for almost two centuries.

The question of protecting news under copyright law meant that newspaper proprietors and editors joined the growing number of increasingly organised groups lobbying systematically for reform of copyright law in the last decades of the nineteenth century. The various Bills introduced during these years, and the discussions of the Select Committees concerning them, provided another forum in which ideas could crystallise and be debated. Despite the emergence of consensus regarding the duration of copyright, there was little agreement on where other boundaries should be drawn. In some areas, the problems arose from conflicts between the interests of authors and publishers; in others it arose from the conflict between the expansionist urges of copyright owners and public interest concerns for dissemination of knowledge, as well as recognition of the benefits to be gained by secondary users from weaker copyright protection.

In the end, copyright reform was a political decision and, at the end of the century, the Government had little incentive to dive into the morass of copyright law as it then stood. In 1900, Arthur Balfour, first Lord of Treasury and leader of the House of Commons, refused to commit to introducing a Government Bill on

[117] ibid 64.
[118] Copyright HL Bill (1899) 44 s 12.
[119] Copyright HL Bill (1900) 295 s 12.
[120] *The Author* (1 March 1902) 142–43.

copyright, citing lack of information as to the attitudes of the colonies.[121] Canada had re-emerged as a problem, by introducing a Bill in 1889 that included a manufacturing clause similar to that in the Chace Act as well as a licensing clause, and threatening to withdraw from the Berne Convention. As it was in conflict with Imperial law, this Act required the approval of the Governor-General which was not forthcoming. After heavy lobbying on both sides of the Atlantic and much diplomatic negotiation, in which key roles were played by Daldy and, on behalf of the Society of Authors, the writer Hall Caine, the 1899 Act was eventually abandoned and a less objectionable Act was passed in 1900. However, Canada continued to feel resentment at not receiving reciprocal protection in the United States, as well as at her lack of legislative autonomy on copyright matters.[122]

After Lord Thring's Bill of 1900 was withdrawn from Parliament, copyright reform was relegated to the back burner. In 1902 a deputatation of representatives from the Publishers' Association, the Society of Authors, the Copyright Association and the Music Publishers' Association was received by Gerald Balfour, President of the Board of Trade[123]. He promised that if the Canadian objections were removed, a Bill would be introduced in the next session.[124] Neither event occurred. The Society of Authors did its best to keep the project of codification alive, but was continually disappointed. In 1906, it was bemoaned in the pages of its journal, *The Author*, that copyright 'had been mentioned in the speech from the Throne at the opening of Parliament in 1901. It has not been mentioned since. It appears to have expired of senile decay'.[125] The following year, another author wondered wistfully: 'Is it too much to hope that a new government, having among its members an unusual number of well-known authors, may be able to find time to introduce and pass a new Copyright Act?'[126] However, as one writer in the *Author* noted, those who thought a Copyright Bill could easily be taken through the House 'ignore utterly the colonial questions that may arise, the questions under the Berne Convention, and under other existing treaties, the many wheels within wheels'.[127]

At the turn of the century, the problem of copyright law remained intractable. The interests involved were too varied to be easily reconciled and the interplay of colonial and international aspects was too complex to be resolved in a private members' Bill. Only Government action would be able to create the necessary consensus and momentum needed to carry a Bill, but there were few inducements for the Government to take up such a thorny issue.

[121] Parl Deb HC vol 87 col 790 (6 August 1900).

[122] For the full story of Canada's involvement in copyright at the end of the century, see Seville, *Internationalisation* 116–35.

[123] And brother of Arthur Balfour, referred to above.

[124] Kingsford, *The Publishers Association* 18–19.

[125] *The Author* (1 April 1905) 208.

[126] *The Author* (1 March 1906) 169.

[127] *The Author* (1 May 1907) 206.

II. A MUSICAL INTERLUDE

A. The Problem of Piracy

While thorough codifying reform proved elusive in the early years of the new century, one specific interest group met with more success: music publishers.[128] Music piracy was not, of course, a new practice even at the start of the twentieth century. In the 1870s and 1880s the large, established music publishing firms, such as Boosey & Co and Novello & Co, were very concerned about piracy—but it was American piracies that caused the publishers sleepless nights. In 1881, Thomas Chappell called a meeting of the major London music publishers and the Music Publishers' Association (MPA) was formed. The object of the MPA was to protect the interests of the trade against piracies in America and the colonies, as well as pursuing domestic copyright reform.[129] In 1891 the Chace Act took the pressure off the American situation to a large degree, and music publishers could turn their attention back home.

This was fortunate because at home a new problem was beginning to emerge—mass-produced illegitimate copies of sheet music. The end of the nineteenth century was the golden age of music halls, and saw the creation of the first mass audiences and the birth of popular music.[130] The popular music boom can be seen in the dramatic increase in output of sheet music.[131] However, it was not cheap. A sheet of music could be priced anywhere between 4s and 1s 4d, and tended to be sold for around 2s or 1s 6d per song. Even John Abbott, loyal long-time employee of Francis, Day & Hunter, conceded this might seem high at a time when £3 was a good weekly wage for a man.[132]

As noted above, the music publishers had been concerned for some time by the problem of private copying, in particular, the multiplication of copies of sheet music in manuscript. Such copies were sometimes advertised in ladies' journals[133] and the music publishers were irritated that the general public seemed unaware that manuscript copies for one's own use were infringements. As the *Musical News* observed in 1893:

[128] For more detail on this story, see I Alexander, 'Criminalising Copyright: A Story of Publishers, Pirates and Pieces of Eight' [2007] *Cambridge Law Journal* 625.

[129] J Coover, *Music Publishing, Copyright and Piracy in Victorian England* (London, Mansell Publishing Limited, 1985) 9.

[130] R Middleton, 'Popular Music of the Lower Classes' in N Temperley (ed), *The Romantic Age 1800–1914* (London, The Athlone Press, 1976) 80–81.

[131] DW Krummel, 'Music Publishing' in Temperley, *The Romantic Age* 49

[132] J Abbott, *The Story of Francis, Day & Hunter*, (London, Francis, Day & Hunter, 1952) 39. According to studies undertaken by the Board of Trade in 1905 the average income of a working man's family was around 36s a week, of which around 60% was spent on food, and most of the remainder on rent, clothing, fuel and light. Such a family would pay around 3–4s a week on bread or flour: Second Series of Memoranda, Statistical Tables and Charts prepared in the Board of Trade with reference to various matters bearing upon British and Foreign Trade and Industrial Conditions (Cd 2337, 1905) 1–9.

[133] *Musical Opinion and Music Trade Review* (August 1882) 115, extracted in Coover, *Music Publishing* 13.

> It cannot be too widely known, and yet the knowledge seems to be by no means general, that the multiplication of copies of any musical composition of which the copyright has not expired, by anyone other than the owner of the copyright or his agent, is absolutely illegal and actionable, no matter in what way such multiplication is made.[134]

Manuscript copies, however, presented only a small threat to music sellers and publishers. The real problems arose with the advent of photolithography. Lithography had been used in music printing throughout the nineteenth century[135] and in the middle of the century it was combined with the new technique of photography. By the end of the century, photographic equipment had become increasingly accessible and affordable. As John Abbott noted, in his history of music publishing firm Francis, Day & Hunter:

> Popular music offered an easy prey to these thieves. Consisting of a few pages they could be photographed, transferred to a lithographic printing press, and copies turned out in any old barn or basement . . . A popular song, say from a musical comedy, could be photographed, printed, and on sale at twopence or fourpence per copy, within a week of the issue of the legitimate edition.[136]

The first approach taken by the publishers was to bring civil proceedings against the various hawkers, many of whom were repeat offenders.[137] However, the majority of such actions were worse than useless; although the publishers were awarded injunctions, these were promptly breached, and because the hawkers were usually 'men of straw' the publishers only very rarely recovered their costs, let alone a damages award.[138] The publishers ended up even more out of pocket than before they began. In December of 1897, the principal publishers met to discuss the matter. What was needed, they decided, was better legislation and the machinery of the criminal law.[139]

[134] *Musical News* (26 August 1893). See also an article reproduced from the *Musical Times* in the *Musical News* (6 April 1895) 323.

[135] Interestingly, its inventor, Alois Senefelder, was an aspiring dramatist in search of a way to produce multiple copies his plays without the intermediary of the publisher. See Stanley Boorman, 'Printing and Publishing of Music' in L Macy (ed), *Grove Music Online*, www.grovemusic.com.

[136] Abbott, *The Story of Francis, Day & Hunter* 31.

[137] *Coote v Ingram*, *The Times* (3 November 1887) 3b. See also Report of the Committee appointed by the Home Secretary to Inquire into the Piracy of Music Publications with Evidence and Appendix (Cd 1960, 1904) (Music Piracy Report (1904)) 27.

[138] David Day claimed that of 12 infringement actions brought between 1897 and 1902, the firm recovered their costs in only 3, despite being awarded injunctions in all of them. Arthur Boosey claimed that Boosey & Co. had brought 12 successful civil actions, at a cost to the company of £500, and only managed to recover any money in 2 cases. Music Piracy Report (1904) 4, 29. One such case was the action against the printers, Poole & Sons, in which Boosey & Co. successfully recovered £115 in damages as well as costs for piracy of *The Holy City*. This was because they have been able to get behind the hawkers to target the printers themselves. See *Musical News* (26 April 1902) 410–11.

[139] MPA Minute Book, vol 1 (23 December 1897). The Fine Arts Act 1862 made the copying of artistic works an offence that could be dealt with by a civil action on the case or by summary proceedings and subject to a penalty of 10*l* (Copyright Act 1842 ss 6, 8) Several criminal prosecutions had been successfully brought under this Act by the art dealer, publisher and printseller, Henry Graves: *Ex parte Beal* (1867–68) LR 3 QB 387; *In re Prince ex parte Graves* (1867–68) LR 3 Ch App 642 CA. In this latter case it was held that the Fine Arts Copyright Act clearly created a criminal offence that could be punished by imprisonment.

In 1899, the publisher David Day, of Francis, Day & Hunter, appeared before the Select Committee considering the Bills on literary and artistic copyright asking that a penalty on hawking pirated music be accompanied by the power to search for and seize unlawful copies in houses and shops.[140] When the Bills proceeded no further Day too was driven to take matters into his own hands. Between January and March 1902, he arranged for a series of raids to be carried out on places that had been identified as storing pirated sheet music. He then set up a new body, the Musical Copyright Association, in March of the same year which adopted similar tactics, engaging ex-police officers as agents to 'clear the streets' by seizing music and tearing it up.[141]

B. Achieving Effective Legislation

However, working outside the law was unsatisfactory and, once again, the publishers turned to Parliament for assistance. In 1902, the music publishing firm of Frank Dean and Co engaged the lawyer Edward Cutler to make another attempt at drafting a Bill to present to Parliament. Cutler, whose involvement with copyright law has been noted above,[142] had a considerable practice in copyright law, particularly musical copyright law.[143] His Bill was based on Lord Thring's Copyright Bill of 1900. It included a penalty of £5 for every infringing copy and gave constables the power to seize, without warrant, any pirated copies being hawked about upon the authority of either the court or the copyright owner.[144] Cutler's Bill was introduced into the House of Lords by Lord Monkswell on 17 March 1902. Lord Monkswell, as we have seen, had also been involved in copyright reform for many years,[145] and had been heavily lobbied by Boosey & Co and other music publishers.[146]

The Bill passed in the House of Lords, and in the House of Commons.[147] However, before it was enacted, the Commons removed the penalty clauses, thereby rendering the statute toothless. Matters were made still worse for the publishers when a Marylebone Police Court Magistrate refused to make an order in a piracy case because no summons had been served upon the person upon whom the music had been found and the decision was upheld by the Divisional Court.[148] Lord Alverstone noted in his judgment that 'under this Act a far greater privilege is conferred upon the owners of musical copyright than is enjoyed by other

[140] Select Committee Report (1899) 58–62.
[141] Music Piracy Report (1904) 33.
[142] See above: text to n 25.
[143] He more often acted against the music publishers than for them, most notably acting for Whight, the Aeolian manufacturers, in the case of *Boosey v Whight* [1899] 1 Ch 836.
[144] Musical Copyright HL Bill (1902) 178.
[145] See above: nn 21, 24, 30, 34.
[146] Parl Deb HL vol 106 col 456 (17 April 1902).
[147] Musical (Summary Proceedings) Copyright Act 1902 (2 Edw VII c 15).
[148] *Ex parte Francis and Others* [1903] 1 KB 275.

persons in cases where their rights of property are infringed'.[149] He also pointed out that proof of infringement might 'involve considerations of very nice questions of copyright law'.[150] Thus, it was not a necessary implication that the magistrate should act *ex parte*, and if Parliament had so intended the Act would have contained express language to that effect.[151]

As hawkers were generally vagrant persons of no fixed address, this decision dealt a serious blow to enforcement of the Act. In May 1903, the Earl of Lytton[152] introduced a Bill to amend the 1902 Act, claiming that, far from halting the piracy, the 1902 Act had led to its increase. He stated that futile attempts to enforce the Act ' have merely acted as an advertisement of the very lucrative nature of the trade; and the utter failure of its administration has given confidence to the classes engaged in it'.[153] The House of Lords passed the Bill, but it stalled in the House of Commons.

At this time, the united front presented by the music publishers began to fracture. The MPA had originally supported the establishment of the Musical Copyright Association and applauded its activities, particularly as its meager funds had been seriously depleted contesting the Aeolian case, *Boosey v Whight.*[154] In August 1903, friction began to develop between the two bodies but this was soon resolved and it was decided that a new organisation, called the Musical Defence League, would be formed for the purpose of bringing pressure to bear on Parliament.[155] Following this crisis, the MPA began to take a more active role in stamping out piracy. Arthur Preston, an employee of Boosey & Co, was among those employed to travel the countryside tracking down provincial pirates. Preston made large captures, including 7,000 piratical copies in Liverpool and 6,000 in Manchester.[156] In Liverpool, however, the prosecution failed on the basis that the copies had been seized from a house, and the 1902 Act specifically referred to copies being 'offered for sale'.[157] Preston and his colleague Mabe continued their travels around the countryside, bringing prosecutions in towns including Doncaster, Sheffield, Chester, Leicester, Belfast and Torquay. Most of the subsequent prosecutions were successful. The hawkers were fined and costs orders were

149 ibid 280.

150 ibid.

151 ibid 281.

152 Lytton's grandfather, Edward Bulwer-Lytton, had been responsible for introducing the Dramatic Copyright Act of 1833; see above: ch 4.

153 Parl Deb HL vol 122 col 1049 (19 May 1903).

154 *Boosey v Whight* (1899) 1 Ch 836.

155 MPA Minute Book, vol 1 (23 September 1903).

156 For detail on Preston's activities, see the scrapbook in the British Library (Music Library, M55) which contains clippings from provincial papers on seizures by Preston and other agents of the MPA and MCA. The book is labelled 'Press Cuttings related to pirated music ca 1883–1926' (hereafter, 'Press Cuttings'). Adrian Johns refers to this as Preston's scrapbook and Preston is the most likely person to have compiled it. However, I have been unable to find any concrete evidence that he is indeed the creator of the book. See A Johns, 'Pop Music Pirate Hunters' (2002) 131 *Daedalus* 72.

157 Musical Copyright Act 1902 s 2. Chappell & Co subsequently brought a civil prosecution that was successful. See Press Cuttings.

awarded in the MPA's favour. Hawkers who failed to pay were gaoled and the illegitimate copies were destroyed.[158]

In December 1903, the music publishers' supporters in the Commons at last convinced Arthur Balfour, now Prime Minister, to establish a Departmental Committee to further examine the issue of piracy.[159] Its members included a Metropolitan Police Magistrate, Edward Fenwick; the publisher, John Murray; and the barrister, TE Scrutton, who was counsel to the Musical Copyright Association but officially representing the Board of Trade. Two Members of Parliament were also on the Committee; they were William Galloway, an engineer and a Conservative, who supported the case of the music publishers; and James Caldwell, a Liberal member, who had opposed the 1902 Act and Lytton's 1903 Bill.[160]

The Committee heard evidence from numerous music publishers and two well-known composers, Lionel Monckton and Michael Maybrick (who composed under the name of Stephen Adams). The publishers explained to the Committee the nature and extent of the piracy problem, informing the members of their difficulties in bringing actions against the pirates and their inability to recover damages from them. The composer Lionel Monckton gave evidence that he was 'some hundreds of pounds out of pocket since the piracy began'.[161] Maybrick relied on his natural rights in his compositions to attack the pirates, stating:

> My view is this: These people are taking my property; they are picking my pocket. They are taking my daily bread out of my mouth; they are taking advantage of my brains and using them for themselves to make money with, and I look upon that as robbery on me personally.[162]

The most surprising witness to give evidence was James Frederick Willetts, the self-styled 'King of the Pirates'. Willetts presented himself before the Committee as a sort of musical Robin Hood. He introduced himself as the manager of the People's Music Publishing Company and claimed his sole aim was reform of copyright law. He stated:

> The cause of piracy, I say, is the extortionate price charged to the public by the publishers of copyright music—a price which I consider is altogether beyond the reach of the general public, by whom there is a great and pressing demand—and a price which is out of all reason considering the cost of production, even after making the most handsome allowance for the labour of the author and composer . . . The cause also is a general agitation for the reduction in the price of music.[163]

158 See Press Cuttings.

159 Parl Deb HC vol 130 cols 1163–64 (26 Feburary 1904).

160 Over the next four years, Caldwell was to become a vilified figure in the musical press, with the *Musical Times* likening him to the unprincipled and politically opportunistic Mr Gregsbury MP in Dickens' *Nicholas Nickleby*. *Musical Times* (1 August 1904) 519.

161 Music Piracy Report (1904) 25.

162 ibid 45.

163 ibid 76.

Willetts argued that the aim of the various copyright Acts was the encouragement of learning and contended that copyrights were privileges 'conferred I take it by Parliament as much in the interests, if indeed not more in the interests, of the public than in that of the author or composer himself'.[164] As well as claiming that his editions made music available to the working classes, many of whom now owned pianos, Willetts proposed that authors and composers should let any publisher print their works subject to payment of a royalty, which harked back to discussions before the 1878 Royal Commission.[165] Willetts' proposal was not looked upon favourably by the Committee, and nor was Willetts himself. Scrutton subjected him to a searing cross-examination as to his motives in publishing pirated works and the genuineness of his belief in his moral rectitude. Finally, he undermined Willetts' credibility by introducing his conviction for embezzlement from his former employer, the publishers Messrs Whittingham.[166]

The majority of the Committee was convinced by the case made by the music publishers and composers. In their report, they concluded that a widespread system of piracy had grown up that was causing considerable damage to composers and publishers and which the existing legislation was unable to prevent. They recommended that fresh legislation be introduced, including a summary power to inflict remedies on printers and sellers of infringing works, a power to arrest offenders, and a power of search.[167]

James Caldwell MP, however, was not convinced and delivered a separate report. He took a different view of copyright to that of the majority, stating:

> A slight consideration will show that copyright is not such an absolute right of property as is claimed, but is a 'liberty' or privilege, conferred by Parliament, with the view of encouraging music in the general community, into which the public interest enters as well as that of the owner of copyright, and over the exercise of which by the owner of the copyright, Parliament has and exercises a right of control.[168]

Caldwell's view of copyright was similar to that of Willetts before the Committee. But where Willetts' view was dismissed by the majority as a sham and cover for his piratical activities, Caldwell, a lawyer and wealthy calico merchant by trade, was not so easily neutralised. Although he did not deny that piracy was occurring, Caldwell believed that its increase could be traced to the enormous difference between the prices paid by the public for music compared to the cost of production, and the existence of a

> great and ever increasing market for music, which, owing to the present exorbitant prices charged to the public, is practically shut out, and is demanding music at prices quite compatible with the fullest recognition of the royalty paid to the author and composer.[169]

164 ibid 76.
165 ibid 79.
166 ibid 85.
167 ibid 9.
168 ibid 11.
169 ibid 15.

The publishers were dismissive of Caldwell's notion that there was a public interest in copyright. When asked whether he thought the public had any interest in being supplied with a copyright song at a reasonable price, Arthur Boosey retorted that the public had nothing to do with it. He argued that publishers spend thousands of pounds on making songs popular, and very few songs became popular at all. Thus, they had a perfect right to charge any price they choose.[170] Caldwell did not, however, base his opposition solely on appeals to the public interest. He also asserted that cheaper music would serve the interests of composers, who would receive a larger income owing to the greater demand and, therefore, sales of cheap music.[171] In a memorandum published in July 1903, Caldwell expressed his distaste for the publishers' attempts to elide their interests with those of composers. He noted that this was a case

> of a powerful and wealthy Association, able to spend £1,000 a week in the protection of their valuable interests as owners of copyright, pushing forward a Bill in their own pecuniary interests, which I do not deny is a perfectly legitimate object. But it becomes necessary to refer to that fact, as the Promoters have been putting in the forefront the interests of the Composers of Music, thereby attempting to arouse sympathy in favour of the Bill—a proceeding somewhat analogous to that of putting a row of women and children in front of a line of soldiers.[172]

The composers, however, were happy to close ranks with the publishers in the fight against the pirates. In the middle of 1904, the Musical Defence League called its first meeting. Present were not just the usual music publisher protagonists, William and Arthur Boosey and David Day, but also the composers Sir Edward Elgar, Michael Maybrick and Lionel Monckton.[173] The broader world of publishing and printing also joined the fray. John Murray, Frederick Macmillan, Reginald Smith (the President of the Book Publishers' Association) were present, as were delegates from the London Society of Compositors, the London Society of Lithographic Printers and the London Printing Machine Managers' Trade. Scrutton, Galloway and several other Members of Parliament attended, and others, including Lord Knutsford, Lord Lytton and Gladstone sent letters. Letters of sympathy were also received from Sir Arthur Conan Doyle and Rudyard Kipling, as well as the Members of Parliament TP O'Connor and Herbert Gladstone.[174] The meeting, which was widely reported in the press, was opened by the Duke of Argyll who drew attention to the problem of piracy, emphasising the loss it caused to musical composers, which he estimated at £37,000.[175] Sir Edward Elgar was among those who also spoke, saying that he had come to the meeting 'to ask that his livelihood might be spared to him'.[176]

[170] ibid 301.
[171] ibid 19.
[172] Memorandum (27 July 1903), BT 209/454.
[173] *Musical Times* (1 August 1904) 534 (from *Standard* (5 July 1904)). Copy of article from the *London Musical Courier* (9 July 1904) in HO 45/10298/115994.
[174] *Musical Times* (1 August 1904) 535.
[175] *The Times* (6 July 1904) 15c.
[176] ibid.

A new Bill was introduced into the House of Commons in 1904 and committed to a Standing Committee, but was blocked by Caldwell and his supporters.[177] The music publishers, led by William Boosey, continued heavy lobbying of MPs and the Home Office.[178] They also continued to pursue litigation against the hawkers. In March 1905, the Master Music Printers also began lobbying, sending a letter to the Prime Minister complaining that piracy was having a disastrous effect on employment in the industry.[179] Responsibility for the Bill in Parliament was taken over by TP O'Connor, a leading journalist, lover of music, and Irish Nationalist MP, but he made little progress in the face of Caldwell's opposition and the Government's reluctance to support a contentious measure.[180]

At the end of 1905, the music publishers adopted yet another new tactic, which had originally been suggested by Sir Harry Poland KC before the Departmental Committee of 1904.[181] The firm of Chappell & Co commenced a prosecution against Willetts and several of his associates. The defendants were charged with the common law offence of conspiracy. Counsel for Willetts argued that Willetts had no criminal intent, but merely acted contrary to the civil law, and that he should be allowed to take a civil risk without being branded a criminal.[182] Nevertheless, after a trial lasting eight days, Willetts and his associates were all found guilty. Willetts was sentenced to nine months' imprisonment without hard labour.[183] Chappell & Co followed their London success with a conspiracy prosecution in Leeds and this time they were able to include the hawkers in the action.[184] Once again they were successful, but it was something of a Pyrrhic victory. A meeting of the Music Publishers' Association noted that 'An immense number of copies of piratical works have been seized and plates destroyed, but unfortunately fresh offenders spring up in one neighbourhood as soon as they are stopped in another'.[185] Chappell & Co had spent £4,000 in obtaining the convictions and appealed to the trade for donations to help cover their losses.[186]

Nevertheless, the trial of Willetts provided considerable publicity for the music publishers' cause. It was reported in depth not only in the musical press, but also in such national papers as the *Daily Telegraph* and *The Times*. Meanwhile, the Musical Copyright Bill continued to be debated in the House of Commons. It was an issue that cut across party lines, despite attempts to make it an anti-radical

[177] Parl Deb HC vol 129 col 480 (5 February 1904); vol 130 cols 1156 ff (26 February 1904); vol 132 col 596 (24 March 1904); vol 135 cols 1372 ff (10 June 1904); vol 139 cols 564, 579 (2 August 1904).

[178] Parl Deb HC vol 144 cols 1018–19 (10 April 1905); vol 144 col 1407 (12 April 1905); vol 148 col 551 (29 June 1905). See letter from Boosey to Balfour in PRO document HO 45/10298/115994.

[179] *Musical News* (18 March 1905) 252.

[180] Parl Deb HC vol 148 cols 551–52 (29 June 1905).

[181] Music Piracy Report (1904) 60.

[182] *The Times* (19 January 1906) 3f.

[183] *The Times* (20 January 1906) 9a.

[184] *Musical Opinion and Music Trade Review* (March 1906) 464, extracted in Coover, *Music Publishing* 129.

[185] MPA Minute Book, vol 1 (5 April 1906.)

[186] ibid.

platform in the lead up to the 1906 election.[187] In May 1906, O'Connor once more introduced the Bill, this time with cross-party support.[188] Unlike Balfour's Conservative Government, which had long refused to take up the Bill,[189] the new Liberal Government was prepared openly to support it. After considerable further debate, the Bill at last passed the House of Commons, and the House of Lords, and received Royal Assent on 4 August 1906.

C. Victory At Last?

The new Musical Copyright Act provided that any person who printed, reproduced, or sold, or exposed, offered, or had in his possession for sale, any pirated copies of a musical work, or had in his possession any plates for the purpose of printing copies of a musical work would be guilty of an offence and punishable on summary conviction.[190] The punishment for a first offence was a maximum fine of £5, and upon subsequent convictions a maximum fine of £10 and a term of imprisonment not exceeding two months.[191] Constables were given the power to arrest anyone selling or possessing pirated copies of musical works,[192] and provision was made for general search warrants to be granted by a court.[193] Copies proven to be pirated would be forfeited or destroyed or otherwise dealt with as the court should see fit.[194]

The Act that finally came into force fully satisfied neither its supporters nor its opponents. Caldwell had been largely unsuccessful in inserting provisions aimed at protecting the public against high prices and unjust criminal convictions. The music publishers, on the other hand, had not had things all their own way. The onus of establishing *mens rea* was thrown onto the prosecution for first offenders, but the publishers were pleased with the strength of the search powers.[195] In 1907, Chappell & Co reported in the *Musical Times* that their costs in securing the prosecution of Willetts had come to 3,000 guineas, the Leeds prosecution had cost

[187] Leslie Stuart, a popular music hall singer and vigorous campaigner against the pirates, had written to the *Daily Telegraph* in January 1906 urging the music trade to vote against the radicals, including Caldwell. Messrs Chappell & Co had responded that it should not be made a party issue, as Conservatives, Liberals and even Home Rulers supported the Bill. *Musical News* (13 January 1906) 40–41.

[188] Parl Deb HC vol 158 col 101 (28 May 1906). The other sponsors of the Bill were Conservatives AJ Balfour and Sloan, the Nationalist Redmond, Labour members Keir-Hardie and Enoch Edwards, and the Liberals Alfred Thomas and Crombie.

[189] A letter from Balfour to Galloway on 1 October 1904 explained that the Government was not willing to take up the Bill because whenever the Government brings in a Bill 'anxiously desired by particular interests, and it does not pass, those people suspect treachery or incompetence on the part of the Government' (HO 45/10298/115994).

[190] Musical Copyright Act 1906 s 1.

[191] ibid s 1.

[192] ibid s 1(2).

[193] ibid s 2(1).

[194] ibid s 2(2).

[195] MPA Minute Book, vol 1 (17 July 1905).

1,000 guineas, and the parliamentary expenses in securing the Act had amounted to £2,500. The total was therefore £6,700.[196] Overall, the 1906 Act could be considered a victory for the music publishers, but it had certainly not come cheap.

The key to the eventual enactment of the Bill appears to be the role of O'Connor. An Irish Nationalist with radical views, by 1906 he been a Member of Parliament for 26 years and, following the 1906 election, he became the lynchpin between the Liberals and the Irish party. These two factors gave O'Connor considerable influence in the House of Commons which, in turn, provided the momentum necessary to get the measure through the House. Musical copyright did not present issues that naturally recommended it to one or other party and this is no doubt one reason why the struggle continued for as long as it did. While it is possible to trace broader Liberal and Radical concerns with social reform in the Parliamentary and committee discussions of the Bills in the years between 1904 and 1906, they were not so clearly defined as to unite either party behind the Bill. Indeed, most of the opposition came from the Liberal benches.

Instead, the debates in the House of Commons revolved around two issues in copyright law: first, the nature of the right conferred; and secondly, protection of the public interest. It was Caldwell and his supporters who moved these issues to the centre of the debate and feelings ran high because the demand for criminal sanctions not only went to the very root of both issues but also raised the stakes considerably. For Caldwell, copyright was not a property right but

> an interest conferred by Parliament for the promotion of music among the community, while at the same time giving reasonable remuneration to the composer. It was not property in the same sense as a watch which a man could use, sell, or deal with as he pleased for all eternity.[197]

For them, the proposed Bill was, in the words of the Liberal MP James Galloway Weir 'a shameful attempt to bolster up a rich and powerful combination to the detriment of the public'.[198] Those who opposed the Bill also pointed out that although the Bill was presented as protecting the interests of the composer,

> the poor musical composer . . . only got a royalty of about twopence a copy from the publisher from his song, while the publisher robbed him and would continue to rob him under the *aegis* of this Bill of the other profits of his work.[199]

Rejecting the characterisation of copyright as a property right was significant because it justified tipping the scales away from copyright owners. However, throughout the debates, Caldwell maintained that he was not opposed to stringent laws to put down piracy, provided the interests of the public were properly recognised.[200] He stated in 1904 that

[196] *Musical Times* (1 February 1907) 111.
[197] Parl Deb HC vol 135 col 1406 (10 June 1904).
[198] ibid col 1393.
[199] Parl Deb HC vol 161 col 513 (19 July 1906) (TM Healy, Nationalist).
[200] Parl Deb HC vol 135 col 1407 (10 June 1904).

> if copyright owners were to have these drastic powers, which were not possessed by owners of anything else in the kingdom; if they were to be given powers of obtaining search warrants, and such penalties as could be inflicted under this bill, then at least they ought to show before the magistrates that the reasonable requirements of the public were being satisfied'.[201]

One safeguard that Caldwell proposed was to make registration of musical works compulsory. He argued that 'when they were creating penal offences registration should be made compulsory because a man should know before an offence was committed exactly what was copyright and what was not'.[202]

Another aspect of the proposed legislation to which Caldwell and others were strenuously opposed was the publishers' desire for a reversal of the burden of proof. Ignoring the fundamental principle of 'innocent until proven guilty', consecutive versions of the Bill provided that a person found selling or possessing pirated copies of a musical work would be guilty unless he proved his innocence. As George Harwood, Liberal MP for Bolton, pointed out to the House, 'It was a very serious step to take against persons belonging to the poorest and least educated class to put them in the dock and say, "we assume you guilty unless you prove your innocence." '[203] The reversal of the burden of proof was one of the most objectionable aspects of the Bill for many Liberal, Nationalist and Radical members. In the end, a compromise was reached. The general provision was that the burden of proving innocence was placed upon the defendant. However, if the defendant had no previous convictions, and could prove that the copies in issue had printed upon the title page the name and address of a printer or publisher, then the prosecution had to prove his guilty knowledge that the copies were pirated.[204]

The third aspect of Caldwell's attempt to protect the public interest stemmed from his belief that the underlying cause of piracy was the high price of music. Other members were also convinced that the music publishers had combined to keep the price of music high.[205] They saw music publishing as a monopolistic trade combination which militated against the public interest. As Weir argued, 'for the masses of the people there should be an edition at a price within their reach. Why should the jaded shop or factory girl who found a solace in music be unable to cultivate her taste?'[206] Caldwell suggested giving the Privy Council the power to compel licences or cancel copyright if the public interest were not satisfied. A similar point was made in 1904 by Llewellyn Atherley-Jones MP, a lawyer on the radical wing of the Liberal party. He had proposed several possible amendments. One was a clause providing that any person may present a petition to the Board of Trade alleging that the reasonable requirements of the public with respect to a

[201] ibid col 1399.
[202] ibid col 1375.
[203] Parl Deb HC vol 160 col 1453 (16 June 1904).
[204] Musical Copyright Act 1906 s 1(1).
[205] Parl Deb HC vol 135 cols 1390, 1392, 1403 (10 June 1904).
[206] Parl Deb HC vol 135 col 1393 (10 June 1904).

copyright have not been satisfied, and seeking the grant of a compulsory licence, or the revocation of the copyright. This clause was lifted directly from the Patents Amendment Act of 1902.[207] However, the Board of Trade was opposed to such a clause, on the basis that if it applied to music it must also apply to books and other copyright subjects.[208] Atherley-Jones also suggested inserting an amendment which gave the Court discretion to refuse a search warrant if it appeared that the 'reasonable requirements of the public with reference to such musical work have not been satisfied'.[209] The House, however, voted against the clause and no provision protecting the public from high prices was enacted.

One further restriction was made to the powers sought by the music publishers, in the form of an amendment introduced by the Liberal Home Secretary Herbert Gladstone. Gladstone objected to the provision of the Bill that allowed a constable to enter a house without a warrant. However, his amendment also expanded the police powers by providing that a constable having entered premises could seize any piece of music he believed to be pirated, not just those specified on the warrant.[210] The amendment was accepted and became part of the Act.

Those arguing in favour of the Bill tended to emphasis the effect of piracy on the income of composers, a strategy to which the various composers involved did not object. Those who supported the publishers in Parliament also elided their interests with those of composers. As Thomas Cochrane told the House of Commons in 1904, 'The composer and publisher, having invested their brains and money, had a right to look for some protection'.[211] Another MP, Ian Malcolm, informed the House that Caldwell was wrong to say that the privileges of copyright were granted to protect the public; 'they were granted to protect the brain-property of British citizens, who had as much right to that property as people had to material property'.[212] By highlighting the injury to composers, the supporters of the Bill appealed, once again, to the ideology of romantic authorship and the inviolability of property rights. However, it was not just composers who were cast as the victims, but also small-scale retailers. The Earl of Lytton, when introducing his Bill, had informed the House of Lords that the sufferers were not just musical authors, but also the 'class of small shopkeepers who have sought to act honestly . . . but who

[207] Musical (Summary Proceedings) Copyright Act 1902 s 3. The link between this Act and the proposed compulsory licensing clauses may provide some insight into why Caldwell took such an interest in the musical copyright debates. Caldwell was a former calico merchant and the Calico Printers' Association had given evidence to the Fry Committee, which was reviewing aspects of the patents laws. The calico printers complained about the practice of foreigners who took out patents in the United Kingdom on dyes which were manufactured outside the country, and then re-sold into the country at high prices for them. They considered that a clause that would impose compulsory licences if a patent was not worked in the United Kingdom would protect their interests and those of the public. Report of the Departmental Committee appointed to inquire into the working of the Patent Acts on certain specified questions (Cd 506, 1901), 91. Caldwell had made a similar point in Parliament. Parl Deb HC vol 110 cols 858–59 (4 July 1902).

[208] BT 209/454.

[209] Parl Deb HC vol 135 col 1391 (10 June 1904).

[210] Parl Deb HC vol 160 cols 1477–83 (16 July 1906).

[211] Parl Deb HC vol 130 col 1192 (26 February 1904).

[212] ibid col 1188.

have found it quite impossible to meet the pressure of competition of musical pirates'.[213] The musical press similarly drew attention to printers and dealers suffering financially due to the pirates.[214]

A second tactic which buttressed this approach was the use of the language of theft, likening the pirates' activities to criminal violations of physical property. As previously noted, Maybrick had told the 1904 Committee that the pirates were 'taking my property; they are picking my pocket'.[215] The language of theft was queried by Caldwell when Arthur Boosey complained before the same Committee that 'if you see people with stolen goods you should be able to do something'.[216] Caldwell told him that the law did not treat piracy as theft, but Scrutton disagreed, saying that the Act treated songs as Boosey's property.[217] Both Boosey and Scrutton, however, recognised they had a difficult task convincing the public that purchasing pirated music was wrong. Boosey admitted that not only had piano tuners mentioned finding copies of pirated music in respectable houses, but he also knew that friends of his had pirated copies in their possession.[218] And at the Musical Defence League meeting Scrutton noted in his speech that:

> Respectable people who would look with scorn if they were asked to buy a watch because it was stolen and it was cheap, or vegetables from their greengrocer because they were stolen from his neighbour's garden, think nothing of buying musical pieces and books because they can get them so cheap.[219]

A final important element of the arguments of the Bill's supporters, which was linked to the second, was the characterisation of copyright piracy as not merely a breach of a private property right but also a threat to the very social and moral fabric of society. In 1904, Galloway emphasised the fact that the hawkers would often operate out of public houses, noting: 'He made that statement because it might be agreeable to the advocates of temperance reform'.[220] He also informed the House of Commons that hawkers were 'mostly of the criminal class' and that a large number were alien Jews.[221] In a similar vein was Scrutton's discreditation of Willetts' evidence before the 1904 Committee by introducing his previous conviction for embezzlement, a fact which Galloway made sure to bring to the attention of the House of Commons.[222]

It seems that these rhetorical strategies were effective in achieving greater protection against the pirates. The various objections made by Caldwell and others opposed to the publishers' Bill on the basis of public interest may have failed to halt the legislation, but they did squarely place the public interest on centre stage for

[213] Parl Deb HL vol 122 col 1051 (19 May 1903).
[214] See *Musical News* (18 March 1905) 252, (3 July 1905) 30.
[215] Music Piracy Report (1904) 45.
[216] ibid 77.
[217] ibid.
[218] Music Piracy Report (1904) 7.
[219] HO 45/10298/115994, article from *London Musical Courier* (9 July 1904).
[220] Parl Deb HC vol 130 vol 1173 (26 February 1904).
[221] ibid col 1171.
[222] ibid cols 1169–70.

the first time since the 1878 Commission. At a more practical level, they slowed the legislation's progress considerably and placed limits on the powers granted. In this way they prevented the Act from becoming excessively draconian through high penalties and a reverse burden of proof for first time offenders. After a mere two decades of lobbying, the music publishers were largely successful. While the larger project of consolidation and codification languished in the wings, a powerful and organised group had been able to shape the law in their favour, demonstrating that at this point in time it was still easier for the legislature to deal with copyright on a subject-specific basis.

III. THE IMPERIAL COPYRIGHT ACT OF 1911

Complete reform and codification of copyright law remained a low priority for the Government for several years after the Musical Copyright Act of 1904. But in 1908 the Berne Convention was significantly altered at the Berlin Revision Conference. A number of the revisions agreed upon were incompatible with British domestic law, including the addition of works of architecture as a subject of protection, the principle of absence of formalities, the assimilation of translation rights with copyright and protection lasting for the life of the author and 50 years thereafter.[223]

The Berlin Revision forced the Government's hand. In order for Britain to continue as a member of the Union, it would need to amend its domestic laws. The Society of Authors had sought to influence the Board of Trade's position at the negotiations and once again their intermediary was Sir Henry Bergne who, to the members' great sorrow, died suddenly while in Berlin. When the delegates returned from the conference, the secretary of the Society met with a Board of Trade Official and the Society's Committee of Management called together a joint committee, which also included representatives from the Music Publishers' Association, the Publishers's Association and the Copyright Association.[224] All of the bodies agreed to support the terms of the Berlin Convention, as did the Dramatic Copyright Sub-Committee of the Society of Authors.[225] Meanwhile, the Government appointed a Departmental Committee, under the chairmanship of Lord Gorell[226] and reporting to the President of the Board of Trade, Winston S Churchill, to examine the ways in which the current law would need to be revised in order to give effect to the Berlin Convention.[227]

The membership of the Departmental Committee (known as the Gorell Committee) reflected the variety of groups now interested in copyright reform. The lawyers and long-term players Thomas Scrutton and Edward Cutler were

223 Ricketson and Ginsburg, *International Copyright* 92–102. Note that the duration for life and fifty years was not mandatory at this point, but merely agreed in principle.

224 *The Author* (1 July 1909) 273–74.

225 ibid 274. The music publishers had some objections but withdrew them for the sake of unanimity: ibid 274.

226 John Gorell Barnes was a former judge and became a law lord in 1909.

227 Report of the Committee on the Law of Copyright (Cd 4976, 1910) (Gorell Committee)

present. The interests of music publishers and sellers were represented by Henry Reginald Clayton and William Boosey. Art was represented by painter Lawrence Alma-Tadema; drama by actor and director Harley Granville Barker; literature by the poet Henry Cust, the novelist (and lawyer) Anthony Hope Hawkins and the literary scholar, Walter Raleigh. Literary publishing was represented by Frederick Macmillan. The interests of the sound recording companies were upheld by E Trevor Williams, founder of the Gramophone Company. TP O'Connor MP represented the interests of journalism, but played no role in the drafting of the report and CW Bowerman, another MP, was the Parliamentary Secretary of the London Society of Compositors. The other members were George Ranken Askwith, head of the Statistical Department at the Board of Trade who had accompanied Bergne to Berne and taken over his duties after his death there (and whose wife had published two novels); Algernon Law, of the Foreign Office; and William Joynson-Hicks, a Conservative MP and a solicitor, known for his interest in the latest technology.[228]

The instructions given to the Gorell Committee were to consider whether the provisions of the Berlin Revision of the Berne Convention were in accordance with the law of Great Britain and, if not, whether it would be advisable to alter the law in order to give effect to the Revised Convention.[229] Those giving evidence before the Committee were drawn overwhelmingly from the copyright-owning industries, such as authors, literary publishers, music publishers and artists. They were joined by a large contingent of makers of and dealers in mechanical musical instruments. Two witnesses spoke on behalf of the printing industry and one spoke about newspapers. Having heard all the evidence, the Committee reported that it was in favour of ratifying the Convention, although reservations were expressed by some members of the Committee on some matters.

The next step was to achieve the acquiescence of Britain's self-governing colonies. An Imperial Copyright Conference was held in May 1910, and was presided over by the new President of the Board of Trade, Sydney Buxton.[230] The Imperial Conference also recommended that the Revised Convention be ratified. A draft Bill for consolidating and amending the law was submitted to the Conference, and was generally approved.[231] The Dominions' approval meant that the Bill could move forward and, on 26 July 1910, Buxton introduced it into the House of Commons, not with a view to its passing, but in order to allow those with an interest in it to consider its details.[232] He withdrew the Bill in November,[233] but re-introduced an amended version on 30 March 1911,[234] which went to a

[228] Interestingly, a partner of the law firm Joynson-Hicks founded in 1888 published a book in 1989, commenting on the Copyright, Designs and Patents Act 1988, entitled *Joynson-Hicks on Copyright.*

[229] Gorell Committee 2.

[230] No 3 Copyright Conference (Dominions) (Cd 5272, 1910).

[231] ibid 8.

[232] Parl Deb HC vol 19 cols 1945–50 (26 July 1910).

[233] Parl Deb HC vol 20 col 235 (21 November 1910).

[234] Parl Deb HC vol 23 col 1534 (30 March 1911).

Standing Committee.[235] The Bill was far from uncontroversial, and it was discussed at length in both Houses of Parliament.[236] Almost every clause was the subject of objection and debate. Outside Parliament, pressure for copyright legislation had been maintained for some time through a number of articles published in the major periodicals of the day, many of them authored by GH Thring of the Society of Authors[237] and, while the Bill was before Parliament, interested parties kept up a constant stream of letters to *The Times*. In the course of this extended discussion and debate, many of the issues that had arisen during the nineteenth century re-emerged as controversial. Likewise, the rhetoric of romantic authorship, property rights and the public interest were again employed to support a variety of positions.

A. A New and Expansive Law?

One of the most important changes required by the Berlin Revision was the alteration of the term of copyright protection to a period that included the life of the author and 50 years thereafter. Although the increase of copyright term to the life of the author and a fixed period thereafter had not been contentious in the 1890s (when the fixed term in each of the various Bills was 30 years), it now re-emerged as a source of conflict.

Unsurprisingly, the majority of witnesses who gave evidence to the Gorell Committee were in favour of the extension. The Committee concluded that it would not be prejudicial to the public interest to adopt the new term, and in fact 'it would tend to beneficial assistance in the development and progress of literature and art'.[238] Joynson-Hicks dissented from the Committee's recommendation, arguing that 'the only two witnesses who were called on this point representing the general public, or at all events, the non-copyright division of the community' were opposed to the extension. As these witnesses were from the Federation of Master Printers, and the Users of Mechanical Instruments, Joynson-Hicks' characterisation of them as representing the 'general public' was disingenuous. Vane Stow, from the Master Printers Federation, claimed that an increased period was contrary to the interests of workers in the trade, and that it would also affect the public by inhibiting the dissemination of cheap literature.[239] JE Hough, representing the Users of Mechanical Instruments, also had an interest in keeping periods of protection short, particularly in the face of growing pressure to bring the

[235] ibid col 2587.

[236] Parl Deb HC vol 28 col 1902 ff (28 July 1911); HC vol 29 cols 2133 ff (17 August 1911); HC vol 32 cols 2447 ff (13 December 1911); HL vol 10 cols 39 ff (31 October 1911), cols 113 ff (14 November 1911), 168 ff (15 November 1911), 451 ff (4 December 1911).

[237] WM Colles, 'Copyright At Home and Abroad' (1909) 65 *The Nineteenth Century* 1056, 'Copyright Law Reform' (1910) 213 *Quarterly Review* 483, 'The Copyright Question' (1910) 212 *Edinburgh Review* 310; GH Thring, 'Imperial Copyright' (1910) 88 *Fortnightly Review* 688, 'The Copyright Bill, 1911' (1911) 89 *Fortnightly Review* 901.

[238] Gorell Committe 16.

[239] Minutes of Evidence. Report of the Committee on the Law of Copyright (Cd 5051, 1910) (Gorell Committee Evidence) 201.

rights to reproduce music mechanically within the gift of the composer or owner. Hough accused composers and publishers of 'cupidity and jealousy',[240] and claimed that phonographs gave amusement in working-class homes which otherwise would have no access to music.[241] Once again, the interests of the public were brought in to mask the interests of the trade.

When the question of extension was debated again in Parliament in 1911, those supporting and those opposing the extension had their rhetoric already laid out for them. The Members arguing in favour invoked the names of great authors. Buxton pointed to Wagner, Herbert Spencer and George Meredith as examples of creators whose works were not immediately popular, and who would have benefited from increased terms of protection. He argued, 'An author may write for fame, but he also writes to pay the butcher, the baker, and the candlestickmaker, and to provide, as far as possible, for his children'.[242] Arthur Lynch, physician, author and Irish nationalist, invoked the spirits of Wordsworth, Byron, Shelley and Keats,[243] while Augustine Birrell, the author of *Seven Lectures on Copyright Law*, appealed to the long-standing example of Milton as a harshly treated author.[244]

Those arguing against the increased term espoused the cause of the general public. Joynson-Hicks argued that the Bill was 'a still further approximation to perpetual copyright, contrary, as I believe, to the interests of the public and the public domain'.[245] He gave the example of the loss to school children of Tennyson's works due to copyright protection,[246] and expressed anxiety about the difficulty of tracing copyright owners after such a long period.[247] George Roberts, Labour MP for Norwich, feared that an extension of term would restrict the publication of cheap reprints, and that the legislation would 'retard the dissemination of that literature, and the extensions of popular books and culture among the working classes'.[248] Frederick Booth, a Liberal member, claimed that the Labour conferences were all against the proposal, asking 'How are the great bulk of our people to get on who have been denied the privilege of education in the battle of life and become useful citizens unless they have access to cheap literature?'[249] Another Liberal member, George Radford, an author as well as a solicitor, characterised the extension as an encroachment on the public domain that would deprive the public, and particularly the poor, of cheap literature.[250]

Buxton met these criticisms by pointing to the second part of the extension clause, which provided that 25 years after the death of an author, a work could be reproduced upon the giving of notice to the copyright owner, and payment of

[240] ibid 232.
[241] ibid 112.
[242] Parl Deb HC vol 23 col 2600 (7 April 1911).
[243] ibid col 2630.
[244] ibid col 2647.
[245] ibid col 2616.
[246] ibid col 2626.
[247] ibid col 2619.
[248] ibid col 2637.
[249] Parl Deb HC vol 28 col 1963 (28 July 1911).
[250] ibid col 1958.

copyright royalties at a rate of 10 per cent.[251] This clause was permissible under the Berlin Revision as the extension to life plus 50 years was not a mandatory provision. Buxton asserted that the object of this clause was to 'protect the public'.[252] There was some objection to this provision[253] but still more controversial was a second clause, also aimed at protecting the public in the situation where books were unduly withheld.[254] This clause provided that a complaint could be made to the Judicial Committee of the Privy Council at any time after the death of the author where the copyright owner had refused to reproduce the work 'and that by reason of the refusal the work is withheld from the public'.[255] In such circumstances the copyright owner could be ordered to grant a licence for the reproduction of the work.[256]

A number of the Members objected to this clause. Sir Gilbert Parker, an author of numerous books, criticised the clause allowing appeal to a third party as a fundamental mistake in the Bill which struck at the rights of private property,[257] and accused Buxton of bowing to pressure from the Dominions who would use the clause to obtain cheap books.[258] Sir Henry Craik, nephew of the literary scholar George Lillie Craik and himself a writer whose literary activities included editing a series for Macmillan, also opposed the clause, arguing that books were already produced as cheaply as was consistent with fair remuneration to the publisher.[259] The publishers and the Society of Authors were deeply opposed to such a provision,[260] with Thring referring to the position as 'preposterous'.[261]

When the Bill was read for a second time, the discussion in the Commons focused almost exclusively on the extension of term and lasted for five hours.[262] Although the House eventually agreed to the second reading, the debates on duration were re-opened when the particular clause relating to it was discussed.[263] However, when the House divided to vote, the term of 50 years was accepted by a majority of 153 to 35 against.[264] The compulsory licence provisions were accepted without a vote. As in 1842, the ideology of romantic authorship had been partially successful in increasing the term of protection, but a significant compromise had also been made.

Clause one of the Act brought two further changes, which occasioned some discussion and resistance. First, the Act was expressly stated to cover unpublished as

[251] Copyright Act 1911 (1 & 2 Geo 5 c 46) s 3.

[252] Parl Deb HC vol 28 col 1961 (28 July 1911).

[253] See the letter from H Rider Haggard in *The Times* (6 June 1911) 7c

[254] Parl Deb HC vol 23 col 2602 (7 April 1911).

[255] Copyright Act, 1911 s 4. In earlier versions, the appeal was to be made to the Comptroller-General of Patents Designs and Trade Marks: Bill 149, 30 March 1911 s 4; Bill 93, 22 March 1910.

[256] Copyright Act, 1911 s 4.

[257] Parl Deb HC vol 23 col 2611 (7 April 1911).

[258] ibid col 2609.

[259] ibid col 2642.

[260] Letter from CJ Longman, *The Times* (17 April 1911) 8f.

[261] Thring, 'The Copyright Bill, 1911' 904.

[262] Parl Deb HC vol 23 cols 2587–63 (7 April 1911).

[263] Parl Deb HC vol 28 cols 1953–66 (28 July 1911).

[264] ibid col 1966.

well as published works. Booth and Josiah Wedgwood, another Liberal member and descendant of the master potter, objected to this, believing this to be an unwarranted extension of the law. Booth considered it inimical to the cause of cheap literature, while Wedgwood argued it would prevent scientific discoveries from being made available to the public.[265] The Solicitor-General explained that under the current law unpublished works had perpetual protection and the amendment was negatived.[266] Booth and Wedgwood also objected to the use of the word 'original' and a similar objection had been made in the Standing Committee by Sir George Agnew, a Liberal MP, former art dealer and past president of the Printsellers' Association. Agnew objected that including the word would result in reproductions of artistic works by old masters not being protected on the basis they were not original designs.[267] In the House of Commons, the Solicitor-General informed the Members that 'Originality in the language of the law of copyright is not the same thing as novelty'. He explained:

> [B]efore a man can claim protection of the law of copyright that that which he claims to protect as his should really be his in the sense that his is the brain that has first of all applied itself to the subject matter and produced the composition, or, at any rate, that his is the brain which, thought it has not produced the composition, has expressed it in a new form. In one sense you may say a photograph of an existing picture is not original, but that is not the sense in which the word is understood by a lawyer in connection with copyright. I can assure the House that is not the way in which it would be understood by the courts hereafter. What would be understood by originality would be that there must be either in the form or in the composition itself some element of originality, a requirement that would not exclude derivative works from the ambit of the Bill.

This broad approach to originality, which followed that in *Walter v Lane*,[268] satisfied the objectors and the word remained in the Bill to become law.

Another important change was the abolition of formalities. The Gorell Committee had little time for registration, stating:

> The Committee fail to see what advantage to the public can be expected from systems of registration which are particularly onerous in the case of foreign authors, and if abolished for them, should be abolished for authors of our own country.[269]

The Imperial Conference agreed that formalities should be abolished. However, it did recognise a public interest purpose of registration in relation to proving innocence in the case of infringement, and recommended that provision be made to protect innocent infringers from being liable for damages.[270] The 1910 Bill contained a section that allowed for voluntary registration,[271] and provided that it

265 Parl Deb HC vol 28 cols 1911–14 (28 July 1911).
266 ibid col 1916.
267 *The Times* (28 April 1911) 7c.
268 *Walter v Lane* (1899) 2 Ch 749; [1900] AC 539. See above: ch 6 text to n385.
269 Gorell Committee 12.
270 Copyright Conference (1910) 7.
271 Copyright HC Bill 1910 [282] s 17.

would not be possible to claim innocence if registration had occurred.[272] This created inconsistency with the abolition of formalities[273] and the section as to registration was removed in the 1911 Bill, while the innocent infringer provision remained and was enacted into law.[274]

The abolition of formalities occasioned little discussion in Parliament. In the House of Lords, Lord Courtney of Penwith proposed an amendment which would have continued the current legal requirement that the owners of musical works who wished to reserve the performance right place such a notice on the title page.[275] He withdrew the amendment when it was pointed out that this would be inconsistent with the Berlin Revision, but continued to protest that such a clause would be in the interests of the public, owners and innocent infringers.[276] Outside Parliament, however, the abolition of formalities excited considerable opposition, which was expressed in a number of letters to *The Times*. Some of this opposition derived from the introduction of the principle that copyright would run from the death of the author, with Dundas White MP pointing out that the public were entitled to an easy means of ascertaining copyright's duration.[277] Opposition also came from Whorlow, the secretary to the Newspaper Society, who argued the abolition of compulsory registration would expose the press to copyright challenges,[278] and the Council of the Library Association, for whom registration gave the opportunity of creating an official and complete list of publications to the advantage of librarians and bibliographers.[279]

A related and more explosive issue was the question of library deposit. This re-emerged as a point of serious contention when a deputation, led by Lord Kenyon, met with Buxton to request the inclusion of the recently formed National Library of Wales as one of the deposit libraries.[280] This was followed by the submission of a Memorandum that argued that intellectual activity in Wales was being crippled by the want of an adequate public library and that the Welsh were being unfairly treated and were handicapped by the nation's poverty.[281] Perhaps more influential in getting the case heard was the threat by Edgar Jones MP in the House of Commons that the Welsh members would oppose the Bill if Wales were not included.[282]

Unsurprisingly, the Publishers' Association was in violent opposition to the proposal, and turned the full might of its lobbying machine onto Parliament's consideration of this issue. John Murray, T Fisher Unwin, Frederick Macmillan and

272 ibid s 6.

273 See objection in the House of Commons, Parl Deb HC vol 23 cols 2625–26 (7 April 1911).

274 Copyright Act 1911 (1& 2 Geo V c 46) s 8.

275 Parl Deb HL vol 10 cols 123–24 (14 November 1911).

276 ibid col 126.

277 *The Times* (26 April 1911) 8c.

278 *The Times* (29 May 1911) 12a; (3 November 1911) 10f.

279 *The Times* (1 November 1911) 14g. See also the letter from RA Peddie, *The Times* (19 August 1910) 5c.

280 RCB Partridge, *The History of the Legal Deposit of Books* (London, The Library Association, 1938) 107.

281 ibid.

282 Parl Deb HC vol 23 cols 2655–56 (7 April 1911).

William Heinemann fired off numerous letters to *The Times*, arguing that, while they did not begrudge the British Library its deposit copies, the copies delivered to the other libraries represented a heavy burden and an unjust tax.[283] When the Bill went before the House of Lords, the Publishers' Association circulated a memorandum, asking not only that no further burden be placed upon them, but also that some kind of guarantee be given that the other libraries would ask only for books of 'academic value'.[284] Once again, the publishers expressed their annoyance at the libraries for claiming every published book, despite assurances given as long ago as 1819 that they would ask only for those that were necessary.[285]

Faced with the possibility of losing its deposit privileges, the University of Cambridge addressed its own memorandum to the House of Lords, emphasising the 'national importance of preserving a record of the national literature' and claiming that one copy in the British Library was insufficient to achieve this aim.[286] Within the Lords, Earl Curzon, the Chancellor of Oxford University, championed the interests of the Bodleian Library. In the end, the compromise agreed in the House of Commons remained, namely, that the British Museum should receive a copy of every published book, while the libraries of Oxford, Cambridge, the Library of the Faculty of Advocates, Edinburgh and the Library of Trinity College Dublin would request books by written demand. The National Library of Wales was subject to further restrictions which would be set out in regulations by the Board of Trade.[287]

The abolition of registration while retaining the duty of library deposit finally severed any remaining links between the two elements of the old censorship regime. Deposit was now purely a matter of serving the needs of the public libraries. The 1911 Act also did away with two other formalities: the notice that was required to be printed on musical pieces, reserving the performing right; and the need to notify two justices of the peace in order to claim protection for lectures. There was some objection to including lectures fully within the scope of copyright law in the Standing Committee. Wedgwood objected on the basis it would adversely affect newspapers, but Sir Gilbert Parker countered that failing to protect lectures would deprive learned societies of the services of lecturers.[288] The matter would arise again in relation to copyright exceptions.[289]

Thus, the Act completed the assimilation of the performing right and the lecturing right to copyright by including within the owner's exclusive rights the right to 'perform, or in the case of a lecture, to deliver' the work.[290] However, the Act

[283] *The Times* (7 July 1911) 7g; (8 July 1911) 9c; (13 July 1911) 6a; (14 July 1911) 7b; (21 November 1911) 14e; (23 November 1911) 11b; (25 November 1911) 8g; (30 November 1911) 4g.

[284] *The Times* (13 November 1911) 3e.

[285] *The Times* (13 November 1911) 3e. See also Parl Deb HL vol 10 cols 178, 181 (15 November 1911).

[286] *The Times* (20 November 1911) 10c.

[287] Copyright Act 1911 s 15.

[288] *The Times* (28 April 1911) 7c.

[289] See below: n 390.

[290] Copyright Act 1911 s 1(2).

went still further, as it now protected works irrespective of their material form; indeed, they did not need to have any physical existence at all. Protection had moved definitively away from the 'book' to the more abstract and intangible 'work'. Works not published as 'books' were classed as 'unpublished works' and the Act resolved the long-stading ambiguities regarding unpublished works and the common law by bringing them squarely within the statutory regime.[291] The Act was, however, silent on the issues of immoral, seditious and libellous books, something that is somewhat surprising, as each of the Bills of 1898, 1899 and 1900 had explicitly provided that copyright would not exist in such works.

The 1911 Act also expanded the scope of copyright by expressly including architecture as a subject for copyright protection. Architects had been agitating for protection since the Royal Copyright Commission of 1878 and the addition of architecture to copyright works at the Berlin Revision Conference meant that Britain had to take these claims seriously. There was some resistance to this by Members of Parliament on public interest grounds. Joynson-Hicks characterised it as 'copyright run mad'[292] and Sir George Croyden Marks, an engineer and patent expert, feared it would 'harass every man's home and . . . prevent architecture from extending as it ought to extend from the adoption of features which are good'.[293] However, the House voted to include the clause and it was adopted.[294]

Copyright was also expressed in the Act to cover 'records, perforated rolls and other contrivances by means of which sounds may be mechanically reproduced'.[295] This was less contentious than the provisions regarding the rights of composers in relation to mechanical instruments, which are described in further detail below. Joynson-Hicks had actually supported this expansion, and won over some opposition by demonstrating that British industry was threatened by the import of thousands of records from Russia.[296] The Berlin Conference had also approved a French suggestion for the inclusion of cinematographic works to be protected as literary or artistic works.[297] This was uncontroversial before Parliament and the Act included them in the definition of 'dramatic work'.[298] The creation of 'neighbouring rights' was thus achieved without any real objection by those opposed to other expansions of copyright law.

One candidate for protection, however, was not so lucky. The question of granting a limited right in news, which had received favourable attention in 1900, was completely abandoned by 1911. The Berne Convention, as revised in Berlin, allowed the reproduction of articles which were not serial stories or tales in news-

291 ibid s 1(1)(b).
292 Parl Deb HC vol 28 col 2609 (28 July 1911).
293 ibid col 1936.
294 Copyright Act 1911 ss 1(1), 35. For the full story of architecture's inclusion within the scope of copyright legislation, see K Weatherall, 'Bringing Architecture into the Copyright System in the UK' (forthcoming).
295 Copyright Act 1911 s 19(1).
296 *Musical Opinion and Music Trade Review* (August 1911) 803; Parl Deb HC vol 29 col 2168 (17 August 1911).
297 Ricketson and Ginsburg, *International Copyright* 100.
298 Copyright Act 1911 ss 1, 35(1).

papers, unless they were expressly forbidden by the newspaper.[299] However, a further clause set out that the Convention's protection would not apply to 'news of the day or miscellaneous information which is simply of the nature of items of news',[300] thus leaving Member States to make their own provision for such matters.

The Gorell Committee recommended the adoption of the Berlin article and made no mention of the proposals of 10 years earlier to grant a limited right to protect news.[301] Nor was it mentioned at the Imperial Conference or by the Members of Parliament discussing the Bill. One explanation for this is that it may have appeared in the intervening period that news carried in telegrams could be adequately protected by the common law.[302] Another is the death of Moberly Bell who had been most distressed by the removal of the section protecting news in the earlier Bills; in fact, he died of a heart attack while writing letters on that very subject.[303] As the journalist John Cabburn wrote in letter to *The Times*, 'had he been spared he would have rendered good service in securing that the Copyright Bill came into law in a form that would secure a lasting and satisfactory settlement of the vexed question of copyright in news'.[304] Instead, a deputation of newspaper proprietors lobbied the Board of Trade for the inclusion of a section expressly setting out that copyright should *not* subsist in news,[305] but this was not included either. However, the 1911 Act did not enact the Berlin Revision's article on newspapers and, as a consequence, the protection given to British newspapers was greater than the protection required by the Berlin Revision. Newspapers were also granted the right to publish lectures, discussed in further detail below,[306] and a right to publish reports of political speeches.[307] Both of these sections embodied the argument made long before by Thomas Wakley that speeches were intended to be made available to the public rather than locked up by copyright law.[308]

Overall, the 1911 Act considerably expanded the rights of creators and owners. Moreover, by providing that these rights could be exercised in relation to different formats, whether it were translation, dramatisation, performance or film adaptation, it completed the law's move away from reliance on material form. The Act now referred to 'works' rather than 'books', 'paintings', 'sculptures' and so on. The publishers had already begun to divide up their products into distinct markets and the Act confirmed the legitimacy of such practices, as well as extending their possibilities by moving beyond the limits placed on them by the common law. However, in one field in particular there was considerable resistance to the

299 Ricketson and Ginsburg, *International Copyright* 98. Berne Convention, revised by Berlin Conference, art 9.
300 Berne Convention art 9.
301 Gorell Committee 20.
302 *The Exchange Telegraph Co v Howard* [1905–10] Mac CC 36; *The Times* (22 March 1906).
303 *The Times* (6 April 1911) 9g.
304 *The Times* (8 April 1911) 13b.
305 BT 209/619 (March 1911).
306 See below: n 390.
307 Copyright Act 1911 s 20.
308 See above: ch 4 nn 68 ff.

extension of copyright to cover transformative works—the treatment of music and its recording—and it is to this that the chapter now turns.

B. Music and Mechanical Instruments

The treatment of mechanical musical instruments was another issue that caused feelings to run high in debates over the new Act. Despite victory in the courts[309] the mechanical instrument industry was marshalling its forces against international threats to the business. Predicting that their ability to make and sell records of copyright music would be curtailed, members of the 'Talking Machine' industry engaged in heavy lobbying at the Berlin Convention.[310] The music publishing industry, on the other hand, claimed that failure to grant them protection against such reproductions would lead to their ruin.[311] As a compromise, the Convention expressly recognised the rights of copyright owners in relation to reproduction and public performance of works by mechanical musical instruments. However, it left the application of the article subject to such 'reservations and conditions' as the domestic legislation of the Union member countries should apply.[312] *The Times* appeared somewhat bemused by the time spent discussing the problem at Berlin. It reported that:

> The gramophone and cinematograph articles, important as they are to some people, will chiefly strike the reader as an amusing instance of the way in which science now invades and pervades all. Some of us may by this time be a little tired of these marvels—for marvels of the first rank they undoubtedly are—but none the less they have such a vogue, and it is so likely to continue, that it takes a whole International Convention to deal with the wrongs which they may, if left alone, inflict upon owners of property.[313]

The matter was discussed in considerable detail before the Gorell Committee. Several representatives of the music publishing industry, as well as composers, advocated granting musical copyright owners the ability to control the use of their works by the manufacturers of musical instruments, and the right to receive royalties from such sales. Most of the witnesses were concerned with being able to participate in the large profits being realised by the makers of phonographic records and other aspects of the mechanical instrument industry. The composer William Wallace, however, seemed more concerned with controlling the integrity of his works, claiming that the works taken for mechanical production were often 'mangled and tortured'.[314]

309 *Newmark v National Phonograph Co (Ltd) and Edison Manufacturing Co (Ltd)* (1907) 23 TLR 439 (for details, see above: ch 5).

310 See BT 209/618 for lobbying of the Board of Trade by the Gramophone Company in October 1907.

311 Ricketson and Ginsburg, *International Copyright*, vol 1, p 99.

312 ibid.

313 *The Times* (14 November 1908) 13d.

314 Gorell Committee Evidence 206.

Representatives from the mechanical instrument industry appeared before the Committee in even greater numbers than did music publishers and composers. They requested that some consideration be shown towards an industry which had invested considerable amounts of money based upon the judicial decisions holding that it was no infringement to reproduce music on records or perforated rolls.[315] Consequently, they requested that a compulsory licence be created, which would allow them to continue manufacturing such items, with the amount payable under the licence to be fixed by law,[316] and that any changes made should not have retrospective application.[317] The mechanical instrument manufacturer's claim for a compulsory licence was based on a clause of the 1909 Copyright Act of the United States which provided that, where the owner of a musical copyright work had used or permitted the use of the work on a mechanical instrument, any other person might make similar use of the work on payment of a royalty of two cents for each 'part' manufactured.[318]

While most of the mechanical instrument makers pleaded that granting composers and publishers rights in the records and rolls would ruin their businesses, others linked their own interests to more general social concerns. Sir Herbert Marshall, proprietor of several companies that manufactured player pianos, argued that the result could be to create a serious monopoly which would be against the interests of the community, and claimed that his business created labour for the people.[319] JE Hough[320] claimed that records performed an important function in bringing music to homes of the lower classes, and argued that their manufacturers should pay no royalty at all to composers.[321]

The Committee, however, was more persuaded by the claims of authorship, concluding that

> there can be no doubt but that it is right in principle that the authors of works capable of adaptation to mechanical instruments should have the exclusive right of authorising the adaptation of their works to such instruments—that it is in reality part of the literary property which they have in the product of their own brains.[322]

[315] In 1909, *Boosey v Whight* was followed in another case involving perforated rolls: *Mabe v Connor* [1909] 1 KB 515. The following year, Joyce J dismissed the claim of the composer Lionel Monckton to prevent his works being reproduced as gramophone records: *Monckton v The Gramophone Company (Limited)*, *The Times* (6 December 1910) 3c; (7 December 1910) 3c. The decision was upheld by the Court of Appeal: (1912) 28 TLR 205.

[316] See esp, Gorell Committee Evidence 227, 235.

[317] ibid 235, 237.

[318] ibid 23–24. This clause had been achieved as the result of a deal between composers, publishers and manufacturers of piano rolls and talking machines: see J Litman, 'Copyright, Legislation and Technological Change' (1989) 68 *Oregon Law Review* 275, 286–88.

[319] Gorell Committee Evidence 99, 233.

[320] Hough was the director of a company which was the relic of the Edison Bell Phonographic Company, whose assets Hough had purchased, and which produced records, phonographs and graphophones.

[321] Gorell Committee Evidence 232.

[322] Gorell Committee 24.

With one dissent, the Committee rejected the imposition of compulsory licences, stating that freedom of contract was the preferred approach in relation to growing industries.[323] Nonetheless, a majority also considered that any manufacturer who had already adapted a work for a mechanical instrument might continue to do so in respect of that work.[324]

Notwithstanding these recommendations, the second Bill of 1911 showed more sympathy to the plight of mechanical instrument manufacturers. It provided that the right to make a record, perforated roll or other mechanical contrivance was one of the exclusive rights of the copyright owner[325] but once the copyright owner had given consent to, or had acquiesced in, the making of a mechanical contrivance, any other person could make such a contrivance, upon giving notice to the owner and payment of a royalty fixed by the legislation.[326] It also provided that the consent or acquiescence did not authorise any alterations in the work.[327] With respect to works which had already been published prior to the Act, consent was still required but the royalty to be paid was lower and the provision as to making alterations did not apply.[328]

The music publishers responded by petitioning Winston Churchill at the Board of Trade. William Boosey was appalled by Churchill's response, which reasoned that pianola discs were an infringement because they could be read by experts, but gramophone discs could not be read, and therefore were not infringements.[329] In the House of Commons, debate centred on the retroactive operation of the Bill's provisions. Mr Cassel spoke on behalf of the manufacturers who had petitioned him[330] and proposed that the clause be amended to provide that no copyright would subsist at all in works made prior to the Act.[331] His amendment was seconded by Dundas White, who characterised the manufacturers as mere members of the public being denied justice. He stated, 'I think the public ought not to be excluded from doing what they can do now as regards existing works',[332] and added, 'We wish to safeguard the rights of the public to existing works'.[333]

Heavy lobbying also took place in the letters pages of *The Times*. Here the mechanical musical instrument makers' arguments did not solely rely on the legal decisions in their favour, but went further, taking a strictly positivist legal view. As James Van Allen Shields, of the Columbia Phonograph Company, argued, 'The authorities say that "copyright can only exist by virtue of some statute." No statute

[323] ibid 25. The dissenter, unsurprisingly, was Trevor Williams, founder of the Gramophone Company.

[324] ibid.

[325] Copyright HC Bill 1911 [296] s 1(2)(c).

[326] ibid s 19.

[327] ibid s 19(2)(i).

[328] ibid s 19(7).

[329] W Boosey, *Fifty Years of Music* (London, Ernest Benn Limited, 1931) 148.

[330] Parl Deb HC vol 29 cols 2159–63 (17 August 1911).

[331] ibid col 2158.

[332] ibid col 2163.

[333] ibid col 2164.

at present embraces mechanical playing devices within its provisions'.[334] Drummond Robertson made a similar point, arguing that

> as a consequence of this state of the law, all works for the purpose of mechanical reproduction have been in public domain and belong to the public just as freely as do copyright works generally as soon as the term of protection prescribed by statute has expired.[335]

The second strand of the mechanical musical instrument makers' argument was that making records did not amount to making 'copies', which was the same approach that the courts had taken.[336] As Drummond Robertson further put it, a record is not a copy but

> a special rendering of the work by a performer . . . The record is illegible and useless until it is made audible by mechanical means. It consists in fact of a combination of the author's work, the performer's talent, and the mechanician's skill, and we therefore contend that the author plays a limited part, and often a very limited part, in the production of the finished record, and that he is not entitled to claim the record as his sole creation, and to enjoy without due regard to the interests of his fellow-workers the exclusive benefit of mechanical reproduction.[337]

The argument that the record was not a copy because it was the product of new labour employed the same reasoning as the 'new work' principle. The arguments of the composers and publishers, on the other hand, employed the language of property, theft and unfair competition, thereby casting morally deserving composers as the victims of the piece. The composer William Wallace claimed in *The Times* that the record-making industry had 'appropriated the raw material without paying for it',[338] while George Bernard Shaw wrote that the gramophone makers had been operating on 'the assumption that musical material could be stolen with impunity'.[339] In his memoir, William Boosey, argued that 'The composer should have the absolute right to deal with his mechanical rights as he does with his printing rights'.[340] In the House of Commons, TP O'Connor, long-time ally of the music publishers,[341] argued that the clause 'will give the poor authors and composers a little earlier opportunity of getting their rights, which the Bill, after all, gives with a very niggardly hand'.[342] Others were not to be fooled by such arguments, at least on the part of publishers. John Ward MP noted that the reward could not be called beggarly or miserly, but was rather a generous grant of a new right. Furthermore, he added:

[334] *The Times* (17 August 1910) 10e. See also the letter from Edward Sullivan, *The Times* (27 April 1911) 7f.

[335] *The Times* (2 May 1911) 10b. See also *The Times* (9 May 1911) 4d.

[336] See *Mabe v Connor* [1909] KB 515, following *Boosey v Whight* [1900] 1 Ch 122.

[337] *The Times* (2 May 1911) 10b.

[338] *The Times* (28 April 1911) 7c.

[339] *The Times* (4 May 1911) 7f.

[340] Boosey, *Fifty Years of Music* 149.

[341] See above: section II.

[342] Parl Deb HC vol 29, col 2168 (17 August 1911).

> I do not suppose the composer will get one-thousandth part of the gift we are making. It is people who by some means—some great musical publisher gets hold of the copyright in a particular music to which reference has been made—it is really that vested interest we are creating on this occasion.[343]

In the end, the clause drafted in the 1911 Bill was adopted, with the further compromise offered to manufacturers of mechanical instruments of the lapse of another two years before they would be required to pay royalties on records they had already manufactured.[344]

C. Infringement and Exceptions

Clause two of the 1911 Act introduced yet another dramatic change: for the first time the law of infringement was defined in legislation. The first important provision, however, came in clause 1, which provided that the owner's exclusive right would cover acts done to the whole of the work or to a 'substantial part thereof'.[345] Following the development of the case law, this principle was uncontroversial. However, the Berlin Revisions required some more significant adjustments to the law of infringement. The first change was to provide that authors should have the exclusive right to translate their works during the term of copyright protection.[346] By this time, granting the translation right to the copyright owner was considerably less controversial than it had previously been. The Gorell Committee recommended the adoption of the clause without discussion, and the definition of copyright in the 1910 Bill and early drafts of the 1911 Bill included the right to reproduce a work in any material form and in any language whatsoever.[347] A contributor to the *Musical Opinion and Music Trade Review* complained that the new Bill of 1911 gave the author 'a sort of dog in the manger right'[348] that would last after his death, and calling it 'unthinkable'[349] that a British statesman should prevent the public from having translations. However, this was a rare voice of dissent. The House of Lords altered the drafting of the translation provision,[350] but the right remained in the Bill and ultimately became law.[351]

Other, more contentious, changes to the permissible uses of works were also required. The 1908 Berlin Revision retained the Berne Convention article allow-

[343] ibid col 2171.
[344] Copyright Act 1911 s 19(7)(b).
[345] ibid s 1(2).
[346] Berne Convention, revised by Berlin Conference, art 8.
[347] Copyright HC Bill 1910 [282] s 1(2); Copyright HC Bill 1911 [149] s 1(2); Copyright HC Bill 1911 (as amended in Committee) [296] s 1(2).
[348] *Musical Opinion and Music Trade Review* (June 1911) 655.
[349] ibid 656.
[350] Parl Deb HL vol 10 col 114 (14 November 1911).
[351] Imperial Copyright Act 1911 s 1(2)(a).

ing extracts for educational purposes and chrestomathies,[352] as well as a modified version of Berne article 10 (now article 12) which provided:

> The following shall be specially included among the unlawful reproductions to which the present Convention applies:—Unauthorized indirect appropriations of a literary or artistic work, such as adaptations, musical arrangements, transformations of a novel, tale, or piece of poetry into a dramatic piece, and vice versa, etc, when they are only the reproduction of that work, in the same form or in another form, without essential alterations, additions, or abridgments, and do not present the character of a new original work.[353]

The first inconsistency between this article and British law was with respect to dramatisations. The extended discussions regarding dramatisation in the 1890s had settled the thinking on this matter in favour of including dramatisation as a right of the copyright owner. Some witnesses appeared before the Gorell Committee to speak in favour of adopting the article,[354] and it was included in the 1911 Act with little further fuss.

A more difficult question arose in relation to the exception expressed in favour of works which were both 'indirect appropriations' as well as 'new original works'. As noted above, the Bills of the 1890s had ignored this provision, including abridgments in the scope of the authors' rights.[355] The Gorell Committee gave it more consideration. Its Report stated: 'According to British law, the presence of additions, however ingenious and novel, will not remove the taint of piracy, if any substantial feature or part of the original work has been copied'.[356] This was the view of copyright law for which Scrutton, who was one of the members of the Committee, had expressed a preference in his 1883 treatise.[357] The Report went on to claim that adoption of that part of the article would involve the abolition of a 'well settled' rule, would raise questions of 'great nicety' and 'be the source of copious litigation'.[358] However, there was some suggestion that the Committee realised that this might overstate the clarity of British law on the question, because the Report's author also added 'But see the cases of *Wilkins v Aikin* . . . and *Spiers v Brown*'.[359] In the end, the Committee resolved that they were not required to follow that part of the article.[360]

Ironically, in light of the fact that the Convention left open the possibility of retaining or reinvigorating the 'new work' principle, the Committee's discussion sounded its death knell in British law. An indication of the principle's demise is the fact that the drafters of the 1911 Act did not see the need to include abridgments

352 Art 8 in the Berne Convention, revised by Paris Conference 1896, but art 10 following the Berlin Revisions. The Berne version discussed above: text to n 59.
353 Berne Convention, revised by the Berlin Conference, art 12.
354 Gorell Committee Evidence 187.
355 See above: text to nn 41 ff.
356 Gorell Committee 22.
357 See quotation at ch 6, n 453.
358 Gorell Committee 22.
359 ibid.
360 ibid.

specifically as an exclusive right of the copyright owner, unlike those drafting the Bills of the 1890s. With the new-work principle discredited, there was no longer any need for such a section, as abridgments would fall to be treated as any other infringement, and would be judged on the amount and quality of the taking, rather than the merits of the work thereby produced.

Clause one, then, pushed back the boundaries of infringement by drawing into the owner's rights translations, performances, dramatisations and mechanical reproduction. As GH Thring pointed out, in his article commenting on the Act, section one 'in all cases tends to widen the author's control of his possessions'.[361] Having widened the scope of the author's rights, the next task was to define what would now amount to infringement, thereby following the subtle shift in approach initiated by the courts.

The most contentious matter was whether private uses of works should be allowed. The 1910 Bill contained a clause similar to that contained in the 1900 Bill in respect of exceptions to infringement:

> [C]opyright shall not be infringed by making for private use an abridgment or translation of a literary or dramatic work, or an adaptation, transposition, arrangement or setting of a musical work, or studies or sketches from an artistic work, or by making fair extracts from or otherwise fairly dealing with the contents of any such work for the purposes of criticism or review.[362]

The music publishers were vehemently opposed to this clause. Henry Reginald Clayton called it 'a most dangerous innovation' which was likely to undermine all copyright property, especially music.[363] It threatened them most because sheet music sellers relied on selling large numbers of songs of only a few sheets each. Single sheets were much easier to copy than entire books and could be passed around between groups of friends, which would severely affect the music trade. Another important market was church choirs and musical societies, which purchased large numbers of the same song and whose activities were more likely to be characterised as private than commercial.

The Board of Trade consulted the Copyright Association, the Publishers' Association, the Music Publishers' Association and the Society of Authors on the 1910 draft. All of these groups were opposed to the private use exception.[364] The reference to 'private use' was accordingly removed in the 1911 Bill, and the clause was altered to provide that

> the following acts shall not constitute an infringement of copyright:–
>
>> Any fair dealing with any work for the purposes of private study, research, criticism, or review.[365]

[361] GH Thring, 'Advantages and Defects of the Copyright Act, 1911' (1912) 91 *Fortnightly Review* 1132, 1135.

[362] Copyright HC Bill (1910) [282] s 1(2)(i).

[363] Memorandum on 1910 Bill, BT 209/477.

[364] BT 209/477.

[365] Copyright HC Bill (1911) [149] s 2(1)(i).

Thus, private study and research were added to the list of permissible uses, and private abridgments, translations and adaptations removed.

Some attempts were made to expand the clause in Committee. The words 'or newspaper summary' were added and accepted after some discussion.[366] Joynson-Hicks suggested inserting the words 'or any reasonable quotation, provided that the work deals with some subject of public importance and the source from which it is taken is acknowledged, unless such quotation is prohibited by notice and published at the head of the work'.[367] Birrell objected that quotation was already covered by the clause, as you could not review without quoting. Hubert Carr-Gomm, a Liberal Member, proposed: 'Provided that the whole, or even a material part thereof, shall not be reproduced in the review without the author's consent'.[368] George Toulmin, another Liberal Member and a newspaper proprietor, proposed adding: 'and that such work is not made by the author for the purpose of publication in competition with the original work'.[369] Toulmin's objective was to allow the newspapers to retain their practice of excerpting articles from *The Times*, the *Telegraph* and the *Fortnightly Review*.[370] These proposed amendments were not adopted.

There is little direct evidence of the reasoning of the Board of Trade's draftsmen in choosing the examples of fair dealing exceptions that they did, nor as to why they altered the phrase from 'making fair extracts or otherwise fairly dealing with' to 'any fair dealing with'. Certainly, the 1911 Act seemed to restrict more closely and explicitly the permissible uses to the five purposes set out. However, as Burrell has argued, there is considerable evidence that the 1911 Act was not intended to mark a break from the past, nor to usher in a new and more restrictive approach to protecting copyright than had previously existed.[371]

In Parliament, Viscount Haldane, who had introduced the Bill into the House of Lords, stated:

> the principle of fair dealing is a principle which the Courts have applied with greatest care . . . All that is done here is to make a plain declaration of what the law is and to put all copyright works under the same wording.[372]

An internal, confidential memorandum from the Board of Trade stated that the modes of 'fairly dealing' set out in the 1910 Bill had been criticised as too limited and that the 1911 Bill contained corresponding provisions 'in a shorthand and amended form which substantially reproduces the existing law'.[373] A later version

[366] *The Times* (3 May 1911) 6b.

[367] Report from Standing Committee A on the Copyright Bill with the proceedings of the committee (1911) 223, 5.

[368] ibid 6.

[369] ibid 6.

[370] *The Times* (3 May 1911) 6c.

[371] R Burrell and A Coleman, *Copyright Exceptions: The Digital Impact* (Cambridge, Cambridge University Press, 2005) 258.

[372] Parl Deb HL vol 10 col 117 (14 November 1911).

[373] BT 209/474.

of the same document omits this statement, but another internal document comparing the 1911 Bill with the current law, noted that the new section and the current law were 'substantially [the] same'.[374] These two documents establish that the intention of the Board of Trade when drafting the Bill was to enact the current state of the law regarding infringement. The use of the word 'shorthand' in the memorandum suggests that it was not considered that the four uses set out in the Bill (later to be joined by the fifth, newspaper summary) were to be strictly interpreted, but were intended to be understood synecdochically as standing in for a variety of permissible uses.

This is also the way that the Act was interpreted by contemporary commentators. JM Easton, in the 1915 edition of Copinger's work on copyright, considered:

> It is not very clear why the provision authorising fair dealing with any work for the purposes above mentioned should have been expressly inserted in the Act, for fair dealing for other purposes has always been . . . permitted and, presumably, it was not intended to cut down the rights of fair user previously enjoyed under the old law.[375]

EJ Macgillivray, in his commentary on the 1911 Act, had an explanation:

> The protection granted under the general definition of copyright in sect 1 is so absolutely prohibitive of any use in the nature of a reproduction of the whole or any part of the author's work, that it is necessary to introduce the exceptions specified in sub-section (i). It would hardly have been safe to have left it entirely to the Court to say what exceptions should or should not be admitted upon the analogy of the case law decided under the Copyright Act, 1842.[376]

However, he also considered that the old law could be used to interpret the section.[377] Interestingly, Macgillivray also referred to the permitted uses as 'being in the public domain'.[378] Although the expression 'public domain' had been in currency for some time as describing the status of works in which the copyright had expired, its application in the context of fair dealing reveals that Macgillivray considered that the permitted uses had a public function. Nevertheless, according to Macgillivray, that public interest was limited in favour of commercial considerations, as he added, 'Probably, the limits of fair dealing are exceeded whenever the user is such that it must naturally compete with and injure the sale of the original work'.[379] GH Thring was less sanguine, noting that 'the words 'fair dealing' are likely to lead to considerable litigation'.[380]

The drafting of the fair dealing exceptions in the 1911 Act demonstrates yet again the way that groups with vested interests sought to shape the Act in a way that would favour them. The provisions that were introduced may have appeared more

374 ibid.

375 JM Easton (ed), *The Law of Copyright by WA Copinger*, 5th edn (London, Stevens & Haynes, 1915) 144.

376 EJ Macgillivray, *The Copyright Act, 1911, Annotated* (London, Stevens & Sons, Ltd, 1912) 27.

377 ibid 28.

378 ibid 27.

379 ibid.

380 Thring, 'Advantages and Defects' 1136.

restrictive than the contemporary common law, looking at them with hindsight, and bearing in mind the way that they were developed subsequently.[381] However, it seems that the legislators had no intention of restricting the existing law; they were merely unsure as to how to embody it in the legislation. The drafters of the fair-dealing provisions attempted to replicate the common law by making use of the two categories that had developed in the case law, and adding three other categories that dealt with private use and news reporting in ways acceptable to those with vested interests. This reliance on categories followed the pattern established by the courts in their findings on infringement. It had the advantage of giving the law the appearance of simplicity, certainty and clarity. The disadvantages were that the flexibility of the common law was lost and the ability of other people to deal with copyright works was forced into specific categories of acceptable purposes, resulting in an expansion of the rights of copyright owners.

In addition to the fair dealing clause, the first of the non-infringing acts in section two, five further categories of acts that would not amount to infringement were also added. Subsection (ii) related to artistic works, and provided that it would not be an infringement for an artist, who was not a work's owner, to use moulds, sketches etc made for the purpose of the work, as long as he did not reproduce the 'main design' of the work.[382] This responded to concerns that had been aired before the 1878 Commission, and enacted its recommendation on the subject.[383] The third non-infringing act was making paintings, drawings, engravings or photographs of works of sculpture or artistic craftsmanship in public places, or of architectural works.[384] This provision occasioned some discussion in the House of Lords, when the Earl of Malmesbury expressed the concerns of the Imperial Arts League regarding it. The League claimed that this clause would deprive them of 'a considerable proportion of their means of livelihood', and this would be particularly disadvantageous to sculptors.[385] Viscount Haldane, who had charge of the Bill in the Lords, responded by pointing out that the Bill actually improved the position of artists, because under the current law anyone could make a sketch of a statue, while the Bill limited this to public places—a limitation he claimed to be in the 'public interest'.[386]

The fourth specific exception related to the use of extracts in collections of works for use in schools. A similar exception had been proposed to the Select Committee in 1900, but rejected. The clause was first proposed by Wedgwood in Committee. Birrell objected to it, on the basis that publishers already had all the works that had fallen out of copyright at their disposal, and that most living authors would have no objection to giving permission to make extracts if they were 'decently asked'. He observed that surely an author was 'entitled to have a cut out

381 See Burrell and Coleman, *Copyright Exceptions* 259–63.
382 Copyright Act 1911 s 2(1)(ii).
383 Royal Copyright Commission (1878) xxi.
384 Copyright Act 1911 s 2(1)(iii).
385 Parl Deb HL vol 10 col 118 (14 November 1911).
386 ibid col 120.

of his own mutton?'[387] In the House of Commons, Radford also opposed the clause on the grounds that it made an exception to the Bill's purpose of securing copyright to authors based on 'sentimental appeal'.[388] However, after much discussion over its drafting, the following clause was adopted:

> The publication in a collection, mainly composed of non-copyright matter, bona fide intended for the use of schools, and so described in the title and in any advertisements issued by the publisher, of short passages from literary works not themselves published for the use of schools in which copyright subsists: Provided that not more than two of such passages from works by the same authors are published by the same publisher within five years, and that the source from which such passages are taken is acknowledged.[389]

The final two categories of non-infringing act operated to limit the new rights in respect of lectures and performances. By subsection (v) publication of lectures delivered in public in newspapers was permitted unless expressly prohibited by notice.[390] Toulmin, speaking in the Standing Committee on behalf of the Newspaper Society, had advocated giving rights to print lectures to newspapers and Martin, another Committee member, had proposed that such rights should apply not just to newspapers but to everyone. He considered it was a matter of public interest and no harm to the lecturer. Sir Henry Craik countered that such an approach would have destroyed the livelihood of such great men as Thackeray, Carlyle and Dickens; and Edgar Jones expressed surprise that Labour Members should take the part of wealthy newspaper owners over that of the poor lecturer.[391]

Subsection (vi) allowed the reading or recitation in public of a reasonable extract of a permitted work.[392] This provision had been proposed by Joynson-Hicks[393] and illustrates the shift in the law's approach. Prior to 1911, the law did not prohibit any reading or recitation on the basis it did not amount to a 'performance'.[394] Now, this was reduced to the status of an 'exception' and limited to a reasonable amount. The wording of each of these categories had been the subject of amendment and discussion in the Standing Committee, and other additional clauses were also been proposed. One such suggestion, which was reiterated by Joynson-Hicks in the House of Commons, was an exception which would allow the publication of letters in cases where such publication was in the public interest, or necessary to preserve or establish the rights or reputation of the recipient or his family.[395] However, Sir John Simon, the Solicitor-General, persuaded him to withdraw the amendment on the basis it was unnecessary.

[387] *The Times* (10 May 1911) 5f.

[388] Parl Deb HC vol 28 cols 1949–50 (28 July 1911).

[389] Copyright Act 1911 s 2(1)(iv). After the passing of the Act, the Publishers' Association was quick to introduce guidelines, following consultation with the Society of Authors, that required notice to be given to the copyright owner and setting out suggested lengths that would be considered to be 'short passages'. Easton, *Law of Copyright* 143 n.

[390] Imperial Copyright Act 1911 s 2(1)(v).

[391] *The Times* (5 May 1911) 4e.

[392] Imperial Copyright Act 1911 s 2(1)(vi).

[393] *The Times* (5 May 1911) 4e.

[394] See above: ch 5, text to n 152.

[395] Parl Deb HC vol 28 col 1951 (28 July 1911).

The legislative enactment of certain exceptions to copyright cannot be seen as the recognition by Parliament of the claims or interests of the public in general. It seems that Parliament was prepared to recognise some specific claims by particular users of copyright, if they could fit their demands into 'public interest' rhetoric, as in the case of educational publishers. The other sections, however, dealt with quite different claims. Subsection (ii) mediated between the claims of artists and owners and subsection (iii) reconciled the competing claims of different kinds of artist. Subsection (v) could be seen as recognising the interest of the public in obtaining information delivered in lectures, but also worked to the benefit of newspaper owners, and subsection (vi) turned something that had previously fallen outside the scope of the law into a mere 'exception' to it.

It is not surprising that authors and copyright owners were generally pleased with the outcome. However, one aspect of the infringement clause which had occasioned no discussion in Parliament but was not welcomed by the Society of Authors, was the inclusion of the requirement that to commit a secondary infringement, the infringer had to have knowledge of that fact.[396] In his commentary on the Act, GH Thring wrote that this was 'a step of retrogression, not of progression. It will give security to the careless editor and publisher, the manager of a theatre, the purloiner of artistic values . . . It is the one serious fault in an Act which should otherwise receive commendation'.[397]

D. Overview of the 1911 Act

Eventually the Bill was passed by both Houses and received royal assent on 16 December 1911.[398] The Society of Authors held a dinner to celebrate the passing of the 1911 Copyright Act, at which Joseph Comyns Carr[399] stated: 'The present Act is the largest instalment of justice that has even been conferred on literature by the Parliament of England'.[400] In many ways, the 1911 Act achieved the goal of reform towards which authors, publishers and others had been striving since the Royal Copyright Commission delivered its report in 1878. Duration of copyright was extended to last for the life of the author and a generous period thereafter, and all the works which had been given copyright, or copyright-like, protection were brought together within a single statute. However, even this latter, fundamental element of the new Act was contested until the end. The publishers remained unconvinced that artistic, literary and musical copyright could happily be married into a single piece of legislation, with both John Murray

396 Imperial Copyright Act 1911 s 2.

397 Thring, 'Advantages and Defects' 1137

398 Parl Deb HC vol 32 col 2846 (16 December 1911).

399 Joseph Comyns Carr's interests cut right across the breadth of copyright—he was a journalist, director of the Grosvenor Gallery, friend of the Pre-Raphaelites, dramatist and theatre manager.

400 Thring, 'Advantages and Defects' 1142.

and Heinemann expressing scepticism in the early months of 1911.[401] Even Morris Colles, a member of the Society of Authors, was unconvinced, noting in 1909 that 'Uniformity, whether international or domestic, can be attempted at a cost which is wholly disproportionate to any practical advantages likely to result. The point illustrates the inconvenience of attempting to sweep so many categories of property into the copyright net'.[402]

Notwithstanding these objections, by the end of the first decade of the twentieth century, copyright law was at last accepted by the Government to be a matter of sufficient public importance as to call for legislative reform. The various groups of authors and publishers which had formed towards the end of the previous century agreed. The nature of this highly significant public interest, however, was not a simple and straightforward matter. Indeed, there were many different public interests operating in different spheres, not all of which were pushing reform in the same direction. One point of intersection was national and international interests. While the Berne Convention was essentially an instrument for codifying the norms of authorship, and thus not directly concerned with the claims of the public, being involved in the Convention was a matter of public interest for the United Kingdom. While there was an international interest involved in being a party to such a significant Convention there were also national gains flowing from beneficial trade outcomes, as well as the advantages of codifying and simplifying the domestic law of copyright.

In the course of various discussions and debates over the form that the Act should take public interest considerations appeared in a variety of guises. One serious source of opposition to the Act came from Labour and Liberal Members opposed to copyright on an ideological basis. In particular, the Liberal Members Booth, Leach and Wedgwood contested many sections on the basis that they would harm the poorer members of society by maintaining and encouraging high prices of books and music. Many of their objections betrayed fundamental misconceptions of copyright law, but they subjected almost every section of the Act to scrutiny. Those aligned to the interests of authors or copyright owners greatly resented their intrusions. GH Thring complained that

> [t]he chief opposition came from the Labour members on the Committee. It seems strange that the very men who are recognized as such strong fighters for the rights of those who live by manual labour, should not have been equally capable of recognising an equal right in the producer of intellectual property.[403]

An editorial comment in *The Times* further observed that the Labour Members

> are scrutinizing every line of the Bill to see whether any provision in it may deprive some poor child of the opportunity of acquiring knowledge, oblivious of the consideration that the poor author is as worthy of his hire as the artisan.[404]

401 See the comment by Murray in the *Publishers' Circular* (11 February 1911) 169 and the report of Heinemann's address to the Publishers' Association in the *The Times* (31 March 1911) 7c.

402 Colles, 'Copyright at Home and Abroad' 1061.

403 Thring, 'Advantages and Defects' 1134.

404 *The Times* (13 May 1911) 9g.

Macgillivray was also critical of Labour's involvement:

> It may be said that the Government has made too many concessions, both to the socialistic demands of the Labour Party, who believe that there should be no copyright, and to the demands of the makers of mechanical instruments, who appealed to the Government to save a great industry from possible bankruptcy. It was obvious, however, after the first few days in Committee, that it had become a question of passing the bill with these concessions or abandoning it altogether. The Government were right in choosing the former course.[405]

These comments illustrate some of the many different ways that 'the public' was conceptualised in the copyright reform debates. While for one group it could be a community of learning individuals or a disadvantaged segment of the community seeking to improve itself, for another it was a group of authors or creators, benefiting from greater state protection and international norms. In other contexts, the public might be the nation state with an interest in the balance of trade, or indeed the consumer as a purchaser of gramophone records. It might be the audience at an educational lecture, or those unable to attend in person but hoping to read the lecture in a newspaper; it might equally be the group of those seeking to give lectures, or societies seeking to entice lecturers to appear before it.

Believing their rightful claims had been sacrificed to political expediency, the authors who had lobbied so long and so hard for the Act were not entirely satisfied with it. Although Comyns Carr had called it 'the largest instalment of justice' to authors, he added 'I have spoken of this Bill as an instalment, because I am not here to admit that even the great concessions we have obtained exhaust the legitimate demands and aspirations of the authors of this country'.[406] However, the 1911 Act was far from being a carefully crafted balance of competing demands and interests. In fact, the process of expanding the rights of authors and owners, while recognising certain public interest concerns, had caused a significant shift in the shape of copyright law; a shift that the players involved did not, indeed probably could not, see. Their focus was on the detail, the micro-narrative of copyright law. Whilst they did recognise that copyright had expanded, they could not have anticipated the dramatic change that resulted from freeing copyright from its physical form in the 'book', namely, that copyright could be traced through new formats and more markets in its conception as a 'work' that at times did not even require material fixation.

Another shift in the scope of copyright came from the Act's provisions regarding infringement. Taking a step back from the competing interests and rhetoric, it becomes apparent that by extending the rights of copyright owners to cover all uses of works, and setting out the acts that would not amount to infringement as specific categories of permissible behaviour, the question asked of infringement was no longer 'what is protected?' but 'what is allowed?' Prior to the Act, copyright had been a territory of shifting and uncertain boundaries. To invert Jane

[405] Macgillivray, *Copyright Act, 1911* vi.
[406] *The Author* (1 January 1911) 106.

Ginsburg's aquatic metaphor,[407] in 1911 the copyright tide came up and left islands of permissible uses jutting out of a sea of owners' rights. Arguments relying on 'public interest' had failed to hold back the waves except when it could be reduced to specific examples. As a general concept, then, public interest was less persuasive than the rhetoric of authorship, particularly in light of the fact that the claims of authorship could themselves be reconfigured in public interest terms. Thus, it is important that the power of authorship is not overstated either; the claims of authors had failed to provide the necessary impetus for copyright reform for over three decades, and nor had they had it all their own way when reform finally arrived. It was only when Britain was compelled by international pressure to take action that reform was finally brought about. Copyright law was thus the product of concerns regarding trade, colonial and international relations, authorship and the public interest. The 1911 Act expressed all of these impulses without resolving them into a comprehensive or unified whole. Augustine Birrell predicted this outcome in the course of debate when he observed, 'Copyright is necessarily a subject which gives rise to a very wide field of discussion. In some of its aspects it goes down deep into human affairs and raises questions of a subtle character which mankind will ever dispute'.[408]

[407] J Ginsburg, '"Une Chose Publique"? The Author's Domain and the Public Domain in Early British, French and US Copyright Law' [2006] *Cambridge Law Journal* 636, 642 (see above: ch 1, quotation cued to n 188).

[408] Parl Deb HC vol 23 col 2644 (7 April 1911).

8

Conclusion

WRITING IN 1899, Augustine Birrell lamented that '[t]he question of copyright has, in these latter days, with so many other things, descended into the market-place, and joined the wrangle of contending interests and rival greedinesses'.[1] Birrell is not alone in his nostalgia for an imaginary time when copyright dealt only with deserving works of creative authorship rather than being driven by commercial interests. Over one hundred years later, Hector MacQueen likewise commented that the 1911 Copyright Act (and the 1956 and 1988 Acts) was preceded by a 'deliberative reform process' which, in the last decade of the twentieth century, was displaced by a 'piecemeal, issue-driven approach within the European Union'.[2]

Another popular trope adopted by commentators on copyright law is it expansion. The story of copyright's development can be, and frequently is, portrayed as an 'inexorable march'[3] over new territories and the colonisation of new forms of cultural work in the interests of the copyright owner.[4] This narrative has inspired some evocative metaphors, from WR Cornish's 'spreading . . . rash'[5] to Jessica Litman's 'billowing white goo'.[6] Many place the beginning of copyright's expansion in the twentieth century,[7] and, in particular, as reaching new heights in its final decades.[8] Some ascribe responsibility for this expansion to the growing role of lobby groups formed by those with vested interests,[9] others to the widespread

[1] A Birrell, *Seven Lectures on the Law and History of Copyright in Books* (London, Cassell & Company Limited, 1899) 195.

[2] H MacQueen, 'Copyright Law Reform: Some Achievable Goals?' Oxford Intellectual Property Research Centre, Seminar Paper (2005), www.oiprc.ox.ac.uk/EJWP0406.pdf.

[3] D Vaver, 'Intellectual Property: The State of the Art' (2000) 116 *Law Quarterly Review* 621, 624.

[4] See eg, H Laddie, 'Copyright: Over-strength, Over-regulated, Over-rated?' (1996) 5 *European Intellectual Property Review* 253; R Sackville, 'Monopoly versus Freedom of Ideas: The Expansion of Intellectual Property' (2005) 16 *Australian Intellectual Property Journal* 65; H MacQueen, 'Extending Intellectual Property: Producers v Users' (1994) 45 *Northern Ireland Legal Quarterly* 30.

[5] WR Cornish, *Intellectual Property: Omnipresent, Distracting, Irrelevant*, (Oxford, Oxford University Press, 2004) 1.

[6] J Litman, 'Billowing White Goo' (2008) 31 *Columbia Journal of Law & the Arts* 587.

[7] eg Laddie, 'Copyright: Over-strength'.

[8] See NW Netanel, 'Why Has Copyright Expanded? Analysis and Critique' in F Macmillan (ed), *New Directions in Copyright Law*, vol 6 (Cheltenham, UK, Edward Elgar, 2008) 3; J Litman, 'Copyright Legislation and Technological Change' (1989) 68 *Oregon Law Review* 275.

[9] See Netanel, 'Why Has Copyright Expanded?'; Litman, 'Copyright Legislation'.

use of property rhetoric.[10] Implicitly, they hark back to a happier time, when copyright policy was developed more rationally, perhaps with greater attention to such ideals as the nurturing of authorship or the promotion of social welfare.

This supposed golden age of copyright law is, like most golden ages, a myth. Copyright emerged from the marketplace for printed books as a law that sought to regulate the market for printed books. Its expansion began with the Statute of Anne and, by the nineteenth century, was gathering a considerable head of steam. At the start of that century, literary copyright covered only books, calico designs, sculptures and engravings, lasted only twenty-eight years and infringement was largely a matter of reprinting or making identical copies. By 1911, copyright covered a broad variety of cultural products, lasted for fifty years after the death of an author and prevented all secondary uses of such works, except those which fell into certain specific and fixed categories. The rhetoric of property was not new in the twentieth century[11] and nor was the involvement of interested parties in seeking to influence the shape of the law.

One of the aims of this book has been to draw out the role played by various interest groups in shaping different areas of copyright law and policy. An explanation for this process is offered by Peter Drahos' Marxian-inspired analysis of copyright law. Drahos contends that intellectual property rights, including copyright, have a 'dangerous inner logic'[12] which invites 'socially costly levels of opportunistic behaviour'.[13] Drahos tells a tale of 'mildly opportunistic actors' who seek to maximise the benefits that can be drawn from intellectual property rights in their favour.[14] Two preventative strategies that they use are 'rights expanding' and 'bargaining chip' strategies.[15] The copy-owning booksellers of the eighteenth century and the powerful, established publishing houses of the nineteenth century can be cast in the role of these opportunistic actors and their use of rights-expanding strategies can be seen in their litigious activities, as well as their lobbying of Government for new legislation.

One of the main strategies employed by those with a stake in the copyright industries was the use of the rhetoric of Romantic authorship, emphasising the natural rights of authors, often in combination with a Lockean labour-based theory of property. These arguments were used so extensively that authorship and copyright became joined in a way that those drafting the Statute of Anne had barely contemplated. In an article on the birth of the public domain, Rose argues that in the eighteenth and nineteenth centuries English lawyers developed a strong discourse of property rights, while the public domain discourse remained

[10] See M Lemley, 'Romantic Authorship and the Rhetoric of Property' (1996–97) 75 *Texas Law Review* 873.

[11] See J Hughes, 'Copyright and Incomplete Historiographies: Of Piracy, Propertization, and Thomas Jefferson' (2006) 79 *Southern California Law Review* 993.

[12] P Drahos, *A Philosophy of Intellectual Property* (Aldershot, Dartmouth, 1996) 119.

[13] ibid.

[14] ibid 123.

[15] ibid 133–36.

weak.[16] An examination of various developments during the nineteenth century shows that, at some points in copyright's history, the ideology of romantic authorship does appear to have been a successful rights-expanding strategy.

However, if Rose's claims regarding the strength of the discourse of property rights are correct, why was it not able to win over the courts and the legislature on the matter of duration in *Donaldson v Becket*, in 1842, and in the years after 1878? Why was it not successful in convincing the legislature to reduce significantly the number of legal deposit libraries? A story of copyright's expansion which relies solely on the rhetoric of romantic authorship, whilst illuminating in some respects, fails to reveal the historical contingency and complexity of the developments in copyright law during this period. It ignores the lack of single causative effects, the lack of stark oppositions, the lack of simple victories.

The central concern of this book has been to place the concept of public interest alongside norms such as authorship and property in copyright law.[17] The answer that is sometimes given to explain the lack of success, or partial success, of appeals to the natural rights of authors in the eighteenth and nineteenth centuries is that priority was given to the interest of the public in education and access to knowledge.[18] This book has sought to subject the concept of public interest to greater scrutiny than has hitherto occurred. In particular, it has argued that in the eighteenth and nineteenth centuries, the 'public interest' was not a simple, fixed concept. Appeals to a general belief in the desirability of learning appeared in the preamble to the Statute of Anne, and were quickly adopted by litigants and judges for its persuasive force. As proponents of evangelical religion and utilitarianism linked their educative ideals to copyright and social welfare, the discourse of public interest became still more powerful. Resort was made to public interest concerns in parliamentary discussions over book prices, extension of copyright duration and legal deposit, as well as in the case law concerning the rights of foreign authors and infringement. However, the 'public interest' is not the same in each of these examples. At times, particularly at the start of the period, it was expressed in antipathy to monopolies and extolling the virtues of healthy competition; at other times it was the interests of the reading public in cheap books or access to books in libraries, the interests of the 'improving' public in access to lectures and educational publications, or the general economic benefits to be gained from protecting local manufacturers.

A very different version of the public interest, however, can be seen in the contradictory attitudes towards education for the masses. This is illustrated in the

[16] M Rose, 'Nine-Tenths of the Law: The English Copyright Debates and the Rhetoric of the Public Domain' (2003) 66 *Law and Contemporary Problems* 75, 85.

[17] Following squarely in the footsteps of most of those who have gone before, the book has concentrated almost exclusively on literary copyright. The central theme being investigated, that of the concept of the public interest, can be illustrated by reference to literary copyright and for reasons of timing and space the book is limited in this manner. There is without doubt a need for more research to be done into the development of copyright law in other areas of creative endeavour, which would certainly enrich understanding of the area, as well as highlighting other important elements of copyright's history.

[18] See Deazley, *On the Origin* 226 (for example).

development by Lord Eldon of the rule that copyright would not protect immoral, blasphemous or seditious works. This also emphasises that the encouragement of learning referred to in the Statute of Anne was not directed at the entire population of Britain, but at that small sector of it that had the leisure to read and write, as well as sufficient wealth to afford a luxury commodity such as books. As education and standards of living improved, questions arose as to whether the encouragement should extend to the masses at all.

Towards the end of the nineteenth century, other public interests emerged. In the context of increasing internationalisation of copyright law, the public's interest in protecting local industry was pitted against the public interest in achieving international trade standards and consistency. New consumer groups emerged, such as the potential buyers of gramophone records. Even authors could present themselves as part of an international community which would benefit from international norms. Thus, not only might public interests align with private interests, but a private interest could *become* a public interest if viewed from a certain perspective.

This book has sought to draw out the way that different public interests were articulated and the impact that they had in different areas of copyright law, looking in particular at the way that they interacted with arguments based on the rhetoric of romantic authorship. One such area is the law of infringement. Although arguments based on the property rights of authors were not always a trump card in the debates over duration, when divorced from notions of the natural rights of authors the labour-based concept of property was more influential in forming the law of infringement. As Oren Bracha has persuasively argued, the nineteenth century publishing market sought to capture consumer demand and markets in new ways, but when they came to translate their interests into legal demands, the ideology of authorship was 'one of the main vehicles at hand'.[19] This ideology was employed to represent copyright as protecting an 'intellectual entity created by the author' which could take a number of physical forms.[20]

However, while publishers might have been able to draw on the notion of an idealised romantic author creating for his own personal fulfilment, their claims remained firmly located in the marketplace. The continuing emphasis on the economic nature of the property over any authorial attributes it might possess, such as genius or artistic originality, meant that copyright law continued to cover a broad range of subject matter bearing a closer resemblance to fact compilation than creation, just as it had done prior to the Statute of Anne. The failure of various attempts to link subsistence of copyright to a criterion of creative or inventive originality demonstrates that the main objective of copyright law, as far as the publishers were concerned, was to prevent others from competing in an unfair manner in the same or related markets; that is, to reap where they had not sown.

[19] O Bracha, 'Owning Ideas: A History of Anglo-American Intellectual Property' (unpublished SJD Dissertation Harvard Law School, June 2005), www.obracha.net/oi/or.htm, 591.

[20] ibid 592.

Despite the claims of many commentators that the law of infringement represents a balance between the interests of the public and those of the copyright owner, this book highlights the central role of competition and the demands of the market in the law's development.

The weight placed on private property rights and competition can also be seen in the decisions concerned with partial taking. In the early cases, the judges injected elements of the public interest in the creation and circulation of new works into the question, as in the rule that abridgments and other new works would not be considered infringements. By the second half of the century these principles were no longer applied in practice, and the courts had increasingly come to focus on the matter that was copied and the effect such copying would have on the market for the original work.

However, although general concerns for the public interest in the creation of new works had lost ground in cases of partial copying from one book to another, they still held sway in cases of transformative copying from one medium to another. It was only concerted lobbying from dramatic authors, composers and publishers that altered this principle in the 1911 Act. Even then, it seems likely that in the absence of international pressure being placed on Great Britain to conform to the revised Berne Convention copyright reform would have taken still longer to achieve and may have taken a different shape. Robert Burrell's characterisation of judges as only too willing to listen to the pleas of copyright owners for expanded rights[21] therefore requires some adjustment.

It was the demands of trade that played the most significant role in shaping the infringement doctrine of substantial taking and the permitted categories of fair uses of works. These factors were relevant to the extent of damage which the second work would inflict upon the market for the first and, when combined with the breadth of protection granted to works of fact and information, resulted in copyright law performing many of the same functions that a separate tort of unfair competition might carry out.[22] This goes some way to explaining why Britain developed no such tort, unlike her neighbours France and Germany and her former colony, the United States of America.[23]

[21] R Burrell and A Coleman, *Copyright Exceptions: The Digital Impact* (Cambridge: Cambridge University Press, 2005) 255–56.

[22] However, this was not true of designs in manufactured products. The problem of protecting designs was the subject of a compromise in the 1911 Copyright Act, which was intended to exclude designs from the territory of copyright law, leaving it to be protected only through the registered designs system. Unregistered designs were, therefore, left without the protection that a law of unfair competition might have given them.

[23] The Supreme Court of America recognised a right to prevent unfair competition in *International News Service v Associated Press* 248 US 215 (1918). However, its reception in the law has been rocky, leaving it with an unclear and restricted role. See, eg, Z Chafee, 'Unfair Competition' (1940) 53 *Harvard Law Review* 1289; A Kamperman-Sanders, *Unfair Competition Law: The Protection of Intellectual and Industrial Creativity* (Oxford, Clarendon Press, 1997); WJ Derenberg, 'The Influence of the French Code Civil on the Modern Law of Unfair Competition' (1955) 4 *American Journal of Comparative Law* 1 and W Morison, 'Unfair Competition at Common Law' (1951–53) 2 *University of Western Australia Law Review* 34.

The close relationship between infringement and unfair competition has been noted before.[24] However, the expansive scope of protection also has the potential to be anti-competitive itself, as was found to be the case in the late twentieth century in relation to television listings.[25] The interplay between competition laws and the law of copyright is a new battleground where the interests of copyright owners are seen as being incompatible with the interests of the general public. Once again, concerns about the monopolising effects of copyright law, and the social and economic damage caused thereby, come to the fore in copyright debates.[26]

The crucial roles played by owners, rather than authors, can be seen in other areas of copyright's expansion, such as the achievement of international copyright, greater protection against music piracy and the introduction of new categories for protection. In all of these cases the claims of owners were supported by those of authors, or other relevant creators, which made credible the authorship rhetoric employed by owners. However, these interested parties also had recourse to arguments based on public interest. Here the claim was that increasing protection was good for the public in general because it would encourage authors to produce more and better quality works. While such a claim may be largely unverifiable as a factual proposition[27] it is hard to disagree with the argument that there is a public interest in promoting authorship and creativity, as well as in a strong market for books and a healthy and competitive trade in creative products. Similarly, in the debates over legal deposit, owners employed rhetoric based on property as well as the public interest. Here, the public interest was achieved in the more roundabout manner of relieving the burdens on publishers so that they had more funds available to publish more books at lower prices.

[24] S Ricketson, 'Reaping Without Sowing: Unfair Competition and Intellectual Property Rights in Anglo-Australian Law' (1984) *University of New South Wales Law Journal* 1. See also *Victoria Park Racing and Recreation Grounds Co. Ltd v Taylor* (1937) 58 CLR 479, 509 per Dixon J.

[25] *Radio Telefis Eireann and Independent Television Publications Ltd v Commission of the European Communities* [1995] ECR I-743 (*Magill* case). Still more recently, see obiter dicta of Gummow, Hayne and Heydon JJ in *IceTV Pty Limited v Nine Network Australia Pty Limited* [2009] HCA 14 (High Court of Australia) [166].

[26] The relationship between copyright and competition is an area in which we may expect to see further development. See eg, I Maher, 'Competition Law and Intellectual Property Rights: Evolving Formalism' in P Craig and G De Burca (eds), *The Evolution of EU Law* (Oxford, Oxford University Press, 1999); K Lindgren, 'The Interface between Intellectual Property and Antitrust: Some Current Issues in Australia' (2005) 16 *Australian Intellectual Property Journal* 76; F Houwen and R Neville, 'Risky Business: Current Challenges in the Relationship between Competition Law and Copyright' (2009) 8 *Competition Law Journal* 18.

[27] There is, however, a considerable law and economics literature attempting to assess this claim. See (for the tip of the iceberg), A Plant, 'The Economic Aspects of Copyright in Books' (1934) 2 *Economica* 167; S Breyer, 'The Uneasy Case for Copyright: A Study of Copyright in Books, Photocopies and Computer Programs' (1970) 84 *Harvard Law Review* 281; WM Landes and RA Posner, 'An Economic Analysis of Copyright Law' (1989) 18 *Journal of Legal Studies* 325; WM Landes and RA Posner, 'Indefinitely Renewable Copyright' (2003) 70 *University of Chicago Law Review* 471. For an overview of more of the literature, see RA Towse, C Hadke, P Stepan, 'The Economics of Copyright Law: A Stocktake of the Literature' (2008) 5 *Review of Economic Research on Copyright Issues* 1, concluding that 'there is nothing in all the literature we surveyed here to guide us towards the "optimal" copyright standard' (16).

What is significant for rhetorical purposes is the order in which the factors are placed. To take some examples from the present day, a declaration drawn up by copyright scholars arguing against a restrictive interpretation of the 'three-step test',[28] states, 'Copyright law aims to benefit the public interest. It produces important incentives for creation and dissemination of new works of authorship to the general public'.[29] By contrast, as noted in chapter one, an EU Directive providing for an increase in copyright term, sets out that copyright 'ensures the maintenance and development of creativity in the interest of authors, cultural industries, consumers and society as a whole'.[30] Thus, those seeking greater protection for owners tend to put the claims of authors first. However, it is also important to note that the claims of authorship might also be used to argue for lower levels of protection, by limiting protection to works that show real creativity or originality,[31] or by recognising the interests of 'second generation' authors in broader exceptions or a shorter term of protection.[32]

Therefore, Ginsburg is both right and wrong when she states that the opposition of authors and public is 'specious':[33] right, because it is a fallacy, a sleight of hand often employed to advance the interests of copyright owners or users against the other; yet also wrong, because such opposition has had an important role historically in developing copyright law, and should not be readily dismissed. The real strength of public interest discourse in the past has been, as it is today, its ability to be pressed into service for a variety of purposes. Public interest rhetoric has a long and distinguished history in copyright law, which has adapted itself to different demands and situations due to its very opacity. The nature of the public interests which copyright has the capacity to serve may not be the same today as they were three hundred years ago, but they should not be forgotten, nor should they be subsumed into the rather more narrow issue of 'users' rights'.

This latter expression, and its close relation 'user interests', is increasingly commonly elided with, or substituted for, considerations of the public interest, particularly in discussions of copyright's balancing function and in relation to the exceptions to copyright. The 1977 Whitford Committee reported that 'copyright protection not infrequently involves a conflict between public and private interests' concluding that, overall, 'the balance between the rights of the copyright owner on the one hand and the exceptions in favour of the user on the other is about right'.[34] More recently, the European Council also referred to users in the Information Society Directive, stating:

28 Berne Convention for the Protection of Literary and Artistic Works, art 9(2).

29 C Geiger, J Griffiths, RM Hilty, 'Towards a Balanced Interpretation of the "Three-Step Test" in Copyright Law' [2008] *European Intellectual Property Review* 489, 493.

30 Directive 2006/116/EC of the European Parliament and of the Council of 12 December 2006 on the term of protection of copyright and certain related rights, recital 11.

31 Ricketson, as quoted above: n 2.

32 L Bently, '*R. v The Author:* From Death Penalty to Community Service' (2008) 32 *Columbia Journal of Law & the Arts* 1, 98–100.

33 J Ginsburg, 'Authors and Users in Copyright' (1997) 45 *Journal of the Copyright Society of the USA* 1, 4.

34 Report of the Committee to consider the Law on Copyright and Designs, Chairman: the Hon. Mr Justice Whitford, Cmnd. 6732 (1976–77) 4.

> A fair balance of rights and interests between the different categories of right-holders, as well as between the different categories of right-holders and users of protected subject-matter must be safeguarded.[35]

The Supreme Court of Canada has gone so far as to describe the fair dealing exception as a 'user's right.[36]

It has been noted that there are two general categories of 'user': consumers[37] who buy or borrow the work, or those, like teachers, who make copies for distribution; and, users who take extracts or parts of works in order to create other works.[38] However, focusing solely on these groups, even if their claims are elevated to 'rights' rather than 'interests' runs the risk of ignoring other elements of copyright law that may affect society in general. The interests of the latter could include: living in a society where there are many and varied creative works and works of information available; having such works available at affordable prices; having such works widely disseminated; information about such works being available; works being of high quality; works being of a kind that foster morality or education; and creators of works being free from the controlling hand of state or private patronage.[39] An examination of the discussions and debates that reform of copyright law gave rise to in the nineteenth century reminds us that all of these interests have been and continue to be relevant.

A study of the history of copyright law and the concept of public interest leads one right into the abyss at the heart of copyright law—its lack of a universally accepted, morally sustainable and philosophically consistent foundation. An historical investigation of copyright law demonstrates that this void has existed in copyright law from the time that the first cases were brought under the Statute of Anne. However, it has often proved a boon to litigants and lobbyists seeking to cast the goals of copyright in the image of the result they are seeking. If we are looking to history to find the true goal of copyright law, we need to be aware that the story of copyright in the eighteenth and nineteenth centuries can offer a variety of plausible foundations, aims and aspirations. For the future, it might prove more profitable to recognise that copyright was born of contingency and that its early development owes more to the particular economic, social and political conditions of its era than to the expression of timeless values.

Close study of the history of copyright law shows that the way in which copyright law has developed in Britain, and the countries to which she exported her law, up to and after 1911, was not an inevitable progression. We can look at the decade prior to the passing of the Imperial Copyright Act as providing evidence of what the law might have been and in many areas it is clear that there were no

[35] Directive 2001/29/EC of 22 May 2001 on the harmonisation of certain aspects of copyright and related rights in the information society, recital 31.

[36] *CCH Canadian Ltd v Law Society of Upper Canada* [2004] 339, [48], [51].

[37] Or those whom Ginsburg somewhat worryingly calls 'consumptive users': Ginsburg, 'Authors and Users' 3.

[38] Sometimes called transformative or productive users: ibid.

[39] For a theory of copyright's role in sustaining democracy, see NW Netanel, 'Copyright and a Democratic Civil Society' (1996) 106 *Yale Law Journal* 283.

foregone conclusions. For example, it was not apparent at the birth of sound recording technology that the right to make recordings would be granted to composers rather than the makers of such machines. Moreover, the various Select Committees and legislative drafts experimented with a number of shapes for the law, including a general private fair dealing exception, short-term protection for news, compulsory licensing, different formulations for the permitted purpose exceptions, and different periods of protection for different kinds of works. Calls for reform of copyright law today often advocate the adoption of one of more of these approaches.[40]

As technology continues to change and society alters its views on what is valuable, both in terms of creativity and economics, the question of how copyright law deals with such developments will recur time and again. However, it seems certain that the new challenges will mirror the old: which subject matters or commodities should be protected? To what extent will the public be able to access or make use of works created by others? There will be new ways of infringing but equally, as recent developments have shown, new ways of tracking and halting infringement.

By emphasising the different forms that copyright law might have taken, and the forces that acted upon it, this book seeks to free us from the shackles of copyright's commonly received history. This is not to say that history is not important. On the contrary, in a rapidly changing technological environment, it is more important than ever to be aware of how we got where we are. This is particularly the case when we see industry lobby groups putting forward the same arguments for increased protection that were made by their predecessors of one hundred years ago, and we find consumer protection bodies and other user groups making the same responses. It seems that despite the historical specificity of copyright law's development, some aspects of it *are* timeless.

The shackles from which liberation is sought are those versions of copyright history that cast it as developing inexorably by reference to a single principle such as 'authorship' or 'public interest'. Instead, we can recognise that copyright law has been about all of these things, and at different times and in different ways they have all played influential roles. The object of this book has not been to dismiss the language of public interest as being mere empty rhetoric. Rather, it has sought to make it more accurate, to advocate its use more carefully and, in consequence, to make it richer and more valuable to copyright debates today. Recognising the centrality of the market underpinnings of copyright law, the fact that there has been no single line of development, and the elements of continuity and discontinuity with the present, means that we can choose our future more freely. Instead of professing allegiance to notions of what copyright has been about in the past, we should ask what we want it to be about in the future, what goals it should fulfil, and how it can be crafted in order to achieve them.

[40] See eg, NS Nadel, 'How Current Copyright Law Discourages Creative Output: The Overlooked Impact of Marketing' (2004) 19 *Berkeley Technology Law Journal* 785.

Bibliography

Abbott, J, *The Story of Francis, Day & Hunter* (London, Francis, Day & Hunter, 1952).

Abrams, HB, 'The Historical Foundation of American Copyright Law: Exploding the Myth of Common Law Copyright' (1983) 29 *Wayne Law Review* 119.

Alderson, B and Immel, A, 'Mass Markets: Children's Books' in D McKitterick (ed), *The Cambridge History of the Book in Britain,* vol 6: *1830–1914* (Cambridge, Cambridge University Press, 2009) 382–415.

Alexander, I, 'Criminalising Copyright: A Story of Publishers, Pirates and Pieces of Eight' [2007] *Cambridge Law Journal* 625.

Altick, RD, *The English Common Reader: A Social History of the Mass Reading Public 1800–1900* (Chicago, University of Chicago Press, 1957).

Amory, H, '"*De facto* Copyright?" Fielding's *Works* in Partnership, 1769–1821' (1984) 17 *Eighteenth Century Studies* 449.

Arber, E, *A Transcript of the Registers of the Company of Stationers of London, 1554–1640*, 5 vols (London, privately printed, 1875–1894) vol 1.

Ardagh, P, 'St Andrews University Library and the Copyright Acts' (1948–55) 3 *Edinburgh Bibliographical Society Transactions* 183.

Arnold, M, 'Copyright' (1880) 49 *Fortnightly Review* 319.

Astbury, R, 'The Renewal of the Licensing Act in 1693 and its Lapse in 1695' (1978) 33 *The Library* 296.

Atto, C, 'The Society for the Encouragement of Learning' (1938) 19 *The Library* 261.

Baloch, T, 'Law Booksellers and Printers as Agents of Unchange' [2007] *Cambridge Law Journal* 389.

Barnard, J, 'Introduction' in J Barnard and DF McKenzie (eds), *The Cambridge History of the Book in Britain*, vol 4: *1557–1695* (Cambridge, Cambridge University Press, 2002) 1–27.

Barnard, J and Bell, M, 'The English Provinces' in J Barnard and DF McKenzie (eds), *The Cambridge History of the Book in Britain,* vol 4: *1557–1695*, (Cambridge, Cambridge University Press, 2002) 665–86.

Barnard, J and McKenzie, DF (eds), *The Cambridge History of the Book in Britain 1557–1695*, vol 4 (Cambridge, Cambridge University Press, 2002).

Barnes, JJ, *Authors, Publishers and Politicians: The Quest for an Anglo-American Copyright Agreement 1815–1854* (London, Routledge & Kegan Paul, 1974).

Barnes JJ, *Free Trade in Books: A Study of the London Book Trade since 1800* (Oxford, Clarendon Press, 1964).

Barnes, JJ and Barnes, PP, 'Reassessing the Reputation of Thomas Tegg, London Publisher, 1776–1846' (2000) 3 *Book History* 45.

Barratt, D, 'The Dramatic Authors' Society (1833–1883) and the Payment of English Dramatists' (1988) 7 *Essays in Theatre* 19.

Belanger, T, 'Booksellers' Sales of Copyright: Aspects of the London Book Trade 1718–1768' (PhD Dissertation, Columbia University, 1970).

Belanger, T, 'Booksellers' Trade Sales, 1718–1768' (1975) 30 *The Library* 281.

Bell, E, '*The Times* Book Club and the Publishers' Association' in F Macmillan, *The Net Book Agreement 1899 and the Book War 1906–8* (Glasgow, MacLehone & Co., 1924) 34–67.
Bently, L, 'Copyright and the Victorian Internet: Telegraphic Property Laws in Colonial Australia' (2004) 38 *Loyola Law Review of Los Angeles* 71.
Bently, L, 'Copyright, Translations, and Relations Between Britain and India in the Nineteenth and Early Twentieth Centuries' (2007) 82 *Chicago-Kent Law Review* 1181.
Bently, L, '*R. v The Author*: From Death Penalty to Community Service' (2008) 32 *Columbia Journal of Law & the Arts* 1.
Bently, L and Kretschmer, M (eds), *Primary Sources on Copyright (1450–1900)* www.copyrighthistory.org.
Bently, L and Sherman, B, 'Great Britain and the Signing of the Berne Convention in 1886' (2001) 48 *Journal of the Copyright Society of the USA* 311.
Bently, L and Sherman, B, *Intellectual Property Law* (Oxford, Oxford University Press, 2001).
Bergne, JHG, 'The International Copyright Union' (1887) 3 *Law Quarterly Review* 14.
Besant, W, *Essays and Historiettes* (London, Chatto and Windus, 1903).
Beven, T, 'The Appellate Jurisdiction of the House of Lords' (1901) 17 *Law Quarterly Review* 155.
Birrell, A, *Seven Lectures on the Law and History of Copyright in Books* (London, Cassell & Co Ltd, 1899).
Black, J, *The English Press, 1621–1861* (Stroud, Sutton Publishing Limited, 2001).
Blackstone, W, *Commentaries on the Laws of England*, 4 vols, 1st edn (Oxford, Clarendon Press, 1765–1769).
Blagden, C, 'Booksellers' Trade Sales 1718–1768' (1951) 5 *The Library*, 5th series, 243.
Blagden, C, *The Stationers' Company: A History 1403–1959* (London, George Allen & Unwin Ltd, 1960).
Blagden, C, 'Thomas Carnan and the Almanack Monopoly' (1961) 14 *Studies in Bibliography* 23.
Blann, R, *Throwing the Scabbard Away: Byron's Battle Against the Censors of 'Don Juan'* (New York, Peter Lang, 1991).
Bonham-Carter, V, *Authors by Profession* (London, Spottiswoode Ballantyne Press, 1978).
Bonnell, TF, 'John Bell's *Poets of Great Britain*: The "Little Triffling Edition" Revisited' (1887) 85 *Modern Philology* 128.
Boorman, S, 'Printing and Publishing of Music' in L Macy (ed), *Grove Music Online*, www.grovemusic.com.
Boosey, W, *Fifty Years of Music* (London, Ernest Benn Limited, 1931).
Booth, BA, 'Trollope, Reade and 'Shilly-Shally' (Part I)' (1947) 1 *The Trollopian* 45.
Booth, BA, 'Trollope, Reade and 'Shilly-Shally' (Part II)' (1947) 2 *The Trollopian* 43.
Booth, MR, 'Public Taste, the Playwright and the Law' in C Leech and TW Craik (eds), *The Revels History of Drama in English*, vol 6: *1750–1880* (London, Methuen & Co Ltd, 1975) 29–57.
Bowrey, K, 'On Clarifying the Role of Originality and Fair Use in Nineteenth Century UK Jurisprudence: Appreciating the "Humble Grey Which Emerges as a Result of Long Controversy"' in L Bently, G D'Agostino, C Ng (eds), *The Common Law of Intellectual Property: Essays in Honour of Professor David Vaver* (Oxford, Hart Publishing, forthcoming 2010).
Bowrey, K and Fowell, N, 'Digging Up Fragments and Building IP Franchises' (2009) 31 *Sydney Law Review* 185.
Boyle J, 'The Second Enclosure Movement and the Construction of the Public Domain' (2003) 66 *Law and Contemporary Problems* 33.
Bracha, O, 'The Ideology of Authorship Revisited: Authors, Markets, and Liberal Values in Early American Copyright' (2009) 118 *Yale Law Journal* 186.

Bracha, O, 'Owning Ideas: A History of Anglo-American Intellectual Property' (unpublished SJD Dissertation Harvard Law School, June 2005), available at www.obracha.net/oi/oi.htm.

Brack, OM (ed), *Writers, Books and Trade* (New York, AMS Press, 1994).

Bradshaw, D, '"Fair Dealing" as a Defence to Copyright Infringement in UK Law: An Historical Excursion from 1802 to the *Clockwork Orange* Case 1993' (1995) *Denning Law Journal* 67.

Brantlinger, P, *The Reading Lesson: The Threat of Mass Literacy in Nineteenth-Century British Fiction* (Bloomington, Indiana University Press, 1998).

Brewer, J, 'Commercialisation and Politics' in N McKendrick, J Brewer and JH Plumb (eds), *The Birth of a Consumer Society: The Commercialisation of Eighteenth-Century England* (London, Hutchinson, 1983) 197–262.

Breyer, S, 'The Uneasy Case for Copyright: A Study of Copyright in Books, Photocopies and Computer Programs' (1970) 84 *Harvard Law Review* 281.

Briggs, A, *The Age of Improvement 1737–1867*, 2nd edn (Harlow, UK, Longman, 2000).

Briggs, W, *The Law of International Copyright (with Special Sections on the Colonies and The United States of America)* (London, Stevens & Haynes, 1906).

Britton, J, *The Rights of Literature; or an Inquiry into the Policy and Justice of the Claims of Certain Public Libraries on all the Publishers and Authors of the United Kingdom for Eleven Copies on the Best Paper of Every New Publication* (London, AJ Valpy, 1814).

Brougham, H, *Practical Observations upon the Education of the People, Addressed to the Working Classes and their Employers* (London, Richard Taylor, 1825).

Brydges E, *Answer to the Further Statement ordered by the Syndics of the University of Cambridge* (London, Barnard and Farley, 1818).

Brydges, E, *Reasons for a further Amendment of the Act Geo III c156 being an Act to amend the Copyright Act of Queen Anne* (London, Nichols, Son and Bently, 1817).

Brydges, E, *A Summary Statement of the Great Grievance imposed on Authors and Publishers and the Injury Done to Literature by the Late Copyright Act* (London, Longman, Hurst, Rees, Orme and Brown, 1818).

Brydges E, *A Vindication of the Pending Bill for the Amendment of the Copyright Act, from the Misrepresentations and Unjust Comments of the Syndics of the University Library at Cambridge* (London, Longman, Hurst, Rees, Orme and Brown, 1818).

Bryson, WH, *The Equity Side of the Exchequer* (Cambridge, Cambridge University Press, 1975).

Burrell R, 'The Future of the Copyright Exceptions' in D McClean and K Schubert (eds), *Dear Images* (London, ICA, 2002) 455–71.

Burrell, R, 'Reining in Copyright Law: Is Fair Use the Answer?' (2001) *Intellectual Property Quarterly* 361.

Burrell, R and Coleman, A, *Copyright Exceptions: The Digital Impact* (Cambridge, Cambridge University Press, 2005).

Bynum, WF, 'Wakley, Thomas (1795–1862)', *Oxford Dictionary of National Biography* (Oxford University Press, 2004) www.oxforddnb.com/view/article/28425.

Campbell, J, *Lives of the Lord Chancellors*, vol 6 (London, John Murray, 1868).

Carter, H, *A History of the Oxford University Press*, vol 1 (Oxford, Clarendon Press, 1975).

'The Cases of the Appellants and Respondents in the Cause of Literary Property wherein the Decree of Lord Chancellor Apsley was Reversed, &c, by a Gentleman of the Inner Temple' in S Parks (ed), *The Literary Property Debate: Six Tracts 1764–1774* (New York, Garland Publishing Inc, 1975).

'Cases of *Walcot v Walker, Southey v Sherwood, Murray v Benbow* and *Lawrence v Smith*' (1822) 27 *Quarterly Review* 127.
Chafee, Z, 'Coming into Equity with Clean Hands' (1947) *Michigan Law Rreview* 1065.
Chafee, Z, 'Unfair Competition' (1940) 53 *Harvard Law Review* 1289.
Chard, LF, 'Bookseller to Publisher: Joseph Johnson and the English Book Trade, 1760–1810' (1977) 32 *The Library* 138.
Christian, E, *A Vindication of the Right of the Universities of Great Britain to a Copy of Every New Publication* (Cambridge, University Press, 1807).
Christian, E, *A Vindication of the Right of the Universities of Great Britain to a Copy of Every New Publication*, 3rd edn (Cambridge, University Press, 1818).
Clarkson, CL, *The First Magazine: A History of the Gentleman's Magazine* (Providence, RI, Brown University, 1938) 63.
Cochrane, JG, *The Case Stated between the Public Libraries and the Booksellers* (London, J Moyes 1813).
Colclough W, 'Distribution' in D McKitterick(ed), *The Cambridge History of the Book in Britain*, vol 6: *1830–1914* (Cambridge, Cambridge University Press, 2009) 238–80.
Colles, WM, 'Copyright at Home and Abroad' (1909) 65 *The Nineteenth Century* 1056.
Colles, WM, 'Copyright Law Reform' (1910) 213 *Quarterly Review* 483.
Colles, WM, 'The Copyright Question' (1910) 212 *Edinburgh Review* 310.
Collins, AS, *Authorship in the Days of Johnson: Being a Study of the Relationship Between Author, Patron, Publisher and Public, 1726–1780* (London, Robert Holden & Co Ltd, 1927).
Collins, AS, *The Profession of Letters: A Study of the Relation of Author to Patron, Publisher, and Public, 1780–1832* (London, George Routledge & Sons Ltd, 1928).
Coover, J, *Music Publishing, Copyright and Piracy in Victorian England* (London, Mansell Publishing Limited, 1985).
Copinger, WA, *The Law of Copyright in Works of Literature and Art*, 1st edn (London, Stevens & Haynes, 1870).
Copinger, WA, *The Law of Copyright in Works of Literature and Art*, 2nd edn (London, Stevens & Haynes, 1881).
Copyright Asoociation, *Report of the Copyright Association for the year 1874–5* (London, Longmans, Green & Co, 1875).
Cornish, WR, 'The Author's Surrogate: the Genesis of British Copyright' in K O'Donovan and GR Rubin (eds), *Human Rights and Legal History* (New York, Oxford University Press, 2000) 254–70.
Cornish, WR, 'The Copyright History of What Must-have-been' in G Roussel et al (eds), *Mélanges Victor Nabhan* (Montreal, Editions Yvon Blais, 2004) 61–74.
Cornish, WR, *Intellectual Property: Omnipresent, Distracting, Irrelevant*, (Oxford, Oxford University Press, 2004).
Craig, P and De Burca, G (eds), *The Evolution of EU Law* (Oxford: Oxford University Press, 1999).
Curtis, GT, *A Treatise on the Law of Copyright* (London, Maxwell & Son, 1847).
Curtis, SJ, *History of Education in Great Britain*, 7th edn (London, University Tutorial Press, 1967).
Cutler, E et al, *The Law of Musical and Dramatic Compositions* (London, Cassell & Co, 1890).
Davies, G, *Copyright and the Public Interest*, 2nd edn (London, Sweet & Maxwell, 2002).
de Zwart, M, 'An Historical Analysis of the Birth of Fair Dealing and Fair Use: Lessons for the Digital Age' [2007] *Intellectual Property Quarterly* 60.

de Zwart, M, 'Seriously Entertaining: *The Panel* and the Future of Fair Dealing' (2003) 8 *Media and Arts Law Review* 1.

Deazley, R, 'Commentary on *Copyright Act* 1814' in L Bently and M Kretschmer (eds), *Primary Sources on Copyright (1450–1900)* www.copyrighthistory.org.

Deazley, R, 'The Myth of Copyright at Common Law' (2003) 62 *Cambridge Law Journal* 106.

Deazley R, *On the Origin of the Right to Copy: Charting the Movement of Copyright Law in the Eighteenth Century (1695–1775)* (Oxford, Hart Publishing, 2004).

Deazley, R, 'Re-reading Donaldson (1774) in the Twenty-First Century and Why it Matters' [2003] *European Intellectual Property Review* 270.

Deazley, R, *Rethinking Copyright: History, Theory, Language* (Cheltenham, UK, Edward Elgar, 2006).

'The Decision of the Court of Session Upon the Question of Literary Property in the case Hinton against Donaldson, &c, Published by James Boswell' in S Parks (ed), *The Literary Property Debate: Six Tracts 1764–1774* (New York, Garland Publishing Inc, 1975).

Derenberg, WJ, 'The Influence of the French Code Civil on the Modern Law of Unfair Competition' (1955) 4 *American Journal of Comparative Law* 1.

Dicey, E, 'The Copyright Question' (1876) 19 *Fortnightly Review* 126.

Drahos, P, *A Philosophy of Intellectual Property* (Aldershot, Dartmouth, 1996).

Drahos, P with Braithwaite J, *Information Feudalism* (New York, New Press, 2003).

Dugas, D-J, 'The London Book Trade in 1709 (Part Two)' (2001) 95 *Papers of the Bibliographical Society of America* 157.

Duppa, R, 'An Address to the Parliament of Great Britain on the Claims of Authors to their own Copyright' (1813) 2 *The Pamphleteer* (published anonymously).

Dworkin, G, 'Copyright, The Public Interest and Freedom of Speech: A UK Copyright Lawyer's Perspective' in J Griffiths and U Suthersanen (eds), *Copyright and Free Speech: Comparative and International Analysis* (Oxford, Oxford University Press, 2005) 153–70.

Easton, JM (ed), *The Law of Copyright by WA Copinger*, 5th edn (London, Stevens & Haynes, 1915).

Eden, R, *A Treatise on the Law of Injunctions* (London, Butterworth & Cooke, 1821).

Farrer, TH, 'The Principle of Copyright' (1878) 24 *Fortnightly Review* 836.

Feather, J, *A History of British Publishing* (London, Routledge, 1988).

Feather, J, 'Publishers and Politicians: The Remaking of the Law of Copyright in Britain 1775–1842. Part I: Legal Deposit and the Battle of the Library Tax' (1988) 24 *Publishing History* 49.

Feather, J, *Publishing, Piracy and Politics: An Historical Study of Copyright in Britain* (London, Mansell, 1994).

Feltes, NN, *Modes of Production of Victorian Novels* (Chicago, University of Chicago Press, 1986).

Fitzball, E, *Thirty-five Years of a Dramatic Authors' Life*, 2 vols (London, TC Newby, 1859) vol 1.

Fordham, SGH, 'Paterson's Roads: Daniel Paterson, His Maps and Itineraries' (1925) 5 *The Library*, 4th series, 333.

Foucault, M, 'What is an Author?' in JV Harari (ed) *Textual Strategies: Perspectives in Post-Structuralist Criticism* (Ithaca, NY, Cornell University Press 1979) 141–60.

Foxon, D, *The Stamp Act of 1712: Sandars Lectures 1978* (unpublished, copy in Cambridge University Library).

Fraser, A, 'John Murray's Colonial and Home Library' (1997) 91 *Papers of the Bibliographical Society of America* 339.

Froude, JA, 'Report of the Copyright Commission' (1878) 304 *Edinburgh Review* 295.
Fyfe, A, 'The Information Revolution' in D McKitterick(ed), *The Cambridge History of the Book in Britain,* vol 6: *1830–1914* (Cambridge, Cambridge University Press, 2009) 567–94.
Garnett, K, Davies, G and Harbottle, G, *Copinger and Skone James On Copyright,* 15th edn (London, Sweet & Maxwell, 2005).
Geiger, C, Griffiths, J and Hilty, RM, 'Towards a Balanced Interpretation of the "Three-Step Test" in Copyright Law' [2008] *European Intellectual Property Review* 489.
George, RP (ed), *The Autonomy of Law: Essays on Legal Positivism* (Oxford, Clarendon Press, 1996).
Ginsburg, J, 'Authors and Users in Copyright' (1997) 45 *Journal of the Copyright Society of the USA* 1.
Ginsburg, J, '"Une chose publique"? The Author's Domain and the Public Domain in Early British, French and US Copyright Law' [2006] *Cambridge Law Journal* 636.
Godson, R, *A Practical Treatise on the Law of Patents for Inventions and of Copyright, with an Introduction book on Monopolies,* 1st edn (London, Butterworth & Sons, 1823).
Gomez-Arostegui, T, 'What History Teaches Us about Copyright Injunctions and the Inadequate-Remedy-at-Law Requirement' (2008) 81 *Southern California Law Review* 1197.
Griest, GL, *Mudie's Circulating Library and the Victorian Novel* (Newton Abbot, Devon, David & Charles (Publishers) Ltd, 1970).
Griffiths, J, 'Copyright Law After Ashdown: Time to Deal Fairly with the Public' (2002) *Intellectual Property Quarterly* 240.
Griffiths, J, 'Preserving Judicial Freedom of Movement: Interpreting Fair Dealing in Copyright Law' (2000) *Intellectual Property Quarterly* 240.
Griffiths, J and Suthersanen, U (eds), *Copyright and Free Speech: Comparative and International Analysis* (Oxford, Oxford University Press, 2005).
Hamlyn, HM, 'Eighteenth-century Circulating Libraries in England' (1946–47) 1 *The Library* 197.
Hanson, L, *Government and the Press 1695–1763* (Oxford, Oxford University Press, 1936).
Harari, JV (ed), *Textual Strategies: Perspectives in Post-Structuralist Criticism* (Ithaca, NY, Cornell University Press 1979).
Hettinger, C, 'Justifying Intellectual Property' (1989) 18 *Philosophy and Public Affairs* 31.
Hobsbawm, E, *The Age of Capital 1848–1875* (London, Weidenfeld and Nicholson, 1975).
Hobsbawm, E, *The Age of Empire 1875–1914* (London, Weidenfeld and Nicholson, 1987).
Hobsbawm, E, *The Age of Revolution 1789–1848* (London, Weidenfeld and Nicholson, 1962).
Hodgson, N and Blagden, C, *The Notebook of Thomas Bennet and Henry Clements* (Oxford, Oxford University Press, 1956).
Hoftijzer, PG, 'British Books Abroad: The Continent' in J Barnard and DF Mackenzie (eds), *History of the Book in Britain,* vol 4: *1557–1695* (Cambridge, Cambridge University Press, 2002) 735–43.
Holdsworth, W, *A History of English Law,* vol 4, 3rd edn, (London, Methuen & Co, 1922).
Houwen, F and Neville, R, 'Risky Business: Current Challenges in the Relationship between Competition Law and Copyright' (2009) 8 *Competition Law Journal* 18.
How, J, *Some Thoughts on the Present State of Printing and Bookselling* (London, 1709).
Hughes, J, 'Copyright and Incomplete Historiographies: Of Piracy, Propertization, and Thomas Jefferson' (2006) 79 *Southern California Law Review* 993.
Hunt, A, 'Book Trade Patents' in A Hunt, G Mandelbrote and A Shell (eds), *The Book Trade and its Customers, 1450–1900* (Winchester, St Paul's Bibliographies, 1997) 27–54.

Hunt, A, Mandelbrote, G and Shell, A (eds), *The Book Trade and its Customers, 1450–1900* (Winchester, St Paul's Bibliographies, 1997).

Jackson, WA, *Records of the Court of the Stationers' Company 1602–1640* (London, The Bibliographical Society, 1957).

Jaszi, P, 'Toward a Theory of Copyright: The Metamorphoses of "Authorship"' (1991) *Duke Law Journal* 455.

Jaszi, P, and Woodmansee, M, 'Introduction' in M Woodmansee and P Jaszi (eds), *The Construction of Authorship: Textual Appropriation in Law and Literature* (Durham, NC, Duke University Press, 1994) 1–13.

Johns, A, 'Pop Music Pirate Hunters' (2002) 131 *Daedalus* 72.

Johnson, S, 'Considerations [by the late Dr Samuel Johnson] on the Case of Dr T[rapp']s Sermons, abridged by Mr Cave, 1739' (1787) *Gentleman's Magazine* 555.

Kamperman-Sanders, A, *Unfair Competition Law: The Protection of Intellectual and Industrial Creativity* (Oxford, Clarendon Press, 1997).

Kaplan, B, *An Unhurried View of Copyright* (New York, Columbia University Press, 1967).

Kingsford, RJL, *The Publishers Association 1896–1946* (Cambridge, Cambridge University Press, 1970).

Kishlansky, M, *A Monarchy Transformed: Britain 1603–1714* (London, Penguin Books Ltd, 1996).

Korshin, PJ (ed) *The Widening Circle: Essays on the Circulation of Literature in Eighteenth-Century Europe* (Philadelphia, University of Pennsylvania Press, 1976).

Krummel, DW, 'Music Publishing' in N Temperley (ed), *The Romantic Age 1800–1914* (London, The Athlone Press, 1976).

Laddie, H, 'Copyright: Over-strength, Over-regulated, Over-rated?' (1996) 5 *European Intellectual Property Review* 253.

Laddie, H et al, *The Modern Law of Copyright and Designs* (London, Butterworths, 2000).

Landes, WM and Posner, RA, 'An Economic Analysis of Copyright Law' (1989) 18 *Journal of Legal Studies* 325.

Landes, WM and Posner, RA, 'Indefinitely Renewable Copyright' (2003) 70 *University of Chicago Law Review* 471.

'Late Judgments of the Lord Chancellor' (1823) 38 *Edinburgh Review* 300.

Law, E, *Observations Occasioned by the Contest about Literary Property by Dr Law, Bishop of Carlisle* (Cambridge, J Archdeacon, 1770).

Law, G and Patten, RL, 'The Serial Revolution' in D McKitterick (ed), *The Cambridge History of the Book in Britain,* vol 6: *1830–1914* (Cambridge, Cambridge University Press, 2009) 144–71.

Leary, P and Nash, A, 'Authorship' in D McKitterick(ed), *The Cambridge History of the Book in Britain,* vol 6: *1830–1914* (Cambridge, Cambridge University Press, 2009) 172–213.

Leech, C and Craik, TW (eds), *The Revels History of Drama in English,* vol 6: *1750–1880* (London, Methuen & Co. Ltd, 1975).

Leeming, M, 'Hawkworth's *Voyages*: The First "Australian" Copyright Litigation' (2004) 9 *Australian Journal of Legal History* 159.

Lemley, M, 'Romantic Authorship and the Rhetoric of Property' (1996–97) 75 *Texas Law Review* 873.

'Letters of Timothy Tickler to Eminent Literary Characters' (1823) 9 *Blackwood's Edinburgh Magazine* 214.

Lieberman, D, *The Province of Legislation Determined* (Cambridge, Cambridge University Press, 1989).

Lindgren, K, 'The Interface between Intellectual Property and Antitrust: Some Current Issues in Australia' (2005) 16 *Australian Intellectual Property Journal* 76.
Litman, J, 'Billowing White Goo' (2008) 31 *Columbia Journal of Law & the Arts* 587.
Litman, J, 'Copyright, Legislation and Technological Change' (1989) 68 *Oregon Law Review* 275.
Litman, J, *Digital Copyright* (New York, Prometheus Books, 2001).
Lobban, M, 'From Seditious Libel to Unlawful Assembly: Peterloo and the Changing Face of Political Crime c1770–1820' (1990) *Oxford Journal of Legal Studies* 10.
Locke, J, *The Second Treatise of Civil Government*, ed JW Gough (Oxford, Blackwell, 1948; reprint of the 1690 edition).
Loewenstein, J, *The Author's Due: Printing and the Pre-history of Copyright* (Chicago, University of Chicago Press, 2002).
Longman, T, *Some Observations on Copyright and our Colonies* (London, Longmans, Green & Co, 1872).
Lowndes, JJ, *An Historical Sketch of the Law of Copyright; with remarks on Sergeant Talfourd's Bill* (London, Saunders & Benning, 1840).
Luke, JH (Jnr), 'The Publishing of Byron's *Don Juan*' (1965) 80 *Publications of the Modern Language Association of America* 199.
Macfarlane, R, *Original Copy* (Oxford, Oxford University Press, 2007).
Macfie, RA, *Copyright and Patents for Inventions* (Edinburgh, T & T Clark, 1879).
Macgillivray, EJ, *The Copyright Act, 1911, Annotated* (London, Stevens & Sons, Ltd, 1912).
Macgillivray, EJ, *A Treatise upon the Law of Copyright* (London, John Murrary, 1902).
Machlup, F and Penrose, E, 'The Patent Controversy of the Nineteenth Century' (1950) 10 *Journal of Economic History* 1.
Macmillan, F, *The Net Book Agreement 1899 and the Book War 1906–8* (Glasgow, MacLehone & Co, 1924).
Macmillan, F (ed), *New Directions in Copyright Law*, vol 6 (Cheltenham, UK, Edward Elgar, 2008).
MacQueen, H, 'Copyright Law Reform: Some Achievable Goals?' Oxford Intellectual Property Research Centre, Seminar Paper (2005), www.oiprc.ox.ac.uk/EJWP0406.pdf
MacQueen, H, 'Extending Intellectual Property: Producers v Users' (1994) 45 *Northern Ireland Legal Quarterly* 30.
MacQueen, H, Waelde, C and Laurie, GT, *Contemporary Intellectual Property: Law and Policy* (Oxford, Oxford University Press, 2008).
Maher, I, 'Competition Law and Intellectual Property Rights: Evolving Formalism' in Craig P and De Burca G (eds), *The Evolution of EU Law* (Oxford: Oxford University Press, 1999).
Manley, KA, 'Brydges, Sir (Samuel) Egerton, First Baronet, styled Thirteenth Baron Chandos (1762–1837)' in *Oxford Dictionary of National Biography* (Oxford, Oxford University Press, 2004) www.oxforddnb.com/view/article/3809.
Marchand, LA (ed), *Byron's Letters and Journals*, vol 7 (London, John Murrary, 1976).
Marston, E, *Copyright: National and International with Some Remarks on the Position of Authors and Publishers, by a Publisher* (London, Sampson Low, Marston, Searle & Rivington, 1887).
Maugham, R, *A Treatise on the Laws of Literary Property* (London, Longman et al, 1828).
McFarlane, G, *Copyright: The Development and Exercise of the Performing Right* (Eastbourne, John Offord (Publications) Ltd, 1980).
McKeen Wiles, R, 'The Relish for Reading in Provincial England Two Centuries Ago' in PJ Korshin (ed), *The Widening Circle: Essays on the Circulation of Literature in Eighteenth-Century Europe* (Philadelphia, University of Pennsylvania Press, 1976) 95.

McKendrick, N, Brewer, J and Plumb, JH (eds), *The Birth of a Consumer Society: The Commercialisation of Eighteenth-Century England* (London, Hutchinson, 1983).
McKitterick, D (ed), *The Cambridge History of the Book in Britain*, vol 6: *1830–1914* (Cambridge, Cambridge University Press, 2009).
McKitterick, D, *Cambridge University Library. A History. Eighteenth and Nineteenth Centuries* (Cambridge, Cambridge University Press, 1986).
McKitterick, D, 'Changes in the Look of the Book' in D McKitterick (ed), *The Cambridge History of the Book in Britain*, vol 6: *1830–1914* (Cambridge, Cambridge University Press, 2009) 75–116.
McKitterick, D, *Print, Manuscript and the Search for Order, 1450–1830* (Cambridge, Cambridge University Press, 2003).
Middleton, R, 'Popular Music of the Lower Classes' in N Temperley (ed), *The Romantic Age 1800–1914* (London, The Athlone Press, 1976) 63–91.
Milsom, SFC, *Historical Foundations of the Common Law*, 2nd edn (London, Butterworths, 1981).
Mitchell, BR, *British Historical Statistics* (Cambridge, Cambridge University Press, 1988).
Mitford, J, *A Treatise on the Pleadings in Suits in the Court of Chancery by English Bill* (London, Owen, 1780).
Montagu, B, *Enquiries and Observations Regarding the University Library* (Cambridge, 1805).
Montefiore, J, *The Law of Copyright* (London, James Wallis, 1802).
Morison, W, 'Unfair Competition at Common Law' (1951–53) 2 *University of Western Australia Law Review* 34.
Nadel, NS, 'How Current Copyright Law Discourages Creative Output: The Overlooked Impact of Marketing' (2004) 19 *Berkeley Technology Law Journal* 785.
Netanel, NW, 'Copyright and a Democratic Civil Society' (1996) 106 *Yale Law Journal* 283.
Netanel, NW, 'Why Has Copyright Expanded? Analysis and Critique' in F Macmillan (ed), *New Directions in Copyright Law*, vol 6 (Cheltenham, UK, Edward Elgar, 2008) 3–34.
Nichols, J, *Literary Anecdotes of the Eighteenth Century*, vol 3 (London, Nichols, 1812).
Nimmer, MB and Nimmer, D, *Nimmer on Copyright: A Treatise on the Law of Literary, Musical and Artistic Property, and the Protection of Ideas* (New York, Matthew Bender, 1996).
'Notes' (1893) 9 *Law Quarterly Review* 16.
Nowell-Smith, S, *International Copyright Law and the Publisher in the Reign of Queen Victoria* (Oxford, Oxford University Press, 1968).
O'Donovan, K and Rubin, GR (eds), *Human Rights and Legal History* (New York, Oxford University Press, 2000).
O'Gorman, F (ed), *Victorian Literature and Finance* (Oxford, Oxford University Press, 2007).
Oakes, JL, 'Copyrights and Copyremedies: Unfair Use and Injunctions' (1990) 18 *Hofstra Law Review* 983.
Oates, JCT, 'Cambridge University and the Reform of the Copyright Act, 1805–1813' (1972) 27 *The Library* 275.
Parkes, J, *A History of the Court of Chancery* (London, Longman, Rees, Orme Browne and Green, 1828).
Parks, S (ed), *Horace Walpole's Political Tracts (1747–1748)* (New York, Garland Publishing Inc, 1974)
Parks, S (ed), *The Literary Property Debate: Six Tracts 1764–1774* (New York, Garland Publishing Inc, 1975).
Partridge, RCB, *The History of the Legal Deposit of Books* (London, The Library Association, 1938).

Patry WF, *The Fair Use Privilege in Copyright Law*, 2nd edn (Washington DC, BNA Books, 1995).
Patry, WF, 'Metaphors and Moral Panics in Copyright: The Stephen Stewart Memorial Lecture, November 13, 2007' [2008] *Intellectual Property Quarterly* 1.
Patterson, LR, *Copyright in Historical Perspective* (Nashville, Vanderbilt University Press, 1968).
Patterson, LR and Joyce, C, 'Monopolizing the Law: The Scope of Copyright Protection for Law Reports and Statutory Compilations' (1988–89) 36 *University of California at Los Angeles Law Review* 719.
Pearce, EH, *Sion College and Library* (Cambridge, Cambridge University Press, 1913).
Phillips, CP, *The Law of Copyright in Works of Literature and Art and in the Application of Designs* (London, V & R Stevens, Sons & Haynes, 1863).
Pickering, W, *Booksellers' Monopoly, Address to the Trade and the Public* (London, Whittingham, 1832).
Planché, JR, *The Reflections and Recollections of JR Planché*, 2 vols (London, Tinsley Brothers, 1872) vol 1.
Plant, A, 'The Economic Aspects of Copyright in Books' (1934) 2 *Economica* 167.
Plant, M, *The English Book Trade: An Economic History of the Making and Sale of Books*, 2nd edn (London, Unwin & Allen Ltd, 1965).
Pollard, G, 'The English Market for Printed Books: The Sandars Lectures 1959' (1978) 4 *Publishing History* 8.
Puri, K, 'Fair Dealing with Copyright Material in Australia and New Zealand' (1983) *Victoria University of Wellington Law Review* 277.
Ransom, H, *The First Copyright Statute* (Austin, University of Texas Press, 1956).
Raven, J, 'The Book Trades' in I Rivers (ed), *Books and their Readers in Eighteenth Century England: New Essays* (London, Leicester University Press, 2001) 1–34.
Raven, J, *The Business of Books: Booksellers and the English Book Trade 1450–1850* (New Haven, Yale University Press, 2007).
Raven, J, 'Selling One's Life: James Lackington, Eighteenth-Century Booksellers and the Design of Autobiography' in OM Brack (ed), *Writers, Books and Trade* (New York, AMS Press, 1994) 1–23.
Ricketson, S, 'Reaping Without Sowing: Unfair Competition and Intellectual Property Rights in Anglo-Australian Law' (1984) *University of New South Wales Law Journal* 1.
Ricketson, S and Ginsburg, J, *International Copyright and Neighbouring Rights: The Berne Convention and Beyond*, 2nd edn, 2 vols (Oxford, Oxford University Press, 2006) vol. 1.
Rivers, I (ed), *Books and their Readers in Eighteenth Century England: New Essays* (London, Leicester University Press, 2001).
Rogers, P, *Robinson Crusoe* (London, G Allen & Unwin, 1979).
Rose, M, 'The Author as Proprietor: *Donaldson v Becket* and the Genealogy of Modern Authorship' in B Sherman and A Strowel (eds), *Of Authors and Origins: Essays on Copyright Law* (Oxford, Oxford University Press, 1994) 23–55.
Rose, M, 'The Author in Court: *Pope v Curl* (1741)' in M Woodmansee and P Jaszi (eds), *The Construction of Authorship: Textual Appropriation in Law and Literature* (Durham, NC, Duke University Press, 1994) 211–30.
Rose, M, *Authors and Owners: The Invention of Copyright* (Cambridge, MA, Harvard University Press, 1993).
Rose, M, 'Nine-Tenths of the Law: The English Copyright Debates and the Rhetoric of the Public Domain' (2003) 66 *Law and Contemporary Problems* 75.
Ross, T, 'Copyright and the Invention of Tradition (1992) 26 *Eighteenth Century Studies* 1.
Roussel, G et al (eds), *Mélanges Victor Nabhan* (Montreal, Editions Yvon Blais, 2004).

Sackville, R, 'Monopoly versus Freedom of Ideas: The Expansion of Intellectual Property' (2005) 16 *Australian Intellectual Property Journal* 65.

Saint-Amour, PK, *The Copywrights: Intellectual Property and the Literary Imagination* (Ithaca, NY, Cornell University Press, 2003).

Saunders, D, *Authorship and Copyright* (London, Routledge, 1992).

Saunders, D, 'Dropping the Subject: An Argument for a Positive History of Authorship and the Law of Copyright' in B Sherman B and A Strowel (eds), *Of Authors and Origins: Essays on Copyright Law* (Oxford, Oxford University Press, 1994) 93–110

Scrutton, TE, *The Law of Copyright*, 4th edn (London, William Cloves & Sons, 1903).

Scrutton, TE, *The Laws of Copyright*, 1st edn (London, John Murray, 1883).

Seville, C, 'Edward Bulwer Lytton Dreams of Copyright: "It might make me a rich man"' in F O'Gorman F (ed), *Victorian Literature and Finance* (Oxford, Oxford University Press, 2007) 55–72.

Seville, C, *The Internationalisation of Copyright Law* (Cambridge, Cambridge University Press, 2006).

Seville, C, *Literary Copyright Reform in Early Victorian England* (Cambridge, Cambridge University Press, 1999).

Sher, RB, 'Corporatism and Consensus in the Late Eighteenth-Century Book Trade: The Edinburgh Booksellers' Society in Comparative Perspective' (1998) 1 *Book History* 32.

Sherman, B and Bently, L, *The Making of Modern Intellectual Property Law: The British Experience, 1760–1911* (Cambridge, Cambridge University Press, 1999).

Sherman, B and Strowel, A (eds), *Of Authors and Origins: Essays in Copyright Law* (Oxford, Clarendon Press, 1994).

Siebert, FS, *Freedom of the Press in England* (Urbana, University of Illinois Press, 1952).

Smiles, S, *A Publisher and his Friends: Memoir and Correspondence of the Late John Murray*, vol 1 (London, John Murrary 1997).

Soper, P, 'Law's Normative Claims' in RP George (ed), *The Autonomy of Law: Essays on Legal Positivism* (Oxford, Clarendon Press, 1996) 215–47.

St Clair, W, *The Reading Nation in the Romantic Period* (Cambridge, Cambridge University Press, 2004).

Stevens, JR, *The Censorship of English Drama 1824–1901* (Cambridge, Cambridge University Press, 1980).

Stevens, JR, *The Profession of the Playwright* (Cambridge, Cambridge University Press, 1992).

Stevens, R, *Law and Politics: The House of Lords as a Judicial Body, 1800–1976* (London, Weidenfeld and Nicolson, 1979).

Stewart-Murphy, CA, *A History of British Circulating Libraries* (Newtown, Bird & Bull Press, 1992).

Story, J, *Commentaries on Equity Jurisprudence*, 2nd edn, vol 2 (London, Maxwell, 1839).

Strowel, A, '*Droit d'auteur* and Copyright: Between History and Nature' in B Sherman and A Strowel (eds), *Of Authors and Origins: Essays on Copyright Law* (Oxford: Clarendon Press, 1994) 235–53.

Sturt, M, *The Education of the People: A History of Primary Education in England and Wales in the Nineteenth Century* (London, Routledge & Kegan Paul, 1967).

Sutherland, J, 'The British Book Trade and the Crash of 1826' (1987) 9 *The Library* 148.

Sutherland, JA, *Victorian Novelists and Publishers* (London, Athlone Press, 1976).

Tegg, T, *Remarks on the Speech of Sergeant Talfourd on Moving for Leave to Bring in a Bill to Consolidate the Laws relating to Copyright and to Extend the Term of its Duration* (London, Thomas Tegg & Son, 1837).

Temperley, N (ed), *The Romantic Age 1800–1914* (London, The Athlone Press, 1976).
Thomas, D, *A Long Time Burning: The History of Literary Censorship in England* (New York, Frederick A Praegar, 1969).
Thomas, W, *The Philosophic Radicals: Nine Studies in Theory and Practice 1817–1841* (Oxford, Clarendon Press, 1979).
Thring, GH, 'Advantages and Defects of the Copyright Act, 1911' (1912) 91 *Fortnightly Review* 1132.
Thring, GH, 'The Copyright Bill, 1911' (1911) 89 *Fortnightly Review* 901.
Thring, GH, 'Imperial Copyright' (1910) 88 *Fortnightly Review* 688.
Thring GH, 'Recent Attempts at Copyright Legislation (1898) 63 *Fortnightly Review* 461.
Tompson, RS, 'Scottish Judges and the Birth of British Copyright' (1992) *Juridical Review* 18.
Torremans, P, *Holyoak and Torremans Intellectual Property Law*, 4th edn (Oxford, Oxford University Press, 2005).
Towse, RA, Hadke, C, Stepan, P, 'The Economics of Copyright Law: A Stocktake of the Literature' (2008) 5 *Review of Economic Research on Copyright Issues* 1.
Treadwell, M, 'The Stationers and the Printing Acts at the End of the Seventeenth Century' in J Barnard and DF Mackenzie (eds), *The Cambridge History of the Book in Britain*, vol 4: *1557–1695* (Cambridge, Cambridge University Press, 2002) 755–78.
Trusler, J, *An Essay on Literary Property containing comments on the Statute of Queen Anne and Animadversion on that Statute* (London, 1798).
Turner, S, *Reasons for a Modification of the Act of Anne respecting the Delivery of Books and Copyright* (London, Nichols, Son and Bentley, 1813).
Underdown, EM, 'The Copyright Question' (1886) 2 *Law Quarterly Review* 213.
Vaver, D, 'Abridgements and Abstracts: Copyright Implications' (1995) 5 *European Intellectual Property Review* 225.
Vaver, D, *Copyright Law* (Toronto, Irwin Law, 2000).
Vaver, D, 'Intellectual Property: The State of the Art' (2000) 116 *Law Quarrterly Review* 621.
Vincent, D, *The Rise of Mass Literacy: Reading and Writing in Modern Europe* (Cambridge, Polity Press, 2000).
Walters, G, 'The Booksellers in 1759 and 1774: The Battle for Literary Property' (1974) 29 *The Library* 287.
Warburton, W, 'An Enquiry into the Nature and Origin of Literary Property' (London, 1762) in S Parks (ed), *Horace Walpole's Political Tracts (1747–1748)* (New York, Garland Publishing Inc, 1974).
Watt, I, *The Rise of the Novel: Studies in Defoe, Richardson and Fielding* (London, Penguin, 1963).
Weatherall, K, 'Bringing Architecture into the Copyright System in the UK' (forthcoming).
Webb, W, *Observations on the Copyright Bill, printed by order of the Vice-Chancellor, Heads of College &c of the University of Cambridge* (1818).
Weedon, A, 'From Three-Deckers to Film Rights: A Turn in British Publishing Strategies, 1870–1930' (1999) *Book History* 188.
Weedon, A, *Victorian Publishing: The Economics of Book Publishing for a Mass Market, 1836–1914* (Ashgate, Aldershot, 2003).
Wilkinson, B, 'Recent Developments' (1978) *Fordham Law Review* 1037.
Woodmansee, M, 'The Genius and the Copyright: Economic and Legal Conditions of the Emergence of the Author (1984) 17 *Eighteenth Century Studies* 425.
Woodmansee, M, 'On the Author Effect: Recovering Collectivity' in M Woodmansee and P Jaszi (eds), *The Construction of Authorship: Textual Appropriation in Law and Literature* (Durham, NC; London, Duke University Press, 1994) 15–28.

Woodmansee, M and Jaszi, P (eds), *The Construction of Authorship: Textual Appropriation in Law and Literature* (Durham, NC; London, Duke University Press, 1994).
Woodward, L, *The Age of Reform 1815–1870* (Oxford: Clarendon Press, 1962).
Zachs, W, *The First John Murray and the Late Eighteenth-Century London Book Trade* (Oxford, Oxford University Press, 1998).

Index

www.ingramcontent.com/pod-product-compliance
Ingram Content Group UK Ltd.
Pitfield, Milton Keynes, MK11 3LW, UK
UKHW020237290926
15470UKWH00002B/586

9 781841 137865